A General

HISTORY

of the

ROBBERIES AND MURDERS

of the

MOST NOTORIOUS

PIRATES

A GENERAL HISTORY

of the

ROBBERIES AND MURDERS

of the

MOST NOTORIOUS

PIRATES

by DANIEL DEFOE

CARROLL & GRAF PUBLISHERS, INC.
NEW YORK

First Carroll & Graf edition 1999

Carroll & Graf Publishers, Inc.
19 West 21st Street
New York, NY 10010

Library of Congress Cataloging-in-Publication Data is available.
ISBN: 0-7867-0622-8

Manufactured in the United States of America

Contents

Contents

INTRODUCTION
TO THE 1999
EDITION

A GENERAL HISTORY *of the Robberies and Murders of the Most Notorious Pirates* has been the source of our best-loved seagoing adventure stories from *Treasure Island* and *Peter Pan* to Hollywood's *Captain Blood* and *The Black Swan*. But the author whose work inspired Sir Walter Scott, Robert Louis Stevenson, J. M. Barrie, and Rafael Sabatini has never himself been surely identified. When *A General History* first appeared in May 1724 at Charles Rivington's book shop behind the newly completed Saint Paul's Cathedral, its author was named as Captain Charles Johnson who introduced himself as a widely traveled sailor, but one whose career has never been traced in the maritime or any other archives. Nevertheless the name Captain Johnson appeared on subsequent reprints of *A General History*, even when it was expanded in an edition of 1839 into *The Lives and Actions of the Most Noted Highwaymen, Street-Robbers, Pirates, &c. &c. . . . . The sea dog Johnson was now becoming an expert on crimes committed by landlubbers. So persistent was the tradition that Captain Johnson was once more named as author of A General History,* when the latest edition was published in 1998.

So why have Carroll & Graf decided, correctly as I believe, to depose Captain Johnson and attribute *A General History* to Daniel Defoe, the author of *Robinson Crusoe, Moll Flan-*

ders, *A Journal of the Plague Year, A Tour of Great Britain*, and other acclaimed works of fiction, nonfiction, and something in between the two? The question of who wrote *A General History* was one I had to face in preparing my recent biography *Daniel Defoe: The Life and Strange Surprising Adventures.*

In the modern literary world, the author's name on the title page proclaims his or her copyright and stock-in-trade. In the late seventeenth and early eighteenth centuries, the author's name invited danger because of the controversy that followed the Civil War, the Glorious Revolution of 1688, and frequent uprisings in Scotland and Ireland. The journalist, the pamphleteer, and the author alike lived in fear of arrest, imprisonment, the pillory, or worse. Political and religious hatred did not spare even the most respected poet of the age, John Dryden, who was beaten almost to death by hired goons outside the Lamb and Flag, a still flourishing public house in Covent Garden.

Most of the leading poets and literary men of the age were also polemic journalists and pamphleteers, such as the essayists Joseph Addison and Richard Steele, the authors of *Tatler* and *Spectator*, and Jonathan Swift who wrote the rival *Examiner* besides his satirical masterpiece *Gulliver's Travels.* All lived under threat of sudden arrest and denunciation by their political and religious enemies, not least by one another. Although Addison, Pope, and Matthew Prior were glad to accept the praise for their poems, they tried to conceal the authorship of their more controversial and lucrative writings in prose.

Daniel Defoe whose life (1660–1731) spanned Britain's emergence as a Protestant constitutional monarchy, was shifty and secretive to the point of using a code and disguising his handwriting. As a Nonconformist Christian in 1685 he had joined in the Duke of Monmouth's rebellion against the Roman Catholic King James II and probably fought at the Battle of Sedgemoor. He escaped James's revenge at the subsequent *Bloody Assizes* when hundreds of rebels were hung, drawn and quartered or sent as slaves to the West Indian plantations (like Errol Flynn in Hollywood's *Captain Blood*).

Defoe was facing the same risk when he published his first pamphlet denouncing James in a letter supposedly written to an English Dissenter from a "Friend in the Hague." When the Dutch Protestant William of Orange launched his invasion of England in November 1688, Defoe once more rode west to join a rebellion against King James. Defoe was a friend and admirer of William III and his "Glorious Revolution." He replied to William's xenophobic Tory opponents with a hugely popular verse satire *The True-Born Englishman*, pointing out that the English themselves are a hybrid race from a mixture of all the invading armies. The satire was Defoe's most popular work until the posthumous triumph of *Robinson Crusoe*. Indeed when he wanted to push the sale of a new book or pamphlet, he would ascribe it not to Daniel Defoe but to "the author of *The True-Born Englishman*."

When Queen Anne succeeded William III in 1702, Defoe fell out with the High Church Tories who wanted to bar the Dissenters from public life as a prelude to bringing back a Roman Catholic King. A satirical pamphlet "The Shortest Way with Dissenters" (i.e., hang them all), was taken quite literally by the Tories, by the Dissenters themselves, and by the government, which issued a handsome reward for information leading to Defoe's arrest. He was tried at the Old Bailey before a panel of judges, several of whom he had lampooned in print, accusing one of prostituting his own wife, a second of taking pleasure from whipping half-naked women, and a third of accepting bribes from highwaymen, a theme that recurs in *Moll Flanders*. Not surprisingly these judges sentenced Defoe to three days in the pillory and an indefinite stay in Newgate Prison, which he also describes in *Moll Flanders*:

"That horrid place, my very blood chills at the mention of its name . . . tis impossible to describe the terror of my mind, when I was first brought in and when I looked on myself as lost and that I had nothing to think of but getting out of the world, and that with the utmost infamy; the hellish noise, the roaring, swearing and clamour, the stench and nastiness joined to make the place seem an emblem of hell itself, and a kind of entrance to it."

The Old Bailey judges also bound Defoe to seven years "good behavior," which meant that he could be sent back to prison for publishing anything objectionable to a man or woman in public life, who could prove that Defoe was the author. Understandably he refused to put his name to anything but his philosophical poem "De Jure Divino" and a turgid history of the Union with Scotland. Defoe's natural inclination to secrecy grew stronger when he began to work as a paid propagandist and spy for Robert Harley, the Tory statesman who sprang him from Newgate Prison.

Defoe did not put his name to his first and most famous work of fiction *Robinson Crusoe* (1719) which, like *A General History* appeared as the narrative of a true adventure. During the next few years, he published a number of stories of piracy, war, natural disaster, and crime including the *Farther Adventures of Robinson Crusoe, Captain Singleton, Colonel Jack, Moll Flanders, Roxana, The Memoirs of a Cavalier*, and *A Journal of the Plague Year*.

In 1724, when *A General History* was published, Defoe was at work on what I consider his masterpiece, *A Tour of the Whole Island of Great Britain*, combining accounts of his travels twenty or thirty years earlier, with flights of fantasy and imagination. Although he had almost certainly never left Britain, Defoe compared its towns and countryside with places as far afield as Naples, Belgrade, the Andes, the Plains of Mecca, and Portugal. In one exuberant passage he likens the mountains and the inhabitants of Snowdonia with those of the Alps, although he had almost certainly never visited Switzerland and probably not Wales either.

Although many critics accepted Defoe's accounts of his travels in Europe and Britain's maritime empire at face value, a true explanation appears in a book that was found in his family papers and published in 1890. This is *The Compleat English Gentleman,* in which he advises a self-made man on how to compensate for his lack of an education by buying and reading a library of books. It incidentally shows how Defoe gathered material for his books of overseas travel and adventure, not least *A General History.*

> "If a gentleman has not travelled in his youth, has not made the Grand Tour of Italy and France, he makes his tour of the world in books. He may make himself master of the geography of the universe in maps, atlases and measurements of our mathematicians. He may travel by land with the historians, by sea with the navigators, he may go round the world with Dampier and Rogers, and know a thousand times more in doing it than all those illiterate sailors. He may make all distant places near to him in his reviewing the voyages of those that saw them, and all the past and remote accounts present to him by the histories that they have written of them. The studious geographer and the well-read historian . . . discovers America with Columbus, conquers it with great Cortez and re-plunders it with Sir Francis Drake."

In these words of advice on how to become a "Compleat English Gentleman," Defoe reveals how he wrote with such expertise on all four corners of the discovered world, and especially on the life of pirates. Although he had never traveled farther than Scotland, and then by land rather than sea, he was steeped in the writings of those two "illiterate sailors" William Dampier and Captain Woodes Rogers, both of whom are liberally quoted throughout *A General History.*

Dampier and Rogers were privateers, that is sea captains licensed to raid and plunder enemy shipping in time of war, just as the French and Spanish did to the English merchant fleet. Afterward, both Dampier and Rogers published highly

popular books with the same title *A Voyage Round the World*.
Both Dampier and Rogers were incidentally involved with
the Scottish sailor Alexander Selkirk who was thought the
model for Robinson Crusoe, and certainly was the man on
a desert island in William Cowper's poem:

> *I am monarch of all I survey,*
> *My right there is none to dispute;*
> *From the centre all round to the sea*
> *I am lord of the fowl and the brute.*

Selkirk had joined a privateering expedition led by Dampier in 1704 to attack Spanish ships in the southern and
eastern Pacific. He quarreled with Dampier and asked to be
put ashore on the seldom visited island of Juan Fernandez,
off the Chilean coast. Five years later Captain Rogers, then
leading another expedition against the Spaniards, rescued
Selkirk and brought him back to Britain, where his story was
written up by Steele and other journalists but not by Defoe.

When George I came to the throne in 1714, Defoe was
marginalized as a writer on politics and put his energy in
what we would now call popular tabloid journalism, reporting on crime, natural disasters, and paranormal phenomena
for a number of daily and weekly papers. He specialized in
reporting the trials and executions of murderers, highwaymen, and pirates. Indeed the modern Irish writer Sean
O'Faolain once complained: "It is the greatest pity in the
world that the novel began in the eighteenth century. The
press reporter Defoe laid his stodgy hand on it and his fin-
gerprints are still all over it." (Quoted in J. R. Moore *Defoe
in the Pillory*. p. 189)

When *A General History* first appeared in 1724, the
bookseller-cum-publisher Charles Rivington may have told
his favored customers who was the actual author, but the
subject was topical after a number of recent trials and hang-
ings of pirates at Execution Dock on the Thames. Moreover
the writing was lurid enough to sell on its merits. It was not

till the late eighteenth century that there emerged a reading public that wanted the latest books by its favorite authors such as Fielding, Richardson, Smollett, and Austen. Booksellers were finding too that Defoe's name sold books, and he was slowly given credit for *Moll Flanders, Roxana, The Tour,* and *A Journal of the Plague Year,* as well as for the continually bestselling *Robinson Crusoe.*

Although in the nineteenth century, *A General History* continued to be attributed to the elusive Captain Charles Johnson, it fired the imagination of readers, especially those who were writers themselves. Among these was Sir Walter Scott, whose novel *The Pirate,* published in 1821 was based on the life of James Smith alias Gow.

Another Scots author Robert Louis Stevenson once explained that his immortal pirate story *Treasure Island* was based on the romances of Poe, Defoe, Washington Irving, and "the great Captain Johnson's *History of the Notorious Pirates.*" The Scots dramatist J. M. Barrie claimed that his ever-popular children's play and pantomime *Peter Pan* was also based on Captain Johnson. Ingredients of *A General History* can also be found in the 1920's novels of Rafael Sabatini who in turn inspired Hollywood's *Captain Blood* and *The Black Swan.* Two centuries after its publication *A General History* had created its own world of adventure fantasy, including the skull-and-crossbone flag, walking the plank, black eye patches, parrots, wooden legs, and buried treasure chests bursting with doubloons and pieces of eight.

Before Defoe was credited with *A General History,* he had come to be seen as the first and one of the greatest novelists. Dr. Samuel Johnson deplored Defoe's Nonconformist religion but he recognized him as the author of one of the greatest books apart from the Bible: "Was there ever yet anything written by mere man that was wished longer by its readers except *Don Quixote, Robinson Crusoe* and *Pilgrim's Progress?*" Sir Walter Scott said that *Memoirs of a Cavalier* "reflected additional lustre even on the author of *Robinson Crusoe,*" and that "even if Defoe had never written *Robinson*

Crusoe, he deserved immortality for *A Journal of the Plague Year.*" Robert Louis Stevenson was one of the first to perceive that Crusoe's discovery of a single footprint in the sand was one of the the greatest moments in imaginative literature.

Nineteenth century scholars failed to discover the man behind Captain Charles Johnson. No record of him was found in the well-preserved archives of the Royal Navy and Merchant Marine, nor in early eighteenth century newspapers.

A hack playwright, Charles Johnson was found to have written a drama *The Successful Pirate,* cashing in on the crime wave in the 1720s, but the same Johnson had no knowledge of seagoing life and had written no popular books. Yet as late as the 1920s Captain Charles Johnson still appeared as author of *A General History* in each new edition.

The first suggestion in print that Daniel Defoe had written *A General History* was made in 1932 by the American scholar John Robert Moore, a professor at Indiana University. A Defoe enthusiast as well as an academic, Moore celebrated his hero in works such as *Defoe in the Pillory and other Essays,* of which the title piece remains the best ever examination of Defoe's ordeal in 1703. In his enthusiasm, Moore sometimes accepted Defoe's flights of fancy, such as having lived in Portugal, and he attributed to Defoe several works that were probably by someone else.

When I was doing research for my own biography *Daniel Defoe: The Life and Strange Surprising Adventures,* I found that some of the works on Moore's "checklist" were clearly by other hands, for instance the book on Madagascar containing a glossary of the local language. Even more often, I had to accept Moore's attribution, often with bad grace, since when I sensed that a book was Defoe's, I felt obliged to read it in its entirety. I can well remember opening in the now defunct Reading Room of the British Museum, a book which Moore had said was Defoe's with the mind-boggling title: *A Continuation of Letters written by a Turkish spy at Paris, Giving an Impartial Account to the Diva at Constan-*

*tinople of the most remarkable transactions of Europe and dis-
covering several Intrigues and Secrets of the Christian Courts,
especially of that of Paris, continuous from the year 1687 to the
year 1693. Translated into Italian, and from thence to English.*
This *Turkish Spy* amazingly echoed the style and thoughts
of Defoe, even quoting one of his favorite maxims, compar-
ing the French and English armies: (viz) that of the French,
if the soldiers will but follow, the officers will always lead,
and that of the English, if the officers will but lead, the
soldiers will always follow."

Moore's ever-expanding checklist of books and pamphlets
that he attributed to Defoe was based on a sound understanding of Defoe's racy style, his inquisitive spirit, and joy
in assuming disguises such as a Cavalier in the *Civil War*, a
Londoner in the *Plague Year* of 1665 (when Defoe was only
a small child), a Turkish spy or a wicked lady; such as
naughty Moll Flanders or tragic Roxana, a proto-feminist
who rejected marriage in favor of "women's liberty" and sex-
ual freedom. Moore had an eye for Defoe's flashes of imaginative genius, comparable with Crusoe finding the single
footprint in the sand. Moore singled out a passage in *A Journal of the Plague Year* conveying the terror of London in
1665:

"Passing through Tokenhouse Yard, in Lothbury of a
sudden, a casement violently opened just above my
head, and a woman gave three fearful screeches 'Oh!
death, death death!' in a most inimitable tone, and
which struck me with a horror and a chillness in my
very blood. There was nobody to be seen in the whole
street, neither did any window open, for people had no
curiosity now in any case, nor could anyone help one
another, so I went on to pass into Bell Lane."

Under the influence of Moore, the libraries of the United
States and Britain began to include *A General History* in their
greatly expanded list of books attributed to Defoe, ei-

ther as "possible" or "probable." To me it seemed like Defoe at his racy best, so that I ventured to call it in my biography, "far more readable and exciting than his pirate story *Captain Singleton*, which would not now be in print if it was not a 'novel' by Defoe."

However, Defoe's growing renown as "the father of the English novel" meant that his works were getting onto the syllabi of English language faculties throughout the world. A Defoe industry flourished in academic circles and his writing was scrutinized by partisans of the rival factions, such as Freudianism Marxism, feminism, Afro-American studies, semiotics, magical realism, post-modernism, and what have you. A new generation of Defoe scholars cast a critical eye on the work of pioneers such as Moore, especially his checklist of attributions, now swollen to 570. In 1988, a determined attempt at revisionism was made by P. N. Furbank and W. R. Owens of New York University in their *Canonization of Daniel Defoe*.

In their subsequent *De-Attributions A Critique of J. R. Moore's "Checklist"*, Furbank and Owens listed 252 items from the Defoe canon, which they regarded as suspect, although as Furbank explained in a subsequent article: "What we are saying is not that Defoe could not have written these works but that we know of no good or sufficient reason for supposing that he did."

Among the Furbank and Owens "De-Attributions" was *A General History*. They pointed out inconsistencies between the particular lives and other publications attributed to Defoe such as his pamphlet on Henry Avery, entitled "The King of the Pirates" (1719) and "An Account of the Conduct and Proceedings of the Late John Gow." They question Moore's reliance on an intuitive recognition of Defoe's style and on what they call his tendency to "chain-forging," his practice of building one argument or attribution on top of another without making a proper connection between them.

The arguments of Furbank and Owens convinced the most recent publishers of *A General History* (The Lyons

Press, with an introduction by David Cordingley) that "we must abandon the attractive idea that Defoe wrote [it] and look elsewhere." In his introduction, Mr. Cordingley tends to assume that Captain Charles Johnson was the real name of the author and hopes to find some confirmation that such a person existed. "Unfortunately no record has yet come to light of a sea captain of the right date, and a search of genealogical records has failed to produce anything conclusive, one way or another."

Cordingley speculates that "Captain Johnson may have been a pirate for he sometimes shows a sympathy for and an admiration for some of the pirates which few ordinary sailors and even fewer landlubbers would have felt at that time." Now warming to his theme, Mr. Cordingley insists that the author of Johnson's *History* was a seaman of some experience: "His use of seamen's language always rings true . . . Johnson is entirely conversant with anchor work and moorings. He knows about warping a ship along a river, and understands the importance of careening a ship at regular intervals. . . . Perhaps one day, a letter or log book will be discovered which will reveal his true identity. . . ."

In fact the knowledge of ships displayed in *A General History* was no more than the average in the age of sail and certainly no more than a layman's knowledge of aviation today. With regard to pirates and their world, Defoe would rightly have thought of himself as an expert. Like many nonconformists growing up in the reigns of Charles II and James II, Defoe had a strong fellow-feeling for the Puritans of the New England seaboard whose ships were so often prey in *A General History*. His family preacher Samuel Annesley, and his academic tutor, Charles Morton, both had links with Harvard. The Boston *News Letter* specialized in the stories of piracy from which *A General History* was compiled.

Although he escaped being sent as a slave to Barbados after the failed rebellion of 1685, Defoe had a lifelong interest in this and the other Caribbean islands, notably Cuba, Jamaica, Trinidad, and Tobago, where Crusoe is shipwrecked. In his thrice-weekly *Review*, which he wrote single-handedly from 1704–1713, Defoe often relates how he put forward plans to William III for extending England's empire in the Caribbean. At different times, he proposed the capture and annexation of Cuba, Panama, Venezuela, and even distant Chile.

In his career as a merchant during the 1680s and 1690s Defoe was engaged in trading ventures to the Americas and at least once lost ship and cargo to a French privateer. This disaster led to his bankruptcy in 1692 and later became a recurring terror in his fiction. Defoe was at one time involved in a crackpot scheme for raising sunken treasure off Cornwall and the Spanish Main. Most of his heroes and heroines, including Robinson Crusoe on his island are obsessed with collecting hoards of gold, silver, and pieces of eight and preserving them from capture by pirates.

During the reign of Queen Anne, when Defoe worked as a spy and secret adviser to Robert Harley, later Lord Oxford, he became obsessed with a plan for England's getting control of the Asiento or monopoly of the slave trade from Africa to Latin America. The theme reappears in several of his novels including *Robinson Crusoe*, whose hero is shipwrecked while on his way to purchase a cargo of "servants" for sale to the planters of Brazil. The Asiento figures large in Captain Johnson's introduction to *A General History* and in several stories of individual pirates. Defoe as a journalist often wrote on the West African slave trade and how to supply the North America colonies as cheaply as possible. Again, his special knowledge appears in the accounts of pirates raiding Sierra Leone and the Gambia, from where Alex Hailey traced his ancestors in *Roots*.

Most of the adventures in *A General History* are found in novels like *Robinson Crusoe, Colonel Jack*, and above all *Captain Singleton*, which is based on the same material. But in some ways it surpasses them in the raciness of the writing. In explaining why Captain Teach was known as Blackbeard, the author tells us that he:

"Assumed the cognomen from that large quantity of hair which like a frightful meteor covered his face and frightened America more than any comet that has appeared there in a long time. His beard was black which he suffered to grow to an extravagant length. He was accustomed to twist it into ribbons in small tails, after the manner of our ramilies wigs and turn them about his ears. In time of action he wore a sling over his shoulders, with three brace of pistols hanging in bandoleers, and stuck lighted matches under his hat, which appearing on either side of his face, his eyes naturally looking fierce and wild, made him altogether such a figure that cannot form an idea of a fury out of hell to look more frightful . . ."

In the *Life of Captain England,* "a fellow with a terrible pair of whiskers, and a wooden leg, being stuck round with pistols like the man in the almanack with darts, comes swearing and vaporing upon the quarter deck and asks in a damning manner which was Captain Mackra. The captain expected no less than that this fellow would be his executioner, but when he came near him he took him by the hand, swearing damn him he was glad to see him."

One of Captain Low's rascally crew attacked a passenger "and gave him one blow across the belly with his cutlass that cut out his bowels, and he fell down dead without speaking a word. At the same time another of these rogues, cutting at a prisoner, and Captain Low, standing in his way, very opportunely received the blow upon his under jaw, which laid his teeth bare. Upon this the surgeon was called, who immediately stitched up the wound, but Low, finding fault with this operation, the surgeon being tolerably drunk as it was customary for everyone to be, he struck him such a blow with his fist that broke out all the stitches, and then bid him sew up his chops himself and be damned." As in *Captain Singleton, A General History* makes fun of the Quaker pirates who kill for the sake of booty and even take part in the slave trade. As a Nonconformist, Defoe slyly records in the *Life of Captain Roberts* how an Anglican clergyman was captured by pirates who treated him kindly and "kept nothing which belonged to the Church, except three prayer books and a bottle screw."

The 1724 edition of *A General History* included pictures of Blackbeard and of two then notorious female pirates Mary Reade and Anne Bonny, for Defoe understood the selling value of sex. Their stories include some bedroom romps, but, as in *Moll Flanders,* a skeptical woman's perception of the pleasure involved: "The husband came to bed, and that night played the vigorous lover; but one thing spoiled the diversion on the wife's side, which was the reflection that it was not designed for her; however she was passive, and bore it like a Christian." As in his novel about a feminist, *Roxana,* Defoe hints at a lesbian friendship between the two female pirates.

At least one of the pirates jumps ship on a tropical island to live with a native woman. However, Defoe assumes that few British pirates were "so degenerated as to prefer toad-in-a-shell (as Ward calls turtles) to venison, and negroes to fine English ladies."

A General History mirrors Defoe's old-fashioned (and now politically incorrect) views on crime as well as on race. It tells us that men are driven to rob and rape and murder by their inherently wicked nature rather than by society. It is especially harsh on those who commit wanton cruelty, such as setting fire to a ship with a cargo of shackled slaves, or gang-raping a female prisoner. But *A General History* does not pander to sadism. The worst atrocities attributed to these eighteenth century pirates are mild compared with the horrors that took place twenty years ago in the South China Sea when the Boat People from Vietnam met the Malay pirate fishermen.

—Richard West

The
Preface.

*H*AVING TAKEN *more than ordinary Pains in collecting the Materials which compose the following History,
we could not be satisfied with our selves, if any Thing
were wanting to it, which might render it entirely satisfactory
to the Publick: It is for this Reason we have subjoined to the
Work, a short Abstract of the Laws now in Force against Pyrates,
and made Choice of some particular Cases, (the most curious we
could meet with) which have been heretofore tried, by which it
will appear what Actions have, and what have not been adjudged Pyracy.*

*It is possible this Book may fall into the Hands of some Mas-
ters of Ships, and other honest Mariners, who frequently, by
contrary Winds or Tempests, or other Accidents incident to long
Voyages, find themselves reduced to great Distresses, either
through Scarcity of Provisions, or Want of Stores. I say, it may
be a Direction to such as those, what Lengths they may venture
to go, without violating the Law of Nations, in Case they should
meet other Ships at Sea, or be cast on some inospitable Shore,
which shouldreful a trade with them for such Things as are absolutely necessary for the Preservation of their lives, or the Safety
of the Ship and Cargoe.*

*We have given a few Instances in the Course of this History
of the Inducements Men have to engage themselves headlong in
a Life of so much Peril to themselves, and so destructive to the*

Navigation of the trading World; to remedy which Evil there seems to be but two Ways, either to find Employment for the great Numbers of Seamen turn'd adrift at the Conclusion of a War, and thereby prevent their running into such Undertakings, or to guard sufficiently the Coast of Africa, *the* West-Indies, *and other Places whereto Pyrates resort.*

I cannot but take Notice in this Place, that during this long Peace, I have not so much as heard of a Dutch *Pyrate: It is not that I take them to be honester than their Neighbours; but when we account for it, it will, perhaps, be a Reproach to our selves for our want of Industry: The Reason I take to be, that after a War, when the* Dutch *Ships are laid up, they have a Fishery, where their Seamen find immediate Business, and as comfortable Bread as they had before. Had ours the same Recourse in their Necessities, I'm certain we should find the same Effect from it; for a Fishery is a Trade that cannot be overstock'd; the Sea is wide enough for us all, we need not quarrel for Elbow-room: Its Stores are infinite, and will ever reward the Labourer. Besides, our own Coast, for the most Part, supply the* Dutch, *who employ several hundred Sail constantly in the Trade, and so sell to us our own Fish. I call it our own, for the Sovereignty of the* British *Seas, are to this Day acknowledged us by the* Dutch, *and all the neighbouring Nations; wherefore, if there was a publick Spirit among us, it would be well worth our while to establish a National Fishery, which would be the best Means in the World to prevent Pyracy, employ a Number of the Poor, and ease the Nation of a great Burthen, by lowering the Price of Provision in general, as well as of several other Commodities.*

I need not bring any Proofs of what I advance, viz. that there are Multitudes of Seamen at this Day unemploy'd; it is but too evident by their straggling, and begging all over the Kingdom. Nor is it so much their Inclination to Idleness, as their own hard Fate, in being cast off after their Work is done, to starve or steal. I have not known a Man of War commission'd for several Years past, but three times her Compliment of Men have offer'd themselves in 24 Hours; the Merchants take their Advantage of this, lessen their Wages, and those few who are in Business are poorly paid, and but poorly fed; such Usage breeds Discontents amongst them, and makes them eager for any Change.

I shall not repeat what I have said in the History concerning the Privateers of the West-Indies, *where I have taken Notice they live upon Spoil; and as Custom is a second Nature, it is no Wonder that, when an honest Livlyhood is not easily had, they run into one so like their own; so that it may be said, that Privateers in time of War are a Nursery for Pyrates against a Peace.*

Now we have accounted for their Rise and Beginning, it will be natural to enquire why they are not taken and destroy'd, before they come to any Head, seeing that they are seldom less than twelve Men of War stationed in our American *Plantations, even in Time of Peace; a Force sufficient to contend with a powerful Enemy. This Enquiry, perhaps, will not turn much to the Honour of those concern'd in that Service; however, I hope I may be excus'd if what I hint is with a Design of serving the Publick.*

I say, 'tis strange that a few Pyrates should ravage the Seas for Years, without ever being light upon, by any of our Ships of War; when in the mean Time, they (the Pyrates) shall take Fleets of Ships; it looks as if one was much more diligent in their Affairs, than the other. Roberts *and his Crew, alone, took 400 Sail, before he was destroy'd.*

This Matter, I may probably set right another time, and only observe for the present, that the Pyrates at Sea, have the same Sagacity with Robbers at Land; as the latter understand what Roads are most frequented, and where it is most likely to meet with Booty, so the former know what Latitude to lie in, in order to intercept Ships; and as the Pyrates happen to be in want of Provisions, Stores, or any particular Lading, they cruise accordingly for such Ships, and are morally certain of meeting with them; and by the same Reason, if the Men of War cruise in those Latitudes, they might be as sure of finding the Pyrates, as the Pyrates are to find the Merchant Ships; and if the Pyrates are not to be met with by the Men of War in such a Latitude, then surely down the same Latitude may the Merchant Ships arrive safely to their Port.

To make this a little plainer to my Country Readers, I must observe that all our outward bound Ships, sometime after they leave the Land, steer into the Latitude of the Place they are bound to; if to the West-India *Islands, or any Part of the Main of* America, *as* New-York, New-England, Virginia, &c. *because the Latitude is the only Certainty in those Voyages to be found, and then they sail due West, till they come to their Port, without altering their Course. In this West Way lie the Pyrates, whether it be to* Virginia, &c. *or* Nevis, St. Christophers, Montserat, Jamaica, &c. *so that if the Merchant Ships bound thither, do not fall a Prey to them one Day, they must another: Therefore I say, if the Men of War take the same Track, the Pyrates must unavoidably fall into their Mouths, or be frighted away, for where the Game is, there will the Vermin be; if the latter should be the Case, the trading Ships, as I said before, will pass unmolested and safe, and the Pyrates be reduced to take Refuge in some of their lurking Holes about the uninhabited Islands, where their Fate would be like that of the Fox in his Den, if they should venture out, they would be hunted and taken, and if they stay within they must starve.*

I must observe another Thing, that the Pyrates generally shift their Rovings, according to the Season of the Year; in the Summer they cruise mostly along the Coast of the Continent of America, *but the Winters there, being a little too cold for them, they follow the Sun, and go towards the Islands, at the approach of cold Weather. Every Man who has used the* West-India *Trade, knows this to be true; therefore, since we are so well acquainted with all their Motions, I cannot see why our Men of War under a proper Regulation, may not go to the Southward, instead of lying up all the Winter useless: But I shall proceed too far in this Enquiry, I shall therefore quit it, and say something of the following Sheets, which the Author may venture to assure the Reader that they have one Thing to recommend them, which is Truth; those Facts which he himself was not an Eye-Witness of,* he had from the authentick *Relations* of the *Persons concern'd in taking the Pyrates,* as well as from the *Mouths* of the *Pyrates* themselves, after they were taken, and he conceives no *Man* can produce better *Testimonies* to support the *Credit* of any *History.*

It will be observed, that the *Account* of the *Actions* of *Roberts* runs into a greater *Length,* than that of any other *Pyrate,* for which we can assign two *Reasons, first,* because he ravaged the *Seas* longer than the rest, and of *Consequence* there must be a greater *Scene* of *Business* in his *Life: Secondly,* being resolved not to weary the *Reader,* with tiresome *Repetitions: When* we found the *Circumstances* in *Roberts's Life,* and other *Pyrates,* either as to pyratical *Articles,* or any *Thing* else, to be the same, we thought it best to give them but once, and chose *Roberts' s Life* for that *Purpose,* he having made more *Noise* in the *World,* than some others.

As to the *Lives* of our two female *Pyrates,* we must confess they may appear a little *Extravagant,* yet they are never the less true for seeming so, but as they were publickly try'd for their *Pyracies,* there are living *Witnesses* enough to justify what we have laid down concerning them; it is certain, we have produced some *Particulars* which were not so publickly known, the *Reason* is, we were more inquisitive into the *Circumstances* of their past *Lives,* than other *People,* who had no other *Design,* than that of gratifying their own private *Curiosity: If* there are some *Incidents* and *Turns* in their *Stories,* which may give them a little the *Air* of a Novel, they are not invented or contrived for that *Purpose,* it is a *Kind* of *Reading* this *Author* is but little acquainted with, but as he himself was exceedingly diverted with them, when they were related to him, he thought they might have the same *Effect* upon the *Reader.*

I presume we need make no *Apology* for giving the *Name* of a *History* to the following *Sheets,* though they contain nothing but the *Actions* of a *Parcel* of *Robbers. It* is *Bravery* and *Stratagem* in *War* which make *Actions* worthy of *Record;* in which *Sense* the *Adventures* here related will be thought deserving that *Name.* Plutarch is very circumstantial in relating the *Actions* of Spartacus, *the Slave,* and makes the *Conquest* of him, one of the *greatest Glories of* Marcus Grassus; *and it is probable, if this Slave had liv'd a little longer,* Plutarch *would have given us his Life at large.* Rome, *the Mistress of the World, was no more at first than a Refuge for Thieves and Outlaws; and if the Progress of our Pyrates had been equal to their Beginning; had they all united, and settled in some of those Islands, they might, by this Time, have been honoured with the Name of a Commonwealth, and no Power in those Parts of the World could have been able to dispute it with them.*

If we have seem'd to glance, with some Freedom, at the Behaviour of some Governors of Provinces abroad, it has been with Caution; and, perhaps, we have, not declar'd as much as we knew: However, we hope those Gentlemen in the same Station, who have never given Occasion for the like Censure, will take no Offence, tho' the Word Governor is sometimes made use of.

P.S. *It will be necessary to add a Word or two to this Preface, in order to inform the Reader, that there are several material Additions made to this second Impression, which swelling the Book in Bulk, must of Consequence add a small Matter to its Price.*

The first Impression having been received with so much Success by the Publick, occasioned a very earnest Demand for a second: In the mean Time, several Persons who had been taken by the Pyrates, as well as others who had been concerned in taking of them, have been so kind to communicate several Facts and Circumstances to us, which had escaped us in the first Impression. This occasioned some Delay, therefore if we have not brought it out, as soon as wish'd, it was to render it the more compleat.

We shall not enter into a Detail of all the new Matter inserted here, but the Description of the Islands St. Thome, &c. *and that of* Brasil *are not to be passed by, without a little Notice. It must be observed, that our speculative Mathematicians and Geographers, who are, no doubt, Men of the greatest Learning, seldom travel farther than their Closets for their Knowledge, &c. are therefore unqualified to give us a good Description of Countries: It is for this Reason that all our Maps and Atlasses are so monstrously faulty, for these Gentlemen are obliged to take their Accounts from the Reports of illiterate Men.*

It must be noted also, that when the Masters of Ships make Discoveries this Way, they are not fond of communicating them; a Man's knowing this or that Coast, better than others, recommends him in his Business, and makes him more useful, and he'll no more discover it than a Tradesman will the Mystery of his Trade.

The Gentleman who has taken the Pains to make these Observations, is Mr. Atkins, *a Surgeon, an ingenious Man in his own Profession, and one who is not ty'd down by any narrow Considerations from doing a Service to the Publick, and has been pleased generously to communicate them for the good of others. I don't doubt, but his Observations will be found curious and very serviceable to such as Trade to those Parts, besides a Method of Trade is here laid down with the* Portuguese, *which may prove of great Profit to some of our Countrymen, if followed according to his Plan.*

It is hoped these Things will satisfy the Publick, that the Author of the following Sheets considered nothing so much as making the Book useful;—tho' he has been informed, that some Gentlemen have rais'd an Objection against the Truth of its Contents, viz. *that it seems calculated to entertain and divert.— If the Facts are related with some Agreeableness and Life, we hope it will not be imputed as a Fault; but as to its Credit, we can assure them that the Sea-faring Men, that is all that know the Nature of these Things, have not been able to make the least Objection to its Credit:—And he will be bold to affirm, that there is not a Fact or Circumstance in the whole Book, but he is able to prove by credible Witnesses.*

There have been some other Pyrates, besides those whose History are here related, such as are hereafter named, and their Adventures are as extravagant and full of Mischief, as those who are the Subject of this Book.—The Author has already begun to digest them into Method, and as soon as he receives some Materials to make them compleat, (which he shortly expects from the West-Indies) *If the Publick gives him Encouragement he intends to venture upon a second Volume.*

Introduction

AS THE Pyrates in the *West-Indies* have been so formidable and numerous, that they have interrupted the Trade of *Europe* into those Parts and our *English* Merchants, in particular, have suffered more by their Depredations, than by the united Force of *France* and *Spain*, in the late War: We do not doubt but the World will be curious to know the Original and Progress of these Desperadoes, who were the Terror of the trading Part of the World.

But before we enter upon their particular History, it will not be amiss, by way of Introduction, to shew, by some Examples drawn from History, the great Mischief and Danger which threaten Kingdoms and Commonwealths, from the Increase of these sort of Robbers; when either by the Troubles of particular Times, or the Neglect of Governments; they are not crush'd before they gather Strength.

It has been the Case heretofore, that when a single Pyrate has been suffered to range the Seas, as not being worth the Notice of a Government, he has by Degrees grown so powerful, as to put them to the Expence of a great deal of Blood and Treasure, before he was suppress'd. We shall not examine how it came to pass, that our Pyrates in the *West-Indies* have continually increased till of late; this is an Enquiry which belongs to the Legislature, or Representatives of the People in Parliament, and to them we shall leave it.

Our Business shall be briefly to shew, what from Beginnings, as inconsiderable as these, other Nations have suffered.

In the Times of *Marius* and *Sylla*, *Rome* was in her greatest Strength, yet she was so torn in Pieces by the Factions of those two great Men, that every Thing which concerned the publick Good was altogether neglected, when certain Pyrates broke out from *Cicilia*, a Country of *Asia Minor*, situate on the Coast of the *Mediteranean*, betwixt *Syria* on the East, from whence it is divided by Mount *Tauris*, and *Armenia Minor* on the West. This Beginning was mean and inconsiderable, having but two or three Ships, and a few Men, with which they cruised about the *Greek* Islands, taking such Ships as were very ill arm'd or weakly defended; however, by the taking of many Prizes, they soon increased in Wealth and Power: The first Action of their's which made a Noise, was the taking of *Julius Casar* who was as yet a Youth, and who being obliged to fly from the Cruelties of *Sylla*, who fought his Life, went into *Bithinia*, and sojourned a while with *Nicomedes*, King of that Country; in his Return back by Sea, he was met with, and taken, by some of these Pyrates, near the Island of *Pharmacusa*: These Pyrates had a barbarous Custom of tying their Prisoners Back to Back and throwing them into the Sea: but, supposing *Casar* to be some Person of a high Rank, because of his purple Robes, and the Number of his Attendants, they thought it would be more for their Profit to preserve him, in hopes of receiving a great Sum for his Ransom; therefore they told him he should have his Liberty, provided he would pay them twenty Talents, which they judg'd to be a very high Demand, in our Money, about three thousand six hundred Pounds Sterling; he smiled, and of his own Accord promised them fifty Talents; they were both pleased, and surpriz'd at his Answer, and consented that several of his Attendants should go by his Direction and raise the Money; and he was left among these Ruffians with no more than 3 Attendants. He pass'd eight and thirty Days, and seemed so little concerned or afraid,

that often when he went to sleep, he used to charge them
not to make a Noise, threatening, if they disturbed him, to
hang them all; he also play'd at Dice with them, and sometimes wrote Verses and Dialogues, which he used to repeat,
and also cause them to repeat, and if they did not praise and
admire them, he would call them Beasts and Barbarians,
telling them he would crucify them. They took all these as
the Sallies of a juvenile Humour, and were rather diverted,
than displeased at them.

At length his Attendants return'd with his Ransoni, which
he paid, and was discharged; he sail'd for the Port of *Mile-
tum*, where as soon as he was arriv'd, he used all his Art and
Industry in fitting out a Squadron of Ships, which he
equipp'd and arm'd at his own Charges; and sailing in Quest
of the Pyrates, he surpriz'd them as they lay at Anchor
among the Islands, and took those who had taken him before, with some others; the Money he found upon them he
made Prize of, to reimburse his Charges, and he carry'd the
Men to *Pergamus* or *Troy*, and there secured them in Prison:
In the mean Time, he apply'd himself to *Junius*, then Governor of *Asia*, to whom it belonged to judge and determine
of the Punishment of these Men; but *Junius* finding there
was no Money to be had, answered *Casar*, that he would
think at his Leisure, what was to be done with those Prisoners; *Casar* took his Leave of him, returned back to *Pergamus*, and commanded that the Prisoners should be brought
out and executed, according to Law in that Case provided;
which is taken Notice of, in a Chapter at the End of this
Book, concerning the Laws in Cases of Pyracy: And thus he
gave them that Punishment in Earnest, which he had often
threatened them with in Jest.

Casar went strait to *Rome*, where, being engaged in the
Designs of his own private Ambition, as were almost all the
leading Men in *Rome*, the Pyrates who were left, had Time
to increase to a prodigious Strength; for while the civil Wars
lasted, the Seas were left unguarded, so that *Plutarch* tells us,
that they erected diverse Arsenals full of all manner of war-

like Stores, made commodious Harbours, set up Watch-Towers and Beacons all along the Coasts of *Cilicia*; that they had a mighty Fleet, well equipp'd and furnish'd, with Galliots of Oars, mann'd, not only with Men of desperate Courage, but also with expert Pilots and Mariners; they had their Ships of Force, and light Pinnaces for cruising and making Discoveries, in all no less than a thousand Sail; so gloriously set out, that they were as much to be envied for their gallant Shew, as fear'd for their Force; having the Stern and Quarters all gilded with Gold and their Oars plated with Silver, as well as purple Sails; as if their greatest Delight had been to glory in their Iniquity. Nor were they content with committing Pyracies and Insolencies by Sea, they committed as great Depredations by Land, or rather made Conquests; for they took and sack'd no less than four hundred Cities, laid several others under Contributions, plundered the Temples of the Gods, and inriched themselves with the Offerings deposited in them; they often landed Bodies of Men, who not only plundered the Villages along the Sea Coast, but ransacked the fine Houses of the Noblemen along the *Tiber*. A Body of them once took *Sextillius* and *Bellinus*, two *Roman* Prætors, in their purple Robes, going from *Rome* to their Governments, and carried them away with all their Sergeants, Officers and Vergers; they also took the Daughter of *Antonius* a consular Person, and one who had obtained the Honour of a Triumph, as she was going to the Country House of her Father.

But what was most barbarous, was a Custom they had when they took any Ship, of enquiring of the Person on Board, concerning their Names and Country; if any of them said he was a *Roman*, they fell down upon their Knees, as if in a Fright at the Greatness of that Name, and begg'd Pardon for what they had done, and imploring his Mercy, they used to perform the Offices of Servants about his Person, and when they found they had deceived him into a Belief of their being sincere, they hung out the Ladder of the Ship, and coming with a shew of Courtefy, told him, he had his

Liberty, desiring him to walk out of the Ship, and this in the Middle of the Sea, and when they observed him in Surprize, as was natural, they used to throw him overboard with mighty shouts of Laughter; so wanton they were in their Cruelty.

Thus, while *Rome* was Mistress of the World, she suffered Insults and Affronts, almost at her Gate from these powerful Robbers; but what for a while made Faction cease, and roused the Genius of that People, never used to suffer Wrongs from a fair Enemy, was an excessive Scarcity of Provisions in *Rome*, occasioned by all the Ships loaden with Corn and Provisions from *Sicily, Corsica*, and other Places, being intercepted and taken by these Pyrates, insomuch that they were almost reduced to a Famine: Upon this, *Pompey* the *Great* was immediately appointed General to manage this War; five hundred Ships were immediately fitted out, he had fourteen Senators, Men of Experience in the War, for his Vice-Admirals; and so considerable an Enemy, were these Ruffians become, that no less than an Army of a hundred thousand Foot, and five thousand Horse was appointed to invade them by Land; but it happened very luckily for *Rome*, that *Pompey* fail'd out before the Pyrate had Intelligence of a Design against them, so that their Ships were scattered all over the *Mediterranean*, like Bees gone out from a Hive, some one Way, some another, to bring Home their Lading; *Pompey* divided his Fleet into thirteen Squadrons, to whom he appointed their several Stations, so that great Numbers of the Pyrates fell into their Hands, Ship by Ship, without any Loss; forty Days he passed in scouring the *Mediterranean*, some of the Fleet cruizing along the Coast of *Africk*, some about the Islands, and some upon the *Italian* Coasts, so that often those Pyrates who were flying from one Squadron, fell in with another; however, some of them escaped, and these making directly to *Cilicia*, and acquainting their Confederates on Shore with what had happened, they appointed a Rendezvous of all the Ships that had escaped at the Port of *Coracesium*, in the same Country. *Pompey* finding

the *Mediterranean* quite clear, appointed a Meeting of all his
Fleet at the Haven of *Brundusium*, and from thence failing
round into the *Adriatick*, he went directly to attack these
Pyrates in their Hives; as soon as he came near the *Corecesium*
in *Cilicia*, where the Remainder of the Pyrates now lay, they
had the Hardiness to come and give him Battle, but the
Genius of old *Rome* prevailed, and the Pyrates received an
entire Overthrow, being all either taken or destroyed; but as
they made many strong Fortresses upon the Sea Coast, and
built Castles and strong Holds up the Country, about the
Foot of Mount *Taurus*, he was obliged to besiege them with
his Army; some Places he took by Storm, others surrendered
to his Mercy, to whom he gave their Lives, and at length he
made an entire Conquest.

But it is probable, that had these Pyrates receiv'd sufficient
Notice of the *Roman* Preparation against them, so as they
might have had Time to draw their scattered Strength into
a Body, to have met *Pompey* by Sea, the Advantage appeared
greatly on their Side, in Numbers of Shipping, and of Men;
nor did they want Courage, as may be seen by their coming
out of the Port of *Corecesium*, to give the *Romans* Battle,
with a Force much inferior to their's; I say, had they over-
thrown *Pompey*, it is likely they would have made greater
Attempts, and *Rome*, which had conquer'd the whole World,
might have been subdued by a Parcel of Pyrates.

This is a Proof how dangerous it is to Governments to be
negligent, and not take an early Care in suppressing these
Sea Banditti, before they gather Strength.

The Truth of this Maxim may be better exemplified in
the History of *Barbarouse*, a Native in the City of *Mitylene*,
in the Island of *Lesbos*, in the *Egean* Sea; a Fellow of ordinary
Birth, who being bred to the Sea, first set out from thence
upon the pyrating Account with only one small Vessel, but
by the Prizes he took, he gain'd immense Riches, so that
getting a great Number of large Ships, all the bold and dis-
solute Fellows of those Islands flock'd to him, and listed in
his Service, for the Hopes of Booty; so that his Strength was

increased to a formidable Fleet: With these he perform'd such bold and adventurous Actions, that he became the Terror of the Seas. About this Time it happened that *Selim Eutemi*, King of *Algiers*, having refused to pay the accustomed Tribute to the *Spaniards*, was apprehensive of an Invasion from thence; wherefore he treated with *Barbarouse*, upon the Foot of an Ally, to come and assist him, and deliver him from paying this Tribute; *Barbarouse* readily came into it, and sailing to *Algiers* with a great Fleet, he put part of his Men on Shore, and having laid a Plot to surprize the City, he effected it with great Success, and murder'd *Selim* in a Bath; soon after which, he was himself crowned King of *Algiers*; after this he made War upon *Abdilabde*, King of *Tunis*, and overthrew him in Battle; he extended his Conquests on all Sides; and thus from a Thief became a mighty King: and tho' he was at last kill'd in Battle, yet he had so well established himself upon that Throne, that, dying without Issue, he left the Inheritance of the Kingdom to his Brother, another Pyrate.

I come now to speak of the Pyrates infesting the *West-Indies*, where they are more numerous than in any other Parts of the World, on several Reasons:

First, Because there are so many uninhabited little Islands and Keys, with Harbours convenient and secure for cleaning their Vessels, and abounding with what they often want, Provision; I mean Water, Sea-Fowl, Turtle, Shell, and other Fish; where, if they carry in but strong Liquor, they indulge a Time, and become ready for new Expeditions before any Intelligence can reach to hurt them.

It may here perhaps be no unnecessary Digression, to explain upon what they call Keys in the *West-Indies*: These are small sandy Islands, appearing a little above the Surf of the Water, with only a few Bushes or Weeds upon them, but abound (those most at any Distance from the Main) with Turtle, amphibious Animals, that always chuse the quietest and most unfrequented Place, for laying their Eggs, which are to a vast Number in the Seasons, and would seldom be seen, but for this, (except by Pyrates:) Then Vessels from *Jamaica* and the other Governments make Voyages, called Turtling, for supplying the People, a common and approved Food with them. I am apt to think these *Keys*; especially those nigh Islands, to have been once contiguous with them, and separated by Earthquakes (frequently there) or Inundations, because some of them that have been within continual View, as those nigh *Jamaica*, are observed within our Time, to be entirely wasted away and lost, and others daily wasting. There are not only of the Use above taken Notice of to Pyrates; but it is commonly believed were always in buccaneering pyratical Times, the hiding Places for their Riches, and often Times a Shelter for themselves, till their Friends on the Main, had found Means to obtain Indemnity for their Crimes; for you must understand, when Acts of Grace were more frequent, and the Laws less severe, these Men continually found Favours and Incouragers at *Jamaica*, and perhaps they are not all dead yet; I have been told many of the them still living have been of the same Trade, and left it off only because they can live as well honestly, and gain now at the hazard of others Necks.

Secondly, another Reason why these Seas are chose by Pyrates, is the great Commerce thither by *French, Spaniards, Dutch*, and especially *English* Ships: They are sure in the Latitude of these trading Islands, to meet with Prizes, Booties of Provision, Cloathing, and Naval-Stores, and sometimes Money; there being great Sums remitted this Way to *England*; (the Returns of the Assiento, and private Slave-Trade, to the *Spanish West-Indies*:) And in short, by some one or other, all the Riches of *Potosi*.

A third Reason, is the Inconveniency and Difficulty of being pursued by the Men of War, the many small Inlets, Lagoons and Harbours, on these solitary Islands and Keys, is a natural Security.

'Tis generally here that the Pyrates begin their Enterprizes, setting out at first with a very small Force; and by infesting these Seas, and those of the Continent of *North-America*, in a Year's Time, if they have good luck on their Sides, they accumulate such Strength, as enables them to make foreign Expeditions: The first, is usually to *Guiney*, taking the *Azores* and *Cape de Verd* Islands in their Way, and then to *Brazil* and the *East-Indies*, where if they meet with prosperous Voyages, they set down at *Madagascar*, or the neighboring Islands, and enjoy their ill gotten Wealth, among their elder Brethren, with Impunity. But that I may not give too much Encouragement to the Profession, I must inform my maritime Readers, that the far greater Part of these Rovers are cut short in the Pursuit, by a sudden Precipitation into the other World.

The Rise of these Rovers, since the Peace of *Utrecht*, or at least, the great Encrease of them, may justly be computed to the *Spanish* Settlements in the *West-Indies*; the Governors of which, being often some hungry Courtiers, sent thither to repair or make a Fortune, generally Countenance all Proceedings that bring in Profit: They grant Commissions to great Numbers of Vessels of War, on Pretence of preventing an interloping Trade, with Orders to seize all Ships or Vessels whatsoever, within five Leagues of their Coasts, which our *English* Ships cannot well avoid coming, in their Voyage to *Jamaica*. But if the *Spanish* Captains chance to exceed this Commission, and rob and plunder at Discretion, the Sufferers are allowed to complain, and exhibit a Process in their Court, and after great Expence of Suit, Delay of Time, and other Inconveniencies, obtain a Decree in their Favour, but then when the Ship and Cargo comes to be claim'd, with Costs of Suit, they find, to their Sorrow, that it has been previously condemn'd, and the Plunder divided among the Crew; the Commander that made the Capture, who alone is responsible, is found to be a poor raskally Fellow, not worth a Groat, and, no doubt, is plac'd in that Station for the like Purposes.

The frequent Losses sustain'd by our Merchants abroad, by these Pyrates, was Provocation enough to attempt something by way of Reprisal; and a fair Opportunity offering it self in the Year 1716, the Traders of the *West-Indies*, took Care not to slip it over, but made the best Use of it their Circumstances would permit.

It was about two Years before, that the *Spanish* Galleons, or Plate Fleet, had been cast away in the Gulf of *Florida*; and several Vessels from the *Havana*, were at work, with diving Engines, to fish up the Silver that was on board the Galleons.

The *Spaniards* had recovered some. Millions of Pieces of Eight, and had carried it all to the *Havana*; but they had at present about 350000 Pieces of Eight in Silver, then upon the Spot, and were daily taking up more. In the mean time, two Ships, and three Sloops, fitted out from *Jamaica, Barbadoes &c.* under Captain *Henry Jennings*, sail'd to the Gulf, and found the *Spaniards* there upon the Wreck; the Money before spoken of, was left on Shore, deposited in a Store-House, under the Government of two Commissaries, and a Guard of about 60 Soldiers.

The Rovers came directly upon the Place, bringing their little Fleet to an Anchor, and, in a Word, landing 300 Men, they attack'd the Guard, who immediately ran away; and thus they seized the Treasure, which they carried off, making the best of their Way to *Jamaica*.

In their Way they unhappily met with a *Spanish* Ship, bound from *Porto Bello* to the *Havana*, with a great many rich Goods, *viz.* Bales of Cochineal, Casks of Indico, and 60000 Pieces of Eight more, which their Hands being in, they took, and having rifled the Vessel, let her go.

They went away to *Jamaica* with their Booty, and were followed in View of the Port, by the *Spaniards*, who having seen them thither, went back to the Governor of the *Havana*, with the Account of it, who immediately sent a Vessel to the Governor of *Jamaica* to complain of this Robbery, and to reclaim the Goods.

As it was in full Peace, and contrary to all Justice and Right, that this Fact was committed, they were soon made sensible that the Government at *Jamaica* would not suffer them to go unpunished, much less protect them. Therefore they saw a Necessity of shifting for themselves; so, to make bad worse, they went to Sea again, tho' not without disposing of their Cargo to good Advantage, and furnishing themselves with Ammunition, Provisions, &c. and being thus made desperate, they turn'd Pyrates, robbing not the *Spaniards* only, but their own Countrymen, and any Nation they could lay their Hands on.

It happened about this Time, that the *Spaniards*, with three or four small Men of War, fell upon our Logwood Cutters, in the Bay of *Campeachy*, and Bay of *Honduras*; and after they had made Prizes of the following Ships and Vessels, they gave the Men belonging to them, three Sloops to carry them home, but these Men being made desperate by their Misfortunes, and meeting with the Pyrates, they took on with them, and so encreas'd their Number.

The L I S T of Ships and Vessels taken by the Spanish Men of War in the Year 1716.

The *Stafford,* Captain *Kneck,* from *New-England,*
                          bound for *London.*

Anne, ——	*Gernish,* for ditto.
Dove ——	*Grimstone,* for *New-England.*
A Sloop, ——	*Alden,* for ditto.
A Brigantine, ——	*Mosson,* for ditto.
A Brigantine, ——	*Turfield,* for ditto.
A Brigantine, ——	*Tennis,* for ditto.
A Ship, —— ——	*Porter,* for ditto.
Indian Emperor,	*Wentworth,* for *New-England.*
A Ship, ——	*Rich,* Master.
Ditto, ——	*Bay.*
Ditto, ——	*Smith.*
Ditto, ——	*Stockum.*
Ditto, ——	*Satlely.*

A Sloop, —— ——	*Richards*, belonging to *New-England*.
Two Sloops, —— ——	belonging to *Jamaica*.
One Sloop —— ——	of *Barbadoes*.
Two Ships ——————	from *Scotland*.
Two Ships ——————	from *Holland*.

The Rovers being now pretty strong, they consulted to-gether about getting some Place of Retreat, where they might lodge their Wealth, clean and repair their Ships, and make themselves a kind of Abode. They were not long in resolving, but fixed upon the Island of *Providence*, the most considerable of the *Bahama* Islands, lying in the Latitude of about 24 Degrees North, and to the Eastward of the *Spanish Florida*.

This Island is about 28 Miles long, and eleven where broadest, and has a Harbour big enough to hold 500 Sail of Ships; before which lies a small Island, which makes two Inlets to the Harbour; at either Way there is a Bar, over which no Ship of 500 Tun can pass. The *Bahama* Islands were possess'd by the *English* till the Year 1700, when the *French* and *Spaniards* from *Petit Guavus*, invaded them, took the Fort and Governor in the Island of *Providence*, plunder'd and destroy'd the Settlements, &c. carried off half the Blacks, and the rest of the People, who fled to the Woods, retired afterwards to *Carolina*.

In *March* 1705–6, the House of Lords did in an Address to her late Majesty, set forth,

'That the *French* and *Spaniards* had twice, during the Time of the War, over run and plundered the *Bahama* Islands, that there was no Form of Government there: That the Harbour of the Isle of *Providence*, might be easily put in a Posture of Defence, and that it would be of dangerous Consequence, should those Islands fall into the Hands of the Enemy; wherefore the Lords humbly besought her Majesty to use such Methods as she should think proper for taking the said Island into her Hands, in order to secure the same to the Crown of this Kingdom, and to the Security and Advantage of the Trade thereof.'

But, however it happened, no Means were used in compliance to that Address, for securing the *Bahama* Islands, till the *English* Pyrates had made *Providence* their Retreat and general Recepticle; then 'twas found absolutely necessary, in order to dislodge that troublesome Colony; and Information being made by the Merchants to the Government, of the Mischief they did, and were likely to do, his Majesty was pleased to grant the following Order.

Whitehall September 15, 1716.
'Complaint having been made to his Majesty, by great Number of Merchants, Masters of Ships and others, as well as by several Governors of his Majesty's Islands and Plantations in the *West-Indies*; that the Pyrates are grown so numerous, that they infest not only the Seas near *Jamaica*, but even those of the Northern Continent of *America*; and that, unless some effectual Means be used, the whole Trade from *Great Britain* to those Parts, will not be only obstructed, but in imminent Danger of being lost: His Majesty has, upon mature Deliberation in Council, been pleased, in the first Place, to order a proper Force to be employ'd for the suppressing the said Pyrates, which Force so to be employed, is as follows.

A List of his Majesty's Ships and Vessels employed, and to be employed, at the *British* Governments and Plantations in the *West-Indies*.

Place where. Rates, Ships, Guns.

Place where.	Rates,	Ships,	Guns.	
	5	Adventure,	40	Now there.
		Diamond,	40	Sail'd from hence thither 5th of last Month.
		Ludlow Castle,	40	To carry the Governor
Jamaica,		Swift Sloop,		Now there.
	6	Winohelsea,	20	Surveying the Coast of the West-Indies, and then to return Home; but, during her being at Jamaica, is to join the others, for Security of the Trade, and intercepting Pyrates.
Barbadoes,	5	Scarborough,	30	Now there.
Leeward	6	Seaford,		
Islands,		Tryal Sloop,	6	Now there.
	6	Lime,	20	Now there.
	5	Shoreham,	30	Order'd Home.
Virginia,		Pearl,	40	Sailed thither from Home the 7th of last Month, and is to cruise about the Capes.
New-York,	6	Phoenix,	30	Now there.
New-England,		Squirrel,	20	
		Rose,	20	Order'd Home.

Those at *Jamaica, Barbadoes* and the Leeward Islands, are to join upon Occasion, for annoying the Pyrates, and the Security of the Trade: And those at *New-England, Virginia* and *New-York,* are to do the like.'

Besides these Frigots, two Men of War were ordered to attend Captain *Rogers,* late Commander of the two *Bristol* Ships, called the *Duke* and *Dutchess,* that took the rich *Acapulca* Ship, and made a Tour round the Globe. This Gentleman received a Commission from his Majesty, to be Governor of the Island of *Providence,* and was vested with Power to make Use of all possible Methods for reducing the Pyrates; and that nothing might be wanting, he carried with him, the King's Proclamation of Pardon, to those who should return to their Duty by a certain Time; the Proclamation is as follows;

By the KING,

A PROCLAMATION, for suppressing of PYRATES.

GEORGE R.

Whereas we have received Information, that several Persons, Subjects of Great Britain, *have since the 24th Day of* June, *in the Year of our Lord 1715, committed divers Pyracies and Robberies upon the High-Seas, in the* West-Indies, *or adjoyning to our Plantations, which hath and may Occasion great Damage to the Merchants of* Great Britain, *and others trading into those parts; and tho' we have appointed such a Force as we judge sufficient for suppressing the said Pyrates, yet the more effectually to put an End to the same, we have thought fit, by and with the Advice of our Privy Council, to Issue this our Royal Proclamation; and we do hereby promise, and declare, that in Case any of the said Pyrates, shall on or before the 5th of* September, *in the Year of our Lord 1718, surrender him or themselves, to one of our Principal Secretaries of State in* Great Britain *or* Ireland, *or to any Governor or Deputy Governor of any of our Plantations beyond the Seas; every such Pyrate and Pyrates so surrendering him, or themselves, as aforesaid, shall have our gracious Pardon, of and for such, his or their Pyracy, or Pyracies, by him or them committed before the fifth of* January *next ensuing. And we do hereby strictly charge and command all our Admirals, Captains, and other Officers at Sea, and all our Governors and Commanders of any Forts, Castles, or other Places in our Plantations, and all other our Officers Civil and Military, to seize and take such of the Pyrates, who shall refuse or neglect to surrender themselves accordingly. And we do hereby further declare, that in Case any Person or Persons, on, or after, the 6th Day of* September 1718, *shall discover or seize, or cause or procure to be discovered or seized, any one or more of the said Pyrates, so refusing or neglecting to surrender themselves as aforesaid, so as they may be brought to Justice, and convicted of the said Offence, such Person or Persons, so making such Dis-*

covery or Seizure, or causing or procuring such Discovery or Seizure to be made, shall have and receive as a Reward for the
same, viz. for every Commander of any private Ship or Vessel,
the Sum of 100 l. for every Lieutenant, Master, Boatswain,
Carpenter, and Gunner, the Sum of 40 l. for every inferior Officer, the Sum of 30 l. and for every private Man, the Sum of
20 l. And if any Person or Persons, belonging to and being Part
of the Crew of any such Pyrate Ship or Vessel, shall on or after
the said sixth Day of September 1718, seize and deliver, or
cause to be seized or delivered, any Commander or Commanders,
of such Pyrate Ship or Vessel, so as that he or they be brought to
Justice, and convicted of the said Offence, such Person or Persons,
as a Reward for the same, shall receive for every such Commander, the Sum of 200 l. which said Sums, the Lord Treasurer,
or the Commissioners of our Treasury for the Time being, are
hereby required, and desired to pay accordingly.

Given at our Court, at *Hampton-Court*, the
fifth Day of *September*, 1717, in the
fourth Year of our Regin.
God save the KING.

Before Governor *Rogers* went over, the Proclamation was
sent to them, which they took as *Teague* took the Covenant,
that is, they made Prize of the Ship and Proclamation too;
however, they sent for those who were out a Cruising, and
called a general Council, but there was so much Noise and
Clamour, that nothing could be agreed on; some were for
fortifying the Island, to stand upon their own Terms, and
Treating with the Government upon the Foot of a Commonwealth; others were also for strengthening the Island for
their own Security, but were not strenuous for these Punc-
tillios, so that they might have a general Pardon, without
being obliged to make any Restitution, and to retire, with
all their Effects, to the neighbouring *British* Plantations.

But Captain *Jennings*, who was their Commadore, and
who always bore a great Sway among them, being a Man of
good Understanding, and a good Estate, before this Whim

took him of going a Pyrating, resolved upon surrendering, without more ado, to the Terms of the Proclamation, which so disconcerted all their Measures, that the *Congress* broke up very abruptly without doing any Thing; and presently *Jennings*, and by his Example, about 150 more, came in to the Governor of *Bermudas*, and had their Certificates, tho' the greatest Part of them returned again, like the Dog to the Vomit. The Commanders who were then in the Island, besides Captain *Jennings* abovementioned, I think were these, *Benjamin Hornigold, Edward Teach, John Martel, James Fife, Christopher Winter, Nicholas Brown, Paul Williams, Charles Bellamy, Oliver la Bouche,* Major *Penner, Ed. England, T. Burgess Tho. Cocklyn, R. Sample, Charles Vane,* and two or three others: *Hornigold, Williams Burgess* and *la Bouche* were afterwards cast away; *Teach* and *Penner* killed, and their Crews taken; *James Fife* killed by his own Men; *Martel's* Crew destroyed, and he forced on an uninhabited Island; *Cocklyn, Sample* and *Vane* hanged; *Winter* and *Brown* surrendered to the *Spaniards* at *Cuba,* and *England* lives now at *Madagascar.*

In the Month of *May* or *June* 1718, Captain *Rogers* arrived at his Government, with two of his Majesty's Ships, and found several of the abovesaid Pyrates there, who upon the coming of the Men of War, all surrendered to the Pardon, except *Charles Vane* and his Crew, which happened after this Manner.

I have before described the Harbour to have two Inlets, by Means of a small Island lying at the Mouth of it; at one of which, both the Men of War entered, and left the other open, so that *Vane* flip'd his Cable, set Fire to a large Prize they had there, and resolutely put out, firing at the Man of War as he went off.

As soon as Captain *Rogers* had settled himself in his Government, he built a Fort for his Defence, and garrisoned it with the People he found upon the Island; the *quondam* Pyrates, to the Number of 400, he formed into Companies, appointed Officers of those whom he most confided in, and then set about to settle a Trade with the *Spaniards*, in the Gulf of *Mexico*; in one of which Voyages, Captain *Burgess* abovementioned, died, and Captain *Hornigold*, another of the famous Pyrates, was cast away upon Rocks, a great Way from Land, and perished, but five of his Men got into a Canoe and were saved.

Captain *Rogers* sent out a Sloop to get Provisions, and gave the Command to one *John Augur*, one of the Pyrates, who had accepted of the Act of Grace; in their Voyage they met with two Sloops, and *John* and his Comrades not yet forgetting their former Business, made Use of their old Freedom, and took out of them in Money and Goods, to the Value of about 500 *l*. after this they steered away for *Hispaniola*, not being satisfy'd whether the Governor would admit them to carry on two Trades at once, and so thought to have bidden Favewel to the *Bahama* Islands; but as ill Luck would have it, they met with a violent Turnado, wherein they lost their Mast, and were drove back to one of the uninhabited *Bahama*'s, and lost their Sloop; the Men got all ashore, and lived up and down in the Wood, for a little Time, till Governor *Rogers* happening to hear of their Expedition, and where they had got to, sent out an armed Sloop to the aforesaid Island; the Master of which, with good Words and fair Promises, got them on Board, and brought them all to *Providence*, being a eleven Persons, ten of which were try'd at a Court of Admiralty, convicted, and hanged by the other's Evidence, in the Sight of all their former Companions and fellow Thieves. The Criminals would fain have spirited up the pardoned Pyrates, to rescue them out of the Hands of the Officers of Justice, telling them from the Gallows, that, *They never thought to have seen the Time, when ten such Men as they should be ty'd up and hanged like Dogs, and four hundred of their sworn Friends and Companions quietly standing by to behold the Spectacle.* One *Humphrey Morrice* urged the Matter further than the rest, taxing them with Pusilanimity and Cowardice, as if it were a Breach of Honour in them not to rise and save them from the ignominious

Death they were going to suffer. But 'twas all in vain, they were now told, it was their Business to turn their Minds to another World, and sincerely to repent of what Wickedness they had done in this. *Yes*, answered one of them, *I do heartily repent; I repent I had not done more Mischief, and that we did not cut the Throats of them that took us, and I am extremely sorry that you an't all hang'd as well as we. So do I*, says another: *And I*, says a third; and then they were all turned off, without making any other dying Speeches, except one *Dennis Macarty*, who told the People, *That some Friends of his had often said he should die in his Shoes, but that he would make them Lyars*, and so kicked them off. And thus ended the Lives, with their Adventures, of those miserable Wretches, who may serve as sad Examples of the little Effect Mercy has upon Men once abandoned to an evil Course of Life.

Least I be thought severe in my Animadversions upon the *Spanish* Proceedings in the *West-Indies*, in respect to their Dealings with us; I shall mention an Instance or two, wherein I'll be as concise as possible, and then transcribe some original Letters from the Governor of *Jamaica*, and an Officer of a Man of War, to the *Alcaldees of Trinidado*, on the Island of *Cuba*, with their Answers, translated into *English*, and then proceed to the particular Histories of the Pyrates and their Crews, that have made most Noise in the World in *our own Times*.

About *March* 1722, one of our Men of War trading upon the Coast, *viz.* the *Greyhound* Galley, Captain *Walron*, the said Captain invited some of the Merchants to Dinner, who with their Attendants and Friends came on Board to the Number of 16 or 18 in all; and having concerted Measures, about six or eight dined in the Cabin, and the rest were waiting on the Deck. While the Captain and his Guests were at Dinner, the Boatswain Pipes for the Ship's Company to dine; accordingly the Men take their Platters, receive their Provisions, and down they go between Decks, leaving only 4 or 5 Hands besides the *Spaniards*, above, who were immediately dispatched by them, and the Hatches laid on the rest; those in the Cabin were as ready as their Companions, for they pulled out their Pistols and shot the Captain, Surgeon and another dead, and grievously wounded the Lieutenant; but he geting out of the Window upon a Side-Ladder, thereby saved his Life, and so they made themselves Masters of the Ship in an Instant: But by accidental good Fortune, she was recovered before she was carry'd off; for Captain *Walron* having mann'd a Sloop with 30 Hands out of his Ship's Company, had sent her to Windward some Days before, also for Trade, which the *Spaniards* knew very well; and just as the Action was over they saw this Sloop coming down, before the Wind; towards their Ship; upon which the *Spaniards* took about 10000 *l.* in Specie, as I am informed, quitted the Ship, and went off in their Launch unmolested.

About the same Time, a *Guard le Coast*, of *Porto Rico*, commanded by one *Matthew Luke*, an *Italian*, took four *English* Vessels, and murthered all the Crews: He was taken by the *Lanceston* Man of War, in *May* 1722, and brought to *Jamaica*, were they were all but seven deservedly hanged. It is likely the Man of War might not have meddled with her, but that she blindly laid the *Lanceston* on Board, thinking she had been a Merchant Ship, who thereupon catched a Tartar. Afterwards in rummaging there was found a Cartridge of Powder made up with a Piece of an *English* Journal, belonging, I believe, to the *Crean* Snow; and upon Examination, at last, it was discovered that they had taken this Vessel and murthered the Crew; and one of the *Spaniards*, when he came to die, confessed that he had killed twenty *English* Men with his own Hands:

S. Jago de la Vega, Febr 20.
A Letter from his Excellency Sir Nicolas Laws, *our Governor, to the Alcaldes of* Trinidado *on* Cuba, *dated the 26th of* Jan. 1721–2.

Gentlemen,

'The frequent Depredations, Robberies, and other Acts of Hostility, which have been committed on the King my Royal Master's Subjects, by a Parcel of Banditti, who pretend to have Commissions from you, and in Reality are sheltered under your Government, is the Occasion of my sending the Bearer Captain *Chamberlain*, Commander of his Majesty's Snow *Happy*, to demand Satisfaction of you for so many notorious Robberies which your People have lately committed on the King's Subjects of this Island; particularly by those Traytors, *Nicolas Brown* and *Christopher Winter*, to whom you have given Protection. Such Proceedings as these are not only a Breach of the Law of Nations, but must appear to the World of a very extraordinary Nature, when considered that the Subjects of a Prince in Amity and Friendship with another, should give Countenance and encourage such vile Practices. I confess I have had long Patience, and declined using any violent Measures to obtain Satisfaction, hoping the Cessation of Arms, so happily concluded upon between our respective Sovereigns, would have put an effectual Stop to those Disorders; but on the contrary, I now find the Port of *Trinidado* a Receptacle to Villains of all Nations. I do therefore think fit to acquaint you, and assure you in the King my Master's Name, that if I do meet with any of your Rogues for the future upon the Coast of this Island, I will order them to be hanged directly without Mercy; and I expect and demand of you to make ample Restitution to Captain *Chamberlain* of all the Negroes which the said *Brown* and *Winter* have lately taken off from the North-Side of this Island, and also of such Sloops and other Effects as they have been taken and robbed of, since the Cessation of Arms, and that you will deliver up to the Bearer such *English* Men as are now detained, or otherwise remain at *Trinidado*; and also expect you will hereafter forbear granting any Commissions, or suffer any such notorious

Villains to be equipp'd and fitted out from your Port: otherwise you may depend upon it, those that I can meet with, shall be esteemed Pyrates, and treated as such; of which I thought proper to give you Notice, and am, *&c.*'

A Letter from Mr. Joseph Laws, *Lieutenant of his Majesty's Ship*, Happy *Snow, to the Alcaldes of* Trinidado.

Genlemen,
'I am sent by Commadore *Vernon,* Commander in Chief of all his Majesty's Ships in the *West-Indies,* to demand in the King our Master's Name, all the Vessels, with their Effects, *& c.* and also the Negroes taken from *Jamaica* since the Cessation of Arms; likewise all *Englishmen* now detained, or otherwise remaining in your Port of *Trinidado,* particularly *Nicholas Brown* and *Christopher Winter,* both of them being Traytors, Pyrates and common Enemies to all Nations: And the said Commadore hath ordered me to acquaint you, that he is surprized that the Subjects of a Prince in Amity and Friendship with another, should give Countenance to such notorious Villains. In Expectation of your immediate Compliance, I am, Gentlemen,

Off the River *Trini-*   Your humble Servant,
dado, Feb. 8. 1720.   *Joseph Laws.*'

The Answer of the Alcaldes of Trinidado, *to*
Mr. Law's *Letter.*

Capt. *Laws,*
'In Answer to yours, this serves to acquaint you, that neither in this City, nor Port, are there any Negroes or Vessels which have been taken at your Island of *Jamaica,* nor on that Coast, since the Cessation of Arms; and what Vessels have been taken since that Time, have been for trading in an unlawful Commerce on this

Coast; and as for those *English* Fugitives you mention, they are here as other Subjects of our Lord the King, being brought voluntarily to our holy Catholick Faith, and have received the Water of Baptism; but if they should prove Rogues, and should not comply with their Duty, in which they are bound at present, then they shall be chastized according to the Ordinances of our King, whom God preserve. And we beg you will weigh Anchor as soon as possible, and leave this Port and its Coasts, because upon no Account you shall be suffered to trade, or any Thing else; for we are resolved not to admit thereof. God preserve you. We kiss your Hand.
Trinidado,   Signed,   *Hieronimo de Fuentes,*
Feb. 8, 1722.   *Benette Alfonso del Manzano.'*

Mr. Laws's *Reply to the Alcaldes Letter.*

Gentlmen,
    'Your refusing to deliver up the Subjects of the King my Master, is somewhat surprizing, it being in a Time of Peace, and the detaining them consequently against the Law of Nations. Notwithstanding your trifling Pretence (for which you have no Foundation but to forge an Excuse) to prevent, my making any Enquiry into the Truth of the Facts I have alleged in my former, I must tell you my Resolutions are, to stay on the Coast till I have made Reprizals; and should I meet any Vessels belonging to your Port, I shall not treat them as the Subjects of the Crown of *Spain*, but as Pyrates, finding it a Part of your Religion in this Place to protect such Villains.
Off the River *Trini-*   Your humble Servant,
dado, Feb. 8. 1720.   *Joseph Laws.'*

The Answer of one of the Alcaldes to Mr. Laws's *Reply.*

Captain *Laws*,

'You may assure your self, I will never be wanting in the Duty of my Post. The Prisoners that are here are not in Prison, but only kept here to be sent to the Governor of the *Havana*: If you (as you say) command at Sea, I command on Shoar: If you treat the *Spaniards*, you should happen to take, as Pyrates, I will do the same by every one of your People I can take up: I will not be wanting to good Manners, if you will do the same. I can likewise act the Soldier, if any Occasion should offer that way, for I have very good People here for that purpose. If you pretend any Thing else, you may execute it on this Coast. God preserve you. I kiss your Hand.

Trinidado,   Signed,
Feb. 20. 1720.   *Bennette Alfonso del Menzano*.'

The last Advices we have received from our Plantations in *America*, dated *June* 9th, 1724, gives us the following Account, *viz.* That Captain *Jones* in the Ship *John* and *Mary*, on the 5th of the said Month, met with, near the Capes of *Virginia*, a *Spanish Guard del Coast*, commanded by one *Don Benito*, said to be commissioned by the Governor of *Cuba*: She was manned with 60 *Spaniards*, 18 *French* Men and 18 *English*, and had an *English* Captain as well as *Spanish*, one *Richard Holland*, who formerly belonged to the *Suffolk* Man of War, which he deserted at *Naples*, and took Shelter in a Convent. He served on Board the *Spanish* Fleet under Admiral *Cammock*, in the War in the *Mediterranean*; and after the Cessation of Arms with *Spain*, settled with several of his Countrymen (*Irish*) in the *Spanish West-Indies*. This *Guard del Coast* made Prize of Captain *Jones's* Ship, and kept Possession of her from 5th to the 8th, during which Time she took also the *Prudent Hannah* of *Boston, Thomas Mousell* Master, and the *Dolphin* of *Topsham, Theodore Bare* Master, both laden and bound for *Virginia*: The former they sent away together with three Men and the Mate, under the

Command of a *Spanish* Officer and Crew, the same Day she was taken; the latter they carried off with them, putting the Master and all the Crew aboard Captain *Jones*'s Ship. They plundered Captain *Jones* of thirty six Men Slaves, some Gold-Dust, all his Cloaths, four great Guns and small Arms, and about four hundred Gallons of Rum, besides his Provisions and Stores, computed in all to 1500 *l.* Sterling.

CHAPTER I.

Of
Captain AVERY,
And his CREW.

NONE OF these bold Adventures were ever so much talked of, for a while, as *Avery*; he made as great a Noise in the World as *Meriveis* does now, and was looked upon to be a Person of as great Consequence; he was represented in *Europe*, as one that had raised himself to the Dignity of a King, and was likely to be the Founder of a new Monarchy; having, as it was said, taken immense Riches, and married the *Great Mogul*'s Daughter, who was taken in an *Indian* Ship, which fell into his Hands; and that he had by her many Children, living in great Royalty and State; that he had built Forts, erected Magazines, and was Master of a stout Squadron of Ships, mann'd with able and desperate Fellows of all Nations; that he gave Commissions out in his own Name to the Captains of his Ships, and to the Commanders of his Forts, and was acknowledged by them as their Prince. A Play was writ upon him, called, the *Successful Pyrate*; and, these Accounts obtained such Belief, that several Schemes were offered to the Council for fitting out a Squadron to take him; while others were for offering him and his Companions an Act of Grace, and inviting them to *England*, with all their Treasure, least his growing Greatness might hinder the Trade of *Europe* to the *East-Indies*.

Yet all these were no more than false Rumours, improved by the Credulity of some, and the Humour of others who

love to tell strange Things; for, while it was said, he was
aspiring at a Crown, he wanted a Shilling; and at the same
Time it was given out he was in Possession of such prodigious Wealth in *Madagascar*, he was starving in *England*.

No doubt, but the Reader will have a Curiosity of knowing what became of this Man, and what were the true
Grounds of so many false Reports concerning him;
therefore, I shall, in as brief a Manner as I can, give his
History.

He was born in the West of *England* near *Plymouth* in
Devonshire, being bred to the Sea, he served as a Mate of a
Merchant-Man, in several trading Voyages: It happened be-
fore the Peace of *Ryswick*, when there was an Alliance be-
twixt *Spain, England, Holland, &c.* against *France*, that the
French in *Martinico*, carried on a smugling Trade with the
Spaniards on the Continent of *Peru*, which by the Laws of
Spain, is not allowed to Friends in Time of Peace, for none
but native *Spaniards* are permitted to Traffick in those Parts,
or set their Feet on Shore, unless at any Time they are
brought as Prisoners; wherefore they constantly keep certain
Ships cruising along the Coast, whom they call *Guards del
Casta*, who have the Orders to make Prizes of all Ships they
can sight of within five Leagues of Land. Now the *French*
growing very bold in Trade, and the *Spaniards* being poorly
provided with Ships, and those they had being of no Force,
it often fell out, that when they light of the *French* Smuglers,
they were not strong enough to attack them, therefore it was
resolv'd in *Spain*, to hire two or three stout foreign Ships for
their Service, which being known at *Bristol*, some Merchants
of that City, fitted out two Ships of thirty odd Guns, and
120 Hands each, well furnished with Provision aud Ammunition, and all other Stores; and the Hire being agreed
for, by some Agents for *Spain*, they were commanded to sail
for *Corunna* or the *Groine*, there to receive their Orders, and
to take on Board some *Spanish* Gentlemen, who were to go
Passengers to *New-Spain*.

Of one of these Ships, which I take to be call'd the *Duke*,

Capt. *Gibson* Commander, *Avery* was first Mate, and being
a Fellow of more Cunning than Courage, he insinuated himself into the good Will of several of the boldest Fellows on
Board the other Ship, as well as that which he was on Board
of; having sounded their Inclinations before he opened himself, and finding them ripe for his Design, he, at length,
proposed to them, to run away with the Ship, telling them
what great Wealth was to be had upon the Coasts of *India*:
It was no sooner said than agreed to, and they resolved to
execute their Plot at Ten a Clock the Night following.

It must be observ'd, the Captain was one of those who
are mightily addicted to Punch, so that he passed most of
his Time on Shore, in some little drinking Ordinary; but this
Day he did not go on Shore as usual; however, this did not
spoil the Design, for he took his usual Dose on Board, and
so got to Bed before the Hour appointed for the Business:
The Men also who were not privy to the Design, turn'd into
their Hammocks, leaving none upon Deck but the Conspirators, who, indeed, were the greatest Part of the Ship's
Crew. At the Time agreed on, the *Dutchess*'s Long-Boat appear'd, which *Avery* hailing in the usual Manner, was answered by the Men in her, *Is your drunken Boatswain on
Board?* Which was the Watch-Word agreed between them,
and *Avery* replying in the Affirmative, the Boat came aboard
with sixteen stout Fellows, and joined the Company.

When our Gentry saw that all was clear, they secured the
Hatches, so went to work; they did not slip the Anchor, but
weigh'd it leisurely, and so put to Sea without any Disorder
or Confusion, tho' there were several Ships then lying in the
Bay, and among them a *Dutch* Frigate of forty Guns; the
Captain of which was offered a great Reward to go out after
her; but *Mynheer*, who perhaps would not have been willing
to have been served so himself, could not be prevail'd upon
to give such Usage to another, and so let Mr. *Avery* pursue
his Voyage, whither he had a Mind to.

The Captain, who by this Time, was awaked, either by
the Motion of the Ship, or the Noise of working the Tackles,

rung the Bell; *Avery* and two others went into the Cabin; the Captain, half asleep, and in a kind of Fright, ask'd, *What was the Matter? Avery* answered cooly, *Nothing;* the Captain replied, *something's the Matter with the Ship, Does she drive? What Weather is it?* Thinking nothing less then that it had been a Storm, and that the Ship was driven from her Anchors: *No, no,* answered *Avery, we're at Sea, with a fair Wind and good Weather. At Sea!* says the Captain, *How can that be? Come,* says *Avery, don't be in a Fright, but put on your Cloaths, and I'll let you into a Secret:*——*You must know, that I am Captain of this Ship now, and this is my Cabin, therefore you must walk out; I am bound to* Madagascar, *with a Design of making my own Fortune, and that of all the brave Fellows joined with me.*

The Captain having a little recovered his Senses, began to apprehend the meaning; however, his Fright was as great as before, which *Avery* perceiving, bad him fear nothing, for, says he, if you have a Mind to make one of us, we will receive you, and if you'll turn sober, and mind your Business, perhaps in Time I may make you one of my Lieutenants, if not, here's a Boat a-long-side, and you shall be set ashore.

The Captain was glad to hear this, and therefore accepted of his Offer, and the whole Crew being called up, to know who was willing to go on Shore with the Captain, and who to seek their Fortunes with the rest; there were not above five or six who were willing to quit this Enterprize; wherefore they were put into the Boat with the Captain that Minute, and made their Way to the Shore as well as they could.

They proceeded on their Voyage to *Madagascar,* but I do not find they took any Ships in their Way; when they arrived at the N.E. Part of that Island, they found two Sloops at Anchor, who, upon seeing them, slip'd their Cables and run themselves ashore, the Men all landing, and running into the Woods; these were two Sloops which the Men had run away with from the *West-Indies,* and seeing *Avery,* they supposed him to be some Frigate sent to take them, and therefore not being of Force to engage him, they did what they could to save themselves.

He guessed where they were, and sent some of his Men on Shore to let them know they were Friends, and to offer they might join together for their common Safety; the Sloops Men were well arm'd, and had posted themselves in a Wood, with Centinels just on the out-side, to observe whether the Ship landed her Men to pursue them, and they observing only two or three Men to come towards them without Arms, did not oppose them, but having challenged them, and they answering they were Friends, they lead them to their Body, where they delivered their Message; at first, they apprehended it was a Stratagem to decoy them on Board, but when the Ambassadors offered that the Captain himself, and as many of the Crew as they should name, would meet them on Shore without Arms, they believed them to be in Earnest, and they soon entered into a Confidence with one another; those on Board going on Shore, and some of those on Shore going on Board.

The Sloops Men were rejoiced at the new Ally, for their Vessels were so small, that they could not attack a Ship of any Force, so that hitherto they had not taken any considerable Prize, but now they hop'd to fly at high Game; and *Avery* was as well pleased at this Reinforcement, to strengthen them for any brave Enterprize, and tho' the Booty must be lessened to each, by being divided into so many Shares, yet he found out an Expedient not to suffer by it himself, as shall be shewn in its Place.

Having consulted what was to be done, they resolved to sail out together upon a Cruize, the Galley and two Sloops; they therefore fell to work to get the Sloops off, which they soon effected, and steered towards the *Arabian* Coast; near the River *Indus*, the Man at the Mast-Head spied a Sail, upon which they gave Chace, and as they came nearer to her, they perceived her to be a tall Ship, and fancied she might be a *Dutch East-India* Man homeward bound; but she proved a better Prize; when they fired at her to bring too, she hoisted *Mogul's* Colours, and seemed to stand upon her Defence; *Avery* only canonaded at a Distance, and some of his Men began to suspect that he was not the Hero they took him for: However, the Sloops made Use of their Time, and coming one on the Bow, and the other on the Quarter, of the Ship, clapt her on Board, and enter'd her, upon which she immediately struck her Colours and yielded; she was one of the *Great Mogul's* own Ships, and there were in her several of the greatest Persons of his Court, among whom it was said was one of his Daughters, who were going on a Pilgrimage to *Mecca*, the *Mahometans* thinking themselves obliged once in their Lives to visit that Place, and they were carrying with them rich Offerings to present at the Shrine of *Mahomet*. It is known that the Eastern People travel with the utmost Magnificence, so that they had with them all their Slaves and Attendants, their rich Habits and Jewels, with Vessels of Gold and Silver, and great Sums of Money to defray the Charges of their Journey by Land; wherefore the Plunder got by this Prize, is not easily computed.

Having taken all the Treasure on Board their own Ships, and plundered their Prize of every Thing else they either wanted or liked, they let her go; she not being able to continue her Voyage, returned back: As soon as the News came to the *Mogul*, and he knew that they were *English* who had robbed them, he threatened loud, and talked of sending a mighty Army with Fire and Sword, to extirpate the *English* from all their Settlements on the *Indian* Coast. The *East-India* Company in *England*, were very much alarmed at it; however, by Degrees, they found Means to pacify him, by promising to do their Endeavours to take the Robbers, and deliver them into his Hands; however, the great Noise this Thing made in *Europe*, as well as *India*, was the Occasion of all these romantick Stories which were formed of *Avery's* Greatness.

In the mean Time our successful Plunderers agreed to make the best of their Way back to *Madagascar*, intending to make that Place their Magazine or Repository for all their Treasure, and to build a small Fortification there, and leave a few Hands always ashore to look after it, and defend it from any Attempts of the Natives; but *Avery* put an End to this Project, and made it altogether unnecessary.

As they were Steering their Course, as has been said, he sends a Boat on Board of each of the Sloops, desiring the Chief of them to come on Board of him, in order to hold a Council; they did so, and he told them he had something to propose to them for the common Good, which was to provide against Accidents; he bad them consider the Treasure they were possess'd of, would be sufficient for them all if they could secure it in some Place on Shore; therefore all they had to fear, was some Misfortune in the Voyage; he bad them consider the Consequences of being separated by bad Weather, in which Case, the Sloops, if either of them should fall in with any Ships of Force, must be either taken or sunk, and the Treasure on Board her lost to the rest, besides the common Accidents of the Sea; as for his Part he was so strong, he was able to make his Party good with any Ship they were like to meet in those Seas; that if he met with any Ship of such Strength, that he could not take her, he was safe from being taken, being so well mann'd; besides his Ship was a quick Sailor, and could carry Sail, when the Sloops could not, wherefore, he proposed to them, to put the Treasure on Board his Ship, to seal up each Chest with 3 Seals, whereof each was to keep one, and to appoint a Rendezvous, in Case of Separation.

Upon considering this Proposal, it appeared so seasonable to them, that they readily came into it, for they argued to themselves, that an Accident might happen to one of the Sloops and the other escape, wherefore it was for the common Good. The Thing was done as agreed to, the Treasure put on Board of *Avery*, and the Chests seal'd; they kept Company that Day and the next, the Weather being fair, in which Time *Avery* tampered with his Men, telling them they now had sufficient to make them all easy, and what should hinder them from going to some Country, where they were not known, and living on Shore all the rest of their Days in Plenty; they understood what he meant: And in short, they all agreed to bilk their new Allies, the Sloop's Men, nor do I find that any of them felt any Qualms of Honour rising in his stomach, to hinder them from consenting to this Piece of Treachery. In fine, they took Advantage of the Darkness that Night, steer'd another Course, and, by Morning, lost Sight of them.

I leave the Reader to judge, what Swearing and Confusion there was among the Sloop's Men, in the Morning, when they saw that *Avery* had given them the Slip; for they knew by the Fairness of the Weather, and the Course they had agreed to steer, that it must have been done on purpose: But we leave them at present to follow Mr. *Avery*.

Avery, and his Men, having consulted what to do with themselves, came to a Resolution, to make the best of their Way towards *America*; and none of them being known in those Parts, they intended to divide the Treasure, to change their Names, to go ashore, some in one Place, some in other, to purchase some Settlements, and live at Ease. The first Land they made, was the Island of *Providence*, then newly settled; here they staid some Time, and having considered that when they should go to *New-England*, the Greatness of their Ship, would cause much Enquiry about them, and possibly some People from *England*, who had heard the Story of a Ship's being run away with from the *Groine*, might suspect them to be the People; they therefore took a Resolution of disposing of their Ship at *Providence*: Upon which, *Avery* pretending that the Ship being fitted out upon the privateering Account, and having had no Success, he had received Orders from the Owners, to dispose of her to the best Advantage, he soon met with a Purchaser, and immediately bought a Sloop.

In this Sloop, he and his Companions embarq'd, they touch'd at several Parts of *America*, where no Person suspected them; and some of them went on Shore, and dispersed themselves about the Country, having received such Dividends as *Avery* would give them; for he concealed the greatest Part of the Diamonds from them, which in the first Hurry of plundering the Ship, they did not much regard, as not knowing their Value.

At length he came to *Boston*, in *New-England*, and seem'd to have a Desire of settling in those Parts, and some of his Companions went on Shore there also, but he changed his Resolution, and proposed to the few of his Companions who were left, to sail for *Ireland*, which they consented to: He found out that *New-England* was not a proper Place for him, because a great deal of his Wealth lay in Diamonds; and should he have produced them there, he would have certainly been seiz'd on Suspicion of Pyracy.

In their Voyage to *Ireland*, they avoided St. *George*'s Channel, and sailing North about, they put into one of the Northern Ports of that Kingdom; there they disposed of their Sloop, and coming on Shore they separated themselves, some going to *Cork*, and some to *Dublin*, 18 of whom obtain'd their Pardons afterwards of K. *William*. When *Avery* had remain'd some Time in this Kingdom, he was afraid to offer his Diamonds to sale, least an Enquiry into his Manner of coming by them should occasion a Discovery; therefore considering with himself what was best to be done, he fancied there were some Persons at *Bristol*, whom he might venture to trust; upon which, he resolved to pass over into *England*; he did so, and going into *Devonshire*, he sent to one of these Friends to meet him at a Town called *Biddiford*; when he had communicated himself to his Friends, and consulted with him about the Means of his Effects, they agreed, that the safest Method would be, to put them in the Hands of some Merchants, who being Men of Wealth and Credit in the World, no Enquiry would be made how they came by them; this Friend telling him he was very intimate with some who were very fit for the Purpose, and if he would but allow them a good Commission would do the Business very faithfully.

Avery liked the Proposal, for he found no other Way of managing his Affairs, since he could not appear in them himself; therefore his Friend going back to *Bristol*, and opening the Matter to the Merchants, they made *Avery* a Visit at *Biddiford*, where, after some Protestations of Honour and Integrity, he delivered them his Effects, consisting of Diamonds and some Vessels of Gold; they gave him a little Money for his present Subsistance, and so they parted.

He changed his Name and lived at *Biddiford*, without making any Figure, and therefore there was no great Notice taken of him; yet let one or two of his Relations know where he was, who came to see him. In some Time his little Money was spent, yet he heard nothing from his Merchants; he writ to them often, and after much Importunity they sent him a small Supply, but scarce sufficient to pay his Debts: In fine, the Supplies they sent him from Time to Time, were so small, that they were not sufficient to give him Bread, nor could he get that little, without a great deal of Trouble and Importunity, wherefore being weary of his Life, he went privately to *Bristol*, to speak to the Merchants himself, where instead of Money he met a most shocking Repulse, for when he desired them to come to an Account with him, they silenced him by threatening to discover him, so that our Merchants were as good Pyrates at Land as he was at Sea.

Whether he was frightened by these Menaces, or had seen some Body else he thought knew him, is not known; but he went immediately over to *Ireland*, and from thence sollicited his Merchants very hard for a Supply, but to no Purpose, for he was even reduced to beggary: In this Extremity he was resolved to return and cast himself upon them, let the Consequence be what it would. He put himself on Board a trading Vessel, and work'd his Passage over to *Plymouth*, from whence he travelled on Foot to *Biddiford*, where he had been but a few Days before he fell sick and died; not being worth as much as would buy him a Coffin.

Thus have I given all that could be collected of any Certainty concerning this Man; rejecting the idle Stories which were made of his fantastick Greatness, by which it appears, that his Actions were more inconsiderable than those of other Pyrates, since him, though he made more Noise in the World.

Now we shall turn back and give our Readers some Account of what became of the two Sloops.

We took Notice of the Rage and Confusion, which must have seized them, upon their missing of *Avery*; however, they continued their Course, some of them still flattering themselves that he had only out sailed them in the Night, and that they should find him at the Place of Rendezvous: But when they came there, and could hear no Tydings of him, there was an End of Hope. It was Time to consider what they should do with themselves, their Stock of Sea Provision was almost spent, and tho' there was Rice and Fish, and Fowl to be had ashore, yet these would not keep for Sea, without being properly cured with Salt, which they had no Conveniency of doing; therefore, since they could not go a Cruizing any more, it was Time to think of establishing themselves at Land; to which Purpose they took all Things out of the Sloops, made Tents of the Sails, and encamped themselves, having a large Quantity of Ammunition, and abundance of small Arms.

Here they met with several of their Countrymen, the Crew of a Privateer Sloop which was commanded by Captain *Thomas Tew*; and since it will be but a short Digression, we will give an Account how they came here.

Captain *George Dew* and Captain *Thomas Tew*, having received Commissions from the then Governor of *Bermudas*, to sail directly for the River *Gambia* in *Africa*; there, with the Advice and Assistance of the Agents of the Royal *African* Company, to attempt the taking the *French* Factory at *Goorie*, lying upon that Coast. In a few Days after they sailed out, *Dew* in a violent Storm, not only sprung his Mast, but lost Sight of his Consort; *Dew* therefore returned back to refit, and *Tew* instead of proceeding on his Voyage, made for the *Cape of Good Hope*, and doubling the said Cape, shaped his Course for the Straits of *Babel Mandel*, being the Entrance into the *Red Sea*. Here he came up with a large Ship, richly laden, bound from the *Indies* to *Arabia*, with three hundred Soldiers on Board, besides Seamen; yet *Tew* had the Hardiness to board her, and soon carried her; and, 'tis said, by this Prize, his Men shared near three thousand Pounds a Piece: They had Intelligence from the Prisoners, of five other rich Ships to pass that Way, which *Tew* would have attacked, tho' they were very strong, if he had not been over-ruled by the Quarter-Master and others.—This differing in Opinion created some ill Blood amongst them, so that they resolved to break up pyrating, and no Place was so fit to receive them as *Madagascar*; hither they steered, resolving to live on Shore and enjoy what they got.

As for *Tew* himself, he with a few others in a short Time went off to *Rhode Island*, from whence he made his Peace.

Thus have we accounted for the Company our Pyrates met with here.

It must be observed that the Natives of *Madagascar* are a kind of Negroes, they differ from those of *Guiney* in their Hair, which is long, and their Complexion is not so good a Jet; they have innumerable little Princes among them, who are continually making War upon one another; their Prisoners are their Slaves, and they either sell them, or put them to death, as they please: When our Pyrates first settled amongst them, their Alliance was much courted by these Princes, so they sometimes joined one, sometimes another, but wheresoever they sided, they were sure to be Victorious; for the Negroes here had no Fire-Arms, nor did they understand their Use; so that at length these Pyrates became so terrible to the Negroes, that if two or or three of them were only seen on one Side, when they were going to engage, the opposite Side would fly without striking a Blow.

By these Means they not only became feared, but powerful; all the Prisoners of War, they took to be their Slaves; they married the most beautiful of the Negroe Women, not one or two, but as many as they liked; so that every one of them had as great a Seraglio as the Grand Seignior at *Con-stantinople*: Their Slaves they employed in planting Rice, in Fishing Hunting, *&c.* besides which, they had abundance of others, who lived, as it were, under their Protection, and to be secure from the Disturbances or Attacks of their powerful Neighbours; these seemed to pay them a willing Homage. Now they began to divide from one another, each living with his own Wives, Slaves and Dependants, like a separate Prince; and as Power and Plenty naturally beget Contention, they sometimes quarrelled with one another, and attacked each other at the Head of their several Armies; and in these civil Wars, many of them were killed; but an Accident happened, which obliged them to unite again for their common Safety.

It must be observed that these sudden great Men, had used their Power like Tyrants, for they grew wanton in Cruelty, and nothing was more common, than upon the slightest Displeasure, to cause one of their Dependants to be tied to a Tree and shot thro' the Heart, let the Crime be what it would, whether little or great, this was always the Punishment; wherefore the Negroes conspired together, to rid themselves of these Destroyers, all in one Night; and as they now lived separate, the Thing might easily have been done, had not a Woman, who had been Wife or Concubine to one of them, run near twenty Miles in three Hours, to discover the Matter to them: Immediately upon the Alarm they ran together as fast as they could, so that when the Negroes approached them, they found them all up in Arms; wherefore they retired without making any Attempt.

This Escape made them very cautious from that Time, and it will be worth while to describe the Policy of these brutish Fellows, and to shew what Measures they took to secure themselves.

They found that the Fear of their Power could not secure them against a Surprize, and the bravest Man may be kill'd when he is asleep, by one much his inferior in Courage and Strength, therefore, as their first Security, they did all they could to foment War betwixt the neighbouring Negroes, remaining Neuter themselves, by which Means, those who were overcome constantly fled to there for Protection, otherwise they must be either killed or made Slaves. They strengthened their Party, and tied some to them by Interest, when there was no War, they contrived to spirit up private Quarrels among them, and upon every little Dispute or Misunderstanding, push on one Side or other to Revenge; Instruct them how to attack or surprize their Adversaries, and lend them loaded Pistols or Firelocks to dispatch them with; the Consequence of which was, that the Murderer was forced to fly to them for the safety of his Life, with his Wives, Children and Kindred.

Such as these were fast Friends, as their Lives depended upon the safety of his Protectors; for as we observed before, our Pyrates were grown so terrible, that none of their Neighbours had Resolution enough to attack them in an open War.

By such Arts as these, in the Space of a few Years, their Body was greatly increased, they then began to separate themselves, and remove at a greater Distance from one another, for the Convenience of more Ground, and were divided like Jews, into Tribes, each carrying with him his Wives and Children, (of which, by this Time they had a large Family,) as also their Quota of Dependants and Followers; and if Power and Command be the Thing which distinguish a Prince, these Ruffians had all the Marks of Royalty about them, nay more, they had the very Fears which commonly disturb Tyrants, as many be seen by the extream Caution they took in fortifying the Places where they dwelt.

In this Plan of Fortification they imitated one another, their Dwellings were rather Citadels than Houses; they made Choice of a Place overgrown with Wood, and scituate near a Water; they raised a Rampart or high Ditch round it, so strait and high, that it was impossible to climb it, and especially by those who had not the Use of scaling Ladders: Over this Ditch there was one Passage into the Wood; the

Dwelling, which was a Hut, was built in that Part of the Wood which the Prince, who inhabited it, thought fit, but so covered that it could not be seen till you came at it; but the greatest Cunning lay in the Passage which lead to the Hut, which was so narrow, that no more than one Person could go a Breast, and contrived in so intricate a Manner, that it was a perfect Maze or Labyrinth, it being round and round, with several little cross Ways, so that a Person that was not well acquainted with the Way, might walk several Hours round and cross these Ways without being able to find the Hut; moreover all along the Sides of these narrow Paths, certain large Thorns which grew upon a Tree in that Country, were struck into the Ground with their Points uppermost, and the Path it self being made crooked and serpentine, if a Man should attempt to come near the Hut at Night, he would certainly have struck upon these Thorns, tho' he had been provided with that Clue which *Ariadne* gave to *Theseus* when he entered the Cave of the *Minataur*.

Thus Tyrant like they lived, fearing and feared by all; and in this Scituation they were found by Captain *Woods Rogers*, when he went to *Madagascar*, in the *Delicia*, a Ship of Forty Guns, with a Design of buying Slaves in order to sell to the *Dutch* at *Batavia* or *New-Holland*: He happened to touch upon a Part of the Island, where no Ship had been seen for seven or eight Years before, where he met with some of the Pyrates, at which Time, they had been upon the Island above 25 Years, having a large motly Generation of Children and Grand-Children descended from them, there being about that Time, eleven of them remaining alive.

Upon their first seeing a Ship of this Force and Burthen, they supposed it to be a Man of War sent to take them; they therefore lurked within their Fastnesses, but when some from the Ship came on Shore, without any shew of Hostility, and offering to trade with the Negroes, they ventured to come out of their Holes, attended like Princes, and since they actually are Kings *De Facto*, which is a kind of a Right, we ought to speak of them as such.

Having been so many Years upon this Island, it may be imagined, their Cloaths had long been worn out, so that their Majesties were extreamly out at the Elbows; I cannot say they were ragged, since they had no Cloaths, they had nothing to cover them but the Skins of Beasts without any tanning, but with all the Hair on, nor a Shoe nor Stocking, so they looked like the Pictures of *Hercules* in the Lion's Skin; and being overgrown with Beard, and Hair upon their Bodies, they appeared the most savage Figures that a Man's Imagination can frame.

However, they soon got rigg'd, for they sold great Numbers of those poor People under them, for Cloaths, Knives, Saws, Powder and Ball, and many other Things, and became so familiar that they went aboard the *Delicia*, and were observed to be very curious, examining the inside of the Ship, and very familiar with the Men, inviting them ashore. Their Design in doing this, as they afterwards confessed, was to try if it was not practicable to surprize the Ship in the Night, which they judged very easy, in case there was but a slender Watch kept on Board, they having Boats and Men enough at Command, but it seems the Captain was aware of them, and kept so strong a Watch upon Deck, that they found it was in vain to make any Attempt; wherefore, when some of the Men went ashore, they were for inveigling them, and drawing them into a Plot, for seizing the Captain and securing the rest of the Men under Hatches, when they should have the Night-Watch, promising a Signal to come on Board to join them; proposing, if they succeeded, to go a Pyrating together, not doubting but with that Ship they should be able to take any Thing they met on the Sea: But the Captain observing an Intimacy growing betwixt them and some of his Men, thought it could be for no good, he therefore broke it off in Time, not suffering them so much as to talk together; and when he sent a Boat on Shore with an Officer to treat with them about the Sale of Slaves, the Crew remained on Board the Boat, and no Man was suffered to talk with them, but the Person deputed by him for that Purpose.

Before he sailed away, and they found that nothing was to be done, they confessed all the Designs they had formed against him. Thus he left them as he found them, in a great deal of dirty State and Royalty, but with fewer Subjects than they had, having, as we observed, sold many of them; and if Ambition be the darling Passion of Men, no doubt they were happy. One of these great Princes had formerly been a Waterman upon the *Thames*, where having committed a Murder, he fled to the *West-Indies*, and was of the Number of those who run away with the Sloops; the rest had been all foremast Men, nor was there a Man amongst them, who could either read or write, and yet their Secretaries of State had no more Learning than themselves. This is all the Account we can give of these Kings of *Madagascar*, some of whom it is probable are reigning to this Day.

CHAPTER II.

Of
Captain MARTEL,
And his CREW.

I COME now to the Pyrates that have rose since the Peace of *Utrecht*; in War Time there is no room for any, because all those of a roving advent'rous Disposition find Employment in Privateers, so there is no Opportunity for Pyrates like our Mobs in *London*, when they come to any Height, our Superiors order out the Train Bands, and when once they are raised, the others are suppressed of Course; I take the Reason of it to be, that the Mob go into the tame Army, and immediately from notorious Breakers of the Peace, become, by being put into order, solemn Preservers of it. And should our Legislators put some of the Pyrates into Authority, it would not only lessen their Number, but, I imagine, set them upon the rest, and they would be the likeliest People to find them out, according to the Proverb, *set a Thief to catch a Thief.*

To bring this about, there needs no other Encouragement, but to give all the Effects taken aboard a Pyrate Vessel to the Captors; for the Case of Plunder and Gain, they like it as well from Friends, as Enemies, but are not fond, as Things are carry'd, *of ruining poor Fellowes,* say the *Creoleans, with no Advantage to themselves.*

The Multitude of Men and Vessels, employ'd this Way, in Time of War; in the *West-Indies,* is another Reason, for the Number of Pyrates in a Time of Peace: This cannot be supposed to be a Reflection on any of our *American* Governments, much less on the King himself, by whose Authority such Commissions are granted, because of the Reasonableness, and absolute Necessity, there is for the doing of it; yet the Observation is just, for so many idle People employing themselves in Privateers, for the sake of Plunder and Riches, which they always spend as fast as they get, that when the War is over, and they can have no farther Business in the Way of Life they have been used to, they too readily engage in Acts of Pyracy, which being but the same Practice without a Commission, they make very little Distinction betwixt the Lawfulness of one, and the Unlawfulness of the other.

I have not enquired so far back, as to know the Original of this Rover, but I believe he and his Gang, were some Privateer's Men belonging to the Island of *Jamaica*, in the preceeding War, his Story is but short, for his Reign was so, an End having been put to his Adventures in good Time, when he was growing strong and formidable. We find him Commander of a Pyrate Sloop of eight Guns, and 80 Men, in the Month of *September*, 1716, cruising off *Jamaica*, *Cuba*, *&c.* about which Time he took the *Berkley* Galley, Captain *Saunders*, and plundered him of 1000 *l.* in Money, and afterwards met with a Sloop call'd the *King Solomon*, from whom he took some Money, and Provisions, besides Goods, to a good Value.

They proceeded after this to the Port of Cavena at the Island of *Cuba*, and in their Way took two sloops which they plundered, and let go; and off the Port fell in with a fine Galley, with 20 Guns, call'd the *John* and *Martha*, Captain *Wilson*, which they attacked under the pyratical Black-Flag, and made themselves Masters of her. They put some of the Men ashore, and others they detain'd, as they had done several Times, to encrease their Company; but Captain *Martel*, charged Captain *Wilson*, to advise his Owners, that their Ship would answer his Purpose exactly, by taking one Desk down, and as for the Cargo, which consisted chiefly of Logwood and Sugar, he would take Care it should be carry'd to a good Market.

Having fitted up the aforesaid Ship, as they design'd, they mounted her with 22 Guns, 100 Men, and left 25 Hands in the Sloop, and so proceeded to Cruize off the Leeward Islands, where they met with but too much Success. After the taking of a Sloop and a Brigantine, they gave Chase to a stout Ship, which they came up with, and, at Sight of the Pyrate's Flag, she struck to the Robbers, being a Ship of 20 Guns, call'd the *Dolphin*, bound for *Newfoundland*. Captain *Martel* made the Men Prisoners, and carry'd the Ship with him.

The middle of *December* the Pyrates took another Galley in her Voyage home from *Jamaica*, call'd the *Kent*, Captain *Lawton*, and shifted her Provisions aboard their own Ship, and let her go, which obliged her to Sail back to *Jamaica* for a Supply for her Voyage. After this they met with a small Ship and a Sloop, belonging to *Barbadoes*, out of both they took Provisions, and then parted with them, having first taken out some of their Hands, who were willing to be forced to go along with them. The *Greyhound* Galley of *London*, Captain *Evans*, from *Guiney* to *Jamaica*, was the next that had the Misfortune to fall in their Way, which they did not detain long, for as soon as they could get out all her Gold Dust, Elephant's Teeth, and 40 Slaves, they sent her onwards upon her Voyage.

They concluded now, that 'twas high Time to get into Harbour and refit, as well as to get Refreshments themselves, and wait an Opportunity to dispose of their Cargo; therefore 'twas resolved to make the best of their Way to *Santa Crux*, a small Island in the Lattitude of 18, 30, N. ten Mile long, and two broad, lying South-East of *Porto Rico*, belonging to the *French* Settlements. Here they thought they might lye privately enough for some Time, and fit themselves for further Mischief. They met with a Sloop by the Way which they took along with them, and in the Beginning of the Year

1716-17, they arrived at their Port, having a Ship of 20 Guns, a Sloop of eight, and three Prizes, *viz.* another Ship of 20 Guns, a Sloop of four Guns, and another Sloop last taken; with this little Fleet, they got into a small Harbour, or Road, the N. W. Part of the Island, and warp'd up two Creeks, which were made by a little Island lying within the Bay; (I am the more particular now, because I shall take Leave of the Gentlemen, at this Place.) They had here bare 16 Foot Water, at the deepest, and but 13 or 14, at the shallowest, and nothing but Rocks and Sands without, which secured them from Wind and Sea, and likewise from any considerable Force coming against them.

When they had all got in, the first Thing they had to do, was to Guard themselves in the best Manner they could; they made a Battery of four Guns upon the Island, and another Battery of two. Guns on the North Point of the Road, and warp'd in one of the Sloops with eight Guns, at the Mouth of the Channel, to hinder any Vessels from coming in; when this was done they went to Work on their Ship, unrigging, and unloading, in order to Clean, where I shall leave them a while, till I bring other Company to 'em.

In the Month of *November*, 1716, General *Hamilton*, Commander in chief of all the *Leeward Carribee Islands*, sent a Sloop Express to Captain *Hume*, at *Barbadoes*, Commander of his Majesty's Ship, *Scarborough*, of 30 Guns, and 140 Men, to acquaint him, that two Pyrate Sloops of 12 Guns each, molested the Colonies, having plundered several Vessels. The *Scarborough* had bury'd twenty Men, and had near forty Sick, and therefore was but in ill State to go to Sea: However, Captain *Hume* left his sick Men behind, and sailed to the other Islands, for a supply of Men, taking 20 Soldiers from *Antegoa*; at *Nevis*, he took 10, and 10 at *St. Christophers*, and then sailed to the Island of *Anguilla*, where he learned, that some Time before 2 such Sloops had been at *Spanish-Town*, otherwise called, one of the *Virgin* Islands: Accordingly, the next Day, the *Scarborough* came to *Spanish-Town*, but could hear no News of the Sloops, only, that they had been there about *Christmas*, (it being then the 15th of *January*.)

Captain *Hume*, finding no Account could be had of these Pyrates, designed to go back, the next Day, to *Barbadoes*; but it happened, that Night, that a Boat anchor'd there from *Santa Crux*, and informed him, that he saw a Pyrate Ship of 22 or 24 Guns, with other Vessels, going in to the North West Part of the Island aforesaid. The *Scarborough* weigh'd immediately, and the next Morning, came in Sight of the Rovers, and their Prizes, and stood to them, but the Pilot refused to venture in with the Ship; all the while the Pyrates fir'd red hot Bullets from the Shore. At length, the Ship came to an Anchor, along Side the Reef, near the Channel, and cannonaded for several Hours, both the Vessels and Batteries: About four in the Afternoon, the Sloop that guarded the Channel, was sunk by the Shot of the Man of War; then she cannonaded the Pyrate Ship of 22 Guns, that lay behind the Island. The next Night, *viz.* the 18th, it falling Calm, Captain *Hume* weigh'd, fearing he might fall on the Reef, and so stood off and on for a Day or two, to block them up. On the 20th, in the Evening, they observed the Man of War to stand off to Sea, and took the Opportunity to warp out, in order to slip away from the Island; but at Twelve o'Clock they run a-ground, and when seeing the *Scarborough* about, standing in again, as their Case was desperate, so they were put into the utmost Confusion; they quitted their Ship, and set her on Fire, with 20 Negroes in her, who were all burnt; 19 of the Pyrates made their Escape in a small Sloop, but the Captain and the rest, with 20 Negroes, betook to the Woods, where 'twas probable they might starve, for we never heard what became of 'em afterwards: Captain *Hume* released the Prisoners, with the Ship and Sloop that remained, and then went after the two Pyrate Sloops first mentioned.

CHAPTER III.

Of
Captain TEACH,
alias BLACK-BEARD.

*E*DWARD *TEACH* was a Bristol Man born, but sailed some Time out of *Jamaica* in Privateers, in the late *French* War; yet tho' he had often distinguished himself for his uncommon Boldness and personal Courage, he was never raised to any Command, till he went a-pyrating, which I think was at the latter End of the Year 1716, when Captain *Benjamin Hornigold* put him into a Sloop that he had made Prize of and with whom he continued in Consortship till a little while before *Hornigold* surrendered.

In the Spring of the year 1717, *Teach* and *Hornigold* sailed from Providence for the Main of *America*, and took in their way a Billop from the *Havana*, with 120 Barrels of Flower and also a Sloop from *Bermuda, Thurbar* Master, from whom they took only some Gallons of Wine, and then let him go; and a Ship from *Madera* to *South-Carolina* out of which they got Plunder to a considerable Value.

After cleaning on the Coast of *Virginia*, they returned to the *West-Indies*, and in the Latitude of 24, made Prize of a large *French Guiney* Man, bound to *Martinico*, which by *Hornigold*'s Consent, *Teach* went aboard of as Captain, and took a Cruize in her; *Hornigold* returned with his Sloop to *Providence*, where, at the Arrival of Captain *Rogers*, the Gov-

ernor, he surrendered to Mercy, pursuant to the King's Proclamation.

Aboard of this *Guiney* Man *Teach* mounted 40 Guns, and
named her the *Queen Ann's Revenge*; and cruising near the
Island of *St. Vincent*, took a large Ship, called the *Great Allen*,
Christopher Taylor Commander; the Pyrates plundered her
of what they though fit, put all the Men ashore upon the
Island above mentioned, and then set Fire to the Ship.

A few Days after, *Teach* fell in with the *Scarborough* Man
of War, of 30 Guns who engaged him for some Hours; but
she finding the Pyrate well mann'd, and having tried her
strength, gave over the Engagement, and returned to *Barbadoes*, the Place of her Station; and *Teach* sailed towards the
Spanish America.

In his Way he met with a Pyrate Sloop of ten Guns,
commanded by one Major *Bonnet*, lately a Gentleman of
good Reputation and Estate in the Island of *Barbadoes*,
whom he joyned; but in a few Days after, *Teach*, finding that
Bonnet knew nothing of a maritime Life, with the Consent
of his own Men, put in another Captain, one *Richards*, to
Command *Bonnet's* Sloop, and took the Major on aboard
his own Ship, telling him *that as he had not been used to the
Fatigues and Care of such a Post, it would be better for him to
decline it, and live easy and at his Pleasure, in such a Ship as
his, where he should not be obliged to perform Duty, but follow
his own Inclinations.*

At *Turniff*, ten Leagues short of the Bay of *Honduras*, the
Pyrates took in fresh Water; and while they were at an Anchor there, they saw a Sloop coming in, whereupon, *Richards*
in the Sloop called the *Revenge*, slipped his Cable, and run
out to meet her; who upon seeing the black Flag hoisted,
struck his Sail and came to, under the Stern of *Teach* the
Commadore. She was called the *Adventure*, from *Jamaica*,
David Harriot Master. They took him and his Men aboard
the great Ship, and sent a Number of other Hands with *Israel
Hands*, Master of *Teach's* Ship, to Man the Sloop for the
pyratical Account.

The 9th of *April*, they weighed from *Turniff*, having lain there about a Week, and sailed to the Bay, where they found a Ship and four Sloops, three of the latter belonged to *Jonathan Bernard*, of *Jamaica*, and the other to Captain *James*; the Ship was of *Boston*, called the *Protestant Casar*, Captain *Wyar* Commander. *Teach* hoisted his Black Colours, and fired a Gun; upon which Captain *Wyar* and all his Men, left their Ship, and got ashore in their Boat. *Teach*'s Quarter-Master, and eight of his Crew, took Possession of *Wyar*'s Ship, and *Richards* secured all the Sloops, one of which they burnt out of spight to the Owner; the *Protestant Casar* they also burnt, after they had plundered her, because she belonged to *Boston*, where some Men had been hanged for Pyracy; and the three Sloops belonging to *Bernard* they let go.

From hence the Rovers sailed to *Turkill*, and then to the *Grand Caimanes*, a small Island about thirty Leagues to the Westward of *Jamaica*, where they took a small Turtler, and so to the *Havana*, and from thence to the *Bahama* Wrecks, and from the *Bahama* Wrecks, they sailed to *Carolina*, taking a Brigantine and two Sloops in their Way, where they lay off the Bar of *Charles-Town* for five or six Days. They took here a Ship as she was coming out, bound for *London*, commanded by *Robert Clark*, with some Passengers on Board for *England*; the next Day they took another Vessel coming out of *Charles-Town*, and also two Pinks coming into *Charles-Town*; likewise a Brigantine with 14 Negroes aboard; all which being done in the Face of the Town, struck a great Terror to the whole Province of *Carolina*, having just before been visited by *Vane*, another notorious Pyrate, that they abandoned themselves to Dispair, being in no Condition to resist their Force. They were eight Sail in the Harbour, ready for the Sea, but none dared to venture out, it being almost impossible to escape their Hands. The inward bound Vessels were under the same unhappy Dilemma, so that the Trade of this Place was totally interrupted: What made these Misfortunes heavier to them, was a long expensive War, the

Colony had had with the Natives, which was but just ended when these Robbers infested them.

Teach detained all the Ships and Prisoners, and, being in want of Medicines, resolves to demand a Chest from the Government of the Province; accordingly *Richards*, the Captain of the *Revenge* Sloop, with two or three more Pyrates, were sent up along with Mr. *Marks*, one of the Prisoners, whom they had taken in *Clark*'s Ship, and very insolently made their Demands, threatning, that if they did not send immediately the Chest of Medicines, and let the Pyrate-Ambassadors return, without offering any Violence to their Persons, they would murder all their Prisoners, send up their Heads to the Governor, and set the Ships they had taken on Fire.

Whilst Mr. *Marks* was making Application to the Council, *Richards*, and the rest of the Pyrates, walk'd the Streets publickly, in the Sight of all People, who were fired with the utmost Indignation, looking upon them as Robbers and Murtherers, and particularly the Authors of their Wrongs and Oppressions, but durst not so much as think of executing their Revenge, for fear of bringing more Calamities upon themselves and so they were forced to let the Villains pass with Impunity. The Government were not long in deliberating upon the Message, tho' 'twas the greatest Affront that could have been put upon them; yet for the saving so many Mens Lives, (among them, Mr. *Samuel Wragg*, one of the Council;) they comply'd with the Necessity, and sent aboard a Chest, valued at between 3 and 400 *l.* and the Pyrates went back safe to their Ships.

Blackbeard, (for so *Teach* was generally called, as we shall hereafter shew) as soon as he had received the Medicines and his Brother Rogues, let go the Ships and the Prisoners; having first taken out of them in Gold and Silver, about 1500 *l.* Sterling, besides Provisions and other Matters.

From the Bar of *Charles-Town*, they sailed to *North-Carolina*; Captain *Teach* in the Ship, which they called the Man of War, Captain *Richards* and Captain *Hands* in the

Sloops, which they termed Privateers, and another Sloop serving them as a Tender. *Teach* began now to think of breaking up the Company, and securing the Money and the best of the Effects for himself, and some others of his Companions he had most Friendship for, and to cheat the rest: Accordingly, on Pretence of running into *Topsail* Inlet to clean, he grounded his Ship, and then, as if it had been done undesignedly, and by Accident; he orders *Hands*'s Sloop to come to his Assistance, and get him off again, which he endeavouring to do, ran the Sloop on Shore near the other, and so were both lost. This done, *Teach* goes into the Tender Sloop, with forty Hands, and leaves the *Revenge* there; then takes seventeen others and Marroons them upon a small sandy Island, about a League from the Main, where there was neither Bird, Beast or Herb for their Subsistance, and where they must have perished if Major *Bonnet* had not two Days after taken them off.

Teach goes up to the Governor of *North-Carolina*, with about twenty of his Men, surrender to his Majesty's Proclamation, and receive Certificates thereof, from his Excellency; but it did not appear that their submitting to this Pardon was from any Reformation of Manners, but only to wait a more favourable Opportunity to play the same Game over again; which he soon after effected, with greater Security to himself, and with much better Prospect of Success, having in this Time cultivated a very good understanding with *Charles Eden*, Esq, the Governor above mentioned.

The first Piece of Service this kind Governor did to *Black-Beard*, was, to give him a Right to the Vessel which he had taken, when he was a pyrating in the great Ship called the *Queen Ann's Revenge*; for which purpose, a Court of Vice-Admiralty was held at *Bath-Town*; and, tho' *Teach* had never any Commission in his Life, and the Sloop belonging to the *English* Merchants, and taken in Time of Peace; yet was she condemned as a Prize taken from the *Spaniards*, by the said *Teach*. These Proceedings shew that Governors are but Men.

Before he sailed upon his Adventures, he marry'd a young

Creature of about sixteen Years of Age, the Governor per-
forming the Ceremony. As it is a Custom to marry here by
a Priest, so it is there by a Magistrate; and this, I have been
informed, made *Teach*'s fourteenth Wife, whereof, about a
dozen might be still living. His Behaviour in this State, was
something extraordinary, for while his Sloop lay in *Okerecock*
Inlet, and he ashore at a Plantation, where his Wife lived,
with whom after he had lain all Night, it was his Custom to
invite five or six of his brutal Companions to come ashore,
and he would force her to prostitute her self to them all, one
after another, before his Face.

In *June* 1718, he went to Sea, upon another Expedition,
and steered his Course towards *Bermudas*; he met with two
or three *English* Vessels in his Way, but robbed them only
of Provisions, Stores and other Necessaries, for his present
Expence; but near the Island aforementioned, he fell in with
two *French* Ships, one of them was loaden with Sugar and
Cocoa, and the other light, both bound to *Martinico*; the
Ship that had no Lading he let go, and putting all the Men
of the loaded Ship aboard her, he brought home the other
with her Cargo to *North-Carolina*, where the Governor and
the Pyrates shared the Plunder.

When *Teach* and his Prize arrived, he and four of his Crew
went to his Excellency, and made Affidavit, that they found
the *French* Ship at Sea, without a Soul on Board her; and
then a Court was called, and the Ship condemned: The Governor had sixty Hogsheads of Sugar for his Dividend, and
one Mr. *Knight*, who was his Secretary, and Collector for
the Province, twenty; and the rest was shared among the
other Pyrates.

The Business was not yet done, the Ship remained, and
it was possible one or other might come into the River, that
might be acquainted with her, and so discover the Roguery;
but *Teach* thought of a Contrivance to prevent this, for, upon
a Pretence that she was leaky, and that she might sink, and
so stop up the Mouth of the Inlet or Cove where she lay, he
obtained an Order from the Governor, to bring her out into

the River, and set her on Fire, which was accordingly executed, and she was burnt down to the Water's Edge, her Bottom sunk, and with it, their Fears of her ever rising in Judgment against them.

Captain *Teach*, alias *Black-beard*, passed three or four Months in the River, sometimes lying at Anchor in the Coves, at other Times sailing from one Inlet to another, trading with such Sloops as he met, for the Plunder he had taken, and would often give them Presents for Stores and Provisions took from them; that is, when he happened to be in a giving Humour; at other Times he made bold with them, and took what he liked, without saying, *by your Leave*, knowing well, they dared not send him a Bill for the Payment. He often diverted himself with going ashore among the Planters, where he revelled Night and Day: By these he was well received, but whether out of Love or Fear, I cannot say; sometimes he used them courteously enough, and made them Presents of Rum and Sugar, in Recompence of what he took from them; but, as for Liberties (which 'tis said) he and his Companions often took with the Wives and Daughters of the Planters, I cannot take upon me to say, whether he paid them *ad Valorem*, or no. At other Times he carried it in a lordly Manner towards them, and would lay some of them under Contribution; nay, he often proceeded to bully the Governor, not, that I can discover the least Cause of Quarrel betwixt them, but it seemed only to be done, to shew he dared do it.

The Sloops trading up and down this River, being so frequently pillaged by *Black-beard*, consulted with the Traders, and some of the best of the Planters, what Course to take; they saw plainly it would be in vain to make any Application to the Governor of *North-Carolina*, to whom it properly belonged to find some Redress; so that if they could not be relieved from some other Quarter, *Black-beard* would be like to reign with Impunity, therefore, with as much Secrecy as possible, they sent a Deputation to *Virginia*, to lay the Affair before the Governor of that Colony, and to solicit an armed

Force from the Men of War lying there, to take or destroy this Pyrate.

This Governor consulted with the Captains of the two Men of War, *viz.* The *Pearl* and *Lime*, who had lain in St. *James*'s River, about ten Months. It was agreed that the Governor should hire a couple of small Sloops, and the Men of War should Man them; this was accordingly done, and the Command of them given to Mr. *Robert Maynard*, first Lieutenant of the *Pearl*, an experienced Officer, and a Gentleman of great Bravery and Resolution, as will appear by his gallant Behaviour in this Expedition. The Sloops were well mann'd and furnished with Ammunition and small Arms, but had no Guns mounted.

About the Time of their going out, the Governor called an Assembly, in which it was resolved to publish a Proclamation, offering certain Rewards to any Person or Persons, who, within a Year after that Time, should take or destroy any Pyrate: The original Proclamation being in our Hands, is as follows.

By his Majesty's Lieutenant Governor, and Commander in Chief, of the Colony and Dominion of *Virginia*,

A PROCLAMATION,
Publishing the Rewards given for apprehending, or killing Pyrates.

Whereas, by an Act of Assembly, made at a Session of Assembly, begun at the Capital in Williamsburgh, *the eleventh Day of* November, *in the fifth Year of his Majesty's Reign, entituled,* An Act to encourage the apprehending and destroying of Pyrates: *It is, amongst other Things enacted, that all and every Person, or Persons, who, from and after the fourteenth Day of,* November, *in the Year of our Lord one thousand seven hundred and eighteen, and before the fourteenth Day of* November, *which shall be in the Year of our Lord one thousand seven hundred and nineteen, shall take any Pyrate, or Pyrates, on the Sea* or *Land, or in Case of Resistance, shall kill any such Pyrate, or Pyrates, between the Degrees of thirty four, and thirty nine, of Northern Latitude, and within one hundred Leagues of the Continent of* Virginia, *or within the Provinces of* Virginia, *or* North-Carolina, *upon the Conviction, or making due Proof of the killing of all, and every such Pyrate, and Pyrates, before the Governor and Council, shall be entitled to have, and receive out of the publick Money, in the Hands of the Treasurer of this Colony, the several Rewards following; that is to say, for* Edward Teach, *commonly call'd Captain* Teach, *or* Black-Beard, *one hundred Pounds, for every other Commander of a Pyrate Ship, Sloop, or Vessel, forty Pounds; for every Lieutenant, Master, or Quarter-Master, Boatswain, or Carpenter, twenty Pounds; for every other inferior Officer, fifteen Pounds, and for every private Man taken on Board such Ship, Sloop, or Vessel, ten Pounds; and, that for every Pyrate, which shall be taken by any Ship, Sloop, or Vessel, belonging to this Colony, or* North-Carolina, *within the Time aforesaid, in any Place whatsoever, the like Rewards shall be paid according to the Quality and Condition of such Pyrates. Wherefore, for the Encouragement of all such Persons as shall be willing to serve his Majesty; and their Country, in so just and honourable an Undertaking, as the suppressing a Sort of People, who may be truly called Enemies to Mankind: I have thought fit, with the Advice and Consent of his Majesty's Council, to issue this Proclamation, hereby declaring, the said Rewards shall be punctually and justly paid, in current Money of* Virginia, *according to the Directions of the said Act. And, I do order and appoint this Proclamation, to be published by the Sheriffs, at their respective County-Houses, and by all Ministers and Readers, in the several Churches and Chappels, throughout this Colony.*

Given at our Council-Chamber at *Williamsburgh*, this 24th Day of *November*, 1718, in the fifth Year of his Majesty's Reign.
GOD SAVE THE KING.
A. SPOTSWOOD.

The 17th of *November*, 1718, the Lieutenant sail'd from *Kicquetan*, in *James* River in *Virginia*, and, the 21st in the Evening, came to the Mouth of *Okerecock* Inlet, where he got Sight of the Pyrate. This Expedition was made with all imaginable Secrecy, and the Officer manag'd with all the Prudence that was necessary, stopping all Boats and Vessels he met with, in the River, from going up, and thereby preventing any Intelligence from reaching *Black-Beard*, and receiving at the same time an Account from them all, of the Place where the Pyrate was lurking; but notwithstanding this Caution, *Black-beard* had Information of the Design, from his Excellency of the Province; and his Secretary, *Mr. Knight*, wrote him a Letter, particularly concerning it, intimating, *That he had sent him four of his Men, which were all he could meet with, in or about Town, and so bid him be upon his Guard.* These Men belonged to *Black-beard*, and were sent from *Bath-Town* to *Okerecock* Inlet, where the Sloop lay, which is about 20 leagues.

Black-beard had heard several Reports, which happened not to be true, and so gave the less Credit to this, nor was he convinced till he saw the Sloops: Whereupon he put his Vessel in a Posture of Defence; he had no more than twenty five Men on Board, tho' he gave out to all the Vessels he spoke with, that he had 40. When he had prepared for Battle, he set down and spent the Night in drinking with the Master of a trading Sloop, who, 'twas thought, had more Business with *Teach*, than he should have had.

Lieutenant *Maynard* came to an Anchor, for the Place being shoal, and the Channel intricate, there was no getting in, where *Teach* lay, that Night; but in the Morning he weighed, and sent his Boat a-head of the Sloops to sound; and coming within Gun-Shot of the Pyrate, received his Fire; whereupon *Maynard* hoisted the King's Colours, and stood directly towards him, with the best Way that his Sails and Oars could made. *Black-beard* cut his Cable, and endeavoured to make a running Fight, keeping a continual Fire at his Enemies, with his Guns; Mr. *Maynard* not having any, kept a constant Fire with small Arms, while some of his Men laboured at their Oars. In a little Time *Teach*'s Sloop ran a-ground, and Mr. *Maynard*'s drawing more Water than that of the Pyrate, he could not come near him; so he anchored within half Gun-Shot of the Enemy, and, in order to lighten his Vessel, that he might run him aboard, the Lieutenant ordered all his Ballast to be thrown over-board, and all the Water to be staved, and then weigh'd and stood for him; upon which *Black-beard* hail'd him in this rude Manner: *Damn you for Villains, who are you? And, from whence came you?* The Lieutenant made him Answer, *You may see by our Colours we are no Pyrates. Black-beard* bid him send his Boat on Board, that he might see who he was; but Mr. *Maynard* reply'd thus; *I cannot spare my Boat, but I will come aboard of you as soon as I can, with my Sloop.* Upon this, *Black-beard* took a Glass of Liquor, and drank to him with these Words: *Damnation seize my Soul if I give you Quarters, or take any from you.* In Answer to which, Mr. *Maynard* told him, *That he expected no Quarters from him, nor should he give him any.*

By this time *Black-beard*'s Sloop fleeted, as Mr. *Maynard*'s Sloops were rowing towards him, which being not above a Foot high in the Waste, and consequently the Men all exposed, as they came near together, (there being hitherto little or no Execution done, on either Side,) the Pyrate fired a Broadside, charged with all Manner of small Shot.——A fatal Stroke to them! The Sloop the Lieutenant was in, having twenty Men killed and wounded, and the other Sloop nine: This could not be help'd, for there being no Wind, they were oblig'd to keep to their Oars, otherwise the Pyrate would have got away from him, which, it seems, the Lieutenant was resolute to prevent.

After this unlucky Blow, *Black-beard*'s Sloop fell Broadside to the Shore; Mr. *Maynard*'s other Sloop, which was called the *Ranger*, fell a-stern, being, for the present, disabled; so the Lieutenant finding his own Sloop had Way, and

would soon be on Board of *Teach*, he ordered all his Men
down, for fear of another Broadside, which must have been
their Destruction, and the loss of their Expedition. Mr.
Maynard was the only Person that kept the Deck, except the
Man at the Helm, whom he directed to lye down snug, and
the Men in the Hold were ordered to get their Pistols and
their Swords ready for close fighting, and to come up at his
Command; in order to which, two Ladders were placed in
the Hatch-Way for the more Expedition. When the Lieutenant's Sloop boarded the other, Captain *Teach*'s Men
threw in several new fashioned sort of Grenadoes, *viz.* Case
Bottles fill'd with Powder, and small Shot, Slugs, and Pieces
of Lead or Iron, with a quick Match in the Mouth of it,
which being lighted without Side, presently runs into the
Bottle to the Powder, and as it is instantly thrown on Board,
generally does great Execution, besides putting all the Crew
into a Confusion; but by good Providence, they had not that
Effect here; the Men being in the Hold, and *Black-beard*
seeing few or no Hands aboard, told his Men, *That they were
all knock'd on the Head, except three or four; and therefore*, says
he, *let's jump on Board, and cut them to Pieces.*

Whereupon, under the Smoak of one of the Bottles just
mentioned, *Black-beard* enters with fourteen Men, over the
Bows of *Maynard*'s Sloop, and were not seen by him till the
Air cleared; however, he just then gave a Signal to his Men,
who all rose in an Instant, and attack'd the Pyrates with as
much Bravery as ever was done upon such an Occasion:
Black-beard and the Lieutenant fired the first Pistol at each
other, by which the Pyrate received a Wound, and then engaged with Swords, till the Lieutenant's unluckily broke, and
stepping back to cock a Pistol, *Black-beard*, with his Cutlash, was striking at that Instant, that one of *Maynard*'s Men
gave him a terrible Wound in the Neck and Throat, by
which the Lieutenant came off with a small Cut over his
Fingers.

They were now closely and warmly engaged, the Lieutenant and twelve Men, against *Black-beard* and fourteen, till the Sea was tinctur'd with Blood round the Vessel; *Black-beard* received a Shot into his Body from the Pistol that Lieutenant *Maynard* discharg'd, yet he stood his Ground, and fought with great Fury, till he received five and twenty Wounds, and five of them by Shot. At length, as he was cocking another Pistol, having fired several before, he fell down dead; by which Time eight more out of the fourteen dropp'd, and all the rest, much wounded, jump'd over-board, and call'd out for Quarters, which was granted, tho' it was only prolonging their Lives for a few Days. The Sloop *Ranger* came up, and attack'd the Men that remain'd in *Black-beard's* Sloop, with equal Bravery, till they likewise cry'd for Quarters.

Here was an End of that couragious Brute, who might have pass'd in the World for a Heroe, had he been employ'd in a good Cause; his Destruction, which was of such Consequence to the Plantations, was entirely owing to the Conduct and Bravery of Lieutenant *Maynard* and his Men, who might have destroy'd him with much less Loss, had they had a Vessel with great Guns; but they were obliged to use small Vessels, because the Holes and Places he lurk'd in, would not admit of others of greater Draught; and it was no small Difficulty for this Gentleman to get to him, having grounded his Vessel, at least, a hundred times, in getting up the River, besides other Discouragements, enough to have turn'd back any Gentleman without Dishonour, who was less resolute and bold than this Lieutenant. The Broadside that did so much Mischief before they boarded, in all Probability saved the rest from Destruction; for before that *Teach* had little or no Hopes of escaping, and therefore had posted a resolute Fellow, a Negroe, whom he had bred up, with a lighted Match, in the Powder-Room, with Commands to blow up, when he should give him Orders, which was as soon as the Lientenant and his Men could have entered, that so he might have destroy'd his Conquerors: and when the Negro found how it went with *Black-beard*, he could hardly be perswaded from the rash Action, by two Prisoners that were then in the Hold of the Sloop.

What seems a little odd, is, that some of these Men, who behaved so bravely against *Black-beard*, went afterwards a pyrating themselves, and one of them was taken along with *Roberts*; but I do not find that any of them were provided for, except one that was hanged; but this is a Digression.

The Lieutenant caused *Black-beard*'s Head to be severed from his Body, and hung up at the Bolt-sprit End, then he sailed to *Bath-Town*, to get Relief for his wounded Men.

It must be observed, that in rummaging the Pyrate's Sloop, they found several Letters and written Papers, which discovered the Correspondence betwixt Governor *Eden*, the Secretary and Collector, and also some Traders at *New-York*, and *Black-beard*. It is likely he had Regard enough for his Friends, to have destroyed these Papers before the Action, in order to hinder them from falling into such Hands, where the Discovery would be of no Use, either to the Interest or Reputation of these fine Gentlemen, if it had not been his fixed Resolution to have blown up together, when he found no possibility of escaping.

When the Lieutenant came to *Bath-Town*, he made bold to seize in the Governor's Store-House, the sixty Hogsheads of Sugar, and from honest Mr. *Knight*, twenty; which it seems was their Dividend of the Plunder taken in the *French* Ship; the latter did not long survive this shameful Discovery, for being apprehensive that he might be called to an Account for these Trifles, fell-sick with the Fright, and died in a few Days.

After the wounded Men were pretty well recover'd, the Lieutenant sailed back to the Men of War in *James River*, in *Virginia*, with *Black-beard*'s Head still hanging at the Bolt-sprit End, and fifteen Prisoners, thirteen of whom were hanged. It appearing upon Tryal, that one of them, *viz.* *Samuel Odell*, was taken out of the trading Sloop, but the Night before the Engagement. This poor Fellow was a little unlucky at his first entering upon his new Trade, there appearing no less than 70 Wounds upon him after the Action, notwithstanding which, he lived, and was cured of them all. The other Person that escaped the Gallows, was one *Israel Hands*, the Master of *Black-beard*'s Sloop, and formerly Captain of the same, before the *Queen Ann's Revenge* was lost in *Topsail* Inlet.

The aforesaid *Hands* happened not to be in the Fight, but was taken afterwards ashore at *Bath-Town*, having been sometime before disabled by *Black-beard*, in one of his savage Humours, after the following Manner.—One Night drinking in his Cabin with *Hands*, the Pilot, and another Man; *Black-beard* without any Provocation privately draws out a small Pair of Pistols, and cocks them under the Table, which being perceived by the Man, he withdrew and went upon Deck, leaving *Hands*, the Pilot, and the Captain together. When the Pistols were ready, he blew out the Candle, and crossing his Hands, discharged them at his Company; *Hands*, the Master, was shot thro' the Knee, and lam'd for Life; the other Pistol did no Execution.—Being asked the meaning of this, he only answered, by damning them, that *if he did not now and then kill one of them, they would forget who he was.*

Hands being taken, was try'd and condemned, but just as he was about to be executed, a Ship arrives at *Virginia* with a Proclamation for prolonging the Time of his Majesty's Pardon, to such of the Pyrates as should surrender by a limited Time therein expressed: Notwithstanding the Sentence, *Hands* pleaded the Pardon, and was allowed the Benefit of it, and is alive at this Time in *London*, begging his Bread.

Now that we have given some Account of *Teach*'s Life and Actions, it will not be amiss, that we speak of his Beard, since it did not a little contribute towards making his Name so terrible in those Parts.

Plutarch, and other grave Historians have taken Notice, that several great Men amongst the *Romans*, took their Sir-Names from certain odd Marks in their Countenances; as

Cicero, from a Mark or Vetch on his Nose; so our Heroe, Captain *Teach*, assumed the Cognomen of *Black-beard*, from that large Quantity of Hair, which, like a frightful Meteor, covered his whole Face, and frightened *America* more than any Comet that has appeared there a long Time.

This Beard was black, which he suffered to grow of an extravagant Length; as to Breadth, it came up to his Eyes; he was accustomed to twist it with Ribbons, in small Tails, after the Manner of our Ramilies Wiggs, and turn them about his Ears: In Time of Action, he wore a Sling over his Shoulders, with three brace of Pistols, hanging in Holsters like Bandaliers; and stuck lighted Matches under his Hat, which appearing on each Side of his Face, his Eyes naturally looking fierce and wild, made him altogether such a Figure, that Imagination cannot form an Idea of a Fury, from Hell, to look more frightful.

If he had the look of a Fury, his Humours and Passions were suitable to it; we shall relate two or three more of his Extravagancies, which we omitted in the Body of his History, by which it will appear, to what a Pitch of Wickedness, human Nature may arrive, if it's Passions are not checked.

In the Commonwealth of Pyrates, he who goes the greatest Length of Wickedness, is looked upon with a kind of Envy amongst them, as a Person of a more extraordinary Gallantry, and is thereby entitled to be distinguished by some Post, and if such a one has but Courage, he must certainly be a great Man. The Hero of whom we are writing, was thoroughly accomplished this Way, and some of his Frolicks of Wickedness, were so extravagant, as if he aimed at making his Men believe he was a Devil incarnate; for being one Day at Sea, and a little flushed with drink:—*Come*, says he, *let us make a Hell of our own, and try how long we can bear it*; accordingly he, with two or three others, went down into the Hold, and closing up all the Hatches, filled several Pots full of Brimstone, and other combustible Matter, and set it on Fire, and so continued till they were almost suffocated, when some of the Men cried out for Air; at length he opened the Hatches, not a little pleased that he held out the longest.

The Night before he was killed, he set up and drank till the Morning, with some of his own Men, and the Master of a Merchant-Man, and having had Intelligence of the two Sloops coming to attack him, as has been before observed; one of his Men asked him, in Case anything should happen to him in the Engagement with the Sloops, whether his Wife knew where he had buried his Money? He answered, *That no Body but himself and the Devil, knew where it was, and the longest Liver should take all.*

Those of his Crew who were taken alive, told a Story which may appear a little incredible; however, we think it will not be fair to omit it, since we had it from their own Mouths. That once upon a Cruize, they found out that they had a Man on Board more than their Crew; such a one was seen several Days amongst them, sometimes below, and sometimes upon Deck, yet no Man in the Ship could give an Account who he was, or from whence he came; but that he disappeared a little before they were cast away in their great Ship, but, it seems, they verily believed it was the Devil.

One would think these Things should induce them to reform their Lives, but so many Reprobates together, encouraged and spirited one another up in their Wickedness, to which a continual Course of drinking did not a little contribute; for in *Black-beard*'s Journal, which was taken, there were several Memorandums of the following Nature, found writ with his own Hand.—*Such a Day, Rum all out:*—*Our Company somewhat sober:*—*A damn'd Confusion amongst us!*—*Rogues a plotting;*—*great Talk of Separation.*—*So I look'd sharp for a Prize;*—*such a Day took one, with a great deal of Liquor on Board, so kept the Company hot, damned hot, then all Things went well again.*

Thus it was these Wretches passed their Lives, with very little Pleasure or Satisfaction, in the Possession of what they violently take away from others, and sure to pay for it at last, by an ignominious Death.

The Names of the Pyrates killed in the Engagement,
are as follow.
Edward Teach, Commander.
Phillip Morton, Gunner.
Garrat Gibbens, Boatswain.
Owen Roberts, Carpenter.
Thomas Miller, Quarter-Master.
John Husk,
Joseph Curtice,
Joseph Brooks, (1)
Nath. Jackson.

All the rest, except the two last, were wounded and
afterwards hanged in *Virginia.*

John Carnes,	*Joseph Philips*,
Joseph Brooks, (2)	*James Robbins*,
James Blake,	*John Martin*,
John Gills,	*Edward Salter*,
Thomas Gates,	*Stephen Daniel*,
James White,	*Richard Greensail.*
Richard Stiles,	*Israel Hands*, pardoned.
Casar,	*Samuel Odel*, acquited.

There were in the Pyrate Sloops, and ashore in a Tent,
near where the Sloops lay, 25 Hogsheads of Sugar, 11 Teir-
ces, and 145 Bags of Cocoa, a Barrel of Indigo, and a Bale
of Cotton; which, with what was taken from the Governor
and Secretary, and the Sale of the Sloop, came to 2500 *l.*
besides the Rewards paid by the Governor of *Virginia*, pursuant to his Proclamation; all which was divided among the
Companies of the two Ships, *Lime* and *Pearl*, that lay in
James River; the brave Fellows that took them coming in for
no more than their Dividend amongst the rest, and was paid
it within these three Months.

CHAPTER IV.

Of
Major STEDE BONNET,
And his CREW.

THE MAJOR was a Gentleman of good Reputation in the Island of *Barbadoes*, was Master of a plentiful Fortune, and had the Advantage of a liberal Education. He had the least Temptation of any Man to follow such a Course of Life, from the Condition of his Circumstances. It was very surprizing to every one, to hear of the Major's Enterprize, in the Island were he liv'd; and as he was generally esteem'd and honoured, before he broke out into open Acts of Pyracy, so he was afterwards rather pitty'd than condemned, by those that were acquainted with him, believing that this Humour of going a pyrating, proceeded from a Disorder in his Mind, which had been but too visible in him, some Time before this wicked Undertaking; and which is said to have been occasioned by some Discomforts he found in a married State; be that as it will, the Major was but ill qualify'd for the Business, as not understanding maritime Affairs.

However, he fitted out a Sloop with ten Guns and 70 Men, entirely at his own Expence, and in the Night-Time sailed from *Barbadoes*. He called his Sloop the *Revenge*; his first Cruize was off the Capes of *Virginia*, where he took several Ships, and plundered them of their Provisions, Cloaths, Money, Ammunition, &c. in particular the *Anne*, Captain *Montgomery*, from *Glascow*; the *Turbet* from *Bar-*

badoes, which for Country sake, after they had taken out the principal Part of the Lading, the Pyrate Crew set her on Fire; the *Endeavour*, Captain *Scot*, from *Bristol*, and the *Young* from *Leith*. From hence they went to *New-York*, and off the East End of *Long-Island*, took a Sloop bound for the *West-Indies*, after which they stood in and landed some Men at *Gardner's Island*, but in a peaceable Manner, and bought Provisions for the Company's Use, which they paid for, and so went off again without Molestation.

Some Time after, which was in *August* 1717, *Bonnet* came off the Bar of *South-Carolina*, and took a Sloop and a Brigantine bound in; the Sloop belonged to *Barbadoes, Joseph Palmer* Master, laden with Rum, Sugar and Negroes; and the Brigantine came from *New-England, Thomas Porter* Master, whom they plundered, and then dismiss'd; but they sailed away with the Sloop, and at an Inlet in *North-Carolina* careened by her, and then set her on Fire.

After the Sloop had cleaned, they put to Sea, but came to no Resolution what Course to take; the Crew were divided in their Opinions, some being for one Thing, and some another, so that nothing but Confusion seem'd to attend all their Schemes.

The Major was no Sailor as was said before, and therefore had been obliged to yield to many Things that were imposed on him, during their Undertaking, for want of a competent Knowledge in maritime Affairs; at length happening to fall in Company with another Pyrate, one *Edward Teach*, (who for his remarkable black ugly Beard, was more commonly called *Black-Beard*:) This Fellow was a good Sailor, but a most cruel hardened Villain, bold and daring to the last Degree, and would not stick at the perpetrating the most abominable Wickedness imaginable; for which he was made Chief of that execrable Gang, that it might be said that his Post was not unduly filled, *Black-beard* being truly the Superior in Roguery, of all the Company, as has been already related.

To him *Bonnet*'s Crew joined in Consortship, and *Bonnet* himself was laid aside, not withstanding the Sloop was his own; he went aboard *Black-beard*'s ship, not concerning himself with any of their Affairs, where he continued till she was lost in *Topsail* Inlet, and one *Richards* was appointed Captain in his room. The Major now saw his Folly, but could not help himself, which made him Melancholy; he reflected upon his past Course of Life, and was confounded with Shame, when he thought upon what he had done: His Behaviour was taken Notice of by the other Pyrates, who liked him never the better for it; and he often declared to some of them, that he would gladly leave off that Way of Living, being fully tired of it; but he should be ashamed to see the Face of any *English* Man again; therefore if he could get to *Spain* or *Portugal*, where he might be undiscovered, he would spend the Remainder of his Days in either of those Countries, otherwise he must continue with them as long as he lived.

When *Black-beard* lost his Ship at *Topsail* Inlet, and surrendered to the King's Proclamation, *Bonnet* reassumed the Command of his own Sloop, *Revenge*, goes directly away to *Bath-Town* in *North-Carolina*, surrenders likewise to the King's Pardon, and receives a Certificate. The War was now broke out between the *Tripple* Allies and *Spain*; so Major *Bonnet* gets a Clearance for his Sloop at *North-Carolina*, to go to the Island of St. *Thomas*, with a Design (at least it was pretended so) to get the Emperor's Commission, to go a Privateering upon the *Spaniards*. When *Bonnet* came back to *Topsail* Inlet, he found that *Teach* and his Gang were gone, and that had taken all the Money, small Arms and Effect of Value out of the great Ship, and set ashore on a small sandy Island above a League from the Main, seventeen Men, no doubt with a Design they should perish, there being no Inhabitant, or Provisions to subsist withal, nor any Boat or Materials to build or make any kind of Launch or Vessel, to escape from that desolate Place: They remained there two Nights and one Day, without Subsistance, or the least Prospect of any, expecting nothing else but a lingering Death; when to their inexpressable Comfort, they saw Redempt on

Hand; for Major *Bonnet* happening to get Intelligence of their being there, by two of the Pyrates who had escaped *Teach*'s Cruelty, and had got to a poor little Village at the upper End of the Harbour, sent his Boat to make Discovery of the Truth of the Matter, which the poor Wretched seeing, made a signal to them, and they were all brought on Board *Bonnet*'s Sloop.

Major *Bonnet* told all his Company, that he would take a Commission to go against the *Spaniards*, and to that End, was going to St. *Thomas*'s therefore if they would go with him, they should be welcome; whereupon they all consented, but as the Sloop was preparing to sail, a Bom-Boat, that brought Apples and Sider to sell to the Sloop's Men, informed them, that Captain *Teach* lay at *Ocricock* Inlet, with only 18 or 20 Hands. *Bonnet*, who bore him a mortal Hatred for some Insults offered him, went immediately in pursuit of *Black-beard*, but it happened too late, for he missed of him there, and after four Days Cruize, hearing no farther News of him, they steered their Course towards *Virginia*.

In the Month of *July*, these Adventures came off the Capes, and meeting with a Pink with a Stock of Provisions on Board, which they happened to be in Want of, they took out of her ten or twelve barrels of Pork, and about 400 Weight of Bread; but because they would not have this set down to the Account of Pyracy, they gave them eight or ten Casks of Rice, and an old Cable, in lieu thereof.

Two Days afterwards they chased a Sloop of sixty Ton, and took her two Leagues off of Cape *Henry*; they were so happy here as to get a Supply of Liquor to their Victuals, for they brought from her two Hogsheads of Rum, and as many of Molosses, which, it seems, they had need of, tho' they had not ready Money to purchase them: What Security they intended to give, I can't tell, but *Bonnet* sent eight Men to take Care of the Prize Sloop, who, perhaps, not caring to make Use of those accustom'd Freedoms. Took the first Opportunity to go off with her, and *Bonnet* (who was pleased to have himself called Captain *Thomas*,) saw them no more.

After this, the Major threw off all Restraint, and though he had just before received his Majesty's Mercy, in the Name of *Stede Bonnet*, he relaps'd in good Earnest into his old Vocation, by the Name of Captain *Thomas*, and recommenced a down-right Pyrate, by taking and plundering all the Vessels he met with: He took off Cape *Henry*, two Ships from *Virginia*, bound to *Glascow*, out of which they had very little besides an hundred Weight of Tobacco. The next Day they took a small Sloop bound from *Virginia* to *Bermudas*, which supply'd them with twenty Barrels of Pork, some Bacon, and they gave her in return, two Barrels of Rice, and a Hogshead of Molossus; out of this Sloop two Men enter'd voluntarily. The next they took was another *Virginia* Man, bound to *Glascow*, out of which they had nothing of Value, save only a few Combs, Pins and Needles, and gave her instead thereof, a Barrel of Pork, and two Barrels of Bread.

From *Virginia* they sailed to *Philadelphia*, and in the Latitude of 38 North, they took a Scooner, coming from *North-Carolina*, bound to *Boston*, they had out of her only two Dozen of Calf-Skins, to make Covers for Guns, and two of their Hands and detained her some Days. All this was but small Game, and seem'd as if they design'd only to make Provision for their Sloop against they arrived at St. *Thomas's*; for they hitherto had dealt favourably with all that were so unhappy as so fall into their Hands; but those that came after, fared not so well, for in the Latitude of 32, off of *Delaware* River, near *Philadelphia*, they took two Snows bound to *Bristol*, out of whom they got some Money, besides Goods, perhaps to the Value of 150 Pounds; at the same Time they took a Sloop of sixty Tons bound from *Philadelphia* to *Barbadoes* which after taking some Goods out, they dismissed along with the Snows.

The 29th Day of *July*, Captain *Thomas* took a Sloop of 50 Tons, six or seven Leagues off *Delaware* Bay, bound from *Philadelphia* to *Barbadoes*, *Thomas Read* Master, loaden with Provisions, which they kept, and put four or five of their Hands on Board her. The last Day of *July*, they took another

Sloop of 60 Tons, commanded by *Peter Manwaring*, bound from *Antegoa* to *Philadelphia*, which they likewise kept with all the Cargo, consisting chiefly of Rum, Molosses, Sugar, Cotton, Indigo and about 25 Pound in Money, valued in all to 500 Pound.

The last Day of *July*, our Rovers with the Vessels last taken, left *Delaware* Bay, and sailed to Cape *Fear* River, where they staid too long for their Safety, for the Pyrate Sloop which they now new named the *Royal James*, proved very leaky, so that they were obliged to remain here almost two months, to refit and repair their Vessel: They took in this River a small Shallop, which they ripped up to mend the Sloop, and retarded the further Prosecution of their Voyage, as before mentioned, till the News came to *Carolina*, of a Pyrate Sloop's being there to carreen with her Prizes.

Upon this Information, the Council of *South-Carolina* was alarmed, and apprehended they should receive another Visit from them speedily; to present which, Colonel *William Rhet*, of the same Province, waited on the Governor, and generously offered himself to go with two Sloops to attack this Pyrate; which the Governor readily accepted, and accordingly gave the Colonel a Commission and full Power, to fit such Vessels as he thought proper for the Design.

In a few Days two Sloops were equipped and manned: The *Henry* with 8 Guns and 70 Men, commanded by Captain *John Masters*, and the *Sea Nymph*, with 8 Guns and 60 Men, commanded by Captain *Fayrer Hall*, both under the entire Direction and Command of the aforesaid Colonel *Rhet*, who, on the 14th of *September*, went on Board the *Henry*, and, with the other Sloop, sailed from *Charles-Town* to *Swillivants* Island, to put themselves in order for the Cruize. Just then arrived a small Ship from *Antigoa*, one *Cock Master*, with an Account, that in Sight of the Bar he was taken and plundered by one *Charles Vane*, a Pyrate, in a Brigantine of 12 Guns and 90 Men; and who had also taken two other Vessels bound in there, one a small Sloop, Captain *Dill Master*, from *Barbadoes*; the other a Brigantine, Captain

Thompson Master, from *Guiney*, with ninety odd Negroes, which they took out of the Vessel, and put on Board another Sloop then under the Command of one *Yeats*, his Consort, with 25 Men. This prov'd fortunate to the Owners of the *Guiney* Man, for *Yeats* having often attempted to quit this Course of Life, took an Opportunity in the Night, to leave *Vane* and to run into *North-Edisto* River, to the Southward of *Charles-Town*, and surrendered to his Majesty's Pardon. The Owners got their Negroes, and *Yeats* and his Men had Certificates given them from the Government.

Vane cruised some Time off the Bar, in hopes to catch *Yeats*, and unfortunately for them, took two Ships coming out, bound to *London*, and while the Prisoners were aboard, some of the Pyrates gave out, that they designed to go into one of the Rivers to the Southward. Colonel *Rhet*, upon hearing this, sailed over the Bar the 15th of *September*, with the two Sloops before mentioned; and having the Wind Northerly, went after the Pyrate *Vane*, and scoured the Rivers and Inlets to the Southward; but not meeting with him, tacked and stood for Cape *Fear* River, in Prosecution of his first Design. On the 26th following, in the Evening, the Colonel with his small Squadron, entered the River, and saw, over a Point of Land, three Sloops at an Anchor, which were Major *Bonnet* and his Prizes; but it happened that in going up the River, the Pilot run the Colonel's Sloops aground, and it was dark before they were on Float, which hindered their getting up that Night. The Pyrates soon discovered the Sloops, but not knowing who they were, or upon what Design they came into that River, they manned three Canoes, and sent them down to take them, but they quickly found their Mistake, and returned to the Sloop, with the unwelcomed News. Major *Bonnet* made Preparations that Night for engaging, and took all the Men out of the Prizes. He shewed Captain *Manwaring*, one of his Prisoners, a Letter, he had just wrote, which he declared he would send to the Governor of *Carolina*; the Letter was to this Effect, *viz. That if the Sloops, which then appeared, were sent out against him, by the said Governor, and he should get clear off, that he would burn and destroy all Ships or Vessels going in or coming out of* South-Carolina. The next Morning they got under Sail, and came down the River, designing only a running Fight. Colonel *Rhet*'s Sloops got likewise under Sail, and stood for him, getting upon each Quarter of the Pyrate, with Intent to board him; which he perceiving, edged in towards the Shore, and being warmly engaged, their Sloop ran a-ground: The *Carolina* Sloops being in the same shoal Water, were in the same Circumstances; the *Henry*, in which Colonel *Rhet* was, grounded within Pistol shot of the Pyrate, and on his Bow; the other Sloop grounded right a-head of him, and almost out of Gun-Shot, which made her of little Service to the Colonel, while they lay a-ground.

At this Time the Pyrate had a considerable Advantage; for their Sloop, after she was a-ground, shifted from Colonel *Rhet*'s, by which Means they were all covered, and the Colonel's Sloop lifting the same Way, his Men were much exposed; notwithstanding which, they kept a brisk Fire the whole Time they lay thus a-ground, which was near five Hours. The Pyrates made a Wiff in their bloody Flag, and beckoned several Times with their Hats in Derision to the Colonel's Men, to come on Board, which they answered with chearful Huzza's, and said, *that they would speak with them by and by;* which accordingly happened, for the Colonel's Sloop being first a float, he got into deeper Water, and after mending the Sloop's Rigging, which was much shattered in the Engagement, they stood for the Pyrate, to give the finishing Stroke, and designed to go directly on Board him; which he prevented, by sending a Flag of Truce, and after some Time capitulating, they surrendered themselves Prisoners. The Colonel took Possession of the Sloop, and was extreamly pleased to find that Captain *Thomas*, who commanded her, was the individual Person of Major *Stede Bonnet*, who had done them the Honour several Times to visit their own Coast of *Carolina*.

There were killed in this Action, on Board the *Henry*, ten

Men, and fourteen wounded; on Board the *Sea Nymph*, two killed and four wounded. The Officers and Sailors in both Sloops behaved themselves with the greatest Bravery; and had not the Sloops so unluckily run a-ground, they had taken the Pyrate with much less loss of Men; but as he designed to get by them, and so make a running Fight, the *Carolina* Sloops were obliged to keep near him, to prevent his getting away. Of the Pyrates there were seven killed and five wounded, two of which died soon after of their Wounds Colonel *Rhet* weigh'd the 30th of *September*, from Cape *Fear* River, and arrived at *Charles-Town* the 3d of *October*, to the great Joy of the whole Province of *Carolina*.

Bonnet and his Crew, two Days after, were put ashore, and there not being a publick Prison, the Pyrates were kept at the Watch-House, under a Guard of Militia; but Major *Bonnet* was committed into the Custody of the Marshal, at his House; and in a few Days after, *David Hariot* the Master, and *Ignatius Pell* the Boatswain, who were designed for Evidence against the other Pyrates, were removed from the rest of the Crew, to the said Marshal's House, and every Night two Centinals set about the said House; but whether thro' any Corruption, or want of Care in guarding the Prisoners, I can't say; but on the 24th of *October*, the Major and *Hariot* made their Escape, the Boatswain refusing to go along with them. This made a great Noise in the Province, and People were open in their Resentments, often reflecting on the Governor, and others in the Magistracy, as tho' they had been brib'd, for conniving at their Escape. These Invectives arose from their Fears, that *Bonnet* would be capable of raising another Company, and prosecute his Revenge against this Country, for what he had lately, tho' justly, suffered: But they were in a short Time made easy in those Respects; for as soon as the Governor had the Account of *Bonnet*'s Escape, he immediately issued out a Proclamation, and promised a Reward of 700 Pounds to any that would take him, the Northward and Southward, in pursuit of him.

Bonnet stood to the Northward, in a small Vessel, but

wanting Necessaries, and the Weather being bad, he was forced back, and so return'd with his Canoe, to *Swillivants* Island, near *Charles-Town*, to fetch Supplies; but there being some Information sent to the Governor, he sent for Colonel *Rhet*, and desired him to go in pursuit of *Bonnet*; and accordingly gave him a Commission for that Purpose: Wherefore the Colonel, with proper Craft, and some Men, went away that Night for *Swillivant's* Island, and, after a very diligent Seach, discovered *Bonnet* and *Hariot* together; the Colonel's Men fired upon them, and killed *Hariot* upon the Spot, and wounded one Negro and an *Indian*. *Bonnet* submitted, and surrender'd himself; and the next Morning, being *November* the 6th, was brought by Colonel *Rhet* to *Charles-Town*, and, by the Governor's Warrant, was committed into safe Custody, in order for his being brought to his Tryal.

On the 28th of *October*, 1718, a Court of Vice-Admiralty was held at *Charles-Town*, in *South-Carolina*, and, by several Adjournments, continued to *Wednesday*, the 12th of *November* following, for the Tryal of the Pyrates taken in a Sloop formerly called *the Revenge*, but afterwards *the Royal James* before *Nicholas Trot*, Esq; Judge of the Vice-Admiralty, and Chief Justice of the said Province of *South Carolina*, and other Assistant Judges.

The King's Commission to Judge *Trot* was read and a Grand Jury sworn, for the finding of the several Bills, and a learned Charge given them by the said Judge, wherein he Ist shewed, *That the Sea was given by God, for the Use of Men, and is Subject to Dominion and Property, as well as the Land.*

2dly, He particularly remark'd to them, *the Sovereignty of the King of* England *over the* British *Seas.*

3dly, He observed, *that as Commerce and Navigation could not be carried on without Laws; so there have been always particular Laws, for the better ordering and regulating marine Affairs*; with an historical Account of those Laws, and Origine.

4thly, He proceeded to shew, *that there have been particular Courts and Judges appointed; to whose Jurisdiction mari-*

time Causes do belong, and that in Matters both Civil and Criminal.

And then 5thly, He particularly shewed them, *the Constitution and Jurisdiction of that Court of Admiralty Sessions.*

And lastly, *the Crimes cognizable therein*; and particularly enlarged *upon the Crime of Pyracy*, which was then brought before them.

The Indictments being found, a petit Jury was sworn, and the following Persons arraigned and tried.

Stede Bonnet, alias *Edwards*, alias *Thomas*, late of *Barbadoes*, Mariner.
Robert Tucker, late of the Island of *Jamaica*, Mariner.
Edward Robinson, late of *New-Castle* upon *Tine*, Mariner.
Neal Paterson, late of *Aberdeen*, Mariner.
William Scot, late of *Aberdeen*, Mariner.
William Eddy, alias *Neddy*, late of *Aberdeen*, Mariner.
Alexander Annand, late of *Jamaica*, Mariner.
George Rose, late of *Glascow*, Mariner.
George Dunkin, late of *Glascow*, Mariner.
* *Thomas Nicholas*, late of *London*, Mariner.
John Ridge, late of *London*, Mariner.
Matthew King, late of *Jamaica*, Mariner.
Daniel Perry, late of *Guernsey*, Mariner.
Henry Virgin, late of *Bristol*, Mariner.
James Robbins, alias *Rattle*, late of *London*, Mariner.
James Mulles, alias *Millet*, late of *London*, Mariner.
Thomas Price, late of *Bristol*, Mariner.
James Wilson, late of *Dublin*, Mariner.
John Lopez, late of *Oporto*, Mariner.
Zachariah Long, late of the Province of *Holland*, Mariner.
Job Bayly, late of *London*, Mariner.
John-William Smith, late of *Charles-Town, Carolina*, Mariner.
Thomas Carman, late of *Maidstone* in *Kent*, Mariner.
John Thomas, late of *Jamaica*, Mariner.
William Morrison, late of *Jamaica*, Mariner.

Samuel Booth, late of *Charles-Town*, Mariner.

William Hewet, late of *Jamaica*, Mariner.

John Levit, late of *North-Carolina*, Mariner.

William Livers, alias *Evis.*

John Brierly, alias *Timberhead*, late of *Bath-Town* in *North-Carolina*, Mariner.

Robert Boyd, late of *Bath-Town* aforesaid, Mariner.

* *Rowland Sharp*, of *Bath-Town*, Mariner.

* *Jonathan Clarke*, late of *Charles-Town*, *South Carolina*, Mariner.

* *Thomas Gerrard*, late of *Antegoa*, Mariner.

And all, except the three last, and *Thomas Nicholas*, were found Guilty, and received Sentence of Death.

They were most of them try'd upon two Indictments, as follows.

The Jurors for our Sovereign Lord the King, do upon their Oath present, that Stede Bonnet, *late of* Barbadoes, *Mariner*, Robert Tucker, &c. &c. *The 2d Day of* August, *in the fifth Year of the Reign of our Sovereign Lord* George, &c. *By Force of Arms upon the High-Sea, in a certain Place called Cape* James, &c. *did pyratically, and fellonionsly set upon, break, board, and enter, a certain Merchant Sloop, called the* Frances, Peter Manwaring *Commander, by Force,* &c. *upon the High-Sea, in a certain Place, called Cape* James, *alias Cape* Inlopen, *about two Miles distant from the Shore, in the Lattitude of 39, or thereabouts; and within the Jurisdiction of the Court of Vice-Admiralty, of* South Carolina, *being a Sloop of certain Persons, (to the Jurors, unknown) and then, and there, pyratically, and felloniously did make an Assault, in, and upon the said* Peter Manwaring, *and others his Mariners, (whose Names to the Jurors aforesaid, are unknown,) in the same Sloop, against the Peace of God, and of our said now Sovereign Lord the King, then, and there being, pyratically and felloniously, did put the aforesaid* Peter Manwaring, *and others, his Mariners, of the same Sloop, in the Sloop aforesaid, then being, in corporal Fear of their Lives, then and there, in the Sloop aforesaid, upon the*

High-Sea, *in the Place aforesaid, called Cape* James, alias *Cape*
Inlopen, *about two Miles from the Shore, in the Lattitude of
39, or thereabouts, as aforesaid, and within the Jurisdiction
aforesaid; pyratically, and felloniously, did steal take, and carry
away the said Merchant Sloop, called the* Frances, *and also
twenty six Hogsheads,* &c. &c. &c. *being found in the aforesaid
Sloop, in the Custody and Possession of the said* Peter Manwaring, *and others, his Mariners of the said Sloop, and from
their Custody and Possession, then and there, upon the High-
Sea aforesaid, called Cape* James, alias *Cape* Inlopen, *as aforesaid, and within the Jurisdiction aforesaid, against the Peace of
our now Sovereign Lord the King, his Crown and Dignity.*

This was the Form of the Indictments they were arraigned
upon, and tho' they might have proved several more Facts
upon the major Part of the Crew, the Court thought fit to
prosecute but two; the other was for seizing in a pyratical
and felonious Manner, the Sloop *Fortune, Thomas Read*
Commander; which Indictment running in the same Form
with the above-mentioned, it will be unnecessary to say more
of it.

All the Prisoners arraigned, pleaded Not Guilty, and put
themselves upon their Tryals, except *James Wilson*, and *John
Levit*, who pleaded Guilty to both Indictments, and *Daniel
Perry*, to one only. The Major would have gone through both
the Indictments at once, which the Court not admitting, he
pleaded Not Guilty to both Indictments, but being convicted
of one, he retracted his former Plea to the second Indictment, and pleaded Guilty to it.

The Prisoners made little or no Defence, every one pretending only that they were taken off a Maroon Shore, and
were shipped with Major *Bonnet* to go to St. *Thomas*'s; but
being out at Sea, and wanting Provisions, they were obliged
to do what they did by others; and so did Major *Bonnet*
himself, pretend that 'twas Force, not Inclination, that occasioned what had happened. However, the Facts being
plainly proved, and that they had all shared ten or eleven

Pounds a Man, excepting the three last, and *Thomas Nicholas*, they were all but they, found Guilty. The Judge made a very grave Speech to them, setting forth *the Enormity of their Crimes, the Condition they were now in, and the Nature and Necessity of an unfeigned Repentance*; and then recommended them to the Ministers of the Province, for more ample Directions, to fit them for Eternity, *for* (concluded he) *the Priest's Lips shall keep Knowledge, and you shall seek the Law at their Mouths; for they are the Messengers of the Lord.* Mat. II. 57. *And the Ambassadors of Christ, and unto them is committed the Word* [or Doctrine] *of Reconciliation,* 2 Cor. V. 19. 20. And then pronounced Sentence of Death upon them.

On *Saturday November* the 8th, 1711. *Robert Tucker, Edward Robinson, Neal Paterson, William Scot, Job Bayley, John-William Smith, John Thomas, William Morrison, Samuel Booth, William Hewit, William Eddy,* alias *Neddy, Alexander Annand, George Ross, George Dunkin, Matthew King, Daniel Perry, Henry Virgin, James Robbins, James Mullet,* alias *Millet, Thomas Price, John Lopez,* and *Zachariah Long,* were executed at the *White-Point* near *Charles-Town,* pursuant to their Sentence.

As for the Captain, his Escape protracted his Fate, and spun out his Life a few Days longer, for he was try'd the 10th, and being found Guilty, received Sentence in like Manner as the former; before which Judge *Trot,* made a most excellent Speech to him, rather somewhat too long to be taken into our History, yet I could not tell how to pass by so good and useful a Piece of Instruction, not knowing whose Hands this Book may happen to fall into.

The Lord Chief Justices's SPEECH, *upon his pronouncing Sentence on Major* STEDE BONNET.

Major *Stede Bonnet,* you stand here convicted upon two Indictments of Pyracy; one by the Verdict of the Jury, and the other by your own Confession.

Altho' you were indicted but for *two* Facts, yet you know

that at your Tryal it was fully proved even by an unwilling Witness, that you *pyratically* took and rifled no less than *thirteen* Vessels, since you sail'd from *North-Carolina.*

So that you might have been indicted, and convicted of *eleven* more Acts of *Pyracy*, since you took the Benefit of the King's *Act of Grace*, and pretended to leave that wicked Course of Life.

Not to mention the many *Acts* of *Pyracy* you committed before; for which if your Pardon from *Man* was never so authentick, yet you must expect to answer for them before God.

You know that the Crimes you have committed are *evil* in themselves, and contrary to the *Light* and *Law* of *Nature*, as well as the *Law* of God, by which you are commanded that *you shall not steal*, Exod. 20. 15. And the Apostle St. *Paul* expressly affirms, That *Thieves shall not inherit the King-dom of God*, I Cor. 6. 10.

But to *Theft* you have added a greater Sin, which is *Mur-der.* How many you may have *killed* of those that resisted you in the committing your former *Pyracies*, I know not: But this we all know, That besides the Wounded, you kill'd no less than *eighteen* Persons out of those that were sent by lawful Authority to suppress you, and put a Stop to those Rapines that you daily acted.

And however you may fancy that that was killing Men fairly in open *Fight*, yet this know, that the Power of the *Sword* not being committed into your Hands by any lawful Authority, you were not impowered to use any *Force*, or *fight* any one; and therefore those Persons that fell in that Action, in doing their Duty to their King and Country, were *mur-dered*, and their *Blood* now cries out for *Vengeance* and *Justice* against you: For it is the *Voice of Nature*, confirmed by the *Law* of God, That *whosoever sheddeth Man's Blood, by Man shall his Blood be shed.* Gen. 9. 6.

And consider that Death is not the only Punishment due to *Murderers*; for they are threatened to have *their Part in the Lake which burneth with Fire and Brimstone, which is the sec-*

ond Death, Rev. 21. 8. See *Chap*. 22. 15. Words which carry
that Terror with them, that considering your Circumstances
and your Guilt, surely the Sound of them must make you
tremble; *For who can dwell with everlasting Burnings?* Chap.
33. 14.

As the *Testimony* of your *Conscience* must convince you of
the great and many Evils you have committed, by which you
have highly offended God, and provoked most justly his
Wrath and Indignation against you, so I suppose I need not
tell you that the only Way of obtaining Pardon and Remis-
sion of your Sins from God, is by a true and unfeigned *Repentance* and *Faith* in Christ, by whose meritorious Death
and Passion, you can only hope for Salvation.

You being a Gentleman that have had the Advantage of
a *liberal Education*, and being generally esteemed a Man of
Letters, I believe it will be needless for me to explain to you
the Nature of *Repentance* and *Faith* in Christ, they being so
fully and so often mentioned in the Scriptures, that you cannot but know them. And therefore, perhaps, for that Reason
it might be thought by some improper for me to have said
so much to you, as I have already upon this Occasion; neither
should I have done it, but that considering the Course of
your Life and Actions, I have just Reason to fear, that the
Principles of Religion that had been instilled into you by
your *Education*, have been at least corrupted, if not entirely
defaced, by the *Scepticism* and *Infidelity* of this wicked Age;
and that what Time you allowed for Study, was rather applied to the *Polite Literature*, and the vain *Philosophy* of the
Times, than a serious Search after the *Law* and *Will* of God,
as revealed unto us in the Holy *Scriptures*: For *had your
Delight been in the Law of the Lord, and that you had meditated
therein Day and Night*, Psal. 1. 2. you would then have found
that God's *Word was a Lamp unto your Feet, and a Light to
your Path*, Psal. 119. 105. and that you would account all
other Knowledge but *Loss*, in Comparison of *the Excellency
of the Knowledge of Christ Jesus*, Phil. 3. 8. *who to them that
are called is the Power of God, and the Wisdom of God*, I Cor.

1. 24. *even the hidden Wisdom which God ordained before the World*, Chap. 2. 7.

You would then have esteemed the *Scriptures* as the *Great Charter* of Heaven, and which delivered to us not only the most perfect *Laws* and *Rules* of Life, but also discovered to us the Acts of *Pardon* from God, wherein they have offended those righteous Laws: For in them only is to be found the great *Mystery* of fallen Man's *Redemption, which the Angels desire to look into,* I Pet. I. 12.

And they would have taught you that *Sin* is the debasing of *Human Nature*, as being a *Derivation* from that *Purity, Rectitude,* and *Holiness*, in which God created us, and that *Virtue* and *Religion*, and walking by the Laws of God, were altogether preferable to the Ways of *Sin* and *Satan*; for that the *Ways* of Virtue are *Ways of Pleasantness, and all their Paths are Peace*, Prov. 3. 17.

But what you could not learn from God's Word, by reason of your *carelesly*, or but *superficially* considering the same, I hope that Course of his *Providence*, and the present *Afflictions* that he hath laid upon you, hath now convinced you of the same : For however in your seeming Prosperity you might make a *Mock at your Sins* Prov. 3. 17. yet now that you see that God's Hand hath reached you, and brought you to pub-lick Justice, I hope your present unhappy Circumstances hath made you seriously reflect upon your past Actions and Course of Life; and that you are now sensible of the Great-ness of your Sins, and that you find the Burden of them is intolerable.

And that therefore being thus *labouring, and heavy laden with Sin*, Mat. II. 28. you will esteem that as the most val-uable *Knowledge*, that can shew you how you can be recon-ciled to that Supreme God that you have so highly offended; and that can reveal to you Him who is not only the powerful *Advocate with the Father for you*, 1 John 2. 1. but also who hath paid that Debt that is due for your Sins by his own Death upon the Cross for you; and thereby made full Sat-isfaction for the Justice of God. And this is to be found no where but in God's Word, which discovers to us that *Lamb of God which takes away the Sins of the World,* John 1. 29. which is *Christ* the Son of God: For this know, and be assured, *that there is none other Name under Heaven given among Men, whereby we must be saved,* Acts 4. 12. but only by the Name of the Lord *Jesus.*

But then consider how he invites all Sinners to come unto him, and, *that he will give them rest,* Matt. 11. 28. for he assures us, *that he came to seek and to save that which was lost,* Luke 19. 10, Mat. 18. 11. and hath promised, *that he that cometh unto him, he will in no wise cast out,* John 6. 37.

So that if now you will sincerely turn to him, tho' late, even at the *eleventh Hour,* Mat. 20. 6, 9. he will receive you.

But surely I need not tell you, that the *Terms* of his *Mercy* is *Faith* and *Repentance.*

And do not mistake the *Nature* of Repentance to be only a bare Sorrow for your Sins, arising from the Consideration of the *Evil* and *Punishment* they have now brought upon you; but your Sorrow must arise from the Consideration of your having offended a gracious and merciful God.

But I shall not pretend to give you any particular Directions as to the Nature of Repentance: I consider that I speak to a Person, whose Offences have proceeded not so much from his not *knowing,* as his *slighting* and *neglecting* his *Duty:* Neither is it proper for me to give Advice out of the Way of my own Profession.

You may have that better delivered to you by those who have made Divinity their particular Study; and who, by their Knowledge, as well as their Office, as being the *Ambassadors of Christ,* 2 Cor. 5. 20. are best qualified to give you Instructions therein.

I only heartily wish, that what, in Compassion to your Soul, I have now said to you upon this sad and solemn Occasion, by exhorting you in general to *Faith* and *Repentance,* may have that due Effect upon you, that thereby you may become a true *Penitent.*

And therefore having now discharged my Duty to you as

a *Christian*, by giving you the best Counsel I can, with respect to the Salvation of your Soul, I must now do my Office as a *Judge*.

The *Sentence* that the Law hath appointed to pass upon you for your Offences, and which this Court doth therefore award, is,

That you, the said Stede Bonnet, *shall go from hence to the Place from whence you came, and from thence to the Place of Execution, where you shall be hanged by the Neck till you are dead.*

And the God of infinite Mercy be merciful to your Soul.

CHAPTER V.

Of
Capt. EDWARD ENGLAND,
And his CREW.

*E*DWARD ENGLAND went Mate of a Sloop that sail'd out of *Jamaica*, and was taken by Captain *Winter*, a Pyrate, just before their Settlement at *Providence*; from whence *England* had the Command of a Sloop in the same laudable Employment: It is surprizing that Men of good Understanding should engage in a Course of Life, that so much debases humane Nature, and sets them upon a Level with the wild Beasts of the Forest, who live and prey upon their weaker Fellow Creatures: A Crime so enormous! That it includes almost all others, as Murder, Rapine, Thest, Ingratitude, *&c.* and tho' they make these Vices familiar to them by their daily Practice, yet these Men are so inconsistent with themselves, that a Reflection made upon their Honour, their Justice, or their Courage, is look'd upon as an Offence that ought to be punished with the Life of him that commits it: *England* was one of these Men, who seem'd to have such a Share of Reason, as should have taught him better Things. He had a great deal of good Nature, and did not want for Courage; he was not avaritious, and always averse to the ill Usage Prisoners received: He would have been contented with moderate Plunder, and less mischievous Pranks, could his Companions have been brought to the same Temper, but he was generally over-rul'd, and as he was engaged in that abominable Society, he was obliged to be a Partner in all their vile Actions.

Captain *England* sail'd to the Coast of *Africa*, after the Island of *Providence* was settled by the *English* Government, and the Pyrates surrendered to his Majesty's Proclamation; and took several Ships and Vessels, particularly the *Cadogan* Snow belonging to *Bristol*, at *Sierraleone*, one *Skinner* Master, who was inhumanly murthered by some of the Crew, that had lately been his own Men, and served in the said Vessel. It seems some Quarrel had happened between them, so that *Skinner* thought fit to remove these Fellows on Board of a Man of War, and at the same Time refused them their Wages; not long after they found Means to desert that Service, and shipping themselves aboard a Sloop in the *West-Indies*, was taken by a Pyrate, and brought to *Providence*, and sailed upon the same Account along with Captain *England*.

Assoon as *Skinner* had struck to the Pyrate, he was ordered to come on Board in his Boat, which he did, and the Person that he first cast his Eye upon, proved to be his old Boatswain, who star'd him in the Face like his evil Genius, and accosted him in this Manner.—*Ah, Captain* Skinner! *Is it you? The only Man I wished to see; I am much in your Debt, and now I shall pay you all in your own Coin.*

The poor Man trembled every Joint, when he found into what Company he had fallen, and dreaded the Event, as he had Reason enough so to do; for the Boatswain immediately called to his Consorts, laid hold of the Captain, and made him fast so the Windless, and there pelted him with Glass Bottles, which cut him in a sad Manner; after which they whipp'd him about the Deck, till they were weary, being deaf to all his Prayers and Intreaties, and at last, because he had been a good Master to his Men, they said, he should have an easy Death, and so shot him thro' the Head. They took some few Things out of the Snow, but gave the Vessel and all her Cargo to *Howel Davis* the Mate, and the rest of the Crew, as will be hereafter mentioned in the Chapter of Captain *Davis*.

Captain *England* took a Ship called the *Pearl*, Captain *Tyzard* Commander, for which he exchanged his own Sloop, fitted her up for the pyratical Account, and new christen'd her, the *Royal James*, with which he took several Ships and Vessels of different Nations at the *Azores* and *Cape de Verd Islands.*

In the Spring, 1719, the Rovers returned to *Africa*, and beginning at the River *Gambia*, sailed all down the Coast; and between that and *Cape Corso*, took the following Ships and Vessels.

The *Eagle* Pink, Captain *Rickets* Commander belonging to *Cork*, taken the 25th of *March*, having 6 Guns and 17 Men on Board, seven of which turned Pyrates.

The *Charlotte*, Captain *Oldson*, of *London*, taken *May* the 26th, having 8 Guns and 18 Men on Board, 13 of which turned Pyrates.

The *Sarah*, Captain *Stunt*, of *London*, taken the 27th of *May*, having 4 Guns and 18 Men on Board, 3 of which turned Pyrates.

The *Bentworth*, Captain *Gardener*, of *Bristol*, taken the 27th of *May*, having 12 Guns and 30 Men on Board, 12 of which turned Pyrates.

The *Buck* Sloop, Captain *Sylvester*, of *Gambia*, taken the 27th of *May*, having 2 Guns and 2 Men on Board and both turned Pyrates.

The *Carteret*, Captain *Snow*, of *London*, taken the 28th of *May*, having 4 Guns and 18 Men on Board, of which turned Pyrates.

The *Mercury*, Captain *Maggott*, of *London*, taken the 29th of *May*, having 4 Guns and 18 Men on Board, 5 of which turned Pyrates.

The *Coward* Galley, Captain *Creed*, of *London*, taken the 17th of *June*, having 2 Guns and 13 Men on Board, 4 of which turned Pyrates.

The *Elizabeth* and *Katherine*, Captain *Bridge* of *Barbadoes*, taken *June* the 27th, having 6 Guns and 14 Men on Board, 4 of which turned Pyrates.

The *Eagle* Pink being bound to *Jamaica*, the *Sarah* to *Virginia*, and the *Buck* to *Maryland*, they let them go, but the *Charlotte*, the *Bentworth*, the *Carteret*, and the *Coward* Galley, they burnt; and the *Mercury* and the *Elizabeth* and *Katherine* were fitted up for Pyrate Ships, the former was new nam'd *Queen Ann's Revenge*, and commanded by one *Lane*, and the other was call'd the *Flying King*, of which *Robert Sample* was appointed Captain. These two left *England* upon the Coast, sail'd to the *West-Indies*, where they took some Prizes, clean'd, and sail'd to *Brasil* in *November*, they took several *Portuguese* Ships there, and did a great deal of Mischief, but in the height of their Undertakings, a *Portuguese* Man of War, which was an excellent Sailor, came a very unwelcome Guest to them, and gave them Chace; the Queen *Ann's Revenge* got off, but was lost a little while after upon that Coast; and the *Flying King*, giving herself over for lost, ran ashore: There were then 70 Men on Board, 12 of which were kill'd, and the rest taken Prisoners, of whom the *Portuguese* hang'd 38, of which 32 were *English*, three *Dutch*, two *French*, and one of their own Nation.

England, in going down the Coast, took the *Peterborough* Galley of *Bristol*, Captain *Owen*; and the *Victory*, Captain *Ridout*; the former they detained, but plundered the latter, and let her go. In *Cape Corso* Road, they saw two Sail at Anchor, but before they could reach them, they flipp'd their Cables and got close under *Cape Corso Castle*, these were the *Whydah*, Captain *Prince*, and the *John*, Captain *Rider*. The Pyrates upon this made a fire Ship of a Vessel they had lately taken, and attempted to burn them, as tho' they had been a common Enemy, which if effected, they could not have been one Farthing the better for it; but the Castle firing warmly upon them, they withdrew, and sail'd down to *Whydah* Road, where they found another Pyrate, one Captain *la Bouche*, who getting thither before *England* arrived, had forestall'd the Market, and greatly disappointed their Brethren.

Captain *England*, after this Baulk, went into a Harbour, clean'd his own Ship, and fitted up the *Peterborough*, which he call'd the *Victory*; they liv'd there very wantonly for several Weeks, making free with the Negroe Women, and committing such outragious Acts, that they came to an open Rupture with the Natives, several of whom they kill'd, and one of their Towns they set on Fire.

When the Pyrates came out to Sea, they put it to a Vote what Voyage to take, and the Majority carrying it for the *East-Indies*, they shap'd their Course accordingly, and arrived at *Madagascar*, the Beginning of the Year 1720. They staid not long there, but after taking in Water and Provisions, sail'd for the Coast of *Malabar*, which is a fine fruitful Country in the *East-Indies*, in the Empire of the *Mogul*, but immediately subject to its own Princes: It reaches from the Coast of *Canara* to *Cape Camorin*, which is between 7° 30, and 12° North Lattitude, and in about 75° East Longitude, counting from the Meridian of *London*. The old Natives are Pagans, but there are a great Number of *Mahometans* inhabiting among them, who are Merchants, and generally rich. On the same Coast, but in a Province to the Northward lies *Goa, Surat, Bombay*, where the *English, Dutch*, and *Portuguese* have Settlements.

Hither our Pyrates came, having made a Tour of half the Globe, as the Psalmist says of the Devils, *Going about like roaring Lions, seeking whom they might devour.* They took several Country Ship that is, *Indian* Vessels, and one European, a *Dutch* Ship, which they exchanged for one of their own, and then came back to *Madagascar*.

They set several of their Hands on Shore with Tents, Powder, and Shot, to kill Hogs, Venison and such other fresh Provision as the Island afforded, and a Whim came into their Heads to seek out for the Remains of *Avery*'s Crew, whom they knew to be settled somewhere in the Island.——Accordingly some of them travell'd several Days Journey, without hearing any Intelligence of them, and so were forc'd to return with the Loss of their Labour, for these Men were settled on the other Side of the Island, as has been taken Notice of under the Chapter of *Avery*.

They stay'd not long here, after they had clean'd their Ships, but sailing to *Juanna*; they met two *English*, and one *Ostend India* Men, coming out of that Harbour, one of which, after a desperate Resistance, they took; the Particulars of which Action is at length related in the following Letter, wrote by the Captain from *Bombay*.

A LETTER from Captain *Mackra*, dated at
Bombay, Nov. 16, 1720.

We arrived the 25th of July last, in Company of the Greenwich, *at* Juanna, (*an Island not far from* Madagascar) *putting in there to refresh our Men, we found fourteen Pyrates that came in their Canoes from the* Mayotta, *where the Pyrate Ship to which they belong'd, viz. the* Indian Queen, *two hundred and fifty Tons, twenty eight Guns, and ninety Men, commanded by Capt.* Oliver de la Bouche, *bound from the* Guinea *Coast to the* East-Indies, *had been bulged and lost. They said they left the Captain and 40 of their Men building a new Vessel to proceed on their wicked Design. Capt.* Kirby *and I concluding it might be of great Service to the* East-India *Company to destroy such a Nest of Rogues, were ready to sail for that Purpose the 17th of* August, *about Eight o' Clock in the Morning, when we discovered two Pyrate Ships standing into the Bay of* Juanna, *one of thirty four, and the other of thirty Guns. I immediately went on Board the* Greenwich, *where they seem'd very diligent in Preparations for an Engagement, and I left Capt.* Kirby *with mutual Promises of standing by each other. I then unmoor'd, got under Sail, and brought two Boats a-head to row me close to the* Greenwich; *but he being open to a Valley and a Breeze, made the best of his Way from me; which an* Ostender *in our Company, of 22 Guns, seeing, did the same, though the Captain had promised heartily to engage with us, and I believe would have been as good as his Word, if Capt.* Kirby *had kept his. About half an Hour after Twelve, I called several times to the* Greenwich *to bear down to our Assistance, and fir'd Shot at him, but to no Purpose. For tho' we did not doubt but he would join us, because when he got about a League from us, he brought his Ship to, and look'd on, yet both he and the* Ostender *basely deserted us, and left us engaged with barbarous and inhuman Enemies, with their black and bloody Flags hanging over us, without the least Appearance of escaping being cut to Pieces. But God, in his good Providence, determin'd otherwise; for notwithstanding their Superiority, we engaged 'em both about three Hours, during which, the biggest received some Shot betwixt Wind and Water, which made her keep off a little stop her Leaks. The other endeavoured all she could to board us, by rowing with her Oars, being within half a Ship's Length of us above an Hour; but by good Fortune we shot all her Oars to Pieces, which prevented them, and by consequence saved our Lives.*

About Four o' Clock, most of the Officers and Men posted on the Quarter-Deck being killed and wounded, the Largest Ship making up to us with all Diligence, being still within a Cable's Length of us, often giving us a Broadside, and no hopes of Capt. Kirby's *coming to our Assistance, we endeavoured to run ashoar; and tho' we drew four Foot Water more than the Pyrate, it pleased God that he stuck fast on a higher Ground than we happily fell in with; so was disappointed a second time from boarding us. Here we had a more violent Engagement than before. All my Officers, and most of my Men, behaved with unexpected Courage; and as we had a considerable Advantage by having a Broadside to his Bow, we did him great Damage, so that had Capt.* Kirby *come in then, I believe we should have taken both, for we had one of them sure; but the other Pyrate (who was still firing at us) seeing the* Greenwich *did not offer to assist us, he supplied his Consort with three Boats full of fresh Men. About Five in the Evening, the* Greenwich *stood clear away to Sea, leaving us struggling hard for Life in the very Jaws of Death; which the other Pyrate, that was afloat, seeing, got a-warp out, and was hauling under our Stern; by which time many of my Men being killed and wounded, and no Hopes left us from being all murdered by enraged barbarous Conquerors, I order'd all that could, to get into the Long-Boat under the Cover of the Smoak of our Guns; so that with what some did in Boats, and others by swimming, most of us that were able got a boar by Seven o' Clock. When the Pyrates came aboard, they cut three of our wounded Men to Pieces. I, with a few of my People, made what haste I could to the King's-town, twenty five Miles from us, where I arrived next Day, almost dead with Fatigue and Loss of Blood, having been sorely wounded in the Head by a Musket Ball.*

At this Town I heard that the Pyrates had offered ten thousand Dollars to the Country People to bring me in, which many of them would have accepted, only they knew them king and all his chief People were in my Interest. Mean time, I caused a Report to be spread, that I was dead of my wounds, which much abated their Fury. About ten Days after, being pretty well recovered, and hoping the Malice of our Enemies was nigh over, I began to consider the dismal Condition we were reduced to, being in a Place where we had no Hopes of getting a Passage home, all of us in a manner naked, not having had Time to get another Shirt, or a Pair of Shoes.

Having obtained Leave to go on Board the Pyrates, and a Promise of Safety, several of the Chief of them knew me, and some of them had sailed with me, which I found of great Advantage; because, notwithstanding their Promise, some of them would have cut me, and all that would not enter with them, to Pieces, had it not been for the chief Captain, Edward England, *and some others I knew. They talked of burning one of their Ships, which we had so entirely disabled, as to be no farther useful to them, and to fit the* Cassandra *in her room; but in the End I managed my Tacks so well, that they made me a Present of the said shattered Ship, which was* Dutch *built, called the* Fancy, *about three hundred Tons, and also a hundred and twenty nine Bales of the Company's Cloth, tho' they would not give me a Rag of my Cloathes.*

They sailed the 3d of September; *and with Jury-Masts, and such old Sails as they left me, I made shift to do she like on the 8th, together with forty three of my Ship's Crew, including two Passengers and twelve Soldiers, having but five Tons of Water aboard; and after a Passage of forty eight Days, I arrived here*

October 26, *almost naked and starv'd, having been reduced to a Pint of Water a Day, and almost in despair of ever seeing Land, by Reason of the Calms we met with between the Coast of* Arabia *and* Malabar.—*We had in all thirteen Men killed and twenty four wounded; and we were told, that we had destroyed about ninety or a hundred of the Pyrates. When they left us, they were about three hundred Whites and eighty Blacks in both Ships. I am persuaded, had our Consort the* Greenwich *done his Duty, we had destroyed both of them, and got two hundred thousand Pounds for our Owners and selves; whereas to his deserting us, the Loss of the* Cassandra *may justly be imputed. I have delivered all the Best that were given me into the Company's Warehouse, for which the Governor and Council have ordered me a Reward. Our Governor, Mr.* Boon, *who is extreme kind and civil to me, has ordered me home with this Pacquet; but Captain* Harvey, *who had a prior Promise, being come in with the Fleet, goes in my room. The Governor hath promis'd me a Country Voyage, to help make me up my Losses, and would have me stay to go home with him next Year.*

Captain *Mackra* certainly run a great Hazard, in going aboard the Pyrate, and began quickly to repent his Credulity; for though they had promised, that no Injury should be done to his Person, he found their Words were not to be trusted; and it may be supposed, that nothing but the desperate Circumstances Captain *Mackra* imagined himself to be in, could have prevailed upon him to fling himself and Company into their Hands, perhaps not knowing how firmly the Natives of that Island were attach'd to the *English* Nation; for about 20 Years ago, Captain *Cornwall*, Commadore of an *English* Squadron, assisted them against another Island called *Mohilla*, for which they have ever since communicated all the grateful Offices in their Power, insomuch that it became a Proverb, *That an* Englishman, *and a* Juanna *Man were all one.*

England was inclined to favour Captain *Mackra*; but he was so free to let him know, that his Interest was declining amongst them; and that the Pyrates were so provoked at the Resistance he made against them, that he was afraid he should hardly be able to protect him; he therefore advised him to sooth up and manage the Temper of Captain *Taylor*, a Fellow of a most barbarous Nature, who was become a great Favourite amongst them for no other Reason than because he was a greater Brute than the rest. *Mackra* did what he could to soften this Beast, and ply'd him with warm Punch; notwithstanding which, they were in a Tumult whether they should make an End of him, or no, when an Accident happen'd which turn'd to the Favour of the poor Captain; a Fellow with a terrible pair of Whiskers, and a wooden Leg, being stuck round with Pistols, like the Man in the Almanack with Darts, comes swearing and vapouring upon the Quarter-Deck, and asks, in a damning Manner, which was Captain *Mackra*: The Captain expected no less than that this Fellow would be his Executioner;—but when he came near him, he took him by the Hand, swearing, *Damn him he was glad to see him; and shew me the Man*, says he, *that offers to hurt Captain* Mackra, *for I'll stand by him*; and so with many Oaths told him, *he was an honest Fellow, and that he had formerly sail'd with him*.

This put an End to the Dispute, and Captain *Taylor* was so mellow'd with the Punch, that he consented that the old Pyrate Ship, and so many Bales of Cloth should be given to Captain *Mackra*, and so he fell asleep. *England* advised Captain *Mackra* to get off with all Expedition, least when the Beast should awake, he might repent his Generosity; Which Advice was followed by the Captain.

Captain *England* having sided so much to Captain *Mackra*'s Interest, was a Means of making him many Enemies among the Crew; they thinking such good Usage inconsistent with their Polity, because it looked like procuring Favour at the Aggravation of their Crimes; therefore upon Imagination or Report, that Captain *Mackra* was fitting out against them, with the Company's Force, he was soon *abdicated* or pulled out of his Government and marooned with three more on the Island of *Mauritius*: An Island indeed, not to be complained of, had they accumulated any Wealth by their Villanies that would have afforded some future comfortable Prospect, for it abounds with Fish, Deer, Hogs and other Flesh. Sir *Thomas Herbert*, says, the Shores with Coral and Ambergrease; but I believe the *Dutch* had not deserted it, had there been much of these Commodities to have been found. It was in 1722, resettled by the *French*, who have a Fort at another neighbouring Island, called *Don Mascarine*, and are touched at for Water, Wood, and Refreshments, by *French* Ships bound to, or for *India*; as St. *Helena* and *Cape Bon Esperance*, are by us and the *Dutch*. From this Place, Captain *England* and his Companions having made a little Boat of Staves and old Pieces of Deal left there, went over to *Madagascar*, where they subsist at present on the Charity of some of their Brethren, who had made better Provision for themselves, than they had done.

The Pyrates detained some Officers and Men belonging to Captain *Mackra*, and having repaired the Damages received in their Rigging, they sailed for *India*. The Day before they made Land, saw two Ships to the Eastward, who at first Sight, they took to be *English*, and ordered one of the Prisoners, who had been an Officer with Captain *Mackra*, to tell them the private Signals between the Company's Ships, the Captain swearing he would cut him in pound Pieces, if he did not do it immediately; but unable, was forced to bear their Scurility, till they came up with them, and found they were two *Moor* Ships from *Muscat*, with Horses; they brought the Captain of them, and Merchants, on Board, torturing them, and rifling the Ships, in order to discover Riches, as believing they came from *Mocha*; but being baulked in their Expectation, and next Morning seeing Land, and at the same Time a Fleet in Shore plying to Windward, they were puzzled how to dispose of them; to let them go, was to discover and ruin the Voyage, and it was cruel to sink the Men and Horses with the Ships, (as many of them were inclined to,) therefore, as a Medium, they brought them to an Anchor, threw all their Sails over-board, and cut one of the Ships Masts half through.

While they lay at an Anchor, and were all the next Day employed in taking out Water, one of the aforementioned Fleet bore towards them with *English* Colours, answered with a red Ensign from the Pyrates, but did not speak with one another. At Night they left the *Muscatt* Ships, weighed with the Sea Wind, and stood to the Northward after this Fleet: About four next Morning, just as they were getting under sail, with the Land Wind, the Pyrates came amongst them, made no stop, but fired their great and small Guns very briskly, till they got through; and as Day-Light cleared, were in a great Consternation in their Minds, having all along taken them for *Angria*'s Fleet; what to do was the Point, whether run or pursue? They were sensible of their Inferiority of Strength, having no more than 300 Men in both Ships, and 40 of them Negroes; besides, the *Victory* had then four Pumps at Work, and must inevitably been lost before, had it not been for some Hand-Pumps, and several pair of Standards brought out of the *Cassandra*, to relieve and strengthen her; but observing the Indifferency of the Fleet, chose rather to chase than run; and thought the best Way to save themselves, was to play at Bullbeggar with the Enemy: So they came up with the Sea Wind, about Gun-Shot to Leeward, the great Ships of the Fleet a-head, and some others a-stern; which latter they took for Fire-Vessels: And these a-head gaining from them by cutting away their Boats, they could do nothing more than continue their Course all Night, which they did, and found them next Morning out of Sight, excepting a Ketch and some few Gal-livats, (*small sort of Vessels something like the Feluccas of the* Mediterranean; *and hoists, like them, triangular Sails.*) They bore down, which the Ketch perceiving, transported her People on Board a Gallivat, and set fire to her; the other proved too nimble and made off. The same Day they chased another Gallivat and took her being come from *Gogo*, bound for *Calliĉut* with Cotton. Of these Men they enquired con-

cerning the Fleet, supposing they must have been in it; and
altho' they protested they had not seen a Ship or Boat since
they left *Gogo*, and pleaded very earnestly for Favour; yet they
threw all their Cargo over-board, and squezed their Joints in
a Vice, to extort Confession: But they entirely ignorant of
who or what this Fleet should be, were obliged not only to
sustain this Torment, but next Day a fresh easterly Wind
having split the Gallivats Sails, they put her Company into
the Boat, with nothing but a Trysail, no Provisions, and only
four Gallons of Water, (half of it Salt,) and then out of Sight
of Land, to shift for themselves.

For the better elucidating of this Story, it may be convenient to inform the Reader, who *Angria* is, and what the Fleet
were, that had so scurvily behaved themselves.

Angria is a famous *Indian* Pyrate, of considerable strength
and Territories, that gives continual Disturbance to the *European* (and especially the *English*) Trade: His chief Hold is
Callaba, not many Leagues from *Bombay*, and has one Island
in Sight of that Port whereby he gains frequent Opportunities of annoying the Company. It would not be so insu-
ferable a Difficulty to suppress him, if the Shallowness of
the Water did not prevent Ships of War coming nigh: And
a better Art he has, of bribing the *Mogul*'s Ministers for
Protection, when he finds an Enemy too powerful.

In the Year 1720, the *Bombay* Fleet consisting of four
Grabbs, (Ships built in India *by the Company, and have three
Masts, a Prow like a Row-Galley, instead of a Boltsprit, about
150 Tons; are officered and armed like a Man of War, for Defence and Protection of the Trade,)* the *London, Chandois,* and
two other Ships with Gallivats, who besides their proper
Compliments, carried down 1000 Men to bombard and bat-
ter *Gayra*, a Fort belonging to *Angria*, on the *Malabar* Coast,
which they having performed ineffectually, were returning
to *Bombay*, and, to make amends, fell in with the Pyrates, to
the Purpose has been already related. Captain *Upton*, Commadore of that Fleet, prudently objecting to Mr. *Brown*,
(who went General,) That the Ships were not to be haz-

arded, since they sailed without their Governor *Boon*'s Orders to engage; and besides, that they did not come out with such a Design. This favourable Opportunity of destroying the Pyrates, angered the Governor, and he transferred the Command of the Fleet to Captain *Mackra*, who had Orders immediately to pursue and engage, where ever he met them.

The Vice-Roy of *Goa*, assisted by the English Company's Fleet from *Bombay*, did attempt the Reduction of *Callaba*, his principal Place, landed 8 or 10000 Men the next Year, the *English* Squadron of Men of War being then in those Seas; but having viewed the Fortification well, and expended some of their Army by Sickness and the Fatigues of a Camp, carefully withdrew again.

I return to the Pyrates, who, after they had sent away the Gallivats People, resolved to cruise to the Southward; and the next Day, between *Goa* and *Carwar*, heard several Guns, which brought them to an Anchor, and they sent their Boat on the Scent, who returned about two in the Morning, and brought Word of two Grabs lying at Anchor in the Road. They weighed and ran towards the Bay, till Day-Light gave the Grabs Sight of them, and was but just Time enough to get under *India Diva* Castle, out of their reach; this displeased the Pyrates the more, in that they wanted Water; and some were for making a Descent that Night and taking the Island, but it not being approved of by the Majority, they proceeded to the Southward, and took next in their Way, a small Ship out of *Onnore* Road, with only a *Dutch* Man and two *Portuguese* on Board. They sent one of these on Shore to the Captain, to acquaint him, if he would supply them with some Water, and fresh Provisions, he should have his Ship again; and the Master returned for answer, by his Mate *Frank Harmless*, that if they would deliver him Possession over the Bar, he would comply with their Request; the Proposal the Mate thought was collusive, and they rather jump'd into *Harmless*'s Opinion, (who very honestly entered with them,) and resolved to seek Water at the *Laccadeva* Islands; so having sent the other Persons on Shore, with threats, that

he should be the last Man they would give Quarter to, (by
Reason of this uncivil Usage;) they put directly for the Islands, and arrived there in three Days: Where being informed by a Menchew they took (with the Governor of
Canwars Pass,) of there being no Anchor-Ground among
them, and *Melinda* being the next convenient Island, they
sent their Boats on Shore, to see if there was any Water, and
whether it was inhabited or not; who returned with an Answer to their Satisfaction, *viz.* that there was abundance of
good Water, and many Houses, but deserted by the Men,
who had fled to the neighbouring Islands on the Approach
of Ships, and left only the Women and Children to guard
one another. The Women they forced in a Barbarous Manner to their Lusts, and to requite them, destroyed their
Cocoa Trees, and fired several of their Houses and *Churches.*
(I suppose built by the *Portuguese*, who formerly used there,
in their Voyages to *India.*)

While they were at this Island, they lost three or four
Anchors, by the Rockyness of the Ground, Freshness of
Winds, and at last were forced thence by a harder Gale
than ordinary, leaving 70 People, Blacks and Whites, and
most of their Water Casks: in ten Days they regained the
Island again, filled their Water, and took the People on
Board.

Provisions were very scarce, and they now resolved to visit
their good Friends the *Dutch*, at *Cochin*, who, if you will
believe these Rogues, never fail of supplying Gentlemen of
their Profession. After three Days sail, they arrived off *Tel-
lechery*, and took a small Vessel belonging to Governor *Ad-
ams, John Tawke* Master, whom they brought on Board very
drunk, and he giving an Account of Captain *Mackra's* fitting
out, put them in a Tempest of Passion: *A Villain,* say they,
*that we have treated so civilly, as to give him a Ship and other
Presents, and now to be armed against us, he ought to be hanged;
and since we cannot show our Resentment on him, let us hang
the Dogs his People, who wish him well, and would do the same,
if clear. If it be in my Power, says the* Quarter-Master, *both*

Masters and Officer's of Ships shall be carried with us for the future, only to plague them—d—n England.

Thence they proceeded to *Calicut*, where they endeavoured to take a large *Moor* Ship out of the Road, but was prevented by some Guns mounted on Shore, and discharged at them: Mr. *Lasinby*, who was one of Captain *Mackra*'s Officers, and detained was under the Deck at this Time, and commanded both the Captain and QuarterMaster of Pyrates, to tend the Braces on the Booms, in hopes it was believed, a Shot would take him before they got clear, asking the Reason why he was not then before? And when he would have excused himself, threat'ned on the like Neglect to shoot him; at which the other beginning to expostulate farther and claim their Promise of Putting him ashore, got an unmerciful beating from the Quarter-Master Captain *Taylor*, who was now Successor to *England* and whose Priviledge it was to do so, being lame of his Hands, and unable.

The next Day in their Passage down, came up with a *Dutch* Galliot, bound for *Calicut* with Lime Stone, and aboard of her they put Captain *Tawke*, and sent him away, and several of the People interceeded for *Lasinby* in vain, *For*, says *Taylor* and his Party, *if we let this Dog go, who has heard our Designs and Resolutions, we overset all our well advised Projection, and particularly this Supply we are now seeking for, at the Hands of the* Dutch.

It was but one Day more before they arrived off *Cochin*, where, by a Fishing-Canoe, they sent a Letter on Shore; and in the Afternoon, with the Sea-breeze, ran into the Road and anchored, saluting the Fort with 11 Guns each Ship, and received the Return, in an equal Number; a good Omen of the welcome Reception they found; for at Night there came on Board a large Boat, deeply laden with fresh Provisions and Liquors, and with it a Servant of a favourite Inhabitant) called *John Trumpet*: He told them they must immediately weigh, and run further to the Southward, where they should be applied with all Things they wanted, naval Stores or Provisions.

They had not been long at Anchor again, before they had several Canoes on Board with both black and white Inhabitants, who continued, without Interruption, all good Offices, during their Stay; particularly *John Trumpet* brought a large Boat of Arrack, than which, nothing could be more pleasing (about 90 Legers,) as also 60 Bales of Sugar; an Offering, its presumed, from the Governor and his Daughter, who, in Return, had a fine Table-Clock sent him, (the Plunder of Captain *Mackra*'s ship,) and she a large Gold Watch, Earnests of the Pay they designed to make.

When they had all on Board, they paid Mr. *Trumpet* to his Satisfaction, it was computed, 6 or 7000 *l.* gave him three Cheers, 11 Guns each Ship, and throw'd Ducatoons into his Boat by handfuls, for the Boat-Men to scramble for.

That Night being little Wind, did not weigh, and *Trumpet*, in the Morning, waked them to the Sight of more Arrack, Chests of Piece-Goods, and ready made Clothes, bringing the Fiscal of the Place also with him. At Noon, while those were on Board, saw a Sail to the Southward, which they weighed, and chaced after; but she having a good Offing, got to the Northward of them, and anchored a small Distance from *Cochin* Fort; the aforementioned Gentlemen assuring them, that they would not be molested in taking her from under the Castle, sollicited before hand for the buying her, and advised them to stand in, which they did boldly, to board her, but when they came within a Cable's length or two of the Chace, now near Shore, the Fort fired two small Guns, whose Shot falling nigh their Muzzels, they instantly bore out of the Road, made an easy Sail to the Southward, and anchored at Night in their former Birth, where *John Trumpet*, to engage their Stay a little longer, informed them, that in a few Days a very rich Ship was to pass by, commanded by the General of *Bombay*'s Brother.

This Governor is an Emblem of foreign Power. What Inconvenience and Injury must the Master's Subjects sustain under one who can truckle to such treacherous and base Means, as corresponding and trading with Pyrates to enrich himself? Certainly such a Man will stickle at no Injustice to repair or make a Fortune. He has the *Argumentuns bacillum* always in his own Hands, and can convince, when he pleases, in half the Time of other Arguments, that Fraud and Oppression is Law. That he imploys Instruments in such dirty Work, expresses the Guilt and Shame, but no way mitigates the Crime. *John Trumpet* was the Tool; but, as the Dog said in the Fable, on another Occasion, *What is done by the Master's Orders, is the Master's Actions.*

I cannot but reflect, on this Occasion, what a vile Government *Sancho Pancho* had of it; he had not only such *Perquisites* rescinded, but was really almost starved; the Victuals taken from him almost every Day, and only under a Pretence of preserving his Excellency's Health: But Governments differ.

From *Cochin* some were for proceeding to *Madagascar* directly; others thought it proper to cruize till they got a Store-Ship, and these being the Majority, they ply'd to the Southward, and after some Days saw a Ship in Shore, which being to Windward of them, they could not get nigh, till the Sea Wind, and Night, favouring, they separated, one of the Northward, the other to the Southward, thinking to enclose her between: But to their Astonishment, and contrary to Expectation, when Day broke, instead of the Chace, found themselves very near five Sail of tall Ships, who immediately making a Signal for the Pyrates to bear down, put them in the utmost Confusion, particularly *Taylor's* Ship, because their Consort was at a Distance from them, (at least three Leagues to the Southward) they stood to one another, and joined, and then together made the best of their Way from the Fleet, whom they judged to be commanded by Captain *Mackra*; of whose Courage having Experience, they were glad to shun any farther Taste of.

In three Hours Chace, none of the Fleet gaining upon them, excepting one Grab, their dejected Countenances cleared up again, the more, in that Calm succeeded for the Remainder of that Day; in the Night, with the Land Wind,

they ran directly off Shore, and found next Day, to their great
Consolation, that they had lost Sight of all the Fleet.

This Danger escaped, they proposed to spend *Christmas*
(the *Christmas* of 1720) in Carowzing and Forgetfulness, and
kept it for three Days in a wanton and riotous Way, not only
eating, but wasting their fresh Provisions in so wretched and
inconsiderable a Manner, that when they had agreed after
this to proceed to *Mauritius*, they were in that Passage at an
Allowance of a Bottle of Water *per Diem*, and not above two
Pounds of Beef, and a small Quantity of Rice, for ten Men
for a Day; so that had it not been for the leaky Ship, (which
once they were about to have quitted, and had done, but for
a Quantity of Arrack and Sugar She had on Board,) they
must most of them have perished.

In this Condition they arrived at the Island of *Mauritius*,
about the Middle of *February*, sheathed and refitted the *Victory*, and on the 5th of *April* sailed again, leaving this terrible
Inscription on one of the Walls. *Left this Place the 5th of*
April, *to go to* Madagascar *for Limes*, and this, least (like
Lawyers and Men of Business) any Visits should be paid in
their Absence: However, they did not sail directly for *Madagascar*, but the Island *Mascarine*, and luckily as Rogues
could wish, they found at their Arrival on the 8th; a *Portuguese* Ship at Anchor, of 70 Guns, but most of them thrown
overboard, her Masts lost, and so much disabled by a violent
Storm they had met with in the Latitude of 13° South, that
she became a Prize to the Pyrates, with very little or no
Resistance, and a glorious one indeed, having the *Conde de
Ericeira*, Viceroy of *Goa*, who made that fruitless Expedition
against *Angria*, the *Indian*, and several other Passengers on
Board; who, as they could not be ignorant of the Treasure
she had in, did assert, that in the single Article of Diamonds,
there was to the Value of between three and four Millions
of Dollars.

The Vice-Roy, who came on Board that Morning, in Expectation of the Ships being *English*, was made a Prisoner,
and obliged to ransome; but in Consideration of his great

Loss, (the Prize being Part his own,) they agreed after some Demurrings, to accept of 2000 Dollars, and set him and the other Prisoners ashore, with Promises to leave a Ship that they might Transport themselves, because the Island was not thought in a Condition to maintain so great a Number; and tho' they had learned from them, the Account of an *Ostender* being to Leeward of the Island, which they took on that Information, (being formerly the *Greyhound* Galley of *London*,) and could conveniently have comply'd with so reasonable a Request; yet they sent the *Ostender* with some of their People to *Madagascar*, with News of their Success, and to prepare Masts for the Prize; and followed themselves soon after, without regard to the Sufferers, carrying 200 *Mozambique* Negroes with them in the *Portuguese* Ship.

Madagascar is an Island larger than *Great-Britain*, most of it within the Tropick of *Capricorn*, and lays East from the Eastern Side of *Africa*: It abounds with Provisions of all Sorts, Oxen, Goats, Sheep, Poultry, Fish, Citrons, Oranges, Tamarinds, Dates, Coco-Nuts, Bananas, Wax, Honey, Rice; or in short, Cotton, Indigo, or any other Thing they will take Pains to plant, and have Understanding to manage: They have likewise Ebony, a hard Wood like Brasil, of which they make their Lances; and Gum of several Sorts, Benzin, Dragon's Blood, Aloes, *&c.* What is most incommodious, are the numerous Swarms of Locusts on the Land, and Crocodiles or Alligators in their Rivers. Hither, in St. *Augustin*'s Bay, the Ships sometimes touch for Water, when they take the inner Passage for *India*, and do not design to stop at *Johanna*; and we may observe from the sixth general Voyage set forth by the *East-India* Company, in Confirmation of what is hereafter said in Relation to Currents in general; that this inner Passage or Channel, has its Northern and Southern Currents strongest where the Channel is narrowest, and is less, and varies on different Points of the Compass, the Sea comes to spread again, in the Passage cross the Line.

Since the Discovery of this Island by the *Portuguese*, *A. D.*

1506, the *Europeans*, and particularly Pyrates, have increased
a dark Mulatto Race there, tho' still few in Comparison with
the Natives, who are Negroes, with curled short Hair, Active, and formerly represented malicious and revengeful, now
tractable and communicable, perhaps owing to the Favours
and Generosity in Cloathing and Liquors, they from Time
to Time have received from these Fellows, who live in all
possible Friendship, and can, any single Man of them, command a Guard of 2 or 300 at a Minute's warning: This is
farther the Native's Interest, to cultivate with them, because
the Island being divided into petty Governments and Commands, the Pyrates, settled here, who are now a considerable
Number, and have little Castles of their own, can prepon-
derate where-ever they think fit to side.

When *Taylor* came with the *Portuguese* Prize here, they
found the *Ostender* had played their Men a Trick, for they
took Advantage of their Drink, rife upon them, and (as they
heard afterwards) carried the Ship to *Mozambique*, whence
the Governor ordered her for *Goa*.

Here the Pyrates came, cleaned the *Cassandra*, and divided their Plunder, sharing 42 small Diamonds a Man, or
in less Proportion according to their Magnitude. An ignorant, or a merry Fellow, who had only one in this Division,
as being judged equal in Value to 42 small, muttered very
much at the Lot, and went and broke it in a Morter, swearing
afterwards, he had a better Share than any of them, for he
had beat it, he said, into 43 Sparks.

Those who were not for running the Hazard of their
Necks, with 42 Diamonds, besides other Treasure, in their
Pockets, knocked off, and stay'd with their old Acquaintance
at *Madagascar*, on mutual Agreements, the longer Livers to
take all. The Residue having therefore no Occasion for two
Ships, the *Victory* being leaky, she was burnt, the Men (as
many as would) coming into the *Cassandra*, under the Command of *Taylor*, who we must leave a Time, projecting either
for *Cochin*, to dispose of their Diamonds among their old
Friends the *Dutch*, or else for the *Red* or *China* Seas, to avoid

the Men of War, that continually clamoured in their Ears, a Noise of Danger, and give the *little* Account we are able, of that Squadron, who arrived in *India*, early in the Year 1721.

At *Cape Good Hope*, in *June*, the Commadore met with a Letter, which was left for him by the Governor of *Madras*, to whom it was wrote by the Governor of *Pandicherry*, a *French* Factory, on the *Coromondel* Coast, signifying, the Pyrates at the Writing of it, were then strong in the *Indian* Seas, having 11 Sail and 1500 Men, but that many of them went away about that Time, for the Coast of *Brazil* and *Guinea*; others settled and fortified themselves at *Madagascar, Mauritius, Johanna* and *Mohilla*: And that others under *Conden*, in a Ship called the *Dragon*, took a large *Moor's* Vessel, coming from *Iudda* and *Mocho*, with thirteen Lackies of Rupees on Board, (*i. e.* 1300000 half Crowns,) who having divided the Plunder, burnt their Ship and Prize, and sat down quietly with their other Friends at *Madagascar*.

The Account contain'd several other Things which we have before related.—Commadore *Matthews*, upon receiving this Intelligence, and being fond of the Service he came out for, hastened to those Islands, as the most hopeful Places of Success; at St. *Mary's* would have engaged *England* with Promises of Favour, if he would communicate what he knew, concerning the *Cassandra*, and the rest of the Pyrates, and assist in the Pilotage; but *England* was wary, and thought this was to *surrender at Discretion*, so they took up the *Judda* Ship's Guns that was burnt, and the Men of War dispersed themselves on several Voyages and Cruises afterwards, as was thought likeliest to succeed, tho' to no Purpose: Then the Squadron went down to *Bombay*, were saluted by the Fort, and came home.

The Pyrates, I mean those of the *Cassandra*, now Captain *Taylor*, fitted the *Portuguese* Man of War, and resolved upon another Voyage to the *Indies*, notwithstanding the Riches they had heaped up; but as they were preparing to sail, they heard of the four Men of War coming after them to those

Seas, therefore they altered their Minds, sail'd for the Main of *Africa*, and put in at a little Place called *Delagoa*, near the River *de Spiritu Sancto*, on the Coast of *Monomotapa*, in 26° South Latitude. They believed this to be a Place of Security, in regard that the Squadron could not possibly get Intelligence of them, there being no Correspondence over Land, nor any Trade carried on by Sea, between that and the Cape, where the Men of War were then supposed to be. The Pyrates came to in the Evening, and were surprized with a few Shot from the Shore, not knowing of any Fortification or *European* Settlement in that Part of the World; so they anchored at a Distance that Night, and perceiving, in the Morning, a small Fort of six Guns, they run up to it, and battered it down.

This Fort was built and settled by the *Dutch East-India* Company, a few Months before, for what Purpose, I know not, and having left 150 Men upon the Place, they were then dwindled to a third Part by Sickness and Casualties, and never after received any Relief or Necessaries; so that Sixteen of those that were left, upon their humble Petition, were admitted on Board the Pyrates, and all the rest would have had the same Favour (they said) had they been any other than *Dutch*. I mention this, as an Instance of their Ingratitude, who had been so much obliged to their Countrymen for Support.

Here they staid above four Months, carreened both their Ships, and took their Diversions with Security, till they had expended all their Provisions, and then put to Sea, leaving considerable Quantities of Muslins, Chintzes, and such Goods behind, to the half starved *Dutch* Men, which enabled them to make good Pennyworths to the next that came, to whom they bartered for Provisions, at the Rate of three Farthings an *English* Yard.

They left *Delagoa* the latter End of *December* 1722, but not agreeing where, or how to proceed, they concluded to part, so those who were for continuing that sort of Life, went on Board the *Portuguese* Prize, and steered for *Madagascar* to their Friends, with whom I hear they are now settled; and the rest took the *Cassandra* and sailed for the *Spanish West-Indies.* The *Mermaid* Man of War happening then to be down on the Main with a Convoy, about 30 Leagues from these Pyrates, would have gone and attacked them; but on a Consultation of the Masters, whose Safety he was particularly to regard, they agreed their own Protection was of more Service than destroying the Pyrate, and so the Commander was unwilling withheld. He dispatched a Sloop to *Jamaica*, with the News, which brought down the *Lanceston*, only a Day, or two, too late, they having just before he came, surrendered with all their Riches, to the Governor of *Porto Bello*.

Here they sate down to spend the Fruits of their dishonest Industry, dividing the Spoil and Plunder of Nations among themselves, without the least Remorse or Compunction, satisfying their Conscience with this Salvo, that other People would have done as much, had they the like Opportunitiess. I can't say, but that if they had known what was doing in *England*, at the same Time by the *South-Sea* Directors, and their Directors, they would certainly have had this Reflection for their Consolation, *viz. That what ever Robberies they had committed, they might be pretty sure they were not the greatest Villains then living in the World.*

It is a difficult Matter to make a Computation of the Mischief that was done by this Crew, in about five Years Time, which is much more than the Plunder they gained, for they often sunk or burnt the Vessel they took, as it suited their Humour or Circumstances, sometimes to prevent giving Intelligence, sometimes because they did not leave Men to navigate them, and at other Times out of Wantonness, or because they were displeased at the Master's Behaviour; for any of these, it was but to give the Word, and down went Ships and Cargoes to the Bottom of the Sea.

Since their Surrender to the *Spaniards*, I am informed several of them have left the Place, and dispersed themselves elsewhere; eight of them were shipp'd about *November* last, in one of the *South-Sea* Company's Assiento Sloops, and

passed for Ship-wreck'd Men, came to *Jamaica*, and there
sailed in other Vessels; and I know one of them that came
to *England* this Spring from that Island. 'Tis said that Captain *Taylor* has taken a Commission in the *Spanish* Service,
and commanded the Man of War that lately attack'd the
English Log-Wood Cutters, in the Bay of *Honduras*.

CHAPTER VI.

Of
Captain CHARLES VANE,
And his CREW.

*C*HARLES VANE was one of those who stole away the Silver which the *Spaniards* had fished up from the Wrecks of the Galleons, in the Gulph of *Florida*, and was at *Providence* (as has been before hinted) when Governor *Rogers* arrived there with two Men of War.

All the Pyrates who were found at this Colony of Rogues, submitted, and received Certificates of their Pardon, except Captain *Vane* and his Crew; who, as soon as they saw the Men of War enter, slipp'd their Cable, set Fire to a Prize they had in the Harbour, and sailed out with their pyratical Colours flying, firing at one of the Men of War as they went off.

Two Days after they went out, they met with a Sloop belonging to *Barbadoes*, which they made Prize of, and kept the Vessel for their own Use, putting aboard five and twenty Hands, with one *Yeats* to command them. A Day or two afterwards they fell in with a small interloping Trader, with a Quantity of *Spanish* Pieces of Eight aboard, bound into *Providence*, called the *John* and *Elizabeth*, which they also took along with them. With these two Sloops *Vane* went to a small island and cleaned; where they shared their Booty, and spent some Time in a riotous Manner of Living, as is the Custom of Pyrates.

The latter, End of *May* 1718, they sail'd, and being in

want of Provisions, they beat up for the Windward Islands, and met with a *Spanish* Sloop bound from *Porto Rico* to the *Havana*, which they burnt, and stowed the *Spaniards* in a Boat, and left them to get to the Island, by the Light of their vessel. But steering between St. *Christopher*'s and *Anguilla*, they fell in with a Brigantine and a Sloop, with the Cargo they wanted; from whom they got Provisions for Sea-Store.

Sometime after this, standing to the Northward, in the Track the *Old-England* Ships take, in their Voyage to the *American* Colonies, they took several Ships and Vessels, which they plundered of what they thought fit, and let them pass.

The latter End of *August, Vane*, with his Consort *Yeats*, came off *South-Carolina*, and took a Ship belonging to *Ipswich*, one *Coggershall* Commander, laden with Logwood, which was thought convenient enough for their Prisoners to work, and throw all the Lading over-board; but when they had more than half cleared the Ship, the Whim changed, and then they would not have her; so *Coggershall* had his Ship again, and he was suffered to pursue his Voyage home. In this Cruize the Rover took several other Ships and Vessels, particularly a Sloop from *Barbadoes, Dill* Master; a small Ship from *Antegoa, Cock* Master; a Sloop belonging to *Curacco, Richards* Master; and a large Brigantine, Captain *Thompson*, from *Guiney*, with ninety odd Negroes aboard. The Pyrates plundered them all and let them go, putting the Negroes out of the Brigantine aboard of *Yeat's* Vessel, by which Means they came back again to the right Owners.

For Captain *Vane*, having always treated his Consort with very little Respect, assuming a Superiority over *Yeats* and his small Crew, and regarding the Vessel but as a Tender to his own; gave them a Disgust, who thought themselves as good Pyrates, and as great Rogues as the best of them; so they caball'd together, and resolved to take the first Opportunity to leave the Company; and accept of his Majesty's Pardon, or set up for themselves, either of which they thought more honourable than to be Servants to the former; and the putting aboard so many Negroes, where they found so few Hands to take Care of them, still aggravated the Matter, though they thought fit to conceal or stifle their Resentments at that Time.

A Day or two afterwards, the Pyrates lying off at Anchor, *Yeats* in the Evening slipp'd his Cable, and put his Vessel under Sail, standing into the Shore; which, when *Vane* saw, he was highly provoked, and got his Sloop under Sail to chase his Consort, who, he plainly perceived, had a Mind to have no further Affairs with him: *Vane's* Brigantine sailing best, he gained Ground of *Yeats*, and would certainly have come up with him, had he had a little longer Run for it; but just as he got over the Bar, when *Vane* came within Gun-shot of him, he fired a Broadside at his old Friend, (which did him no Damage,) and so took his Leave.

Yeats came into *North Edisto* River, about ten Leagues Southward of *Charles-Town*, and sent an Express to the Governor, to know if he and his Comrades might have the Benefit of his Majesty's Pardon, and they would surrender themselves to his Mercy, with the Sloops and Negroes; which being granted, they all came up and received Certificates; and Captain *Thompson*, from whom the Negroes were taken, had them restored to him, for the Use of his Owners.

Vane cruised some Time off the Bar, in hopes to catch *Yeats* at his coming out again, but therein he was disappointed; however, he unfortunately for them, took two Ships from *Charles-Town*, bound home to *England*. It happen'd that just at this Time two Sloops well mann'd and arm'd, were equipp'd to go after a Pyrate, which the Governor of *South-Carolina* was informed, lay then in Cape *Fear* River, a cleaning: But Colonel *Rhet*, who commanded the Sloops, meeting with one of the Ships that *Vane* had plundered, going back over the Bar, for such Necessaries as had been taken from her, and she giving the Colonel an Account of her being taken by the Pyrate *Vane*, and also, that some of her Men, while they were Prisoners on Board of him, had heard the Pyrates say, they should clean in one of the Rivers to the Southward; he altered his first Design, and instead of standing to the Northward, in pursuit of the Pyrate in Cape *Fear* River, he turns to the Southward after *Vane*; who had ordered such Reports to be given out, on purpose to send any Force that should come after him, upon a wrong Scent; for in Reality he stood away to the Northward, so that the Pursuit proved to be the contrary Way.

Colonel *Rhet*'s speaking with this Ship, was the most unlucky Thing that could have happened, because it turned him out of the Road, which in all Probability, would have brought him into the Company of *Vane*, as well as of the Pyrate he went after; and so they might have been both destroy'd, whereas, by the Colonel's going a different Way, he not only lost the Opportunity of meeting with one, but if the other had not been infatuated, to lye six Weeks together at Cape *Fear*, he would have missed of him likewise: However, the Collonel having searched the Rivers and Inlets, as directed, for several Days, without Success, at length sailed in Prosecution of his first Design, and met with the Pyrate accordingly, whom he fought and took, as has been before spoken of, in the History of Major *Bonnet*.

Captain *Vane* went into an Inlet to the Northward, where he met with Captain *Thatch*, or *Teach*, otherwise call'd *Blackbeard*, whom he saluted (when he found who he was) with his great Guns, loaded with Shot, (as is the Custom among Pyrates when they meet) which are fired wide, or up into the Air: *Black-beard* answered the Salute in the same Manner; and mutual Civilities passed for some Days; when about the Beginning of *October*, *Vane* took Leave, and sailed further to the Northward.

On the 23rd of *October*, off of *Long Island*, he took a small Brigantine, bound from *Jamaica* to *Salem New-England*, *John Shattock* Master, and a little Sloop; they rifled the Brigantine, and sent her away. From hence they resolved on a Cruize between Cape *Meise* and Cape *Nicholas*, where they spent some Time, without seeing or speaking with any Vessel, till the latter End of *November*; then they fell upon a

Ship, which 'twas expected would have struck as soon as their black Colours were hoisted; but instead of that, she discharged a Broadside upon the Pyrate, and hoisted Colours, which shewed her to be a *French* Man of War. *Vane* desired to have nothing further to say to her, but trimm'd his sails and stood away from the *French* Man; but *Monsieur* having a Mind to be better informed who he was, set all his Sails, and crowded after him. During this Chace, the Pyrates were divided in their Resolutions what to do: *Vane*, the Captain, was for making off as fast as he could, alledging the Man of War was too strong to cope with; but one *John Rackam*, who was an Officer, that had a kind of a Check upon the Captain, rose up in Defence of a contrary Opinion, saying, *That tho' had more Guns, and a greater Weight of Mettal, they might board her, and then the best Boys would carry the Day.* *Rackam* was well seconded, and the Majority was for boarding; but *Vane* urged, *That it was too rash and desperate an Enterprize, the Man of War appearing to be twice their Force; and that their Brigantine might be sunk by her before they could reach on board.* The Mate, one *Robert Deal*, was of *Vane's* Opinion as were about fifteen more, and all the rest joined with *Rackam*, the Quarter-Master. At length the Captain made use of his Power to determine this Dispute, which, in these Cases, is absolute and uncontroulable, by their own Laws, *viz.* in *fighting chasing*, or *being chased*; in all other Matters whatsoever, he is governed by a Majority; so the Brigantine having the Heels, as they term it, of the *French* Man, she came clear off.

But the next Day, the Captain's Behaviour was obliged to stand the Test of a Vote, and a Resolution passed against his Honour and Dignity branding him with the Name of Coward, deposing him from the Command, and turning him out of the Company, with Marks of Infamy and, with him, went all those who did not Vote for boarding the *French* Man of War. They had with them a small Sloop that had been taken by them some Time before, which they gave to *Vane*, and the discarded Members; and, that they might be in a Condition to provide for themselves, by their own honest Endeavours, they let them have a sufficient Quantity of Provisions and Ammunition along with them.

John Rackam was voted Captain of the Brigantine, in *Vane*'s Room, and proceeded towards the *Caribbee Islands*, where we must leave him, till we have finished our Story of *Charles Vane*.

The Sloop sailed for the Bay of *Honduras*, and *Vane* and his Crew put her into as good a Condition as they could by the Way, to follow the old Trade. They cruised two or three Days off the North-West Part of *Jamaica*, and took a Sloop and two Pettiagas, and all the Men entered with them; the Sloop they kept, and *Robert Deal* went Captain of her.

On the 16th of *December* the two Sloops came into the Bay, where they found only one at an Anchor, call'd the *Pearl*, of *Jamaica*, Captain *Charles Rowling* Master, who got under Sail at the Sight of them; but the Pyrate Sloops coming near *Rowling*, and shewing no Colours, he gave them a Gun or two; whereupon they hoisted the black Flag, and fired three Guns each, at the *Pearl*; she struck, and the Pyrates took Possession, and carried her away to a small Island called *Barnacko*, and there they cleaned, meeting in the Way with a Sloop from *Jamaica*, Captain *Wallden* Commander, going down to the Bay, which they also made Prize of.

In *February*, *Vane* sailed from *Barnacko*, in order for a Cruize; but some Days after he was out, a violent Turnado overtook him, which separated him from his Consort, and after two Days Distress; threw his Sloop upon a small uninhabited Island, near the Bay of *Honduras*, where she was staved to pieces, and most of her Men drowned: *Vane* himself was saved, but reduced to great Streights, for want of Necessaries, having no Opportunity to get any Thing from the Wreck. He lived here some Weeks, and was subsisted chiefly by Fishermen, who frequented the Island with small Craft, from the Main, to catch Turtles, *&c.*

While *Vane* was upon this Island, a Ship put in from *Jamaica* for Water, the Captain of which, one *Holford*, an old Buccaneer, happened to be *Vane*'s Acquaintance; he thought this a good Opportunity to get off, and accordingly applied to his old Friend; but he absolutely refused him, saying him, Charles, *I shan't trust you aboard my Ship, less I carry you a Prisoner; for I shall have you caballing with my Men, knock me on the Head, and run away with my Ship a pyrating.* *Vane* made all the Protestation of Honour in the World to him; but, it seems Captain *Holford* was too intimately acquainted with him, to repose any Confidence at all in his words or Oaths. He told him, *He might easily find a way to get off, if he had a Mind to it: I am now going down the Bay,* says he, *and shall return hither in about a Month; and if I find you upon the Island when I come back, I'll carry you to* Jamaica, *and hang you. Which Way can I get away?* Answers *Vane. Are there Fishermen's Dories upon the Beach? Can't you take one of them?* Replies *Holford. What,* says *Vane, would you have me steal a Dory then? Do you make it a Matter of Conscience?* Said *Holford, to steal a Dory, when you have been a common Robber and Pyrate, stealing Ships and Cargoes, and plundering all Mankind that fell in your Way? Stay there, and be d—n'd, if you are so Squeamish*: And so left him.

After Captain *Holford*'s Departure, another Ship put in to the same Island in her Way home for Water; none of whose Company knowing *Vane* he easily passed upon them for another Man, and so was shipp'd for the Voyage. One would be apt to think that *Vane* was now pretty safe, and likely to escape the Fate which his Crimes had merited; but here a cross Accident happen'd that ruin'd all: *Holford*, returning from the Bay, was met with by this Ship; the Captains being very well acquainted together, *Holford* was invited to dine aboard of him, which he did; and as he passed along to the Cabin, he chanced to cast his Eye down the Hold, and there saw *Charles Vane* at work; he immediately spoke to the Captain, saying, *Do you know who you have got aboard here? Why,* say he, *I have shipp'd a Man at such an Island, who was cast away in a trading Sloop, he seems to be a brisk Hand. I tell you,* says Captain *Holford, it is* Vane *the notorious Pyrate.*

If it be him, replies the other, *I won't keep him: Why then*, says *Holford, I'll send and take him aboard, and surrender him at* Jamaica. Which being agreed to, Captain *Holford*, as soon as he returned to his Ship, sent his Boat with his Mate armed, who coming to *Vane*, shewed him a Pistol, and told him, *He was his Prisoner*; which none opposing, he was brought aboard, and put in Irons; and when Captain *Holford* arrived at *Jamaica*, he delivered his old Acquaintance into the Hands of Justice; which Place he was try'd, convicted, and executed, as was, some Time before, *Vane*'s Consort, *Robert Deal*, brought thither by one of the Men of War.

CHAPTER VII.

Of
Captain *JOHN RACKAM*,
And his CREW.

THIS *JOHN* Rackam, as has been mentioned in the last Chapter, was Quarter-Master to *Vane*'s Company, till they were divided and *Vane* turned out for refusing to board and fight the *French* Man of War; then *Rackam* was voted Captain of that Division that remained in the Brigantine. The 24th of *November* 1718, was the first Day of his Command, and his first Cruize was among the *Caribbee Islands*, where he took and plunder'd several Vessels.

We have already taken Notice, that when Captain *Woodes Rogers* went to the Island of *Providence* with the King's Pardon to such as should surrender, this Brigantine, which *Rackam* now commanded, made its Escape, thro' another Passage, bidding Defiance to Mercy.

To Windward of *Jamaica*, a *Madera* Man fell into the Pyrates Way, which they detained two or three Days, till they had made their Market out of her, and then gave her back to the Master, and permitted one *Hosea Tisdell*, a Tavern-Keeper at *Jamaica*, who had been pick'd up in one of their Prizes, to depart in her, she being then bound for that Island.

After this Cruize, they went into a small Island and cleaned, and spent their *Christmas* ashore, drinking and carousing as long as they had any Liquor left, and then went to Sea again for more, where they succeeded but too well, though they took no extraordinary Prize, for above two Months, except a Ship laden with Thieves from *Newgate*, bound for the Plantations, which, in a few Days, was retaken with all her Cargo, by an *English* Man of War.

Rackam stood off towards the Island of *Bermudas*, and took a Ship bound to *England* from *Carolina*, and a small Pink from *New-England*, and brought them to the *Bahama* Islands, where with the Pitch, Tar, and Stores, they clean'd again, and refitted their own Vessel; but staying too long in that Neighbourhood, Captain *Rogers*, who was Governor of *Providence*, hearing of these Ships being taken, sent out a Sloop well mann'd and arm'd, which retook both the Prizes, and in the mean while the Pyrate had the good Fortune to escape.

From hence they sailed to the Back of *Cuba*, where *Rackam* kept a little kind of a Family, at which Place, they staid a considerable Time, living ashore with their Dalilahs, till their Money and Provision were expended, and then they concluded it Time to look out: They repaired to their Vessel, and was making ready to put Sea, when a *Guarda del Costa* came in with a small *English* Sloop, which she had taken as an Interloper on the Coast. The *Spanish* Guardship attack'd the Pyrate, but *Rackam* being close in behind a little Island, she could do but little Execution where she lay, therefore the *Spaniard* warps into the Channel that Evening, in order to make sure of her the next Morning. *Rackam* finding his Case desperate, and hardly any Possibility of escaping, resolved to attempt the following Enterprize: The *Spanish* Prize lying for better Security close into the Land, between the little Island and the Main; *Rackam* takes his Crew into the Boat, with their Pistols and Cutlashes, rounds the little Island, and falls aboard their Prize silently in the dead of the Night, without being discovered, telling the *Spaniards* that were aboard of her, that if they spoke a Word, or made the least Noise, they were dead Men, and so became Master of her; when this was done, he slipt her Cable, and drove out to Sea: The *Spanish* Man of War, was so intent upon their expected Prize, that they minded nothing else, and assoon as Day broke, made a furious Fire upon the empty Sloop but it was not long before they were rightly apprized of the Matter, and cursed themselves for Fools, to be bit out of a good rich Prize, as she prov'd to be, and to have nothing but an old crazy Hull in the room of her.

Rackam and his Crew had no Occasion to be displeased at the Exchange, that enabled them to continue some Time longer in a Way of Life that suited their depraved Tempers: In *August* 1720, we find him at Sea again, scouring the Harbours and Inlets of the North and West Parts of *Jamaica*, where he took several small Craft, which proved no great Booty to the Rovers, but they had but few Men, and therefore they were obliged to run at low Game, till they could encrease their Company.

In the Beginning of *September*, they took seven or eight fishing-Boats in *Harbour Island*, stole their Nets and other Tackle, and then went off the *French* Part of *Hispaniola*, and landed, and took Cattle away, with two or three *French* Men they found near the Water-Side, hunting of wild Hogs in the Evening: The *French* Men came on Board, whether by Consent or Compulsion, I can't say. They afterwards plundered two Sloops, and returned to *Jamaica*, on the North Coast of which Island, near *Porto Maria* Bay, they took a Scooner, *Thomas Spenlow* Master; it was then the 19th of *October*. The next Day, *Rackam* seeing a Sloop in *Dry Harbour* Bay, he stood in and fired a Gun; the Men all run ashore, and he took the Sloop and Lading, but when those ashore found them to be Pyrates, they hailed the Sloop, and let them know they were all willing to come aboard of them.

Rackam's coasting the Island in this Manner, proved fatal to him, for Intelligence came to the Governor, of his Expedition, by a Canoa which he had surprized ashore, in *Ocho* Bay; upon which a Sloop was immediately fitted out, and sent round the Island in quest of him, commanded by Captain *Barnet*, with a good Number of Hands. *Rackam* rounding the Island, and drawing near the Westermost Point,

called Point *Negril*, saw a small Pettiauger, which at sight of
the Sloop, run ashore and landed her Men; when one of
them hailed her, Answer was made, *They were* English *Men*,
and desired the Pettiauger's Men to come on Board, and
drink a Bowl of Punch, which they were prevailed upon to
do; accordingly the Company came all aboard of the Pyrate,
consisting of nine Persons, in an ill Hour; they were armed
with Muskets and Cutlashes, but, what was their real Design
by so doing, I shall not take upon me to say; but they had
no sooner laid down their Arms, and taken up their Pipes,
but *Barnet*'s Sloop, which was in Pursuit of *Rackam*'s, came
in Sight.

The Pyrates finding she stood directly towards her, fear'd
the Event, and weighed their Anchor, which they but lately
let go, and stood off: Captain *Barnet* gave them Chace, and
having the Advantage of little Breezes of Wind, which blew
off the Land, came up with her, and, after a very small Dispute, took her, and brought her into *Port Royal*, in *Jamaica*.

In about a Fortnight after the Prisoners were brought
ashore, *viz. November* 16, 1720, a Court of Admiralty was
held at St. *Jago de la Vega*, before which the following Persons were convicted, and Sentence of Death passed upon
them, by the President, Sir *Nicholas Laws, viz. John Rackam*
Captain, *George Fetherston* Master, *Richard Corner* Quarter-
Master, *John Davis, John Howell, Patrick Carty, Thomas Earl,
James, Dobbin* and *Noah Harwood*. The five first were executed the next Day at *Gallows Point*, at the Town of *Port
Royal*, and the rest, the Day after, at *Kingston; Rackam, Fev-
erston* and *Corner*, were afterwards taken down and hang'd
up in Chains, one at *Plumb Point*, one at *Bush Key*, and the
other at *Gun Key*.

But what was very surprizing, was, the Conviction of the
nine Men that came aboard the Sloop the same Day she was
taken. They were try'd at an Adjournment of the Court, on
the 24th of *January*, waiting all that Time, it is supposed,
for Evidence, to prove the pyratical Intention of going
aboard the said Sloop; for it seems there was no Act of Pyr-

acy committed by them, after their coming on Board, as appeared by the Witnesses against them, who were two *French* Men taken by *Rackam*, off from the Island of *Hispaniola*, and deposed in the following Manner.

That the Prisoners at the Bar, *viz.* John Eaton, *Edward Warner, Thomas Baker, Thomas Quick, John Cole, Benjamin Palmer, Walter Rouse, John, Hanson,* and *John Howard,* came aboard the Pyrate's Sloop at *Negril Point, Rackam* sending his Canoe ashore for that Purpose: That they brought Guns and Cutlashes on Board with them: That when Captain *Barnet* chased them, some were drinking, and others walking the Deck: That there was a great Gun and a small Arm fired by the Pyrate Sloop, at Captain *Barnet*'s Sloop, when he chased her; and that when Captain *Barnet*'s Sloop fired at *Rackam*'s Sloop, the Prisoner's at the Bar went down under Deck. That during the Time Captain *Barnet* chased them, some of the Prisoners at the Bar (but which of them he could not tell) helped to row the Sloop, in order to escape from *Barnet*: That they all seemed to be consorted together.

This was the Substance of all that was evidenced against them, the Prisoners answered in their Defence, That they had no Witnesses: That they had bought a Pettiauger in order to go a Turtleing; and being at *Negril Point*, and just got ashore, they saw a Sloop with a white Pendant coming towards them, upon which they took their Arms, and hid themselves in the Bushes: That one of them hail'd the Sloop, who answer'd, *They were* English *Men*, and desired them to come aboard and drink a Bowl of Punch; which they at first refused, but afterwards with much perswasion, they went on Board, in the Sloop's Canoe, and left their own Pettiauger at Anchor: That they had been but a short Time on Board, when Captain *Barnet*'s Sloop heaved in Sight: That *Rackam* ordered them to help to weigh the Sloop's anchor immediately, which they all refused: That *Rackam* used violent Means to oblige them; and that when Captain *Barnet* came up with them, they all readily and willingly submitted.

When the Prisoners were taken from the Bar, and the

persons present being withdrawn, the Court considered the Prisoners Cases, and the Majority of the Commissioners being of Opinion, that they were all Guilty of the Pyracy and Felonly they were charged with, which was, *the going over with a pyratical and felonious Intent to* John Rackam, &c. *then notorious Pyrates, and by them known to be so*, they all received Sentence of Death; which every Body must allow proved somewhat unlucky to the poor Fellows.

On the 17th of *February, John Eaton, Thomas Quick* and *Thomas Baker*, were executed at *Gallows Point*, at *Port Royal*, and the next Day *John Cole, John Howard* and *Benjamin Palmer*, were executed at *Kingston*; whether the other three were executed afterwards, or not, I never heard.

Two other Pyrates were try'd that belonged to *Rackam's* Crew, and being convicted, were brought up, and asked if either of them had any Thing to say why Sentence of Death should not pass upon them, in like Manner as had been done to all the rest; and both of them pleaded their Bellies, being quick with Child, and pray'd that Execution might be stay'd, whereupon the Court passed Sentence, as in Cases of Pyracy, but ordered them back, till a proper Jury should be appointed to enquire into the Matter.

The LIFE *of* Mary Read.

NOW WE are to begin a History full of surprizing Turns and Adventures; I mean, that of *Mary Read* and *Anne Bonny*, alias *Bonn*, which were the true Names of these two Pyrates; the odd Incidents of their rambling Lives are such, that some may be tempted to think the whole Story no better than a Novel or Romance; but since it is supported by many thousand Witnesses, I mean the People of *Jamaica*, who were present at their Tryals, and heard the Story of their Lives, upon the first discovery of their Sex; the Truth of it can be no more contested, than that there were such Men in the World, as *Roberts* and *Black-beard*, who were Pyrates.

Mary Read was born in *England*, her Mother was married young, to a Man who used the Sea, who going a Voyage soon after their Marriage, left her with Child, which Child proved to be a Boy. As to the Husband, whether he was cast away, or died in the Voyage, *Mary Read* could not tell; but however, he never returned more; nevertheless, the Mother, who was young and airy, met with an Accident, which has often happened to Women who are young, and do not take a great deal of Care; which was, she soon proved with Child again, without a Husband to Father it, but how, or by whom, none but her self could tell, for she carried a pretty good Reputation among her Neighbours. Finding her Burthen grow, in order to conceal her Shame, she takes a formal Leave of her Husband's Relations, giving out, that she went to live with some Friends of her own, in the Country: Accordingly she went away, and carried with her her young Son, at this Time, not a Year old: Soon after her Departure her Son died, but Providence in Return, was pleased to give her a Girl in his Room, of which she was safely delivered, in her Retreat, and this was our *Mary Read*.

Here the Mother liv'd three or four Years, till what Money she had was almost gone; then she thought of returning to *London*, and considering that her Husband's Mother was in some Circumstances, she did not doubt but to prevail upon her, to provide for the Child, if she could but pass it upon her for the same, but the changing a Girl into a Boy, seem'd a difficult Piece of Work, and how to deceive an experienced old Woman, in such a Point, was altogether as impossible; however, she ventured to dress it up as a Boy, brought it to Town, and presented it to her Mother in Law, as her Husband's Son; the old Woman would have taken it, to have bred it up, but the Mother pretended it would break her heart, to part with it; so it was agreed betwixt them, that the Child should live with the Mother, and the supposed

Grandmother should allow a Crown a Week for it's Main-
tainance.

Thus the Mother gained her Point, she bred up her
Daughter as a Boy, and when she grew up to some Sense,
she thought proper to let her into the Secret of her Birth, to
induce her to conceal her Sex. It happen'd that the Grandmother died, by which Means the Subsistance that came
from that Quarter, ceased, and they were more and more
reduced in their Circumstances; wherefore she was obliged
to put her Daughter out, to wait on a *French* Lady, as a Foot-
boy, being now thirteen Years of Age: Here she did not live
long, for growing bold and strong, and having also a roving
Mind, she entered her self on Board a Man of War, where
she served some Time, then quitted it, went over into *Flanders*, and carried Arms in a Regiment of Foot, as a *Cadet*;
and tho' upon all Actions, she behaved herself with a great
deal of Bravery, yet she could not get a Commission, they
being, generally bought and sold; therefore she quitted the
Service, and took on in a Regiment of Horse; she behaved
so well in several Engagements, that she got the Esteem of
all her Officers; but her Comrade who was a *Fleming*, happening to be a handsome young Fellow, she falls in Love
with him, and from that Time, grew a little more negligent
in her Duty, so that, it seems, *Mars* and *Venus* could not be
served at the same Time; her Arms and Accoutrements
which were always kept in the best Order, were quite neglected: 'tis true, when her Comrade was ordered out upon
a Party, she used to go without being commanded, and frequently run herself into Danger; where she had no Business,
only to be near him; the rest of the Trooper little suspecting
the secret Cause which moved her to this Behaviour, fancied
her to be mad, and her Comrade himself could not account
for this strange Alteration in her, but Love is ingenious, and
as they lay in the same Tent, and were constantly together,
she found a Way of letting him discover her Sex, without
appearing that it was done with Design.

He was much surprized at what he found out, and not a

little pleased, taking it for granted, that he should have a Mistress solely to himself, which is an unusual Thing in a Camp, since there is scarce one of those Campaign Ladies, that is ever true to a Troop or Company; so that he thought of nothing but gratifying his Passions with very little Ceremony; but he found himself strangely mistaken, for she proved very reserved and modest, and resisted all his Temptations, and at the same Time was so obliging and insinuating in her Carriage, that she quite changed his Purpose, so far from thinking of making her his Mistress, he now courted her for a Wife.

This was the utmost Wish of her Heart, in short; they exchanged Promises, and when the Campaign was over, and the Regiment marched into Winter Quarters, they bought Woman's Apparel for her, with such Money as they could make up betwixt them, and were publickly married.

The Story of two Troopers marrying each other made a great Noise, so that several officers were drawn by Curiosity to assist at the Ceremony, and they agreed among themselves that every one of them should make a small Present to the Bride, towards House-keeping, in Consideration of her having been their fellow Soldier. Thus being set up, they seemed to have a Desire of quitting the Service, and settling in the World; the Adventure of their Love and Marriage had gained them so much Favour, that they easily obtained their Discharge, and they immediately set up an Eating House or Ordinary, which was the Sign of the *Three Horse-Shoes*, near the Castle of *Breda*, where they soon run into a good Trade, a great many Officers eating with them constantly.

But this Happiness lasted not long, for the Husband soon died, and the Peace of *Reswick* being concluded, there was no Resort of Officers to *Breda*, as usual; so that the Widow having little or no Trade, was forced to give up House-keeping, and her Substance being by Degrees quite spent, she again assumes her Man's Apparel, and going into *Holland*, there takes on in a Regiment of Foot, quarter'd in one of the Frontier Towns: Here she did not remain long, there was no likelihood of Preferment in Time of Peace, therefore she took a Resolution of seeking her Fortune another Way, and withdrawing from the Regiment, ships herself on Board of a Vessel bound for the *West-Indies*.

It happen'd this Ship was taken by *English* Pyrates, and *Mary Read* was the only *English* Person on Board, they kept her amongst them, and having plundered the Ship, let it go again; after following this Trade for some Time, the King's Proclamation came out, and was publish'd in all parts of the *West-Indies*, for pardoning such Pyrates, who should voluntarily surrender themselves by a certain Day therein mentioned. The Crew of *Mary Read* took the Benefit of this Proclamation, and having surrender'd, liv'd quietly on Shore; but Money beginning to grow short, and hearing that Captain *Woods Rogers*, Governor of the Island of *Providence*, was fitting out some Privateers to cruise against the *Spaniards*, she with several others embark'd for the Island, in order to go upon the Privateering Account, being resolved to make her fortune one way or other.

These Privateers were no sooner sail'd out, but the Crews of some of them, who had been pardoned, rose against their Commanders, and turned themselves to their old Trade: In this Number was *Mary Read*. It is true, she often declared, that the Life of a Pyrate was what she always abhor'd and went into it only upon Compulsion, both this time, and before, intending to quit it, whenever a fair Opportunity should offer it self; yet some of the Evidence against her, upon her Tryal, who were forced Men, and had sailed with her, deposed upon Oath, that in Times of Action, no Person amongst them were more resolute, or ready to board or undertake any Thing that was hazardous, as she and *Anne Bonny*; and particularly at the Time they were attack'd and taken, when they came to close Quarters, none kept the Deck except *Mary Read* and *Anne Bonny*, and one more; upon which, she, *Mary Read*, called to those under Deck, to come up and fight like Men, and finding they did not stir, fired her Arms down the Hold amongst them, killing one, and wounding others.

This was part of the Evidence against her, which she denied; which, whether true or no, this much is certain, that she did not want Bravery, nor indeed was she less remarkable for her Modesty, according to her Notions of Virtue: Her Sex was not so much as suspected by any Person on Board, till *Anne Bonny*, who was not altogether so reserved in point of Chastity, took a particular liking to her; in short, *Anne Bonny* took her for a handsome young Fellow, and for some Reasons best known to herself, first discovered her Sex to *Mary Read; Mary Read* knowing what she would be at, and being very sensible of her own Incapacity that Way, was forced to come to a right. Understanding with her and so to the great Disappointment of *Anne Bonny*, she let her know she was a Woman also, but this Intimacy so disturb'd Captain *Rackam*, who was the Lover and Gallant of *Anne Bonny*, that he grew furiously jealous, so that he told *Anne Bonny*, he would cut her new Lover's Throat, therefore, to quiet him, she let him into the Secret also.

Captain *Rackam*, (as he was enjoined,) kept the Thing a Secret from all the Ship's Company, yet notwithstanding all her Cunning and Reserve, Love found her out in this Disguise, and hinder'd her from forgetting her Sex. In their Cruize they took a great Number of Ships belonging to *Jamaica* and other Parts of the *West-Indies*, bound to and from *England*; and when ever they meet any good Artist, or other Person that might be of any great Use to their Company, if he was not willing to enter, it was their Custom to keep him by Force. Among these was a young Fellow of a most engaging Behaviour, or, at least, he was so in the Eye of *Mary Read*, who became so smitten with his Person and Address, that she could neither rest Night or Day; but as there is nothing more ingenious than Love, 'twas no hard matter for her, who had before practised in these wiles, to find a way to let him discover her Sex: she first insinuated herself into his liking, by talking against the life of a Pyrate, which he was altogether averse to, so they became Mess-Mates and strict Companions. When she found he had a Friendship for her, as a Man, she suffered the Discovery to be made, by carelessly showing her Breasts, which were very white.

The young Fellow, who was made of Flesh and Blood, had his Curiosity and Desire so raised by this Sight, that he never ceased importuning her, till she confessed what she was. Now begins the Scene of Love: as he had a Liking and Esteem for her, under her supposed Character, 'twas now turned into Fondness and Desire; her Passion was no less violent than his, and perhaps she expressed it, by one of the most generous Actions that ever Love inspired. It happened this young Fellow had a Quarrel with one of the Pyrates, and their Ship then lying at an Anchor, near one of the Islands, they had appointed to go ashore and fight, according to the Custom of the Pyrates. *Mary Read*, was to the last degree uneasy and anxious, for the Fate of her lover; she would not have had him refuse the Challenge, because she could not bear the thoughts of his being branded with cowardice; on the other side, she dreaded the Event, and apprehended the Fellow might be too hard for him. When Love once enters into the Breast of one who has any Sparks of generosity, it stirs the Heart up to the most noble Actions; in this Dilemma, she showed, that she cared more for his life, than she did for her own; for she took a resolution of quarreling with this fellow herself, and having challenged him ashore, she appointed the Time two Hours sooner than that when he was to meet her Lover, where she fought him at Sword and Pistol, and killed him upon the Spot.

It is true, she had fought before, when she had been insulted by some of those Fellows, but now it was altogether in her Lover's Cause, she stood as it were betwixt him and Death, as if she could not live without him. If he had no regard for her before, this Action would have bound him to her for ever; but there was no Occasion for Ties or Obligations, his Inclination towards her was sufficient; in fine, they applied their Troth to each other, which *Mary Read* said, she look'd upon to be as good a Marriage, in Conscience, as if it had been done by a Minister in Church; and to this was owing her great Belly, which she pleaded to save her Life.

She declared she had never committed Adultery or Fornication with any Man, she commended the Justice of the Court, before which she was tried, for distinguishing the Nature of their Crimes; her Husband, as she call'd him, with several others, being acquitted; and being ask'd, who he was? She would not tell, but, said he was an honest Man, and had no Inclination to such Practices, and that they had both resolved to leave the Pyrates, the first Opportunity, and apply themselves to some honest Livelyhood.

It is no doubt, but many had Compassion for her yet the Court could not avoid finding her Guilty; for among other Things, one of the Evidence against her, deposed, that being taken by *Rackam* and detain'd some Time on Board, he fell accidentally into Discourse with *Mary Read*, whom he taking for a young Man, ask'd her, what Pleasure she could have in being concerned in such Enterprizes where her Life was continually in Danger by Fire or Sword; and not only so, but she must be sure of dying an ignominious Death, if she should be taken alive?——She answer'd, that as to hanging, she thought it no great Hardship, for, were it not for that, every cowardly Fellow would turn Pyrate, and so infest the Seas, that Men of Courage must starve:——That if it was put to the Choice of the Pyrates, they would not have the punishment less than Death, the Fear of which, kept some dastardly Rogues honest; that many of those who are now cheating the Widows and Orphans, and oppressing their poor Neighbours, who have no Money to obtain Justice, would then rob at Sea, and the Ocean would be crowded with Rogues, like the Land, and no Merchant would venture out, so that the Trade, in a little Time, would not be worth following.

Being found quick with Child, as has been observed, her Execution was respited, and it is possible she would have found Favour, but she was seiz'd with a violent Fever, soon after her Tryal, of which she died in Prison.

The LIFE *of* Anne Bonny.

A<small>S WE</small> have been more particular in the Lives of these two Women, than those of other Pyrates, it is incumbent on us, as a faithful Historian, to begin with their Birth. *Anne Bonny* was born at a Town near *Cark*, in the Kingdom of *Ireland*, her Father an Attorney at Law, but *Anne* was not one of his legitimate issue, which seems to cross an old Proverb, which says, *that Bastards have the best Luck*. Her Father was a Married Man, and his Wife having been brought to Bed, contracted an Illness in her lying in, and in order to recover her Health, she was advised to remove for Change of Air; the Place she chose, was a few Miles distance from her Dwelling, where her Husband's Mother liv'd. Here she sojourn'd some Time, her Husband staying at Home, to follow his Affairs. The Servant-Maid, whom she left to look after the House, and attend the Family, being a handsome young Woman, was courted by a young Man of the same Town, who was a *Tanner*; this *Tanner* used to take his Opportunities, when the Family was out of the Way, of coming to pursue his Courtship; and being with the Maid one Day as she was employ'd in the Houshold Business, not having the Fear of God before his Eyes, he takes his Opportunity, when her Back was turned, of whipping three Silver Spoons into his Pocket. The Maid soon miss'd the Spoons, and knowing that no Body had been in the Room, but herself and the young Man, since she saw them last, she charged him with taking them; he very stifly denied it, upon which she grew outragious, and threatened to go to a Constable, in order to carry him before a Justice of Peace: These Menaces frighten'd him out of his Wits, well knowing he could not stand Search; wherefore he endeavoured to pacify her by desiring her to examine the Drawers and other Places, and perhaps she might find them; in this Time he slips into another Room, where the Maid usually lay, and puts the Spoons betwixt the Sheets and then makes his Escape by a back Door, concluding she must find them, when she went to Bed and so next Day he might pretend he did it only to frighten her, and the Thing might be laugh'd off for a Jest.

As soon as she miss'd him, she gave over her Search, concluding he had carried them off, and went directly to the Constable, in order to have him apprehended: The young Man was informed, that a Constable had been in Search of him, but he regarded it but little, not doubting but all would be well next Day. Three or four Days passed, and still he was told, the Constable was upon the Hunt for him, this made him lye concealed, he could not comprehend the Meaning of it, he imagined no less, than that the Maid had a Mind to convert the Spoons to her own Use, and put the Robbery upon him.

It happened, at this Time, that the Mistress being perfectly recovered of her late Indisposition, was return'd Home, in Company with her Mother-in-law; the first News she heard, was of the Loss of the Spoons, with the Manner how; the Maid telling her, at the same Time, that the young Man was run away. The young Fellow had Intelligence of the Mistress's Arrival, and considering with himself, that he could never appear again in his Business, unless this Matter was got over, and she being a good natured Woman, he took a Resolution of going directly to her, and of telling her the whole Story, only with this Difference, that he did it for a Jest.

The Mistress could scarce believe it, however, she went directly to the Maid's Room, and turning down the Bed Cloaths, there, to her great Surprize, found the three Spoons; upon this she desired the young Man to go Home and mind his Business, for he should have no Trouble about it.

The Mistress could not imagine the Meaning of this, she

never had found the Maid guilty of any pilfering, and therefore it could not enter her Head, that she designed to steal the Spoons herself; upon the whole, she concluded the Maid had not been in her Bed, from the Time the Spoons were miss'd, she grew immediately jealous upon it, and suspected, that the Maid supplied her Place with her Husband, during her Absence, and this was the Reason why the Spoons were no sooner found.

She call'd to Mind several Actions of Kindness, her Husband had shewed the Maid, Things that pass'd unheeded by, when they happened, but now she had got that Tormentor, Jealousy, in her Head, amounted to Proofs of their Intimacy; another Circumstance which strengthen'd the whole, was, that tho' her Husband knew she was to come Home that Day, and had had no Communication with her in four Months, which was before her last Lying in, yet he took an Opportunity of going out of Town that Morning, upon some slight Pretence——All these Things put together, confirm'd her in her Jealousy.

As Women seldom forgive Injuries of this kind she thought of discharging her Revenge upon the Maid: In order to this, she leaves the Spoons where she found them, and orders the Maid to put clean Sheets upon the Bed, telling her, she intended to lye there herself that Night, because her Mother in Law was to lye in her Bed, and that she (the Maid) must lye in another part of the House; the Maid in making the Bed, was surprized with the Sight of the Spoons, but there were very good Reasons, why it was not proper for her to tell where she found them, therefore she takes them up, puts them in her Trunk, intending to leave them in some Place, where they might be found by chance.

The Mistress, that every Thing might look to be done without Design, lies that Night in the Maid's Bed, little dreaming of what an Adventure it would produce: After she had been a Bed some Time, thinking on what had pass'd, for Jealousy kept her awake, she heard some Body enter the Room; at first she apprehended it to be Thieves, and was so fright'ned, she had not Courage enough to call out; but when she heard these Words, Mary, *are you awake?* She knew it to be her Husband's Voice; then her Fright was over, yet she made no answer, least he should find her out, if she spoke, therefore she resolved to counterfeit Sleep, and take what followed.

The Husband came to Bed, and that Night play'd the vigorous Lover; but one Thing spoil'd the Diversion on the Wife's Side, which was; the Reflection that it was not design'd for her; however she was very passive, and bore it like a Christian. Early before Day, she stole out of Bed, leaving him asleep, and went to her Mother in Law, telling her what had passed, not forgetting how he had used her, as taking her for the Maid; the Husband also stole out, not thinking it convenient to be catch'd in that Room; in the mean Time, the Revenge of the Mistress was strongly against the Maid, and without considering, that to her she ow'd the Diversion of the Night before, and that one good *Turn* should deserve another; she sent for a Constable, and charged her with stealing the Spoons: The Maid's Trunk was broke open, and the Spoons found, upon which she was carried before a Justice of Peace, and by him committed to Goal.

The Husband loiter'd about till twelve a Clock at Noon, then comes Home, pretended he was just come to Town; as soon as he heard what had passed, in Relation to the Maid, he fell into a great Passion with his Wife; this set the Thing into a greater Flame, the Mother takes the Wife's Part against her own Son, insomuch that the Quarrel increasing, the Mother and Wife took Horse immediately, and went back to the Mother's House, and the Husband and Wife never bedded together after.

The Maid lay a long time in the Prison, it being near half a Year to the Assizes; but before it happened, it was discovered she was with Child; when she was arraign'd at the Bar, she was discharged for want of Evidence; the Wife's Conscience touch'd her, and as she did not believe the Maid Guilty of any Theft, except that of Love, she did not appear against her; soon after her Acquittal, she was delivered of a Girl.

But what alarm'd the Husband most, was, that it was discovered the Wife was with Child also, he taking it for granted, he had had no Intimacy with her, since her last lying in, grew jealous of her, in his Turn, and made this a Handle to justify himself, for his Usage of her, pretending now he had suspected her long, but that here was Proof; she was delivered of Twins, a Boy and a Girl.

The Mother fell ill, sent to her Son to reconcile him to his Wife, but he would not hearken to it; therefore she made a Will, leaving all she had in the Hands of certain Trustees, for the Use of the Wife and two Children lately born, and died a few Days after.

This was an ugly Turn upon him, his greatest Dependance being upon his Mother; however, his Wife was kinder to him than he deserved, for she made him a yearly Allowance out of what was left, tho' they continued to live separate: It lasted near five Years; at this Time having a great Affection for the Girl he had by his Maid, he had a Mind to take it Home, to live with him; but as all the Town knew it to be a Girl, the better to disguise the Matter from them, as well as from his Wife, he had it put into Breeches, as a Boy, pretending it was a Relation's Child he was to breed up to be his Clerk.

The Wife heard he had a little Boy at Home he was very fond of, but as she did not know any Relation of his that had such a Child, she employ'd a Friend to enquire further into it; this Person by talking with the Child, found it to be a Girl, discovered that the Servant-Maid was its Mother, and that the Husband still kept up his Correspondence with her.

Upon this Intelligence, the Wife being unwilling that her Children's Money should go towards the Maintenance of Bastards, stopped the Allowance: The Husband enraged, in a kind of Revenge, takes the Maid home, and lives with her publickly, to the great Scandal of his Neighbours; but he

soon found the bad Effect of it, for by Degrees lost his Practice, so that he saw plainly he could not live there, therefore
he thought of removing, and turning what Effects he had
into ready Money; he goes to *Cork*, and there with his Maid
and Daughter embarques for *Carolina*.

At first he followed the Practice of the Law in that Province, but afterwards fell into Merchandize, which proved
more successful to him, for he gained by it sufficient to purchase a considerable Plantation: His Maid, who passed for
his Wife, happened to dye, after which his Daughter, our
Anne Bonny, now grown up, kept his House.

She was of a fierce and couragious Temper, wherefore,
when she lay under Condemnation, several Stories were reported of her, much to her Disadvantage, as that she had
kill'd an *English* Servant-Maid once in her Passion with a
Case-Knife, while she look'd after her Father's House; but
upon further Enquiry, I found his Story to be groundless: It
was certain she was so robust, that once, when a young Fellow would have laid with her, against her Will, she beat him
so, that he lay ill of it a considerable Time.

While she lived with her Father, she was look'd upon as
one that would be a good Fortune, wherefore it was thought
her Father expected a good Match for her; but she spoilt all,
for without his Consent, she marries a young Fellow, who
belonged to the Sea, and was not worth a Groat; which provoked her Father to such a Degree, that he turned her out
of Doors, upon which the young Fellow, who married her,
finding himself disappointed in his Expectation, shipped
himself and Wife, for the Island of *Providence*, expecting
Employment there.

Here she became acquainted with *Rackam* the Pyrate, who
making Courtship to her, soon found Means of withdrawing
her Affections from her Husband, so that she consented to
elope from him, and go to Sea with *Rackam* in Men's
Cloaths: She was as good as her Word, and after she had
been at Sea some Time, she proved with Child, and beginning to grow big, *Rackam* landed her on the Island of *Cuba*;

and recommending her there to some Friends of his, they took Care of her, till she was brought to Bed: When she was up and well again, he sent for her to bear him Company.

The King's Proclamation being out, for pardoning of Pyrates, he took the Benefit of it, and surrendered; afterwards being sent upon the privateering Account, he returned to his old Trade, as has been already hinted in the Story of *Mary Read*. In all these Expeditions, *Anne Bonny* bore him Company, and when any Business was to be done in their Way, no Body was more forward or couragious than she, and particularly when they were taken; she and *Mary Read*, with one more, were all the Persons that durst keep the Deck, as has been before hinted.

Her Father was known to a great many Gentlemen, Planters of *Jamaica*, who had dealt with him, and among whom he had a good Reputation; and some of them, who had been in *Carolina*, remember'd to have seen her in his House; wherefore they were inclined to shew her Favour, but the Action of leaving her Husband was an ugly Circumstance against her. The Day that *Rackam* was executed, by special Favour, he was admitted to see her; but all the Comfort she gave him, was, *that she was sorry to see him there, but if he had fought like a Man, he need not have been hang'd like a Dog.*

She was continued in Prison, to the Time of her lying in, and afterwards reprieved from Time to Time; but what is become of her since, we cannot tell; only this we know, that she was not executed.

CHAPTER VIII.

Of
Captain HOWEL DAVIS,
And his CREW.

CAPTAIN *HOWEL Davis* was born at *Milford, in Monmouthshire*, and was from a Boy brought up to the Sea. The last Voyage he made from *England*, was in the *Cadogan* Snow of *Bristol*, Captain *Skinner* Commander, bound for the Coast of *Guiney*, of which Snow *Davis* was chief Mate: They were no sooner arrived at *Sierraleon* on the aforesaid Coast, but they were taken by the Pyrate *England*, who plunder'd them, and *Skinner* was barbarously murdered, as has been related before in the Story of Captain *England*.

After the Death of Captain *Skinner, Davis* pretended that he was mightily sollicited by *England* to engage with him; but that he resolutely answered, he would sooner be shot to Death than sign the Pyrates Articles. Upon which, *England*, pleased with his Bravery, sent him and the rest of the Men again on Board the Snow, appointing him Captain of her, in the Room of *Skinner*, commanding him to pursue his Voyage. He also gave him a written Paper sealed up, with Orders to open it when he should come into a certain Latitude and at the Peril of his Life follow the Orders therein set down. This was an Air of Grandeur like what Princes practice to their Admirals and Generais.—It was punctually complied with by *Davis*, who read it to the Ship's Company; it contained no less than a generous Deed of Gift of the Ship

and Cargoe, to *Davis* and the Crew, ordering him to go to
Brasil and dispose of the Lading to the best Advantage, and
to make a fair and equal Dividend with the rest.

Davis proposed to the Crew, whether they were willing
to follow their Directions, but to his great Surprize, found
the Majority of them altogether averse to it, wherefore in a
Rage, he bad them be damn'd, and go where they would.
They knew that Part of their Cargoe was consigned to certain Merchants at *Barbadoes*, wherefore they steered for that
Island. When they arrived, they related to these Merchants
the unfortunate Death of *Skinner*, and the Proposal which
had been made to them by *Davis*; upon which *Davis* was
seized and committed to Prison, where he was kept three
Months; however, as he had been in no Act of Pyracy, he
was discharged without being brought to any Tryal, yet he
could not expect any Employment there; wherefore knowing
that the Island of *Providence* was a kind of Rendevouz of
Pyrates, he was resolved to make one amongst them, if possible, and to that Purpose, found Means of shipping himself
for that Island; but he was again disappointed, for when he
arrived there, the Pyrates had newly surrendered to Captain
Woods Rogers, and accepted of the Act of Grace, which he
had just brought from *England*.

However, *Davis* was not long out of Business, for Captain
Rogers having fitted out two Sloops for Trade, one called the
Buck, the other the *Mumvil Trader; Davis* found an Em-
ployment on Board of one of them; the Lading of these
Sloops was of considerable Value, consisting of *European*
Goods, in order to be exchanged with the *French* and *Span-
iards*; and many of the Hands on Board of them, were the
Pyrates lately come in upon the late Act of Grace. The first
Place they touched at, was the Island of *Martinico*, belonging
to the *French*, where *Davis* having conspired with some oth-
ers, rise in the Night, secured the Master and seized the
Sloop; as soon as this was done, they called to other other
Sloop, which lay a little Way from them, among whom they
knew there were a great many Hands ripe for Rebellion, and

ordered them to come on Board of them; they did so, and the greatest Part of them agreed to join with *Davis*; those who were otherwise inclined, were sent back on Board the *Mumvil* Sloop, to go where they pleased, *Davis* having first taken out of her, every Thing which he thought might be of Use.

After this, a Counsel of War was called over a large Bowl of Punch, at which it was proposed to chuse a Commander; the Election was soon over for it fell upon *Davis* by a great Majority of *legal Pollers*, there was no Scrutiny demanded, for all acquiesced in the Choice: As soon as he was possess'd of his Command, he drew up Articles, which were signed and sworn to by himself and the rest, their he made a short Speech, the sum of which, was a Declaration of War against the whole World.

After this they consulted about a proper Place where they might clean their Sloop, a light Pair of Heels being of great Use either to take, or escape being taken, for this purpose they made Choice of *Coxon's Hole*, at the East End of the Island of *Cuba*, a Place where they might secure themselves from Surprize, the Entrance being so narrow, that one Ship might keep out a hundred.

Here they cleaned with much Difficulty, for they had no Carpenter in their Company, a Person of great Use upon such Exigencies; from hence they put to Sea, making to the North-Side of the Island of *Hispaniola*. The first Sail which fell in their Way, was a *French* Ship of twelve-Guns; it must be observed, that *Davis* had but thirty five Hands, yet Provisions began to grow short with him; wherefore he attacked this Ship, she soon struck, and he sent twelve of his Hands on Board of her, in order to plunder: This was no sooner done, but a Sail was spied a great Way to Windward of them; they enquired of the *French* Man what she might be, he answered, that he had spoke with a Ship, the Day before, of 24 Guns and 60 Men, and he took this to be the same.

Davis then proposed to his Men to attack her, telling them, she would be a rare Ship for their Use, but they looked upon it to be an extravagant Attempt, and discovered no Fondness for it, but he assured them he had a Stratagem in his Head would make all safe; wherefore he gave Chace, and ordered his Prize to do the same. The Prize being a slow Sailor, *Davis* first came up with the Enemy, and standing along Side of them, shewed his pyratical Colours: They, much surpriz'd, called to *Davis*, telling him, they wondered at his Impudence in venturing to come so near them, and ordered him to strike; but he answered, that he intended to keep them in Play, till his Consort came up, who was able to deal with them, and that if they did not strike to him, they should have but bad Quarters; whereupon he gave them a Broad-Side, which they returned.

In the mean Time the Prize drew near, who obliged all the Prisoners to come upon Deck in white Shirts, to make a Shew of Force, as they had been directed by *Davis*; they also hoisted a dirty Tarpawlin, by Way of black Flag, they having no other, and fir'd a Gun: The *French* Men were so intimidated by this Appearance of Force, that they struck. *Davis* called out to the Captain to come Board of him, with twenty of his Hands; he did so, and they were all for the greater Security clape into Irons, the Captain excepted: Then he sent four of his own Men on Board the first Prize, and in order still to carry on the Cheat, spoke aloud, that they should give his Service to the Captain, and desire him to send some Hands on Board the Prize, to see what they had got; but at the same Time gave them a written Paper, with Instructions what to do. Here he ordered them to nail up the Guns in the little Prize, to take out all the small Arms and Powder, and to go every Man of them on Board the second Prize; when this was done, he ordered that more of the Prisoners should be removed out of the great Prize, into the little one, by which he secured himself from any Attempt which might be feared from their Numbers for those on Board of him were fast in Irons, and those in the little Prize had neither Arms nor Ammunition.

Thus the three Ships kept Company for 2 Days, when

finding the great Prize to be a very dull Sailor, he thought
she would not be fit for his Purpose, wherefore he resolved
to restore her to the Captain, with all his Hands; but first,
he took Care to take out all her Ammunition, and every
Thing else which he might possibly want. The *French* Captain was in such a Rage, at being so outwitted, that when he
got on Board his own Ship, he was going to throw himself
over-board, but was prevented by his Men.

Having let go both his Prizes, he steered Northward, in
which Course he took a small *Spanish*, Sloop after this, he
made towards the *Western* Islands but met with no Booty
thereabouts; then he steered for the *Cape de Verde* Islands,
they cast Anchor at St. *Nicholas*, hoisting *English* Colours;
the *Portuguese* inhabiting there, took him for an *English* Privateer, and *Davis* going ashore, they both treated him very
civilly, and also traded with him. Here he remained five
Weeks, in which Time, he and half his Crew, for their Pleasure, took a Journey to the chief Town of the Island, which
was 19 Miles up the Country: *Davis* making a good Appearance, was caressed by the Governor and the Inhabitants,
and no Diversion was wanting which the *Portuguese* could
shew, or Money could purchase; after about a Week's Stay,
he came back to the Ship, and the rest of the Crew went to
take their Pleasure up to the Town, in their Turn.

At their Return they clean'd their Ship, and put to Sea,
but not with their whole Company; for five of them, like
Hannibal's Men, were so charm'd with the Luxuries of the
Place, and the free Conversation of some Women, that they
staid behind; and one of them, whole Name was *Charles
Franklin*, a *Monmouthshire* Man, married and settled himself, and lives there to this Day.

From hence they sailed to *Bonevista*, and looked into that
Harbour, but finding nothing, they steer'd for the Isle of
May: When they arrived here, they met with a great many
Ships and Vessels in the Road, all which they plundered,
taking out of them whatever they wanted; and also
strengthen'd themselves with a great many fresh Hands, who

most of them enter'd voluntarily. One of the Ships they took to their own Use, mounted her with twenty six Guns, and call'd her the *King James*. There being no fresh Water hereabouts, they made towards St. *Jago*, belonging to the *Portuguese*, in order to lay in a Store; *Davis*, with a few Hands, going ashore to find the most commodious Place to water at, the Governor, with some Attendants, came himself and examined who they were, and whence they came. And not liking *Davis*'s Account of himself, the Governor was so plain to tell them, he suspected them to be Pyrates. *Davis* seemed mightily affronted, standing much upon his Honour, replying to the Governor, he scorn'd his Words; however, as soon as his Back was turn'd, for fear of Accidents, he got on Board again as fast as he could. *Davis* related what had happened, and his Men seemed to resent the Affront which had been offered him. *Davis*, upon this, told them, he was confident he could surprize the Fort in the Night; they agreed with him to attempt it, and accordingly, when it grew late, they went ashore well arm'd; and the Guard which was kept, was so negligent, that they got within the Fort before any Alarm was given: When it was too late there was some little Resistance made, and three Men killed on *Davis*'s Side. Those in the Fort, in their Hurry, run into the Governor's House to save themselves, which they barricadoed so strongly, that *Davis*'s Party could not enter it; however, they threw in Granadoe-Shells, which not only ruin'd all the Furniture, but kill'd several Men within.

When it was Day the whole Country was alarm'd, and came to attack the Pyrates; wherefore it not being their Business to stand a Siege, they made the best of their Way on Board their Ship again, after having dismounted the Guns of the Fort. By this Enterprize they did a great Deal of Mischief to the *Portuguese*, and but very little Good to themselves.

Having put to Sea they muster'd their Hands and found themselves near seventy strong; then it was proposed what Course they should steer, and differing in their Opinions,

they divided, and by a Majority it was carried for *Gambia* on
the Coast of *Guiney*, of this Opinion was *Davis*, he having
been employ'd in that Trade, was acquainted with the Coast:
He told them, that there was a great deal of Money always
kept in *Gambia* Castle, and that it would be worth their
while to make an Attempt upon it. They ask'd him how it
was possible, since it was garrisoned? He desired they would
leave the Management of it to him, and he would undertake
to make them Masters of it. They began now to conceive so
high an Opinion of his Conduct, as well as Courage, that
they thought nothing impossible to him, therefore they
agreed to obey him, without enquiring further into his Design.

Having come within Sight of the Place, he ordered all his
Men under Deck, except as many as were absolutely necessary for working the Ship, that those from the Fort seeing a
Ship with so few Hands, might have no Suspicion of her
being any other than a trading Vessel; then he ran close
under the Fort, and there cast Anchor; and having ordered
out the Boat, he commanded six Men in her, in old ordinary
Jackets, while he himself, with the Master and Doctor,
dressed themselves like Gentlemen; his Design being, that
the Men should look like common Sailors, and they like
Merchants. In rowing ashore he gave his Men Instructions
what to say in Case any Questions should be asked them.

Being come to the landing Place, he was received by a File
of Musqueteers, and conducted into the Fort, where the
Governor accosting them civilly, ask'd them who they were,
and whence they came? They answered they were of *Liverpool*, bound for the River of *Sinnegal*, to trade for Gum
and Elephants Teeth, but that they were chaced on that
Coast by two *French* Men of War, and narrowly escaped
being taken, having a little the Heels of them; but now they
were resolved to make the best of a bad Market, and would
Trade here for Slaves; then the Governor ask'd them what
was the chief of their Cargo? They answered, Iron and Plate,
which were good Things there; the Governor told them he

would Slave them to the full Value of their Cargoe, and asked them, if they had any *European* Liquor on Board they answered, a little for their own Use; however, a Hamper should be at his Service. The Governor then very civilly invited them all to stay and dine with him; *Davis* told him, that being Commander of the Ship, he must go on Board to see her well moored, and give some other Orders, but those two Gentlemen might stay, and that he himself would also return before Dinner, and bring the Hamper of Liquor with him.

While he was in the Fort, his Eyes were very busy in observing how Things lay; he took Notice there was a Centry at the Entrance, and a Guard-House just by it, where the Soldiers upon Duty commonly waited, their Arms standing in a Corner, in a Heap; he saw also a great many small Arms in the Governor's Hall; now when he came on Board, he assured his Men of Success, desiring them not to get drunk, and that as soon as they saw the Flag upon the Castle struck, they might conclude he was Master, and send twenty Hands immediately ashore; in the mean Time, there being a Sloop at Anchor near them, he sent some Hands in a Boat, to secure the Master and all the Men, and bring them on Board of him, least they observing any Bustle or arming in his Ship, might send ashore and give Intelligence.

These Precautions being taken, he ordered his Men, who were to go in the Boat with him, to put two Pair of Pistols each under their Cloaths, he doing the like himself, and gave them Directions to go into the Guard-Room, and to enter into Conversation with the Soldiers, and observe when he should fire a Pistol thro' the Governor's Window, to start up at once and secure the Arms in the Guard-Room.

When *Davis* arrived, Dinner not being ready, the Governor proposed that they should pass their Time in making a Bowl of Punch till Dinner-Time: It must be observed, that *Davis*'s Coxen waited upon them, who had an Opportunity of going about all Parts of the House, to see what Strength they had, he whispered *Davis*, there being no Person then

in the Room, but he, (*Davis*) the Master, the Doctor, the
Coxen and Governor; *Davis* on a sudden drew out a Pistol,
clapt it to the Governor's Breast, telling him, he must surrender the Fort and all the Riches in it, or he was a dead
Man. The Governor being no Ways prepared for such an
Attack, promised to be very Passive, and do all they desired,
therefore they shut the Door, took down all the Arms that
hung in the Hall, and loaded them. *Davis* fires his Pistol
thro' the Window, upon which his Men, without, executed
their Part of the Scheme, like Heroes, in an Instant; getting
betwixt the Soldiers and their Arms, all with their Pistols
cock'd in their Hands, while one of them carried the Arms
out. When this was done, they locked the Soldiers into the
Guard-Room, and kept Guard without.

In the mean Time one of them struck the Union Flag on
the Top of the Castle, at which Signal those on Board sent
on Shore a Reinforcement of Hands, and they got Possession
of the Fort without the least Hurry or Confusion, or so much
as a Man lost of either Side.

Davis harangued the Soldiers, upon which a great many
of them took on with him, those who refused, he sent on
Board the little Sloop, and because he would not be at the
Trouble of a Guard for them, he ordered all the Sails and
Cables out of her, which might hinder them from attempt-
ing to get away.

This Day was spent in a kind of Rejoycing, the Castle
firing her Guns to salute the Ship, and the Ship the Castle;
but the next Day they minded their Business, that is, they
fell to plundering, but they found Things fall vastly short of
their Expectation; for they discovered, that a great deal of
Money had been lately sent away; however, they met with
the Value of about two thousand Pounds Sterling in Bar
Gold, and a great many other rich Effects: Every Thing they
liked, which was portable, they brought aboard their Ship;
some Things which they had no Use for, they were so generous to make a Present of, to the Master and Crew of the
little Sloop, to whom they also returned his Vessel again,

and then they fell to work in dismounting the Guns, and demolishing the Fortifications.

After they had done as much Mischief as they could, and were weighing Anchor to be gone, they spy'd a Ship bearing down upon them in full Sail; they soon got their Anchor's up, and were in a Readiness to receive her. This Ship prov'd to be a *French* Pyrate of fourteen Guns and sixty four Hands, half *French*, half Negroes; the Captain's Name was *La Bouse*; he expected no less than a rich Prize, which made him so eager in the Chace; but when he came near enough to see their Guns, and the Number of their Hands upon Deck, he began to think he should catch a *Tartar*, and supposed her to be a small *English* Man of War; however, since there was no escaping, he resolved to do a bold and desperate Action, which was to board *Davis*. As he was making towards her, for this Purpose, he fired a Gun, and hoisted his black Colours; *Davis* returned the Salute, and hoisted his black Colours also. The *French* Man was not a little pleased at this happy Mistake; they both hoisted out their Boats, and the Captains went to meet and congratulate one another with a Flag of Truce in their Sterns; a great many Civilities passed between them, and *La Bouse* desired *Davis*, that they might sail down the Coast together, that he (*La Bouse*) might get a better Ship: *Davis* agreed to it, and very courteously promised him the first Ship he took, fit for his Use, he would give him, as being willing to encourage a willing Brother.

The first Place they touch'd at, was *Sierraleon*, where at first going in, they spied a tall Ship at Anchor; *Davis* being the best Sailor first came up with her, and wondering that she did not try to make off, suspected her to be a Ship of Force. As soon as he came along Side of her, she brought a Spring upon her Cable, and fired a whole Broadside upon *Davis*, at the same Time hoisted a black Flag; *Davis* hoisted his black Flag in like Manner, and fired one Gun to Leeward.

In fine, she proved to be a Pyrate Ship of twenty four Guns, commanded by one *Cocklyn*, who expecting these two would prove Prizes, let them come in, least his getting under Sail might frighten them away.

This Satisfaction was great on all Sides, at this Junction of Confederates and Brethren in Iniquity; two Days they spent in improving their Acquaintance and Friendship, the third Day *Davis* and *Cocklyn*, agreed to go in *La Bouse*'s Brigantine and attack the Fort; they contrived it so, as to get up thither by high Water; those in the Fort suspected them to be what they really were, and therefore stood upon their Defence; when the Brigantine came within Musket-Shot, the Fort fired all their Guns upon her, the Brigantine did the like upon the Fort, and so held each other in Play for several Hours, when the two confederate Ships were come up to the Assistance of the Brigantine; those who defended the Fort, seeing such a Number of Hands on Board these Ships, had not the Courage to stand it any longer, but abandoning the Fort, left it to the Mercy of the Pyrates.

They took Possession of it, and continued there near seven Weeks, in which Time they all cleaned their Ships. We should have observed, that a Galley came into the Road while they were there, which *Davis* insisted should be yielded to *La Bouse*, according to his Word of Honor before given; *Cocklyn* did not oppose it, so *La Bouse* went into her, with his Crew, and cutting away her half Deck, mounted her with twenty four Guns.

Having called a Counsel of War, they agreed to sail down the Coast together, and for the greater Grandeur, appointed a Commadore, which was *Davis*; but they had not kept Company long when drinking together on Board of *Davis*, they had like to have fallen together by the Ears, the strong Liquor stirring up a Spirit of Discord among them, and they quarrelled, but *Davis* put an End to it, by this short Speech: ——*Heark yo, you* Cocklin *and* La Bouse, *I find by strengthening you, I have put a Rod into your Hands to whip my self, but I'm still able to deal with you both; but since we met in Love, let us part in Love, for I find, that three of a Trade can never agree.*——Upon which the other two went on Board their respective Ships, and immediately parted, each steering a different Course.

Davis held on his Way down the Coast, and making Cape *Appollonia*, he met with two *Scotch* and one *English* Vessel, which he plundered, and then let go. About five Days after he fell in with a *Dutch* Interloper of thirty Guns and ninety Men, (half being *English*,) off Cape *Three Points* Bay; *Davis* coming up along Side of her, the *Dutch* Man gave the first Fire, and pouring in a broad-Side upon *Davis*, killed nine of his Men, *Davis* returned it, and a very hot Engagement followed, which lasted from one a Clock at Noon, till nine next Morning, when the *Dutch* Man struck, and yielded her self their Prize.

Davis fitted up the *Dutch* Ship for his own Use, and called her the *Rover*, aboard of which he mounted thirty two Guns, and twenty seven Swivels, and proceeded with her and the *King James* to *Anamaboe*; he entered the Bay betwixt the Hours of twelve and one at Noon, and found there three Ships lying at Anchor, who were trading for Negroes, Gold and Teeth: The Names of these Ships were the *Hink* Pink, Captain *Hall* Commander, the *Princess*, Captain *Plumb*, of which *Roberts*, who will make a considerable Figure in the sequel of this History, was second Mate, and the *Morrice* Sloop, Captain *Fin*; he takes these Ships without any Resistance, and having plundered them, he makes a Present of one of them, *viz.* the *Morrice* Sloop, to the *Dutch* Men, on Board of which alone were found a hundred and forty Negroes, besides dry Goods, and a considerable Quantity of Gold-Dust.

It happened there were several Canoes along Side of this last, when *Davis* came in, who saved them selves and got ashore; these gave Notice at the Fort, that these Ships were Pyrates, upon which the Fort fired upon them, but without any Execution, for their Mettle was not of Weight enough to reach them; *Davis* therefore, by Way of Defiance, hoisted his black Flag and returned their Compliment.

The same Day he sail'd with his three Ships, making his

Way down the Coast towards *Princes*, a *Portuguese* Colony:
But, before we proceed any farther in *Davis*'s Story, we shall
give our Reader an Account of the *Portuguese* Settlements
on this Coast, with other curious Remarks, as they were
communicated to me by an ingenious Gentleman, lately arrived from those Parts.

A Description of the Islands of ST. THOME
DEL PRINCIPE, *and* ANNOBONO.

As the *Portuguese* were the great Improvers of Navigation,
and the first *Europeans* who traded too and settled on the
Coasts of *Africa*, even round to *India*, and made those Discoveries, which now turn so much to the Advantage of other
Nations, it may not be amiss, previously to a Description of
those Islands, to hint on that wonderful Property of the
Loadstone, that a little before had been found out, and enabled them to pursue such new and daring Navigations.

The attractive Power of the Loadstone, was universally
known with the Ancients, as may be believed by its being a
native Fossil of the *Grecians*, (*Magnes a Magnesia*) but its
directive, or polar Virtue, has only been known to us within
this 350 Years, and said to be found out by *John Goia* of
Malphi, in the Kingdom of *Naples, Prima dedit nautis usum
magnetis Amalphi*; tho' others think, and assure us, it was
transported by *Paulus Venetus* from *China* to *Italy*, like the
other famous Arts of modern Use with us, PRINTING and
the Use of GUNS.

The other Properties or Improvements of the Magnet,
viz. Variation, or its Defluction from an exact N. or S. Line,
Variation of that Variation, and its Inclination, were the In-
ventions of *Sebastian Cabot*, Mr. *Gellibrand*, and Mr. *Norman*; the Inclination of the Needle, or that Property whereby
it keeps an Elevation above the Horizon, in all Places but
under the Equator, (where its Parallel) is as surprizing a
Phaenomenon as any, and was the Discovery of our Countrymen; and could it be found regular, I imagine would very

much help towards the Discovery of Longitude, at least would point out better Methods than hitherto known, when Ships drew nigh Land, which would answer as useful an End.

Before the Verticity and Use of the Compass, the *Portuguese* Navigations had extended no farther than Cape *Non*, (it was their *ne plus ultra*,) and therefore so called; distress of Weather, indeed, had drove some Coasters to *Porto Santo*, and *Madera*, before any certain Method of steering was invented; but after the Needle was seen thus inspired, Navigation every Year improved under the great Incouragements of *Henry, Alphonsus*, and *John* II. Kings of *Portugal*, in Part of the 14th and in the 15th Century.

King *Alphonsus* was not so much at leasure as his Predecessor, to pursue these Discoveries, but having seen the Advantages accrued to *Portugal* by them, and that the Pope had confirmed the perpetual Donation of all they should discover between Cape *Bajadore* and *India*, inclusively, he resolved not to neglect the proper Assistance, and farmed the Profits that did or might ensue to one *Bernard Gomez*, a Citizen of *Lisbon*, who was every Voyage obliged to discover 100 Leagues, still farther on: And about the Year 1470 made these Islands, the only Places (of all the considerable and large Colonies they had in *Africa*,) that do now remain to that Crown.

St. *Thome* is the principal of the three, whose Governour is stiled Captain General of the Islands, and from whom the other at *Princes* receives his Commission, tho' nominated by the Court of *Portugal*: It is a Bishoprick with a great many secular Clergy who appear to have neither Learning nor Devotion, as may be judged by several of them being Negroes: One of the Chief of them, invited us to hear Mass, as a Diversion to pass Time away, where he, and his inferior Brethren acted such affected Gestures and Strains of Voice, as shewed to their Dishonour, they had no other Aim than pleasing us; and what I think was still worse, is was not without a View of Interest; for as these Clergy are the chief

Traders, they stoop to painful and scandalous Methods for ingratiating themselves: They and the Government, on this trading Account, maintain as great Harmony, being ever jealous of each other, and practising little deceitful Arts to monopolize what Strangers have to offer for sale, whether Toys or Cloaths, which of all Sorts are ever Commodious with the *Portuguese,* in all Parts of the World; an ordinary Suit of Black will sell for seven or eight Pound; a Turnstle Wig of four Shillings, for a Moidore; a Watch of forty Shillings, for six Pound, *&c.*

The Town is of mean Building, but large and populous, the Residence of the greater Part of the Natives, who, thro' the whole Island, are computed at 10000, the Militia at 3000, and are in general, a rascally thievish Generation, as an old grave Friend of mine can Witness; for he having carried a Bag of second hand Cloaths on Shore, to truck for Provisions, seated himself on the Sand for that Purpose, presently gathered a Crowd round him, to view them; one of which desired to know the Price of a black Suit, that unluckily lay uppermost, and was the best of them, agreeing to the Demand, with little Hesitation, provided it would but fit him; he put them on immediately, in as much hurry as possible, without any *co-licentia Seignor,* and when my Friend was about to commend the Goodness of the Suit, and Exactness they set with, not dreaming of the impudence of running away from a Crowd, the Rascal took to his Heels, my Friend followed and bawled very much, and tho' there was 500 People about the Place, it served to no other End but making him a clear Stage, that the best Pair of Heels might carry it; so he lost the Suit of Cloaths, and before he could return to his Bag, others of them had beat off his Servant, and shared the rest.

Most of the Ships from *Guiney,* of their own Nation, and frequently those of ours, call at one or other of these Islands, to recruit with fresh Provisions, and take in Water, which on the Coast are not so good, nor so conveniently to come by: Their own Ships likewise, when they touch here, are obliged to leave the King his Custom for their Slaves, which is always in Gold, at so much a Head, without any Deduction at *Brasil*, for the Mortality that may happen afterwards; this by being a constant Bank to pay off the civil and military Charges of the Government, prevents the Inconveniency of Remittances, and keeps both it and *Princes* Isle rich enough to pay ready Money for every Thing they want of *Europeans*.

Their Beefs are small and lean, (two hundred Weight or a little more,) but the Goats, Hogs and Fowls very good, their Sugar course and dirty, and Rum very ordinary; as these Refreshments lay most with People who are in want of other Necessaries, they come to us in Way of bartering, very cheap: A good Hog for an old Cutlash; a fat Fowl for a Span of *Brasil* Tobacco, (no other Sort being valued, &c.) But with Money you give eight Dollars *per* Head for Cattle; three Dollars for a Goat; six Dollars for a grown Hog; a Testune and a Half for a Fowl; a Dollar *per* Gallon for Rum; two Dollars a Roove for Sugar; and half a Dollar for a Dozen of Paraquets: Here is Plenty likewise of Corn and Farine, of Limes, Citrons and Yamms.

The Island is reckoned nigh a Square, each Side 18 Leagues long, hilly, and lays under the *Æquinoctial*, a wooden Bridge just without the Town, being said not to deviate the least Part of a Minute, either to the Southward or Northward; and notwithstanding this warm Scituation, and continual vertical Suns, the Islanders are very healthy, imputed by those who are disposed to be merry, in a great Measure to the Want of even so much as one Surgeon or Physician amongst them.

Isle *Del Principe*, the next in Magnitude, a pleasant and delightful Spot to the grave, and thoughtfull Disposition of the *Portuguese*, and Improvement of Country Retirement, in that, this may be a happy and uninterrupted Retreat from the whole World.

I shall divide what I have to say on this Island, into Observations made on our Approach to it, on the Seas round it, the Harbour, Produce of the Island and Seasons, Way of

Living among the Inhabitants, some Custom of the Negroes, with such proper Deductions on each as may illustrate the Description, and inform the Reader.

We were bound hither from *Whydah*, at the latter Part of the Month *July*, when the Rains are over, and the Winds hang altogether S. W. (as they do before the Rains, S. E.) yet with this Wind (when at Sea) we found the Ship gained unexpectedly so far to the Southward, (*i. e.* Windward,) that we could with ease have weathered any of the Islands, and this seems next to impossible should be, if the Currents, which were strong to Leeward, in the Road of *Whydah*, had extended in like Manner cross the Bite of *Benin*: No, it must then have been very difficult to have weathered even Cape *Formosa*: On this Occasion, I shall farther expatiate upon the Currents on the whole Coast of *Guiney*.

The Southern Coast of *Africa* runs in a Line of Latitude, the Northern on an Eastern Line, but both strait, with the fewest Inlets, Gulphs or Bays, of either of the four Continents; the only large and remarkable one, is that of *Benin* and *Calabar*, towards which the Currents of each Coast tend, and is strongest from the Southward, because more open to a larger Sea, whose rising it is (tho' little and indiscernable at any Distance from the Land,) that gives rise to these Currents close in Shore, which are nothing but Tides altered and disturbed by the Make and Shape of Lands.

For Proof of this, I shall lay down the following Observations as certain Facts. That in the Rivers of *Gambia* and *Sierraleon*, in the Straits and Channels of *Benin*, and in general along the whole Coast, the Flowings are regular on the Shores, with this Difference; that, in the abovemention'd Rivers, and in the Channels of *Benin*, where the Shore contract the Waters into a narrow Compass, the Tides are strong and high, as well as regular; but on the dead Coast, where it makes an equal Reverberation, slow and low, (not to above two or three Foot,) increasing as you advance towards *Benin*; and this is farther evident in that at Cape *Corso*, *Succonda* and *Commenda*, and where the Land rounds and gives any Stop, the Tides flow regularly to four Foot and upwards; when on an evener Coast, (tho' next adjoining,) they shall not exceed two or three Foot; and ten Leagues out at Sea, (where no such Interruption is,) they become scarcely, if at all, perceptible.

What I would deduce from this, besides a Confirmation of that ingenious Theory of the Tides, by Captain *Halley*; is first, that the Ships bound to *Angola, Cabenda,* and other Places on the Southern Coast of *Africa*, should cross the *Æquinoctial* from Cape *Palmas*, and run into a Southern Latitude, without keeping too far to the Westward; and the Reason seems plain, for if you endeavour to cross it about the Islands, you meet Calms, southerly Winds and opposite Currents; and if too far to the Westward, the trade Winds are strong and unfavourable; for it obliges you to stand in to 28 or 30° Southern Latitude, till they are variable.

Secondly, On the Northern Side of *Guiney*, if Ships are bound from the *Gold Coast* to *Sierraleon, Gambia,* or elsewhere to Windward, considering the Weakness of these Currents, and the Favourableness of Land Breezes, and Southerly in the Rains, Turnadoes, and even of the Trade Wind, when a-breast of Cape *Palmas*, it is more expeditious to pursue the Passage this Way, than by a long perambulatory Course of 4 or 500 Leagues to the Westward, and as many more to the Northward, which must bebefore a Wind can be obtained, that could recover the Coast.

Lastly, It is, in a great Measure, owning to this want of Inlets, and the Rivers being small and unnavigable, that the Seas rebound with so dangerous a Surff thro' the whole Continent.

Round the Shores of this Island, and at this Season, (*July, August* and *September,*) there is a great Resort of Whale-Fish, tame, and sporting very nigh the Ships as they sail in, always in Pairs, the Female much the smaller, and often seen to turn on their Backs for Dalliance, the Prologue to engendring: It has an Enemy, called the Thresher, a large Fish too, that has its Haunts here at this Season, and encounters the

Whale, raising himself out of the Water a considerable
Heighth, and falling again with great Weight and Force; it
is commonly said also, that there is a Sword Fish in these
Battles, who pricks the Whale up to the Surface again, but
without this, I believe, he would suffocate when put to quick
Motions, unless frequently approaching the Air, to ventilate
and remove the Impediments to a swifter Circulation: Nor
do I think he is battled for Prey, but to remove him from
what is perhaps the Food of both. The Number of Whales
here has put me sometimes on thinking an advantageous
Fishery might be made of it, but I presume they (no more
than those of *Brasil*) are the Sort which yield the prositable
Part, called Whale-Bone: All therefore that the Islanders do,
is now and then to go out with two or three Canoes, and set
on one for Diversion.

The Rocks and outer Lines of the Island, are the Haunts
of variety of Sea-Birds, especially Boobies and Noddies; the
former are of the Big of a Gull, and a dark Colour, named
so from their Simplicity, because they often sit still and let
the Sailors take them up in their Hands; but I fancy this
succeeds more frequently from their Weariness, and the
Largeness of their Wings, which, when they once have
rested, cannot have the Scope necessary to raise and float
them on the air again. The Noddies are smaller and flat
footed also.

What I would remark more of them, is, the admirable
Instinct in these Birds, for the proper Seasons, and the
proper Places for Support. In the aforemention'd Months,
when the large Fish were here, numerous Flocks of Fowl
attend for the Spawn and Superfluity of their Nourishment;
and in *January* few of either; for the same Reason, there are
scarce any Sea Fowl seen on the *African* Coast; Rocks and
Islands being generally their best Security and Subsistance.

The Harbour of *Princes* is at the E. S. E. Point of the
Island; the North-Side has gradual Soundings, but here deep
Water, having no Ground at a Mile off with 140 Fathom of
Line. The Port (when in) is a smooth narrow Bay, safe from

Winds (unless a little Swell when Southerly) and draughted into other smaller and sandy Ones, convenient for raising of Tents, Watering, and hawling the Seam; the whole protected by a Fort, or rather Battery of a dozen Guns on the Larboard-Side. At the Head of the Bay stands the Town, about 1 Mile from the anchoring Place, and consists of two or three regular Streets, of wooden built Houses where the Governor and chief Men of the Island reside. Here the Water grows shallow for a considerable Distance, and the Natives, at every Ebb (having before encompassed every convenient Angle with a Rise of Stones, something like Weirs in *England*) resort for catching of Fish, which, with them, is a daily Diversion, as well as Subsistance, 500 attending with Sticks and wicker Baskets; and if they cannot dip them with one Hand, they knock them down with the other. The Tides rise regularly 6 Foot in the Harbour, and yet not half that Height without the Capes that make the Bay.

Here are constantly two Missionaries, who are sent for six Years to inculcate the Christian Principles, and more especially attend the Conversion of the Negroes; the present are *Venetians*, ingenious Men, who seem to despise the loose Morals and Behaviour of the Seculars, and complain of them as of the Slaves, *ut Color Mores sunt nigri.* They have a neat Conventual-House and a Garden appropriated, which, by their own Industry and Labour, not only thrives with the several Natives of the Soil, but many Exoticks and Curiosities. A Fruit in particular, larger than a Chestnut, yellow, containing two Stones, with a Pulp, or clammy Substance about them, which, when suck'd exceeds in Sweetness, Sugar or Honey, and has this Property beyond them, of giving a sweet Taste to every Liquid you swallow for the whole Evening after. The only Plague infesting the Garden, is a Vermin called Land-Crabs, in vast Numbers, of a bright red Colour, (in other Respects like the Sea ones) which burrough in these sandy Soils like Rabbets, and are as shy.

The Island is a pleasant Intermixture of Hill and Valley;

the Hills spread with Palms, Coco-Nuts, and Cotton-Trees, with Numbers of Monkeys and Parrots among them; the Valleys with fruitful Plantations of *Yamms, Kulalu, Papas,* Variety of Sallating, *Ananas,* or Pine-Apples, *Guavas, Plantanes, Bonanas, Manyocos,* and *Indian* Corn; with Fowls, *Guinea* Hens, *Muscovy* Ducks, Goats, Hogs, Turkies, and wild Beefs, with each a little Village of Negroes, who, under the Direction of their several Masters, manage the Cultivation, and exchange or sell them for Money, much after the same Rates with the People of St. *Thome.*

I shall run a Description of the Vegetables, with their Properties, not only because they are the Produce of this Island, but most of them of *Africa* in general.

The Palm-Trees are numerous on the Shores of *Africa,* and may be reckoned the first of their natural Curiosities, in that they afford them Meat, Drink and Cloathing; they grow very straight to 40 and 50 Foot high, and at the top (only) have 3 or 4 Circles of Branches, that spread and make a capacious Umbrella. The Trunk is very rough with Knobs, either Excrescencies, or the Healings of those Branches that were lopped off to forward the Growth of the Tree, and make it answer better in its Fruit. The Branches are strongly tied together with a *Cortex,* which may be unravelled to a considerable Length and Breadth; the inward *Lonella* of this *Cortex,* I know are wove like a Cloath at *Benin,* and afterwards died and worn: Under the Branches, and close to the Body of the Tree, hang the Nuts, thirty Bunches perhaps on a Tree, and each of thirty Pound Weight, with prickly Films from between them, not unresemsembling Hedge-Hogs; of these Nuts comes a liquid and pleasant scented Oyl, used as Food and Sauce all over the Coast, but chiefly in the Windward Parts of *Africa,* where they stamp, boil and skim it on in great Quantities; underneath, when the Branches fasten, they tap for Wine, called *Cockra,* in this Manner; the Negroes who are mostly limber active Fellows, encompass themselves and the Trees with a Hoop of strong With and run up with a great deal of Agility; at the Bottom of a Branch of Nuts, he makes an Excavation of an Inch and a half over, and tying fast his Calabash, leaves it to destil, which it does to two or three Quarts in a Night's Time, when does he plugs it up, and chooses another; for if suffered to run too much, or in the Day Time, the Sap is unwarily exhausted, and the Tree spoiled: The Liquor thus drawn, is of a wheyish Colour, intoxicating and sours in 24 Hours, but when near drawn, is *pleasantest to thirst and hunger both*: It is from these Wines they draw their Arack in India. On the very Top of the Palm, grows a Cabbage called so, I believe, from some resemblance its Tas is thought to have with ours, and is used like it, the Covering has a Down that makes the best of Tinder, and the Weavings of other Parts are drawn out into strong Threads.

Coco-Nut-Trees are branch'd like, but not so tall as, *Palm* Trees, the Nut like them, growing under the Branches, and close to the Trunk; the milky Liquor they contain, (to half a Pint or more,) is often drank to quench Thirst, but surfeiting, and this may be observed in their Way of Nourishment, that when the Quantity of Milk is large, the Shell and Meat are very thin, and harden and thicken in Proportion, as that loses.

Cotton Trees also are the Growth of all Parts of *Africa*, as well as the Islands, of vast Bigness, yet not so incremental as the Shrubs or Bushes of five or six Foot high; these bear a Fruit (if it may be so called) about the Bigness of Pigeons Eggs, which as the Sun swells and ripens, bursts forth and discovers three Cells loaded with Cotton, and Seeds in the Middle of them: This in most Parts the Negroes know how to spin, and here at *Nicongo* and the Island St. *Fago*, how to weave into Cloths.

Yamms are a common Root, sweeter but not unlike Potato's: *Kulalu*, a Herb like Spinnage: *Papa*, a Fruit less than the smallest Pumkins; they are all three for boiling, and to be eat with Meat; the latter are improved by the *English* into a Turnip or an Apple Tast, with a due Mixture of Butter or Limes.

Guava's, a Fruit as large as a Pipin, with Seeds and Stones in it, of an uncouth astringing Tast, tho' never so much be said in Commendation of it, at the *West-Indies*, it is common for *Creolians*, (who has tasted both), to give it a Preference to Peach or Nectarine, no amazing Thing when Men whose Tasts are so degenerated, as to prefer a Toad in a Shell, (as *Ward* calls Turtle,) to Venison, and Negroes to fine *English* Ladies.

Plantanes and *Bonano's* are Fruit of oblong Figure, that I think differ only *secundum Major & Minus*, if any, the latter are preferable, and by being less, are juicier; they are usually, when stripped of their Coat, eat at Meals instead of Bread: The Leaf of this Plantane is an admirable Detergent, and, externally applied, I have seen cure the most obstinate scorbutick Ulcers.

Manyoco. A Root that shoots its Branches about the heighth of a Currant Bush; from this Root the Islanders make a Farine or Flower, which they sell at three Ryals a Roove, and drive a considerable Trade for it with the Ships that call in. The manner of making it, is first to press the Juice from it, (which is poisonous) done her with Engines, and then the Negroe Women, upon a rough Stone, rub it into a granulated Flower, reserved in their Houses, either to boil, as we do our Wheat, and is a hearty Food for the Slaves; or make it into a Bread, fine, white, and well tasted, for themselves. One thing worth taking Notice about *Manyoco* in this Island, is, that the Woods abound with a wild poisonous and more mortiserous Sort, which sometimes Men, unskilled in the Preparation of it, feed on to their Destruction: This the Missionaries assured me they often experimented in their Hogs, and believed we did in the Mortality of our Sailors.

Indian Corn, is likewise as well as the *Farine de Manyoco* and Rice, the common Victualling of our Slave Ships, and is afforded here at 1000 Heads for two Dollars. This Corn grows eight or nine Foot high, on a hard Reed or Stick, shooting forth at every six Inches Heighth, some long

Leaves; it has always an Ear, or rather Head, at top, of, perhaps, 400 Fold Increase; and often two, three, or more, Midway.

Here are some Tamarind Trees; another called *Cola*, whose Fruit, or Nut (about twice the Bigness of a Chestnut, and bitter) is chewed by the *Portugueze*, to give a sweet Gust to their Water which they drink; but above all, I was shewn the Bark of one (whose Name I do not know) gravely affirm'd to have a peculiar Property of enlarging the Virile Member; I am not fond of such Conceits, nor believe it in the Power of any Vegetables, but must acknowledge, I have seen Sights of this kind among the Negroes very extraordinary; yet, that there may be no Wishes among the Ladies for the Importation of this Bark, I must acquaint them, that they are found to grow less merry, as they encrease in Bulk. I had like to have forgot their Cinnamon Trees; there is only one Walk of them, and is the Entrance of the Governor's Villa; they thrive extreemly well, and the Bark not inferior to our Cinnamon from *India*; why they and other Spice, in a Soil so proper, receive no farther Cultivation, is, probably, their Suspicion, that so rich a Produce, might make some potent Neighbour take a Fancy to the Island.

They have two Winters, or rather Springs, and two Summers: Their Winters, which are the rainy Seasons, come in *September* and *February*, or *March*, and hold two Months, returning that Fatness and generative Power to the Earth, as makes it yield a double Crop every Year, with little Sweat or Labour.

> *Hic Ver Assiduum atque Alienis Mensibus Æsas*
> ——*Bis gravida Pecudes, bis Pomis utilis arbos.*

Their first coming is with *Travado*'s, *i. e.* sudden and hard Gusts of Wind, with Thunder, Lightning and heavy Showers, but short; and the next new or full Moon at those Times of the Year, infallibly introduces the Rains, which once begun, fall with little Intermission, and are observed coldest in

February. Similar to these are rainy Seasons also over all the Coast of *Africa*: If there may be allowed any general Way of calculating their Time, they happen from the Course of the Sun, as it respects the *Æquinoctial* only; for if these *Æqui-noxes* prove rainy Seasons all over the World (as I am apt to think they are) whatever secret Cause operates with that Station of the Sun to produce them, will more effectually do it in those vicine Latitudes; and therefore, as the Sun advances, the Rains are brought on the *Whydah* and Gold Coast, by *April*, and on the Windwardmost Part of *Guiney* by *May*: The other Season of the Sun's returning to the Southward, make them more uncertain and irregular in Northern *Africa*; but then to the Southward again, they proceed in like manner, and are a Cape *Lopez* in *October*, at *Angola* in *November*, *&c*.

The Manner of living among the *Portugueze* here is, with the utmoft Frugality and Temperance, even to Penury and Starving; a familiar Instance of Proof is, in the Voracity of their Dogs, who finding such clean Cupboards at home, are wild in a manner with Hunger, and tare up the Graves of the Dead for Food, as I have often seen: They themselves are lean with Covetousness, and that Christian Vertue, which is often the Result of it, Selfdenyal; and would train up their Cattle in the same way, could they fetch as much Money, or had not they their Provision more immediately of Providence. The best of them (excepting the Governor now and then) neither pay nor receive any Visits of Escapade or Recreation; they meet and sit down at each others Doors in the Street every Evening, and as few of them, in so small an Island, can have their Plantations at any greater Distance, than that they may see it every Day if they will, so the Subject of their Talk is mostly how Affairs went there, with their Negroes, or their Ground, and then part with one another innocently, but empty.

The Negroes have yet no hard Duty with them, they are rather Happy in Slavery; for as their Food is chiefly Vegetables, that could no way else be expended, there is no Mur-

murs bred on that account; and as their Business is Domestick, either in the Services of the House, or in Gardening, Sowing, or Planting, they have no more than what every Man would prefer for Health and Pleasure; the hardest of their Work is the Carriage of their Pateroons, or their Wives, to and from the Plantations; this they do in Hammocks (call'd at *Whydah, Serpentines*) slung cross a Pole, with a Cloath over, to screen the Person, so carried, from Sun and Weather, and the Slaves are at each End; and yet even this, methinks, is better than the specious liberty a Man has for himself and his Heirs to work in a Coal Mine.

The Negroes are, most of them, thro' the Care of their Patroons, Christians, at least nominal, but excepting to some few, they adhere still to many silly Pagan Customs in their Mournings and Rejoycings, and in some Measure, powerful Majority has introduced them with the Vulgar of the *Mulatto* and *Portugueze* Race.

If a Person die in that Colour, the Relations and Friends of him meet at the House, where the Corpse is laid out decently on the Ground and covered (all except the face) with a Sheet; they sit round it, crying and howling dreadfully, not unlike what our Countrymen are said to do in *Ireland*: This Mourning lasts for eight Days and Nights, but not equally intense, for as the Friends, who compose the Chorus, go out and in, are weary, and unequally affected, the Tone lessens daily, and the Intervals of Grief are longer.

In Rejoycings and Festivals they are equally ridiculous; these are commonly made on some Friend's Escape from Shipwreck, or other Danger: They meet in a large Room of the House, with a Strum Strum, to which one of the Company, perhaps, sings wofully; the rest standing round the Room close to the Petitions, take it in their Turns (one or two at a time) to step round, called Dancing, the whole clapping their Hands continually, and hooping out every Minute *Abeo*, which signify no more, than, *how do you*. And this foolish Mirth will continue three or four Days together at a House, and perhaps twelve or sixteen Hours at a time.

The *Portugueze*, tho' eminently abstemious and temperate in all other Things, are unbounded in their Lusts; and perhaps they substitute the former in room of a Surgeon, as a Counterpoison to the Mischiefs of a promiscuous Salacity: They have most of them Venereal Taints, and with Age become meager and hectick: I saw two Instances here of Venereal Ulcers that had cancerated to the Bowels, Spectacles that would have effectually perswaded Men (I think) how Salutary the Restriction of Laws are.

Anaobono is the last, and of the least Consequence of the three Islands; there are Plenty of Fruits and Provisions, exchanged to Ships for old Cloaths and Trifles of any Sort; they have a Governor nominated from St. *Thome*, and two or three Priests, neither of which are minded, every one living at Discretion, and fill'd with Ignorance and Lust.

To return to *Davis*, the next Day after he left *Anamaboe*, early in the Morning, the Man at the Mast-Head espied a Sail. It must be observed, they keep a good Look-out; for, according to their Articles, he who first espies a Sail, if she proves a Prize, is entitled to the best Pair of Pistols on Board, over and above his Dividend, in which they take a singular Pride; and a Pair of Pistols has sometimes been sold for thirty Pounds, from one to another.

Immediately they gave Chace, and soon came up with her; the Ship proved to be a *Hollander*, and being betwixt *Davis* and the Shore, she made all the Sail she could, intending to run aground; *Davis* guessed her Design, and putting out all his small Sails, came up with her before she could effect it, and fired a Broad-side, upon which she immediately struck, and called for Quarter. It was granted, for according to *Davis*'s Articles, it was agreed, that Quarter should be given whenever it was called for, upon Pain of Death.

This Ship proved a very rich Prize, having the Governor of *Acra* on Board, with all his Effects, going to *Holland*; there was in Money to the Value of 15000 *l.* Sterling, besides other valuable Merchandizes, all which they brought on Board of themselves.

Upon this new Success, they restored Captain *Hall* and Captain *Plumb*, before-mentioned, their Ships again, but strengthened their Company with thirty five Hands, all white Men, taken out of these two and the *Morrice* Sloop; they also restored the *Dutch* their Ship, after having plunder'd her, as is mentioned.

Before they got to the Island of *Princes*, one of their Ships, *viz.* that call'd the *King James*, sprung a Leak; *Davis* order'd all Hands out of her, on Board his own Ship, with every thing else of Use, and left her at an Anchor at *High Cameroon*. As soon as he came in Sight of the Island, he hoisted *English* Colours; the *Portuguese* observing a large Ship sailing towards them, sent out a little Sloop to examine what she might be; this Sloop hailing of *Davis*, he told them he was an *English* Man of War, in Quest of Pyrates, and that he had received Intelligence there were some upon that Coast; upon this they received him as a welcome Guest, and piloted him into the Harbour. He saluted the Fort, which they answered, and he came to an Anchor just under their Guns, and hoisted out the Pinnace, Man of War Fashion, ordering nine Hands and a Coxen in it, to row him ashore.

The *Portugueze*, to do him the greater Honour, sent down a File of Musqueteers to receive him, and conduct him to the Governor. The Governor not in the least suspecting what he was, received him very civilly, promising to supply him with whatever the Island afforded; *Davis* thanked him, telling him, the King of *England* would pay for whatever he should take; so after several Civilities pass'd between him and the Governor, he returned again on Board.

It happened a *French* Ship came in there to supply it self with some Necessaries, which *Davis* took in to his Head to plunder, but to give the Thing a Colour of Right, he persuaded the *Portugueze*, that she had been trading with the Pyrates, and that he found several Pyrates Goods on Board, which he seized for the King's Use: This Story passed so well upon the Governor, that he commended *Davis*'s Diligence.

A few Days after, *Davis*, with about fourteen more went privately ashore, and walk'd up the Country towards a Village, where the Governor and the other chief Men of the Island kept their Wives, in tending, as we may suppose, to supply their Husbands Places with them; but being discovered, the Women fled to a neighboring Wood, and *Davis* and the rest retreated to their Ship, without effecting their Design: The Thing made some Noise, but as no body knew them, it passed over.

Having cleaned his Ship, and put all Things in Order, his Thoughts now were turned upon the main Business, *viz*, the Plunder of the Island, and not knowing where the Treasure lay, a Stratagem came into his Head, to get it (as he thought) with little Trouble, he consulted his Men upon it, and they liked the Design: His Scheme was, to make a Present to the Governor, of a Dozen Negroes, by Way of Return for the Civilities received from him, and afterwards to invite thim, with the chief Men, and some of the Friers, on Board his Ship, to an Entertainment; the Minute they came on Board, they were to be secured in Irons, and there kept till they should pay a Ransom of 40000 *l*. Sterling.

But this Stratagem proved fatal to him, for a *Portugueze* Negroe swam ashore in the Night, and discovered the whole Plot to the Governor, and also let him know, that it was *Davis* who had made the Attempt upon their Wives. However, the Governor dissembled, received the Pyrates Invitation civilly, and promised that he and the rest would go.

The next Day *Davis* went on Shore himself, as if it were out of greater Respect to bring the Governor on Board: He was received with the usual Civility, and he, and other principal Pyrates, who, by the Way had assumed the Title of Lords, and as such took upon them to advise or councel their Captain upon any important Occasion; and likewise held certain Priviledges, which the common Pyrates were debarr'd from, as walking the Quarter-Deck, using the great Cabin, going ashore at Pleasure, and treating with foreign Powers, that is, with the Captains of Ships they made Prize of; I say, *Davis* and some of the Lords were desired to walk up to the Governor's House, to take some Refreshment before they went on Board; they accepted it without the least Suspicion, but never returned again; for an Ambuscade was laid, a Signal being given, a whole Volley was fired upon them; they every Man dropp'd, except one, this one fled back, and escaped into the Boat, and got on Board the Ship: *Davis* was shot through the Bowels, yet he rise again, and made a weak Effort to get away, but his Strength soon forsook him, and he dropp'd down dead; just as he fell, he perceived he was followed, and drawing out his Pistols, fired them at his Pursuers; Thus like a game Cock, giving a dying Blow, that he might not fall unrevenged.

※※※※※※※※※※※※※※※※※※※※※※

CHAPTER IX.

of
Captain *BARTHO. ROBERTS,*
And his CREW.

BARTHOLOMEW ROBERTS sailed in an honest
Employ from *London* aboard of the *Princess,* Captain
Plumb Commander, of which Ship he was second
Mate: He left *England, November* 1719, and arrived at *Gui-
ney* about *February* following, and being at *Anamaboe,* taking
in Slaves for the *West-Indies,* was taken in the said Ship by
Captain *Howel Davis,* as mentioned in the preceeding
Chapter. In the beginning he was very averse to this sort of
Life, and would certainly have escaped from them, had a fair
Opportunity presented it self; yet afterwards he changed his
Principles, as many besides him have done upon another
Element, and perhaps for the same Reason too, *viz.* Prefer-
ment,—and what he did not like as a private Man he could
reconcile to his conscience as a Commander.

Davis being cut off in the manner beforemention'd, the
Company found themselves under a Necessity of filling up
his Post, for which there appear'd two or three Candidates
among the select Part of them, that were distinguish'd by
the Title of Lords, such were *Sympson, Ashplant, Anstis,* &c.
and on canvassing this Matter, how shatter'd and weak a
Condition their Government must be without a Head, since
Davis had been remov'd, in the manner beforemention'd, my
Lord *Dennis* propos'd; its said, over a Bowl to this Purpose.

That it was not of any great Signification who was dignify'd

*with Title; for really and in Truth, all good Governments had
(like theirs) the Supream Power lodged with the Community,
who might doubtless depute and revoke as suited Interest or Humour, We are the Original of this claim (says he) and should a
Captain be so sawcy as to exceed prescription at any time,* why
down with Him! *it will be a Caution after he is dead to his
Successors, of what fatal Consequence any sort of assuming may
be. However, it is my Advice, that, while we are sober, we pitch
upon a Man of Courage, and skill'd in Navigation, one, who
by his Council and Bravery seems best able to defend this Commonwealth, and ward us from the Dangers and Tempests of an
instable Element, and the fatal Consequences of Anarchy; and
such a one I take* Roberts *to be. A Fellow; I think, in all Respects,
worthy your Esteem and Favour.*

This Speech was loudly applauded by all but Lord *Sympson,* who had secret Expectations himself, but on this Disappointment, grew sullen; and left them swearing, *he did not
care who they chose Captain, it was not a Papist, for against
them he had conceive'd an irreconcileable Hatred, for that his
Father had been a Sufferer in* Monmouth's *Rebellion.*

Roberts was accordingly elected, tho' he had not been
above six Weeks among them, the Choice was confirm'd
both by the Lords and Commoners, and he accepted of the
Honour saying, *That since he had dipp'd his Hands in muddy
Water, and must be a Pyrate, it was better being a Commander
than a common Man.*

As soon as the Government was settled, by promoting
other Officers in the room of those that were kill'd by the
Portugueze, the Company resolv'd to revenge Captain
Davis's Death, he being more than ordinarily respected by
the Crew for his Affability and good Nature, as well as his
Conduct and Bravery upon all Occasions; and pursuant to
this Resolution about 30 Men were landed in order to make
an Attack upon the Fort, which must be ascended to by a
steep Hill against the Mouth of the Cannon. These Men
were headed by one *Kennedy,* a bold daring Fellow, but very
wicked and profligate; they march'd directly up under the

Fire of their Ship Guns, and as soon as they were discover'd, the *Portugueze* quitted their Post and fled to the Town, and the Pyrates march'd in without Opposition, set Fire to the Fort, and threw all the Guns off the Hill into the Sea, which after they had done, they retreated quietly to their Ship.

But this was not look'd upon as a sufficient Satisfaction for the Injury they received, therefore most of the Company were for burning the Town which *Roberts* said he would yield to, if any Means could be proposed of doing it without their own Destruction, for the Town had a securer Scituation than the Fort, a thick Wood coming almost close to it, affording Cover to the Defendants, who under such an Advantage, he told them, it was to be fear'd, would fire and stand better to their Arms; besides, that bare Houses would be but a slender Reward for their Trouble and Loss. This prudent Advice prevailed; however, they mounted the *French* Ship, they seiz'd at this Place, with 12 Guns and light'ned her, in order to come up to the Town, the Water being shoal, and battered down several Houses; after which they all returned on Board gave back the *French* Ship to those that had most Right to her, and sailed out of the Harbour by the light of two *Portuguese* Ships, which they were pleased to set on Fire there.

Roberts stood away to the Southward, and met with a *Dutch Guiney* Man, which he made Prize of, but after having plundered her, the Skipper had his Ship again: Two Days after, he took an *English* Ship, called the *Experiment*, Captain *Cornet*, at *Cape Lopez*, the Men went all into the pyrate Service, and having no Occasion for the Ship, they burnt her, and then steered for St. *Thomes* but meeting with nothing in their Way, they sailed for *Annabona*, and there water'd, took in Provisions, and put it to a Vote of the Company, whether their next Voyage should be, to the *East-Indies*, or to *Brasil*; the latter being resolved on, they sailed accordingly, and in 28 Days arrived at *Ferdinando*, an uninhabited Island, on the Coast: Here they water'd, boottop'd their Ship, and made ready for the designed Cruise.

Now that we are upon this Coast, I think it will be the

proper Place to present our Readers with a Description of this Country, and some ingenious Remarks of a Friend, how beneficial a Trade might be carried on here by our *West-India* Merchants, at a little Hazard.

A
DESCRIPTION
of
BRASIL, &c.

Brasil (a name signifying the holy Cross) was discovered for the King of *Portugal*, by *Alvarez Cabral, Ann. Dom.* 1501. extending almost from the *Æquinoctial* to 28° South. The Air is temperate and cool, in comparison of the *West-Indies*, from stronger Breezes and an opener Country, which gives less Interruption to the Winds.

The northernmost Part of it stretching about 180 Leagues, (a fine fertile Country,) was taken from the *Portuguese* by the *Dutch West-Indies* Company, *Anno.* 1637 or thereabouts, but the Conquerors, as is natural where there is little or no Religion subsisting, made such heavy Exaction on the *Portuguese*, and extended such Cruelty on the Natives, that prepared them both easily to unite for a Revolt, facilitated by the *Dutch* Mismanagement: For the States being at this Time very intent on their *India* Settlements, not only recalled Count *Morrice* their Governor, but neglected Supplies to their Garrisons; however, tho' the others were countenanced with a Fleet from *Portugal*, and had the Affection of the Natives, yet they found Means to withstand and struggle with this superior Power, from 1643 to 1660, and they was wholly abandoned by them, on Articles dishonorable to the *Portuguese*, viz.

That the *Dutch*, on Relinquishing, should keep all the Places they had conquered in *India* from *Portugal*. That they should pay the States 800000 *l.* and permit them still the Liberty of Trade to *Africa* and *Brasil*, on the same Custom and Duties with the King of *Portugal*'s Subjects. But since that Time, new Stipulations and Treaties have been made; wherein the *Dutch*, who have been totally excluded the *Brasil* Trade, have, in lieu thereof, a Composition of 10 *per Cent.* for the Liberty of trading to *Africa*; and this is always left by every *Portuguese* Ship (before she begins her Slaving) with the *Dutch* General of the *Gold-Coast*, at *Des Minas*.

There are only three principal Towns of Trade on the *Brasil* Coast, St. *Salvadore*, St. *Sebastian*, and *Pernambuca*.

St. *Salvadore* in the *Bahia los todos Santos*, is an Archbishoprick and Seat of the Viceroy, the chief Port of Trade for Importation, where most of the Gold from the Mines is lodged, and whence the Fleets for *Europe* generally depart. The Seas about it abound with Whale-Fish, which in the Season they catch in great Numbers; the Flesh is salted up generally to be the Victualling of their Slave-Ships, and the Train reserved for Exportation, at 30 and 35 Millrays a Pipe.

Rio Janeiro (the Town St. *Sebastian*) is the Southernmost of the *Portuguese*, the worst provided of Necessaries, but commodious for a Settlement, because nigh the Mine, and convenient to supervise the Slaves, who, as I have been told, do usually allow their Master a Dollar *per Diem*, and have the Overplus of their Work (if any) to themselves.

The Gold from hence is esteemed the best, (for being of a copperish Colour,) and they have a Mint to run it into Coin, both here and at *Bahia*; the Moidors of either having the initial Letters of each Place upon them.

Pernambuca (tho' mention'd last) is the second in Dignity, a large and populous Town, and has its rise from the Ruins of *Olinda*, (or the handsome,) a City of a far pleasanter Situation, six Miles up the River, but not so commodious for Traffick and Commerce. Just above the Town the River divides it self into two Branches, not running directly into the Sea, but to the Southward; and in the Nook of the Island made by that Division, stands the Governor's House, a square plain Building of Prince *Maurice*'s, with two Towers, on which are only this Date inscribed, *Anno* 1641. The Avenues to it are every way pleasant, thro' Visto's of tall Coco-Nut Trees.

Over each Branch of the River is a Bridge; that leading to the Country is all of Timber, but the other to the Town (of twenty six or twenty eight Arches) is half of Stone, made by the Dutch, who in their Time had little Shops and gaming Houses on each Side for Recreation.

The Pavements also of the Town are in some Places of broad Tiles, the remaining Fragments of their Conquest. The Town has the outer Branch of the River behind it, and the Harbour before it jetting into which latter are close Keys for the weighing and receiving of Customage on Merchandize, and for the meeting and conferring of Merchants and Traders. The Houses are strong built, but homely, letticed like those of *Lisbon*, for the Admission of Air, without Closets, and what is worse, Hearths; which makes their Cookers consist all in frying and stewing upon Stoves; and that they do till the Flesh become tender enough to shake it to Pieces, and one Knife is then thought sufficient to serve a Table of half a Score.

The greatest Inconvenience of *Pernambuca* is, that there is not one Publick-House in it; so that Strangers are obliged to hire any ordinary one they can get, at a Guinea a Month: And others who come to transact Affairs of Importance, must come recommended, if it were only for the sake of Privacy

The Market is stocked well enough, Beet being at five Farthings *per l.* a Sheep or Goat at nine Shillings, a Turkey four Shillings, and Fowls two Shillings, the largest I ever saw, and may be procured much Cheaper, by hiring a Man to fetch them out of the Country. The dearest in its kind is Water, which being fetch'd in Vessels from *Olinda*, will not be put on Board in the Road under two Crusado's a Pipe.

The *Portuguese* here are darker than those of *Europe*, not only from a warmer Climate, but their many Intermarriages with the Negroes, who are numerous there, and some of them of good Credit and Circumstances. The Women (not unlike the Mulatto Generation every where else) are fond of Strangers; not only the Courtezans, whose Interest may be supposed to wind up their Affections, but also the marryed Women who think themselves obliged, when you favour them with the Secrecy of an Appointment; but the Unhappiness of pursuing Amours, is, that the generallity of both Sexes are touched with veneral Taints, without so much as one Surgeon among them, or any Body skilled in Physick, to cure or palliate the progressive Mischief: The only Person pretending that Way, is an *Irish* Father, whose Knowledge is all comprehended in the Virtues of two or three Simples, and those, with the Salubrity of the Air and Temperance, is what they depend on, for subduing the worst of Malignity; and it may not be unworthy Notice, that tho' few are exempted from the Misfortune of a Running, Eruptions, or the like, yet I could hear of none precipitated into those deplorable Circumstances we see common in unskillful mercurial Processes.

There are three Monasteries, and about six Churches, none of them Rich or Magnificent, unless one dedicated to St. *Antonio*, the Patron of their Kingdom, which shines all over with exquisite Pieces of Paint and Gold.

The Export of *Brasil* (besides Gold) is chiefly Sugars and Tobacco; the latter are sent off in Rowls of a Quintal Weight, kept continually moistened with Mulossus, which, with the Soil it springs from, imparts a strong and peculiar Scent, more sensible in the Snuff made from it, which tho' under Prohibition of importing to *Lisbon*, sells here at *2 s. per l.* as the Tobacco does at about 6 Millraìes a Rowl. The finest of their Sugars fells at 8 *s. per* Roove, and a small ill tasted Rum drawn from the Dregs and Molossus, at two Tustunes a Gallon.

Besides these, they send off great Quantities of Brasil Wood, and Whale Oyl, some Gums and Parrots; the latter are different from the *African* in Colour and Bigness, for as they are blue and larger, these are green and smaller; and the

Females of them ever retain the wild Note, and cannot be brought to talk.

In lieu of this Produce, the *Portuguese*, once every Year by their Fleet from *Lisbon*, import all manner of *European* Commodities; and whoever is unable or negligent of supplying himself at that Season, buys at a very advanced Rate, before the Return of another.

To transport Passengers, Slaves, or Merchandize from one Settlement to another, or in Fishing; they make use of Bark-Logs, by the *Brasilians* called *Fingadahas*: They are made of four Pieces of Timber (the two outermost longest) pinned and fastened together, and sharpened at the Ends: Towards each Extremity a Stool is fixed to sit on for paddling, or holding by, when the Agitation is more than ordinary; with these odd sort of Engines, continually washed over by the Water, do these People, with a little triangular Sail spreeted about the Middle of it, venture out of Sight of Land, and along the Coasts for many Leagues, in any sort of Weather; and if they overset with a Squall (which is not uncommon) they swim, and presently turn it upright again.

The Natives are of the darkest Copper Colour, with thin Hair, of a square strong make, and muscular; but not so well looking as the Wooley Generation: They acquiesce patiently to the *Portuguese* Government, who use them much more humanly and Christian-like than the *Dutch* did, and by that Means have extended Quietness and Peace, as well as their Possessions, three or four hundred Miles into the Country. A Country abounding with fine Pastures and numerous Herds of Cattle, and yields a vast Increase from every thing that is sown: Hence they bring down to us Parrots, small Monkies, Armadillos and Sanguins, and I have been assured, they have, (far In-land,) a Serpent of a vast Magnitude, called *Siboya*, able, they say, to swallow a whole Sheep; I have seen my self here the Skin of another Specie full six Yards long, and therefore think the Story not improbable.

The Harbour of *Pernambuca* is, perhaps, singular, it is made of a Ledge of Rocks, half a Cables length from the

Main, and but little above the Surface of the Water, running
at that equal Distance and Heighth several Leagues, towards
Cape *Augustine*, a Harbour running between them capable
of receiving Ships of the greatest Burthen: The Northermost
End of this Wall of Rock, is higher than any Part of the
contiguous Line, on which a little Fort is built, commanding
the Passage either of Boat or Ship, as they come over the
Bar into the Harbour: On the Starboard Side, (*i. e.* the
Main) after you have entered a little way, stands another Fort
(a *Pentagon*) that would prove of small Account, I imagine,
against a few disciplined Men; and yet in these consists all
their Strength and Security, either for the Harbour or Town:
They have begun indeed a Wall, since their removing from
Olinda, designed to surround the latter; but the slow Progress they make in raising it, leaves Room to suspect 'twill
be a long time in finishing.

The Road without, is used by the *Portugueze*, when they
are nigh sailing for *Europe*, and wait for the Convoy, or are
bound to *Bahia* to them, and by Strangers only when Necessity compels; the best of it is in ten Fathom Water, near
three Miles W.N.W. from the Town; nigher in, is foul with
the many Anchors lost there by the *Portugueze* Ships; and
farther out (in 14 Fathom) corally and Rocky. *July* is the
worst and Winter Season of this Coast, the Trade Winds
being then very strong and dead, bringing in a prodigious
and unsafe Swell into the Road, intermixed every Day with
Squalls, Rain, and a hazey Horizon, but at other times ser-
ener Skies and Sunshine.

In these Southern Latitudes is a Constellation, which
from some Resemblance it bears to a *Jerusalem* Cross, has
the Name of *Crosiers*, the brightest of this Hemisphere, and
are observed by, as the North Star is in the Northern Latitudes; but what I mention this for, is, to introduce the admirable Phænomenon in these Seas of the Megellanick
Clouds, whose Risings and Sittings are so regular, that I have
been assured, the same Nocturnal Observations are made by
them as by the Stars; They are two Clouds, small and whit-

ish, no larger in Appearance than a Man's Hat, and are seen here in *July* in the Latitude of 8° S. about four of the Clock in the Morning; if their Appearance should be said to be the Reflection of Light, from some Stellary Bodies above them, yet the Difficulty is not easily answered, how these, beyond others, become so durable and regular in their Motions.

From these casual Observations on the Country, the Towns, Coast, and Seas of *Brasil*, it would be an Omission to leave the Subject, without some Essay on an interloping Slave Trade here, which none of our Countrymen are adventrous enough to pursue, though it very probably, under a prudent Manager, would be attended with Safety and very great Profit; and I admire the more it is not struck at, because Ships from the Southern Coast of *Africa*, don't lengthen the Voyage to the *West-Indies* a great deal, by taking a Part of *Brasil* in their Way.

The Disadvantages the *Portugueze* are under for purchasing Slaves, are these, that they have very few proper Commodities for *Guiney*, and the Gold, which was their chiefest, by an Edict in *July* 1722, stands now prohibited from being carried thither, so that the Ships employed therein are few, and insufficient for the great Mortality and Call of their Mines; besides, should they venture at breaking so destructive a Law, as the abovementioned (as no doubt they do, or they could make little or no Purchace) yet Gold does not raise its Value like Merchandize in travelling (especially to *Africa*) and when the Composition with the *Dutch* is also paid, they may be said to buy their Negroes at almost double the Price the *English, Dutch*, or *French* do, which necessarily raises their Value extravagantly at *Brasil*; (those who can purchase one, buying a certainer Annuity than *South-Sea* Stock.)

Thus far of the Call for Slaves at *Brasil*; I shall now consider and obviate some Difficulties objected against any Foreigners (suppose *English*) interposing in such a Trade, and they are some on theirs, and some on our Side.

On their Side it is prohibited under Pain of Death, a Lawless effectual to the Prevention of it than pecuniary Mulcts would be, because a Penalty so inadequate and disproportioned, is only *In terrorem*, and makes it merciful in the Governor, or his Instruments, to take a Composition of eight or ten Moidors, when any Subject is catched, and is the common Custom so to do as often as they are found out.

On our Side it is Confiscation of what they can get, which considering, they have no Men of War to guard the Coast, need be very little, without supine Neglect and Carelessness.

I am a Man of War, or Privateer, and being in Want of Provisions, or in Search of Pyrates, put in to *Pernambuca* for Intelligence, to enable me for the Pursuit: The Dread of Pyrates keeps every one off, till you have first sent an Officer, with the proper Compliments to the Governor, who immediately gives Leave for your buying every Necessary you are in want of, provided it be with Money, and not an Exchange of Merchandize, which is against the Laws of the Country.

On this first time of going on Shore, depends the Success of the whole Affair, and requires a cautious and discreet Management in the Person entrusted: He will be immediately surrounded at landing with the great and the small Rabble, to enquire who? and whence he comes? and whether bound? *&c.* and the Men are taught to answer, from *Guiney*, denying any thing of a Slave on Board, which are under Hatches, and make no Shew; nor need they for those who have Money to lay out will conclude on that themselves.

By that time the Compliment is paid to the Governor, the News has spread all round the Town, and some Merchant addresses you, as a Stranger, to the Civility of his House, but privately desires to know what Negroes he can have, and what Price. A Governor may possibly use an Instrument in sisting this, but the Appearance of the Gentleman, and the Circumstance of being so soon engaged after leaving the other, will go a great way in forming a Man's Judgment, and leaves him no room for the Suspicion of such a Snare; however, to have a due Guard, Intimations will suffice, and bring him, and Friends enough to carry off the

best Part of a Cargo in two Nights time, from 20 to 30
Moidors a Boy, and from 30 to 40 a Man Slave. The Hazard
is less at *Rio Janeiro.*

There has been another Method attempted, of settling a
Correspondence with some *Portugueze* Merchant or two,
who, as they may be certain within a Fortnight of any Vessels
arriving on their Coast with Slaves, might settle Signals for
the debarquing them at an unfrequented Part of the Coast,
but whether any Exceptions were made to the Price, or that
the *Portuguese* dread Discovery, and the severest Prosecution
on so notorious a Breach of the Law, I cannot tell but it has
hitherto proved abortive.

However, Stratagems laudable, and attended with Profit,
at no other Hazard (as I can perceive) then loss of Time, are
worth attempting; it is what is every Day practised with the
Spaniards from *Jamaica.*

Upon this Coast our Rovers cruiz'd for about nine Weeks,
keeping generally out of Sight of Land, but without seeing
a Sail, which discourage'd them so, that they determined to
leave the Station, and steer for the *West-Indies*, and in order
thereto, stood in to make the Land for the taking of their
Departure, and thereby they fell in, unexpectedly, with a
Fleet of 42 Sail of *Portuguese* Ships, off the Bay of *los todos
Santos*, with all their Lading in for *Lisbon*, several of them
of good Force, who lay too waiting for two Men of War of
70 Guns each, their Convoy. However, *Roberts* thought it
should go hard with him, but he would make up his Market
among them, and thereupon mix'd with the Fleet, and kept
his Men hid till proper Resolutions could be form'd; that
done, they came close up to one of the deepest, and ordered
her to send the Master on Board quietly, threat'ning to give
them no Quarters, if any Resistance, or Signal of Distress
was made. The *Portuguese* being surprized at these Threats,
and the sudden flourish of Cutlashes from the Pyrates, submitted without a Word, and the Captain came on Board;
Roberts saluted him after a friendly manner, telling him, that

they were Gentlemen of Fortune, but that their Business with him, was only to be informed which was the richest Ship in that Fleet; and if he directed them right, he should be restored to his Ship without Molestation, otherwise, he must expect immediate Death.

Whereupon this *Portuguese* Master pointed to one of 40 Guns, and 150 Men, a Ship of greater Force than the *Rover*, but this no Ways dismayed them, *they were* Portuguese, they said, and so immediately steered away for him. When they came within Hail, the Master whom they had Prisoner, was ordered to ask, *how Seignior Capitain did?* And to invite him on Board, *for that he had a Matter of Consequence to impart to him*, which being done, he returned for Answer, *That he would wait upon him presently*: But by the Bustle that immediately followed, the Pyrates perceived, they were discovered, and that this was only a deceitful Answer to gain Time to put their Ship in a Posture of Defence; so without further Delay, they poured in a Broad-Side, boarded and grapled her; the Dispute was short and warm, wherein many of the *Portuguese* fell, and two only of the Pyrates. By this Time the Fleet was alarmed, Signals of Top-gallant Sheets flying, and Guns fired, to give Notice to the Men of War, who rid still at an Anchor, and made but scurvy hast out to their Assistance; and if what the Pyrates themselves related, be true, the Commanders of those Ships were blameable to the highest Degree, and unworthy the Title, or so much as the Name of Men: For *Roberts* finding the Prize to sail heavy, and yet resolving not to loose her, lay by for the headmost of them (which much out sailed the other) and prepared for Battle, which was ignominiously declined, tho' of such superior Force; for not daring to venture on the Pyrate alone, he tarried so long for his Consort as gave them both time leisurely to make off.

They found this Ship exceeding rich, being laden chiefly with Sugar, Skins, and Tobacco, and in Gold 40000 Moidors, besides Chains and Trinckets, of considerable Value; particularly a Cross set with Diamonds, designed for the

King of *Portugal*; which they afterwards presented to the
Governor of *Caiana*, by whom they were obliged.

Elated with this Booty, they had nothing now to think of
but some safe Retreat, where they might give themselves up
to all the Pleasures that Luxury and Wantonness could be-
stow, and for the present pitch'd upon a Place called the
Devil's *Islands*, in the River of *Surinam*, on the Coast of
Caiana, where they arrived, and found the eivilest Reception
imaginable, not only from the Governor and Factory, but
their Wives, who exchanged Wares and drove a considerable
Trade with them.

They seiz'd in this River a Sloop, and by her gained Intelligence, that a Brigantine had also sailed in Company with
her, from *Rhode-Island*, laden with Provisions for the Coast.
A Welcome Cargo! They growing short in the Sea Store,
and as *Sancho* says, *No Adventures to be made without Belly-
Timber*. One Evening as they were rumaging (their Mine of
Treasure) the *Portuguese* Prize, this expected Vessel was de-
scry'd at Mast-Head, and *Roberts*, imagining no Body could
do the Business so well as himself, takes 40 Men in the
Sloop, and goes in pursuit of her; but a fatal Accident followed this rash, tho' inconsiderable Adventure, for *Roberts*
thinking of nothing less than bringing in the Brigantine that
Afternoon, never troubled his Head about the Sloop's Provision, nor inquired what there was on Board to subsist such
a Number of Men; but out he sails after his expected Prize,
which he not only lost further Sight of but after eight Days
contending with contrary Winds and Currents, found themselves thirty Leagues to Leeward. The Current still opposing
their Endeavours, and perceiving no Hopes of beating up to
their Ship, they came to an Anchor, and inconsiderately sent
away the Boat to give the rest of the Company Notice of
their Condition, and to order the Ship to them, but too soon,
even the next Day, their Wants made them sensible of their
Infatuation, for their Water was all expended, and they had
taken no thought how they should be supply'd, till either the

Ship came, or the Boat returned, which was not likely to be
under five or six Days. Here like *Tantalus*, they almost fam-
ished in Sight of the fresh Streams and Lakes; being drove
to such Extremity at last, that they were forc'd to tare up the
Floor of the Cabin, and patch up a sort of Tub or Tray with
Rope Yarns, to paddle ashore, and fetch off immediate Supplies of Water to preserve Life.

After some Days, the long-wish'd-for Boat came back,
but with the most unwellcome News in the World, for *Kennedy*, who was Lieutenant, and left in Absence of *Roberts*, to
Command the Privateer and Prize, was gone off with both.
This was Mortification with a Vengeance, and you may
imagine they did not depart without some hard Speeches
from those that were left, and had suffered by their Treachery: And that there need be no further mention of this *Kennedy*, I shall leave Captain *Roberts*, for a Page or two, with
the Remains of his Crew, to vent their Wrath in a few Oaths
and Execrations, and follow the other, whom we may reckon
from that Time, as steering his Course towards *Execution
Dock*.

Kennedy was now chosen Captain of the revolted Crew,
but could not bring his Company to any determined Resolution; some of them were for pursuing the old Game, but
the greater Part of them seem'd to have Inclinations to turn
from those evil Courses, and get home privately, (for there
was no Act of Pardon in Force,) therefore they agreed to
break up, and every-Man to shift for himself, as he should
see Occasion. The first Thing they did, was to part with the
great *Portugueze* Prize, and having the Master of the Sloop
(whose Name I think was *Cane*) aboard, who they said was
a very honest Fellow, (for he had humoured them upon every
Occasion,) told them of the Brigantine that *Roberts* went
after; and when the Pyrates first took him, he complemented
them at an odd Rate, telling them they were welcome to his
Sloop and Cargo, and wish'd that the Vessel had been larger,
and the Loading richer for their Sakes: To this good natured

Man they gave the *Portugueze* Ship, (which was then above
half loaded,) three or four Negroes, and all his own Men,
who returned Thanks to his kind Benefactors, and departed.

Captain *Kennedy* in the *Rover*, sailed to *Barbadoes*, near
which Island, they took a very peaceable Ship belonging to
Virginia; the Commander was a Quaker, whose Name was
Knot; he had neither Pistol, Sword, nor Cutlash on Board;
and Mr. *Knot* appearing so very passive to all they said to
him, some of them thought this a good Opportunity to go
off; and accordingly eight of the Pyrates went aboard, and
he carried them safe to *Virginia*. They made the Quaker a
Present of 10 Chests of Sugar, 10 Rolls of *Brasil* Tobacco,
30 Moidors, and some Gold-Dust, in all to the value of
about 250 *l*. They also made Presents to the Sailors, some
more, some less, and lived a jovial Life all the while they
were upon their Voyage, Captain *Knot* giving them their
Way; nor indeed could he help himself, unless he had taken
an Opportunity to surprize them, when they were either
drunk or asleep; for awake they wore Arms aboard the Ship,
and put him in a continual Terror; it not being his Principle
(or the Sect's) to fight, unless with Art and Collusion; he
managed these Weapons well till he arrived at the Capes,
and afterwards four of the Pyrates went off in a Boat, which
they had taken with them, for the more easily making their
Escapes, and made up the Bay towards *Morland*, but were
forced back by a Storm into an obscure Place of the Country,
where meeting with good Entertainment among the Planters, they continued several Days without being discovered to
be Pyrates. In the mean Time Captain *Knot* leaving four
others on Board his Ship, (who intended to go to *North-
Carolina*,) made what hast he could to discover to Mr. *Spotswood* the Governor, what sort of Passengers he had been
forced to bring with him, who by good Fortune got them
seized; and Search being made after the others, who went
revelling about the Country, they were also taken and all
try'd, convicted and hang'd, two *Portuguese* Jews who were
taken on the Coast of *Brasil* and whom they brought with

them to *Virginia*, being the principal Evidences. The latter had found Means to lodge Part of their Wealth with the Planters, who never brought it to Account: But Captain *Knot* surrendered up every Thing that belonged to them, that were taken aboard, even what they presented to him, in lieu of such Thing as they had plundered him of in their Passage and obliged his Men to do the like.

Some Days after the taking of the *Virginia* Man last mentioned, in cruising in the Latitude of *Jamaica*, *Kennedy* took a Sloop bound thither from *Boston*, loaded with Bread and Flower; aboard this Sloop went all the Hands who were for breaking the Gang, and left those behind that had a Mind to pursue further Adventures. Among the former were *Kennedy*, their Captain, of whole Honor they had such a dispicable Notion, that they went about to throw him over-board, when they found him in the Sloop, as fearing he might betray them all, at their return to *England*; he having in his Childhood been bred a Pick-pocket, and before he became a Pyrate, a House-breaker; both Professions that these Gentlemen have a very mean Opinion of. However, Captain *Kennedy*, by taking solemn Oaths of Fidelity to his Companions, was suffered to proceed with them.

In this Company there was but one that pretended to any skill in Navigation, (for *Kennedy* could neither write nor read, he being preferred to the Command merely for his Courage, which indeed he had often signaliz'd, particularly in taking the *Portuguese* Ship,) and he proved to be a Pretender only; for shaping their Course to *Ireland*, where they agreed to land, they ran away to the North-West Coast of *Scotland*, and there were tost about by hard Storms of Wind for several Days, without knowing where they were, and in great Danger of perishing: At length they pushed the Vessel into a little Creek, and went all ashore, leaving the Sloop at an Anchor for the next Comers.

The whole Company refresh'd themselves at a little Village about five Miles from the Place where they left the Sloop, and passed there for Ship-wreck'd Sailors, and no doubt might have travelled on without Suspicion; but the mad and riotous Manner of their Living on the Road, oc-casion'd their Journey to be cut short, as we shall observe presently.

Kennedy and another left them here, and travelling to one of the Sea-Ports, ship'd themselves for *Ireland*, and arrived there in Safety. Six or seven wisely withdrew from the rest, travelled at their pleasure, and got to their much desired Port of *London*, without being disturbed or suspected; but the main Gang alarm'd the Country where-ever they came, drinking and roaring at such a Rate, that the People shut themselves up in their Houses, in some Places, not daring to venture out among so many mad Fellows: In other Vil-lages, they treated the whole Town, squandering their Money away, as if, like *Æsop*, they wanted to lighten their Burthens: This expensive manner of Living procured two of their drunken Straglers to be knocked on the Head, they being found murdered in the Road, and their Money taken from them: All the rest, to the Number of seventeen as they drew nigh to *Edinburgh*, were arrested and thrown into Goal, upon Suspicion, of they knew not what; However, the Mag-istrates were not long at a Loss for proper Accusations, for two of the Gang offering themselves for Evidences were ac-cepted of; and the others were brought to a speedy Tryal, whereof nine were convicted and executed.

Kennedy having spent all his Money, came over from *Ire-land*, and kept a common B——y-House on *Deptford* Road, and now and then, 'twas thought, made an Excursion abroad in the Way of his former Profession, till one of his Houshold W——gave Information against him for a Robbery, for which he was committed to *Bridewell*; but because she would not do the Business by halves, she found out a Mate of a Ship that *Kennedy* had committed Pyracy upon, as he fool-ishly confess'd to her. This Mate, whose Name was *Grant*, paid *Kennedy* a Visit in *Bridewell*, and knowing him to be the Man procured a Warrant, and had him committed to the *Marshalsea* Prison.

The Game that *Kennedy* had now to play was to turn Evidence himself; accordingly he gave a List of eight or ten of his Comrades; but not being acquainted with their Habitations, one only was taken, who, tho' condemn'd, appeared to be a Man of a fair Character, was forc'd into their Service, and took the first Opportunity to get from them, and therefore receiv'd a Pardon; but *Walter Kennedy* being a notorious Offender, was executed the 19th of *July*, 1721, at *Execution Dock*.

The rest of the Pyrates who were left in the Ship *Rover*, staid not long behind, for they went ashore to one of the *West-India* Islands; what became of them afterwards, I can't tell, but the Ship was found at Sea by a Sloop belonging to St. *Christophers*, and carried into that Island with only nine Negroes aboard.

Thus we see what a disastrous Fate ever attends the Wicked, and how rarely they escape the Punishment due to their Crimes, who, abandon'd to such a profligate Life, rob, spoil, and prey upon Mankind, contrary to the Light and Law of Nature, as well as the Law of God. It might have been hoped, that the Examples of these Deaths, would have been as Marks to the Remainder of this Gang, how to shun the Rocks their Companions had split on; that they would have surrendered to Mercy, or divided themselves, for ever from such Pursuits, as in the End they might be sure would subject them to the same Law and Punishment, which they must be conscious they now equally deserved; *impending Law*, which never let them sleep well, unless when drunk. But all the Use that was made of it here, was to commend the Justice of the Court, that condemn'd *Kennedy, for he was a sad Dog* (they said) *and deserved the Fate he met with*.

But to go back to *Roberts*, whom we left on the Coast of *Caiana*, in a grievous Passion at what *Kennedy* and the Crew had done; and who was now projecting new Adventures with his small Company in the Sloop; but finding hitherto they had been but as a Rope of Sand, they formed a Set of Articles, to be signed and sworn to, for the better Conservation of their Society, and doing Justice to one another; excluding all *Irish* Men from the Benefit of it, to whom they had an implacable Aversion upon the Account of *Kennedy.* How indeed *Roberts* could think that an Oath would be obligatory, where Defiance had been given to the Laws of God and Man, I can't tell, but he thought their greatest Security lay in this, *That it was every one's Interest to observe them if they were minded to keep up so abominable a Combination.*

The following, is the Substance of the Articles, as taken from the Pyrates own Informations.

I.

Every Man has a Vote in Affairs of Moment; but equal Title to the fresh Provisions, or strong Liquors, at any Time seized, and use them at pleasure, unless a Scarcity (no uncommon Thing among them) *make it necessary, for the good of all, to vote a Retrenchment.*

II.

Every Man to be called fairly in turn, by List, on Board of Prizes, because, (over and above their proper Share,) *they were on these Occasions allowed a Shift of Cloaths: But if they defrauded the Company to the Value of a Dollar, in Plate, Jewels, or Money,* M A R O O N I N G *was their Punishment.* This was a Barbarous Custom of putting the Offender on Shore, on some desolate or uninhabited Cape or Island, with a Gun, a few Shot, a Bottle of Water, and a Bottle of Powder, to subsist with, or starve. *If the Robbery was only between one another, they contented themselves with slitting the Ears and Nose of him that was Guilty, and set him on Shore, not in an uninhabited Place, but somewhere, where he was sure to encounter Hardships.*

III.

No Person to Game at Cards or Dice for Money.

IV.

The Lights and Candles to be put out at eight o'Clock at Night: If any of the Crew, after that Hour, still remained inclined for Drinking, they were to do it on the open Deck; which *Roberts* believed would give a Check to their Debauches, for he was a sober Man himself, but found at length, that all his Endeavours to put an End to this Debauch, proved ineffectual.

V.

To keep their Piece, Pistols, and Cutlash clean, and fit for Service: In this they were extravagantly nice, endeavouring to outdo one another, in the Beauty and Richness of their Arms, giving sometimes at an Auction (at the Mast,) 30 or 40 *l.* a Pair, for Pistols. These were slung in Time of Service, with different coloured Ribbands, over their Shoulders, in a Way peculiar to these Fellows, in which they took great Delight.

VI.

No Boy or Woman to be allowed amongst them. If any Man were found seducing anny of the latter Sex, and carried her to Sea, disguised, he was to suffer Death; so that when any fell into their Hands, as it chanced in the *Onslow*, they put a Centinel immediately over her to prevent ill Consequences from so dangerous an Instrument of Division and Quarrel; but then here lies the Roguery; they contend who shall be Centinel, which happens generally to one of the greatest Bullies, who, to secure the Lady's Virtue, will let none lye with her but himself.

VII.

To Desert the Ship, or their Quarters in Battle, was punished with Death, or Marooning.

VIII.

No striking one another on Board, but every Man's Quarrels to be ended on Shore, at Sword and Pistol, Thus The Quarter-Master of the Ship, when the Parties will not come to any Reconciliation, accompanied them on Shore with what Assistance he thinks proper, and turns the Disputants Back to Back, at so many Paces Distance: At the Word of Command, they turn and fire immediately, (or else the Piece is knocked out of their Hands:) If both miss they come to their Cutlashes, and then he is declared Victor who draws the first Blood.

IX.

No Man to talk of breaking up their Way of Living, till each had shared a 1000 l. If in order to this, if Man should lose a Limb, or become a Cripple in their Service, he was to have 800 Dollars, out of the publick stock and for lesser Hurts, proportionably.

X.

The Captain and Quarter-Master to receive two Shares of a Prize; the Master, Boat swain, and Gunner, one share and a half, and other Officers, one and a Quarter.

XI.

The Musicians to have Rest on the Sabbath Day, but the other six Days and Nights, none without special Favour.

These, we are assured, were some of *Roberts*'s Articles, but as they had taken Care to throw over-board the Original they had sign'd and sworn to, there is a great deal of Room to suspect, the remainder contained something too horrid to be disclosed to any, except such as were willing to be Sharers in the Iniquity of them; let them be what they will, they were together the Test of all new Comers, who were initiated by an Oath taken on a Bible, reserv'd for that Purpose only, and were subscrib'd to in Presence of the worshipful Mr. *Roberts*. And in Case any Doubt should arise concerning the Construction of these Laws, and it should remain a Dispute whether the Party had infring'd them or no, a Jury is appointed to explain them, and bring in a Verdict upon the Case in Doubt.

Since we are now speaking of the Laws of this Company, I shall go on, and, in as brief a Manner as I can, relate the principal Customs, and Government, of this roguish Common-Wealth; which are pretty near the same with all Pyrates.

For the Punishment of small Offences, which are not provided for by the Articles, and which are not of Consequence enough to be left to a Jury, there is a principal Officer among the Pyrates, called the Quarter-Master, of the Mens own chusing, who claims all Authority this Way, (excepting in Time of Battle:) If they disobey his Command, are quarrelsome and mutinous with one another, misuse Prisoners, plunder beyond his Order, and in particular, if they be negligent of their Arms, which he musters at Discretion, he punishes at his own Arbitrement, with drubbing or whipping, which no one else dare do without incurring the Lash from all the Ships Company: In short, this Officer is Trustee for the whole, is the first on Board any Prize, separating for the Company's Use, what he pleases, and returning what he thinks fit to the Owners, excepting Gold and Silver, which they have voted not returnable.

After a Description of the Quarter-Master, and his Duty, who acts as a sort of a civil Magistrate on Board a Pyrate

Ship; I shall consider their military Officer, the Captain;
what Privileges he exerts in such anarchy and unrulyness of
the Members: Why truly very little, they only permit him to
be Captain, on Condition, that they may be Captain over
him; they separate to his Use the great Cabin, and sometimes
vote him small Parcels of Plate and China, (for it may be
noted that *Roberts* drank his Tea constantly) but then every
Man, as the Humour takes him, will use the Plate and
China, intrude into his Apartment, swear at him, seize a Part
of his Victuals and Drink, if they like it, without his offering
to find Fault or contest it: Yet *Roberts*, by a better Management than usual, became the chief Director in every Thing
of Moment, and it happened thus:—The Rank of Captain
being obtained by the Suffrage of the Majority, it falls on
one superior for Knowledge and Boldness, *Pistol Proof* (as
they call it,) and can make those fear, who do not love him;
Roberts is said to have exceeded his Fellows in these Respects,
and when advanced, enlarged the Respect that followed it
by making a sort of Privy-Council of half a Dozen of the
greatest Bullies; such as were his Competitors, and had Interest enough to make his Government easy; yet even those,
in the latter Part of his Reign, he had run counter to in every
Project that opposed his own Opinion; for which, and because he grew reserved, and would not drink and roar at their
Rate, a Cabal was formed to take away his Captainship,
which Death did more effectually.

The Captain's Power is uncontroulable in Chace, or in
Battle, drubbing, cutting, or even shooting any one who
dares deny his Command. The same Privilege he takes over
Prisoners, who receive good or ill Usage, mostly as he ap-
proves of their Behaviour, for tho' the meanest would take
upon them to misuse a Master of a Ship, yet he would controul herein, when he see it, and merrily over a Bottle, give
his Prisoners this double Reason for it. First, That it preserved his Precedence; and secondly, That it took the Punishment out of the Hands of a much more rash and mad
Sett of Fellows than himself. When he found that Rigour

was not expected from his People, (for he often practised it to appease them,) then he would give Strangers to understand, that it was pure Inclination that induced him to a good Treatment of them, and not any Love or Partiality to their Persons; for, says he, *there is none of you but will hang me, I know, whenever you can clinch me within your Power.*

And now seeing the Disadvantages they were under for pursuing the Account, *viz.* a small Vessel ill repaired, and without Provisions, or Stores; they resolved one and all, with the little Supplies they could get, to proceed for the *West-Indies*, not doubting to find a Remedy for all these Evils, and to retreive their Loss.

In the Latitude of *Deseada*, one of the Islands, they took two Sloops, which supply'd them with Provisions and other Necessaries; and a few Days afterwards, took a Brigantine belonging to *Rhode Island*, and then proceeded to *Barbadoes*, off of which Island, they fell in with a *Bristol* Ship of 10 Guns, in her Voyage out, from whom they took Abundance of Cloaths, some Money, twenty five Bales of Goods, five Barrels of Powder, a Cable, Hawser, 10 Casks of Oatmeal, six Casks of Beef and several other Goods, besides five of their Men and after they had detained her three Days, let her go; who being bound for the abovesaid Island, she acquainted the Governor with what had happened as soon as she arrived.

Whereupon a *Bristol* Galley that lay in the Harbour, was ordered to be fitted out with all imaginable Expedition, of 20 Guns, and 80 Men, there being then no Man of War upon that Station, and also a Sloop with 10 Guns, and 40 Men: The Galley was commanded by one Captain *Rogers*, of *Bristol* and the Sloop by Captain *Graves*, of that Island, and Captain *Rogers* by a Commission from the Governor was appointed Commadore.

The second Day after *Rogers* sailed out of the Harbour, he was discovered by *Roberts*, who knowing nothing of their Design, gave them Chase: The *Barbadoes* Ships kept an easy sail till the Pyrates came up with them, and then *Roberts* gave them a Gun, expecting they would have immediately struck to his pyratical Flag, but instead thereof, he was forced to receive the Fire of a Broadside, with three Huzzas at the same Time; so that an Engagement ensued, but *Roberts* being hardly put to it, was obliged to crowd all the Sail the Sloop would bear, to get off: The Galley sailing pretty well, kept Company for a long while, keeping a constant Fire, which gail'd the Pyrate; however, at length by throwing over their Guns, and other heavy Goods, and thereby light'ning the Vessel, they, with much ado, got clear; but *Roberts* could never endure a *Barbadoes* Man afterwards, and when any Ships belonging to that Island fell in his Way he was more particularly severe to them than others.

Captain *Roberts* sailed in the Sloop to the Island of *Dominico*, where he watered, and got Provisions of the Inhabitants, to whom he gave Goods in Exchange. At this Place he met with 13 *Englishmen*, who had been set ashore by a *French Guard de la Coste*, belonging to *Martinico*, taken out of two *New-England* Ships, that had been seiz'd, as Prize, by the said *French* Sloop: The Men willingly entered with the Pyrates, and it proved a seasonable Recruit.

They staid not long here, tho' they had immediate Occasion for cleaning their Sloop, but did not think this a proper Place, and herein they judg'd right; for the touching at this Island, had like to have been their Destruction, because they having resolved to go away to the *Granada* Islands, for the aforesaid Purpose, by some Accident it came to be known to the *French* Colony, who sending Word to the Governor of *Martinico*, he equipped and manned two Sloops to go in Quest of them. The Pyrates sailed directly for the *Granadilloes*, and hall'd into a Lagoon, at *Corvocoo*, where they cleaned with unusual Dispatch, staying but a little above a Week, by which Expedition they missed of the *Martinico* Sloops, only a few Hours; *Roberts* sailing over Night, that the *French* arrived the next Morning. This was a fortunate Escape, especially considering, that it was not from any Fears of their being discovered, that they made so much hast from the Island; but, as they had the Impudence themselves to own, for the want of Wine and Women.

Thus narrowly escaped, they sailed for *Newfoundland*, and arrived upon the Banks the latter end *of June*, 1720. They entered the Harbour of *Trepassi*, with their black Colours flying, Drums beating, and Trumpets sounding. There were two and twenty Vessels in the Harbour, which the Men all quitted upon the Sight of the Pyrate, and fled ashore. It is impossible particularly to recount the Destruction and Havock they made here, burning and sinking all the shipping, except a *Bristol* Galley, and destroying the Fisheries, and Stages of the poor Planters, without Remorse or Compunction; for nothing is so deplorable as Power in mean and ignorant Hands, it makes Men wanton and giddy, unconcerned at the Misfortunes they are imposing on their Fellow Creatures, and keeps them smiling at the Mischiefs, that bring themselves no Advantage. *They are like mad Men, that cast Fire-Brands, Arrows, and Death, and say, are not we in Sport?*

Roberts mann'd the *Bristol* Galley he took in the Harbour, and mounted 16 Guns on Board her, and cruising out upon the Banks, he met with nine or ten Sail of *French* Ships, all which he destroyed except one of 26 Guns, which they seiz'd, and carried off for their own Use. This Ship they christ'ned *the Fortune*, and leaving the *Bristol* Galley to the *French* Men, they sailed away in Company with the Sloop, on another Cruise, and took several Prizes, *viz.* the *Richard* of *Biddiford*, *Jonathan Whitfield* Master; the *Willing Mind* of *Pool*; the *Expectation* of *Topsham*; and the *Samuel*, Captain *Cary*, of *London*; out of these Ships they encreased their Company, by entring all the Men they could well spare, in their own Service. The *Samuel* was a rich Ship, and had several Passengers on Board who were used very roughly, in order to make them discover their Money, threatening them every Moment with Death, if they did not resign every Thing up to them. They tore up the Hatches and entered the Hold like a parcel of

Furies, and with Axes and Cutlashes, cut and broke open all the Bales, Cases, and Boxes, they could lay their Hands on; and when any Goods came upon Deck, that they did not like to carry aboard instead of tossing them into the Hold again threw them over-board into the Sea; all this was done with incessant cursing and swearing, more like Fiends than Men. They carried with them, Sails, Guns, Powder, Cordage, and 8 or 9000 *l.* worth of the choicest Goods; and told Captain *Coy, That they should accept of no Act of Grace; that the K— and P—t might be damned with their Acts of G— for them; neither would they go to* Hope-Point, *to be hang'd up a Sun drying, as* Kidd's, *and* Braddish's *Company were; but that if they should ever be overpower'd, they would set Fire to the Powder, with a Pistol, and go all merrily to Hell together.*

After they had brought all the Booty aboard, a Consultation was held whether they should sink or burn the Ship, but whilst they were debating the Matter, they spyed a Sail, and so left the *Samuel,* to give her Chace; at Midnight they came up with the same, which proved to be a Snow from *Bristol,* bound for *Boston,* Captain *Bowles* Master: They us'd him barbarously, because of his Country, Captain *Rogers,* who attack'd them off *Barbadoes,* being of the City of *Bristol.*

July the 16th, which was two Days afterwards, they took a *Virginia* Man called the *Little York, James Philips* Master, and the *Love,* of *Leverpool,* which they plundered and let go; the next Day a Snow from *Bristol,* call'd the *Phenix, John Richards* Master, met with the same Fate from them; as also a Brigantine, Captain *Thomas,* and a Sloop called the *Sadbury,* they took all the Men out of the Brigantine, and sunk the Vessel.

When they left the Banks of *Newfoundland,* they sailed for the *West-Indies,* and the Provisions growing short, they went for the Latitude of the Island *Deseada,* to cruise, it being esteemed the likeliest Place to meet with such Ships as (they used in their Mirth to say) were consigned to them, with Supplies. And it has been very much suspected that Ships have loaded with Provisions at the *English* Colonies,

on pretence of Trading on the Coast of *Africa*, when they
have in reality been consigned to them; and tho' a shew of
Violence is offered to them when they meet, yet they are
pretty sure of bringing their Cargo to a good Market.

However, at this Time they missed with their usual Luck,
and Provisions and Necessaries becoming more scarce every
Day, they retired towards St. *Christophers*, where being
deny'd all Succour or Assistance from the Government, they
fir'd in Revenge on the Town, and burnt two Ships in the
Road, one of them commanded by Captain *Cox*, of *Bristol*;
and then retreated farther to the Island of St. *Bartholomew*,
where they met with much handsomer Treatment. The
Governor not only supplying them with Refreshments, but
he and the Chiefs carressing them in the most friendly Manner: And the Women, from so good an Example, endeavoured to outvie each other in Dress, and Behaviour, to
attract the good Graces of such generous Lovers, that paid
well for their Favours.

Sated at length with these Pleasures, and having taken on
Board a good supply of fresh Provisions, they voted unanimously for the Coast of *Guiney*, and in the Latitude of 22
N. in their Voyage thither, met with a *French* Ship from
Martinico, richly laden, and, which was unlucky for the Master, had a property of being fitter for their Purpose, than the
Banker. *Exchange was no Robbery* they said, and so after a
little mock Complaisance to *Monsieur*, for the Favour he had
done them, they shifted their Men, and took leave: This was
their first *Royal Fortune*.

In this Ship *Roberts* proceeded on his designed Voyage;
but before they reached *Guiney*, he proposed to touch at
Brava, the Southermost of *Cape Verd* Islands and clean. But
here again by an intolerable Stupidity and want of Judgment,
they got so far to Leeward of their Port, that despairing to
regain it, or any of the Windward Parts of *Africa*, they were
obliged to go back again with the Trade-Wind, for the *West-
Indies*; which had very near been the Destruction of them
all. *Surinam* was the Place now designed for, which was at

no less than 700 Leagues Distance, and they had but one Hogshead of Water left to supply 124 Souls for that Passage; a sad Circumstance that eminently exposes the Folly and Madness among Pyrates, and he must be an inconsiderate Wretch indeed, who, if he could separate the Wickedness and Punishment from the Fact, would yet hazard his Life amidst such Dangers, as their want of Skill and Forecast made them liable to.

Their Sins, we may presume were never so troublesome to their Memories, as now, that inevitable Destruction seem'd to threaten them, without the least Glympse of Comfort or Alleviation to their Misery; for, with what Face could Wretches who had ravaged and made so many Necessitous, look up for Relief; they had to that Moment lived in Defiance of the Power that now alone they must trust for their Preservation, and indeed without the miraculous Intervention of Providence, there appeared only this miserable Choice, viz. a present Death by their own Hands, or a ling ring one by Famine.

They continued their Course, and came to an Allowance of one single Mouthful of Water for 24 Hours; many of them drank their Urine, or Sea Water, which, instead of allaying, gave them an inextinguishable Thirst, that killed them: Others pined and wasted a little more Time in Fluxes and Apyrexies, so that they dropped away daily: Those that sustain'd the Misery best, were such as almost starved themselves, forbearing all sorts of Food, unless a Mouthful or two of Bread the whole Day, so that those who survived were as weak as it was possible for Men to be and alive.

But if the dismal Prospect they set out with gave them Anxiety, Trouble, or Pain, what must their Fears and Apprehensions be, when they had not one Drop of Water left, or any other Liquor to moisten or animate. This was their Case, when (by the working of Divine Providence, no doubt they were brought into Soundings, and at Night anchored in seven Fathom Water: This was an inexpressible Joy to them, and, as it were, fed the expiring Lamp of Life with fresh Spirits; but this could not hold long. When the Morning came they saw Land from the Mast-Head, but it was at so great a Distance, that it afforded but an indifferent Prospect to Men who had drank nothing for the two last Days; however, they dispatch'd their Boat away, and late the same Night it return'd to their no small Comfort, with a load of Water informing them, that they had got off the Mouth of *Meriwinga* River on the Coast of *Surinam*.

One would have thought so miraculous an Escape should have wrought some Reformation, but alass they had no sooner quenched their Thirst, but they had forgot the Miracle, till Scarcity of Provisions awakened their Senses, and bid them guard against starving; their allowance was very small, and yet they would profanely say, *That Providence which had gave them Drink, would, no doubt, bring them meat also, if they would use but an honest Endeavour.*

In pursuance of these honest Endeavours, they were steering for the Latitude of *Barbadoes*, with what little they had left, to look out for more, Starve; and, in their Way, met a Ship that answered their Necessities, and after that a Brigantine the former was called the *Greyhound*, belonging to St. *Christophers*, and bound to Philadelphia, the Mate of which signed the Pyrate's Articles, and was afterwards Captain of the *Ranger*, Consort to the *Royal Fortune*.

Out of the Ship and Brigantine, the Pyrates got a good supply of Provisions and Liquor, so that they gave over the designed Cruise, and watered at *Tobago*, and hearing of the two Sloops that had been fitted out and sent after them at *Corvocoo*, they sailed to the Island of *Martinico*, to make the Governor some sort of an Equivalent, for the Care and Expedition he had shewn in that Affair.

It is the Custom at *Martinico*, for the *Dutch* Interlopers that have a Mind to Trade with the People of the Island, to hoist their Jacks when they come before the Town: *Roberts* knew the Signal, and being an utter Enemy to them, he bent his thoughts upon Mischief; and accordingly came in with his Jack flying, which, as he expected, they mistook for a good Market, and thought themselves happiest that could soonest dispatch off their Sloops and Vessels for Trade. When *Roberts* had got them within his Power, (one after another,) he told them, he would not have it said that they came off for nothing, and therefore ordered them to leave their Money behind, for that they were a Parcel of Rogues, and hoped they would always meet with such a *Dutch* Trade as this was; he reserved one Vessel to set the Passengers on Shore again, and fired the rest, to the Number of twenty.

Roberts was so enraged at the Attempts that had been made for taking of him, by the Governors of *Barbados* and *Martinico*, that he ordered a new Jack to be made, which they ever after hoisted, with his own Figure pourtray'd, standing upon two Skulls, and under them the Letters *ABH* and *AMH*, signifying a *Barbadian*'s and a *Martinican*'s Head as may be seen in the Plate of Captain *Roberts*.

At *Dominico*, the next Island they touched at, they took a *Dutch* Interloper of 22 Guns and 75 Men and a Brigantine belonging to *Rhode-Island*, one *Norton* Master. The former made some Defence, till some of his Men being killed, the rest were discouraged and struck their Colours. With these two Prizes they went down to *Guadalupe*, and brought out a Sloop, and a *French* Fly-Boat laden with Sugar; the Sloop they burnt, and went on to *Moonay*, another Island, thinking to clean, but finding the Sea ran too high there to undertake it with Safety, they bent their Course for the North Part of *Hispaniola*, where at *Bennet's* key in the Gulf of *Saminah*, they cleaned both the Ship and the Brigantine. For tho' *Hispaniola* be settled by the *Spaniards* and *French*, and is the Residence of a President from *Spain*, who receives, and finally determines Appeals from all the other *Spanish West-Indies* Islands; yet is its People by no Means proportioned to its Magnitude, so that there are many Harbours in it, to which Pyrates may securely resort without Fear of Discovery from the Inhabitants.

Whilst they were here, two Sloops came in and they pretended, to pay *Roberts* a Visit, the Masters, whose Names were *Porter* and *Tuckerman*, addressed the Pyrate, as the Queen of *Sheba* did *Solomon*, to wit, *That having heard of his Fame and Atchievements*, they had put in there to learn his Art and Wisdom in the Business of pyrating, being Vessels of the same honourable Design with himself and hoped with the Communication of his Knowledge they should also receive his Charity, being in want of Necessaries for such Adventures. *Roberts* was won upon by the Peculiarity and Bluntness of these two Men, and gave them Powder, Arms, and what ever else they had Occasion for, spent two or three merry Nights with them, and at parting, said he hoped the L— *would Prosper their handy Works*. They passed some Time here, after they had got their Vessel ready, in their usual Debaucheries; they had taken a considerable Quanty of Rum and Sugar, so that Liquor was as plenty as Water, and few there were, who denied themselves the immoderate Use of it; nay, Sobriety brought a Man under a Suspicion of being in a Plot against the Commonwealth, and in their Sense, he was looked upon to be a Villain that would not be drunk. This was evident in the Affair of *Harry Glasby*, chosen Master of the *Royal Fortune*, who, with two others, laid hold of the Opportunity at the last Island they were at, to move off without bidding Farewel to his Friends. *Glasby* was a reserved sober Man, and therefore gave Occasion to be suspected, so that he was soon missed after he went away; and a Detachment being sent in quest of the Deserters, they were all three brought back again the next Day. This was a Capital Offence, and for which they were ordered to be brought to an immediate Tryal.

Here was the Form of Justice kept up, which is as much as can be said of several other Courts, that have more lawful Commissions for what they do.—Here was no seeing of Council, and bribing of Witnesses was a Custom not known among them; no packing of Juries, no torturing and wresting the Sense of the Law, for bye Ends and Purposes, no puzzling or perplexing the Cause with unintelligible canting Terms, and useless Distinctions; nor was their Sessions burthened with numberless officers, the Ministers of Rapine and Extortion, with ill boding Aspects, enough to fright *Astrea* from the Court.

The Place appointed for their Tryals, was the Steerage of the Ship; in order to which, a large Bowl of Rum Punch was made, and placed upon the Table, the Pipes and Tobacco being ready the judicial Proceedings began; the Prisoners were brought forth, and Articles of Indictment against them read; they were arraigned upon a statue of their own making, and the Letter of the Law being strong against them, and the Fact plainly proved, they were about to pronounce sentence when one of the Judges mov'd, that they should first Smoak t'other Pipe; which was accordingly done.

All the Prisoners pleaded for Arrest of judgment very movingly, but the Court had such an Abhorrence of their Crime, that they could not be prevailed upon to shew Mercy, till one of the Judges, whose Name was *Valentine Ashplant*, stood up, and taking his Pipe out of his Mouth, said he had something to offer to the Court in behalf of one of the Prisoners; and spoke to this Effect,—*By G*—, Glasby *shall not dye; d*—*n me if he shall*. After this learned Speech, he sat down in his Place, and resumed his Pipe. This motion was loudly opposed by all the rest of the Judges, in equivalent Terms; but *Ashplant*, who was resolute in his Opinion, made another pathetical Speech in the following Manner. *G*—*d*—*n ye Gentlemen, I am as good a Man as the best of you; d*—*n my S*—*I if ever I turned my Back to any Man in my Life, or ever will, by G*—*; Glasby is as honest Fellow, notwithstanding this Misfortune, and I love him, D*—*i d*—*n me if I don't: I hope he'll live and repent of what he has done; but d*—*n me if he must dye, I will dye along with him*. And thereupon, he pulled out a pair of Pistols, and presented them to some of the learned Judges upon the Bench; who, perceiving his Argument so well supported, thought it reasonable that *Glasby* should be acquitted; and so they all came over to his Opinion, and allowed it to be Law.

But all the Mitigation that could be obtained for the other

Prisoners, was, that they should have the Liberty of choosing any four of the whole Company to be their Executioners. The poor Wretches were ty'd immediately to the Mast, and there shot dead, pursuant to their villainous Sentence.

When they put to Sea again, the Prizes which had been detained only for fear of spreading any Rumour concerning them, which had like to have been so fatal at *Corvocoo*, were thus disposed of: They burnt their own Sloop, and mann'd *Norton*'s Brigantine, sending the Master away in the *Dutch* Interloper, not dissatisfied.

With the *Royal Fortune*, and the Brigantine, which they christened the *Good Fortune*, they pushed towards the Latitude of *Deseada*, to look out for Provisions, being very short again and just to their Wish, Captain *Hingstone*'s ill Fortune brought him in their Way, richly laden for *Jamaica*; him they carried to *Berbudas* and plundered; and stretching back again to the *West-Indies*, they continually met with some Consignment or other, (chiefly *French*,) which stored them with Plenty of Provisions, and recruited their starving Condition; so that stocked with this sort of Ammunition, they began to think of something worthier their Aim, for these Robberies that only supplied what was in constant Expenditure, by no Means answered their Intentions; and accordingly they proceeded again for the Coast of *Guiney* where they thought to buy Gold-Dust very cheap. In their Passage thither, they took Numbers of Ships of all Nations, some of which they burnt or sunk, as the Carriage or Character of the Masters displeased them.

Notwithstanding the successful Adventures of this Crew, yet it was with great Difficulty they could be kept together, under any kind of Regulation; for being almost always mad or drunk, their Behaviour produced infinite Disorders, every Man being in his own Imagination a Captain, a Prince, or a King. When *Roberts* saw there was no managing of such a Company of wild ungovernable Brutes, by gentle means, nor to keep them from drinking to excess, the Cause of all their Disturbances, he put on a rougher Deportment, and a more magesterial Carriage towards them, correcting whom he thought fit; and if any seemed to resent his Usage, he told them, *they might go ashore and take Satisfaction of him, if they thought fit, as Sword and Pistol, for he neither valu'd or feared any of them.*

About 400 Leagues from the Coast of *Africa*, the Brigantine who had hitherto lived with them, in all amicable Correspondence, thought fit to take the Opportunity of a dark Night, and leave the Commadore, which leads me back to the Relation of an Accident that happened at one of the Islands of the *West-Indies*, where they water'd before they undertook this Voyage, which had like to have thrown their Government (such as it was) off the Hinges, and was partly the Occasion of the Separation: The Story is as follows.

Captain *Roberts* having been insulted by one of the drunken Crew, (whose Name I have forgot,) he, in the Heat of his Passion killed the Fellow on the Spot, which was resented by a great many others, put particularly one *Jones*, a brisk active young Man, who died lately in the *Marshalsea*, and was his Mess-Mate. This *Jones* was at that Time ashore a watering the Ship, but as soon as he came on Board, was told that Captain *Roberts* had killed his Comrade; upon which he cursed *Roberts*, and said, he ought to be served so himself. *Roberts* hearing *Jones*'s Invective, ran to him with a Sword, and ran him into the Body; who, notwithstanding his Wound, seized the Captain, threw him over a Gun, and beat him handsomely. This Adventure put the whole Company in an Uproar, and some taking Part with the Captain, and others against him, there had like to have ensued a general Battle with one another, like my Lord *Thomant*'s Cocks; however, the Tumult was at length appeas'd by the Mediation of the Quarter-Master and as the Majority of the Company were of Opinion that the Dignity of the Captain, ought to be supported on Board; that it was a Post of Honour, and therefore the Person whom they thought fit to conser it on, should not be violated by any single Member; wherefore they sentenced *Jones* to undergo two Lashes from every one of the Company, for his Misdemeanour, which was executed upon him as soon as he was well of his Wound.

This severe Punishment did not at all convince *Jones* that he was in the wrong, but rather animated him to some sort of a Revenge; but not being able to do it upon *Roberts*'s Person, on Board the Ship, he and several of his Comrades, correspond with *Anstis*, Captain of the Brigantine, and conspire with him and some of the principal Pyrates on Board that Vessel, to go off from the Company. What made *Anstis* a Malecontent, was, the inferiority he stood in, with Respect to *Roberts*, who carried himself with a haughty and magisterial Air, to him and his Crew, he regarding the Brigantine only as a Tender, and, as such, left them no more than the Refuse of their Plunder. In short, *Jones* and his Consort go on Board of Captain *Anstis*, on Pretence of a Visit, and there consulting with their Brethren, they find a Majority for leaving of *Roberts*, and so came to a Resolution to bid a soft Farewel, as they call it, that Night, and to throw over-board whosoever should stick out, but they proved to be unanimous, and effected their Design as above-mentioned.

I shall have no more to say of Captain *Anstis*, till the Story of *Roberts* is concluded, therefore I return to him, in the pursuit of his Voyage to *Guiney*. The loss of the Brigantine was a sensible Shock to the Crew, she being an excellent Sailor, and had 70 Hands aboard; however, *Roberts* who was the Occasion of it, put on a Face of Unconcern at this his ill Conduct and Mismanagement, and resolved not to alter his Purposes upon that Account.

Roberts fell in to Windward nigh the *Senegal*, a River of great Trade for Gum, on this Part of the Coast, monopolized by the *French*, who constantly keep Cruisers, to hinder the interloping Trade: At this Time they had two small Ships on that Service, one of 10 Guns and 65 Men, and the other of 16 Guns and 75 Men; who having got a Sight of Mr. *Roberts*, and supposing him to be one of these prohibited Traders, chased with all the Sail they could make, to come up with him; but their Hopes which had brought them very nigh, too late deceived them, for on the hoisting of *Jolly Roger* (the Name they give their black Flag,) their *French* Hearts failed, and they both surrendred without any, or at least very little Resistance. With these Prizes they went into *Sierraleon*, and made one of them their Consort, by the Name of the *Ranger*, and the other a Store-Ship, to clean by.

Sierraleon River disgorges with a large Mouth the Starboard-Side of which, draughts into little Bays, safe and convenient for cleaning and watering; what still made it preferable to the Pyrate is, that the Traders settled here, are naturally their Friends. There are about 30 *English* Men in all, Men who in some Part of their Lives, have been either privateering, buccaneering, or pyrating, and still retain and love the Riots, and humours, common to that sort of Life. They live very friendly with the Natives, and have many of them of both Sexes, to be their *Gremetta's*, or Servants: The Men are faithful, and the Women so obedient, that they are very ready to prostitute themselves to whomsoever their Masters shall command them. The Royal *African* Company has a Fort on a small Island call'd *Bence* Island, but 'tis of little Use, besides keeping their Slaves; the Distance making it incapable of giving any Molestation to their Starboard Shore. Here lives at this Place an old Fellow, who goes by the Name of *Crackers*, who was formerly a noted Buccaneer, and while he followed the Calling, robb'd and plundered many a Man; he keeps the best House in the Place, has two or three Guns before his Door, with which he Salutes his Friends, (the Pyrates, when they put in) and lives a jovial Life with him, all the while they are there.

Here follows a List, of the rest of those lawless Merchants, and their Servants, who carry on a private Trade with the Interlopers, to the great Prejudice of the Royal *African* Company, who with extraordinary Industry and Expence, have made, and maintain, Settlements without any Consideration from those, who, without such Settlements and Forts, would soon be under an Incapacity of pursuing any such private

Trade. Wherefore, 'tis to be hop'd, proper Means will be taken, to root out a pernicious set of People, who have all their Lives, supported themselves by the Labours of other Men.

Two of these Fellows enter'd with *Robert's* Crew, and continued with them, till the Destruction of the Company.

A List of the White-Men, now living on the high-Land of Sierraleon, *and the Craft they occupy.*

JOHN Leadstone, three Boats and Periagoe.
His Man *Tom,*
His Man *John Brown.*
Alexander Middleton, one Long-Boat,
His Man *Charles Hawkins.*
John Pierce,
William Mead, } Partners, one Long-Boat.
Their Man *John Vernon.*
David Charmers, one Long-Boat.
John Chatmers, one Long-Boat.
Richard Richardson, one Long-Boat.
Norton,
Richard Warren, } Partners, two Long-Boats, and
Robert Glynn, } two small Boats.
His Man *John Franks.*
William Waits, and one young Man.
John Bonnerman.
John England, one Long-Boat.
Robers Samples, one Long-Boat.
William Presgrove,
Harry, } one Sloop, two Long-Boats, a
Davis, } small Boat, and Periagoe.
Mitchel,
Richard Lamb,
With *Roquis Rodrigus,* a *Portuguese*
George Bishop.
Peter Brown.

John Jones, one Long-Boat,
His *Irish* young Man.
At *Rio Pungo, Benjamen Gun.*
At *Kidham, George Teats.*
At *Gallyneas, Richard Lemmons.*

The Harbour is so convenient for Wooding and Watering, that it occasions many of our trading Ships, especially those of *Bristol*, to call in there, with large Cargoes of Beer, Syder, and strong Liquors, which they Exchange with these private Traders, for Slaves and Teeth, purchased by them at the *Rio Nune*'s, and other Places to the Northward, so that here was what they call good Living.

Hither *Roberts* came the End of *June*, 1721, and had Intelligence that the *Swallow*, and *Weymouth*, two Men of War, of 50 Guns each, had left that River about a Month before, and designed to return about *Christmas*; so that the Pyrates could indulge themselves with all the Satisfaction in the World, in that they knew they were not only secure whilst there, but that in going down the Coast, after the Men of War, they should always be able to get such Intelligence of their Rendezvous, as would serve to make their Expedition safe. So after six Weeks stay, the Ships being cleaned and fitted, and the Men weary of whoring and drinking; they bethought themselves of Business, and went to Sea the Beginning of *August*, taking their Progress down the whole Coast, as low as *Jaquin*, plundering every Ship they met, of what was valuable in her, and sometimes to be more mischieviously wicked, would throw what they did not want, overboard, accumulating Cruelty to Theft.

In this Range, they exchanged their old *French* Ship, for a fine Frigate built Ship, call'd the *Onslow*, belonging to the Royal *African* Company, Captain *Gee* Commander, which happened to lye at *Sastos* to get Water and Necessaries for the Company. A great many of Captain *Gee*'s Men were ashore, when *Robert*'s bore down, and so the Ship consequently surpriz'd into his Hands, tho' had they been all on

Board, it was not likely the Case would have been otherwise, the Sailors, most of them, voluntarily joyning the Pyrates, and encouraging the same Disposition in the Soldiers, (who were going Passengers with them to *Cape-Corso-Castle*) whose Ears being constantly tickled with the Feats and Gallantry of those Fellows, made them fancy, that *to go*, was only being bound on a Voyage of Knight Errantry (to relieve the Distress'd, and gather up Fame) and so they likewise offer'd themselves; but here the Pyrates were at a Stand, they entertain'd so contemptible a Notion of Landmen, that they put 'em off with Refusals for some time, till at length, being weary'd with Solicitations, and pittying a Parcel of stout Fellows, which they said, were going to starve upon a little Canky and Plantane, they accepted of them, and allow'd them ¼ Share, as it was then term'd out of Charity.

There was a Clergyman on Board the *Onslow*, sent from *England*, to be Chaplain of *Cape-Corso-Castle*, some of the Pyrates were for keeping him, alledging merrily, that their Ship wanted a Chaplain; accordingly they offered him a Share, to take on with them, promising, he should do nothing for his Money, but make Punch, and say Prayers; yet, however brutish they might be in other Things, they bore so great a Respect to his Order, that they resolved not to force him against his Inclinations; and the Parson having no Relish for this sort of Life, excused himself from accepting the Honour they designed him; they were satisfied, and generous enough to deliver him back every Thing he owned to be his: The Parson laid hold of this favourable Disposition of the Pyrates, and laid Claim to several Things belonging to others, which were also given up, to his great Satisfaction; in fine, they kept nothing which belonged to the Church, except three Prayer-Books, and a Bottle-Screw.

The Pyrates kept the *Onslow* for their own Use, and gave Captain *Gee* the *French* Ship, and then fell to making such Alterations as might fit her for a Sea-Rover, pulling down her Bulk-Heads, and making her flush, so that she became, in all Respects, as compleat a Ship for their Purpose, as any they could have found; they continued to her the Name of the *Royal Fortune*, and mounted her with 40 Guns.

She and the *Ranger* proceeded (as I said before,) to *Jaquin*, and from thence to *Old Calabar*, where they arrived about *October*, in order to clean their Ships, a Place the most suitable along the whole Coast, for there is a Bar with not above 15 Foot Water upon it, and the Channel intricate, so that had the Men of War been sure of their being harbour'd here, they might still have bid Defiance to their Strength, for the Depth of Water at the Bar, as well as the want of a Pilot, was a sufficient Security to the Rovers, and invincible Impediments to them. Here therefore they sat easy, and divided the Fruits of their dishonest Industry, *and drank and drove Card away.* The Pilot who brought them into this Harbour, was Captain L—e, who for this, and other Services, was extreamly well paid, according to the Journal of their own Accounts, which do not run in the ordinary and common way, of *Debtor, contra Creditor,* but much more concise, lumping it to their Friends, and so carrying the Debt in their Heads, against the next honest Trader they meet.

They took at *Calabar*, Captain *Loane* and two or three *Bristol* Ships, the Particulars of all which would be an unnecessary Prolixity, therefore I come now to give an Account of the Usage they received from the Natives of this Place. The *Calabar* Negroes did not prove so civil as they expected, for they refused to have any Commerce or Trade with them, when they understood they were Pyrates: An Indication that these poor Creatures in the narrow Circumstances they were in, that without the Light of the Gospel, or the Advantage of an Education, have, notwithstanding, such a moral innate Honesty, as would upbraid and shame the most knowing Christian: But this did but exasperate these lawless Fellows, and so a Party of 40 Men were detach'd to force to Correspondence, or drive: the Negroes to Extremities, and they accordingly landed under the Fire of their own Cannon. The Negroes drew up in a Body of 2000 Men, as if they intended to dispute the Matter with them, and staid till the Pyrates advanced within Pistol-shot; but finding the Loss of two or three made no Impression on the rest, the Negroes thought fit to retreat, which they did, with some Loss: The Pyrates set Fire to the Town, and then return'd to their Ships. This terrified the Natives, and put an entire stop to all the Intercourse between them; so that they could get no supplies, which obliged them, as soon as they had finished the cleaning and triming of their Ships, to lose no Time, but went for Cape *Lopez* and watered, and at *Anna-Bona* took aboard a stock of fresh Provisions, and then sailed for the Coast again.

This was their last and fatal Expedition, which we shall be more particular in, because, it cannot be imagined that they could have had Assurance to have undertaken it, but upon a Presumption that the Men of War, (whom they knew were upon the Coast,) were unable to attack them, or else pursuant to the Rumour that had indiscretionally obtained at *Sierraleon* were gone thither again.

It is impossible at this Time, to think they could know of the weak and sickly Condition they were in, and therefore founded the Success of this second Attempt upon the Coast, on the latter Presumption, and this seems to be confirmed by their falling in with the Coast as low as Cape *Lahou*, (and even that was higher than they designed,) in the beginning of *January*, and took the Ship called the *King Solomon*, with 20 Men in their Boat, and a trading Vessel, both belonging to the Company. The Pyrate Ship happened to fall about a League to Leeward of the *King Solomon*, at Cape *Appollonia*, and the Current and Wind opposing their working up with the Ship, they agreed to send the Long-Boat, with a sufficient Number of Men to take her: The Pyrates are all Volunteers on these Occasions, the Word being always given, *who will go?* And presently the stanch and firm Men offer themselves; because, by such Readiness, they recommend their Courage, and have an Allowance also of a Shift of Cloaths, from Head to Foot, out of the Prize.

They rowed towards the *King Solomon* with a great deal

of Alacrity, and being hailed by the Commander of her; answered *Defiance*, Captain *Trahern*, before this, observing a great Number of Men in the Boat, began not to like his Visitors and prepared to receive them, firing a Musket as they come under his Stern, which they returned with a Volley, and made greater Speed to get on Board. Upon this, he applied to his Men, and ask'd them, whether they would stand by him, to defend the Ship, it being a Shame they should be taken by half their Number, without any repulse. But his Boatswain, *Phillips*, took upon him to be the Mouth of the People, and put an end to the Dispute. He said plainly he would not, laid down his arms in the King's Name, as he was pleased to term it, and called out to the Boat for Quarters, so that the rest, by his example, were misled to the losing of the Ship.

When they came Abroad they brought her under Sail, by an expeditious method of cutting the Cable; *Walden*, one of the Pirates, telling the Master this Hope of heaving up the Anchor was a needless Trouble, when they designed to burn the Ship. They brought her under Commodore *Robert's* Stern, and not only rifled her of what Sails, Cordage, &c. they wanted for themselves, but wantonly throwed the Goods of the Company overboard, like Spend-Thrifts, that neither expected or designed any account.

On the same Day also, they took the *Flushing*, a Dutch Ship, robbed her of Masts, Yards and Stores, and then cut down her Fore-mast; but what sat as heavily as anything with the Skipper, was, their taking some fine Sausages he had on Board, of his Wife's making, and stringing them in a ludicrous Manner round their Necks, till they had sufficiently showed their Contempt of them, and then threw them into the Sea. Others chopped the Heads of his Fowls off to be dressed for their Supper, and courteously invited the Landlord, provided he would find Liquor. It was a melancholy request to the Man, but it must be complied with, and he was obliged, as they grew drunk, to sit quietly, and hear them sing *French* and *Spanish* Songs out of his *Dutch* Prayer

Books, with other Prophanes, that he (though a *Dutch* man) stood amazed at.

In chasing too near in, they alarmed the Coast, and Expresses were sent to the *English* and *Dutch* Factories, giving an Account of it. They were sensible of this Error immediately, and because they would make the best of a bad Market, resolved to keep out of Sight of Land, and lose the Prizes they might expect between that and *Whydah*, to make the more more sure of that port, where commonly is the best booty; all nations trading thither, especially *Portugueze* who purchase chiefly with Gold, the idol their Hearts were bent upon. And notwithstanding this unlikely course, they met and took several Ships between *Axim* and that place; the circumstantial Stories of which, and the pannic Terrors they struck into His Majesty's Subjects, being tedious and unnecessary to relate, I shall pass by, and come to their arrival in that road.

They came to *Whydah* with a St. *George's* ensign, a black silk Flag flying at their mizzen-peak, and a Jack and Pendant of the same. The Flag had a Death in it, with an Hour-Glass in one Hand, and Cross Bones in the other, a Dart by it, and underneath a Heart dropping three drops of Blood. The Jack had a man portrayed in it, with a flaming Sword in his hand, and standing on two Skulls, subscribed *A.B.H.* and *A.M.H. i. e.* a *Barbadian's* and a *Martinican's* Head, as has been before taken notice of. Here they found in Sail in the Road, *English, French,* and *Portugueze*; the *French* were three stout Ships of 30 guns, and upwards of 100 men each, yet when Roberts came to fire, they, with the other Ships, immediately struck their Colours and surrendered to his Mercy. One reason, it must be confessed, of his easy Victory, was, the Commanders and a good part of the Men being ashore, according to the Custom of the Place, to receive the Cargoes, and return the Slaves, they being obliged to watch the Seasons for it, which otherwise, in so dangerous a Sea as here, would be impracticable. These all, except the *Porcupine*, ransomed with him for eight Pound of Gold-Dust, a Ship, not without the trouble of some Letters passing and repassing from the Shore, before they could settle it; and notwithstanding the Agreement and Payment, they took away one of the *French* Ships, tho' with a Promise to return her, if they found she did not sail well, taking with them several of her Men for that End.

Some of the Foreigners, who never had Dealing this Way before, desired for Satisfaction to their Owners, that they might have Receipts for their Money, which were accordingly given, a Copy of one of them, I have here subjoined, *viz.*

This is to certify whom it may or doth concern, that we GEN-TLEMEN OF FORTUNE, *have received eight Pounds of Gold-Dust, for the Ransom of the* Hardey, *Captain* Dittwitt *Commander, so that we Discharge the said Ship,*

Witness our Hands, this	Batt. Roberts,
13th of Jan. 1721–2.	Harry Glasby.

Others were given to the *Portuguese* Captains, which were in the same Form, but being sign'd by two waggish Fellows, *viz. Sutton*, and *Sympson*, they subscribed by the Names of,

Aaron Whifflingpin
Sim. Tugmutton

But there was something so singularly cruel and barbarous done here to the *Porcupine*, Captain *Fletcher*, as must not be passed over without special Remark.

This Ship lay in the Road, almost slaved, when the Pyrates came in, and the Commander being on Shore, settling his Accounts, was sent to for the Ransom, but he excused it, as having no Orders from the Owners; though the true Reason might be, that he thought it dishonourable to treat with Robbers; and that the Ship, separate from the Slaves, towards whom he could mistrust no Cruelty, was not worth the Sum demanded; hereupon, *Roberts* sends the Boat to transport the Negroes, in order to set her on Fire; but being in hast, and finding that unshackling them cost much Time and Labour, they actually set her on Fire, with eighty of those poor Wretches on Board, chained two and two together, under the miserable Choice of perishing by Fire or Water: Those who jumped overboard from the Flames, were seized by Sharks, a voracious Fish, in Plenty in this Road, and, in their Sight, tore Limb from Limb alive. A Cruelty unparalell'd! And for which had every Individual been hanged, few I imagine would think that Justice had been rigorous.

The Pyrates, indeed, were obliged to dispatch their Business here in hast, because they had intercepted a Letter from General *Phips* to Mr. *Baldwin*, the Royal *African* Company's Agent at *Whydah*, (giving an Account, that *Roberts* had been seen to Windward of Cape *Three Points*,) that he might the better guard against the Damages to the Company's Ships, if he should arrive at that Road before the *Swallow* Man of War, which he assured him, (at the Time of that Letter,) was pursuing them to that Place. *Roberts* call'd up his Company, and desired they would hear *Phip*'s Speech, (for so he was pleased to call the Letter,) and notwithstanding their vapouring, perswaded them of the Necessity of moving; for, says he, such brave Fellows cannot be supposed to be frightned at this News, yet that it were better to avoid dry Blows, which is the best that can be expected, if overtaken.

This Advice weigh'd with them, and they got under Sail, having stay'd only from *Thursday* to *Saturday* Night, and at Sea voted for the Island of *Anna Bona*; but the Winds hanging out of the Way, crossed their Purpose, and brought them to Cape *Lopez*, where I shall leave them for their approaching Fate, and relate some further Particulars of his Majesty's Ship the *Swallow, viz.* where it was she had spent her Time, during the Mischief, that was done, and by what Means unable to prevent it; what also was the Intelligence she received, and the Measures thereon formed, that at last brought two such Strangers as Mr *Roberts* and Capt. *Ogle*, to meet in so remote a Corner of the World.

The *Swallow* and *Weymouth* left *Sierraleon, May* 28, where, I have already taken Notice, *Roberts* arrived about a Month after, and doubtless learn'd the Intent of their Voyage, and cleaning on the Coast; which made him set down with more Security to his Diversion, and furnish him with such Intimations, as made his first Range down the Coast in *August*, following, more prosperous; the *Swallow* and *Weymouth* being then at the Port of *Princes* a cleaning.

Their Stay at *Princes* was from *July* 28 to *Sept.* 20, 1721, where, by a Fatality, common to the Irregularities of Seamen, (who cannot in such Cases be kept under due Restraints,) they buried 100 Men in three Weeks time, and reduced the Remainder of the Ships Companies into so sickly a State, that it was with Difficulty they brought them to sail; and this Misfortune was probably the Ruin of *Roberts*, for it prevented the Men of War's going back to *Sierraleon*, as it was intended, there being a Necessity of leaving his Majesty's Ship *Weymouth* (in much the worse Condition of the two) under the Guns of Cape *Corso*, to impress Men, being unable at this Time, either to hand the Sails, or weigh her Anchor; and *Roberts* being ignorant of the Occasion or Alteration of the first Design, fell into the Mouth of Danger, when he thought himself the farthest from it; for the Men of War not endeavouring to attain further to Windward (when they came from *Princes*) then to secure Cape *Corso* Road under their Lee, they luckily hovered in the Track he had took.

The *Swallow* and *Weymouth* fell in with the Continent at Cape *Appollonia, Octo.* 20th, and there received the ungrateful News from one Captain *Bird*; a Notice that awaken'd and put them on their Guard; but they were far from expecting any Temerity should ever bring him a second Time on the Coast, while they were there; therefore the *Swallow* having seen the *Weymouth* into Cape *Corso* Road *Nov.* 10th, she ply'd to Windward as far as *Bassam*, rather as an Airing to recover a sickly Ship's Company, and shew herself to the Trade, which was found every where undisturb'd, and were for that Reason, returning to her Consort, when accidently meeting a *Portuguese* Ship, she told her, that the Day before she saw two Ships Chace into *Junk*, an *English* Vessel, which she believed must have fallen into their Hands. On this Story, the *Swallow* clung her Wind, and endeavoured to gain that Place, but receiving soon after (*Octo.* the 14th) a contrary Report from Captain *Plummer*, an intelligent Man, in the *Jason* of *Bristal*, who had come further to Windward, and neither saw or heard any Thing of this; she turned her Head down the second Time, anchored at Cape *Appollonia* the 23d, at Cape *Tres Puntas* the 27th, and in *Corso* Road *January* the 7th, 1721-2.

They learned that their Consort the *Weymouth*, was, by the Assistance of some Soldiers from the Castle, gone to Windward, to demand Restitution of some Goods or Men belonging to the *African* Company, that were illegally detained by the *Dutch* at *Des Minas*; and while they were regretting so long a Separation, an Express came to General *Phips*, from *Axim*, the 9th, and followed by another from *Dixcove*, (an *English* Factory,) with Information that three Ships had chased and taken a Galley nigh *Axim* Castle, and a trading Boat belonging to the Company: No doubt was made, concerning what they were, it being taken for granted they were Pyrates, and supposed to be the same that had the *August* before infested the Coast. The natural Result therefore, from these two Advices, was, to hasten for *Whydah*; for it was concluded the Prizes they had taken, had informed them how nigh the *Swallow* was, and withal, how much better in Health than she had been for some Months past; so that unless they were very mad indeed, they would (after being discovered) make the best of their Way for *Whydah*, and secure the Booty there, without which, their Time and Industry had been entirely lost; most of the Gold lying in that Corner.

The *Swallow* weighed from *Cape-Corso, January* the 10th, but was retarded by waiting some Hours on the *Margaret*, a Company's Ship, at *Accra*, again on the *Portugal*, and a whole Day at *Apong*, on a Person they used to stile *Miss Betty*; A Conduct that Mr. *Phips* blamed, when he heard the Pyrates were miss'd at *Whydah*, altho' he had given it as his Opinion, they could not be passed by, and intimated, that to stay a few Hours would prove no Prejudice.

This, however, hinder'd the *Swallow*'s catching them at *Whydah*, for the Pyrates came into that Road, with a fresh Gale of Wind, the same Day the *Swallow* was at *Apong*, and sail'd the 13th of *January* from thence, that she arrived the 17th She gained Notice of them by a *French* Shallop from *Grand Papa*, the 14th at Night, and from *Little Papa* next Morning by a *Dutch* Ship; so that the Man of War was on all Sides, as she thought, sure of her Purchase, particularly when she made the Ships, and discovered three of them to get under Sail immediately at Sight of her, making Signals to one another, as tho' they designed a Defence; but they were found to be three *French* Ships; and those at Anchor, *Portuguese* and *English*, all honest Traders, who had been ransack'd and ransom'd.

This Disappointment chagreen'd the Ship's Company, who were very intent upon their Market; which was reported to be an Arm-Chest full of Gold, and kept with three Keys; tho' in all liklyhood, had they met with them in that open Road, one or both would have made their Escapes; or if they had thought fit to have fought, an Emulation in their Defence would probably have made it desperate.

While they were contemplating on the Matter, a Letter was received from Mr. *Baldwin*, (Governor here for the Company,) signifying, that the Pyrates were at *Jaquin*, seven Leagues lower. The *Swallow* weighed at two next Morning, *January* the 16th, and got to *Jaquin* by Day-Light, but to no other End, than frightening the Crews of two *Portuguese* Ships on Shore, who took her for the Pyrate that had struck such Terror at *Whydah*. She returned therefore that Night, and having been strengthened with thirty Voluntiers, *English* and *French*, the discarded Crews of the *Porcupine*, and the *French* Ship they had carried from hence, she put to Sea again *January* the 19th, conjecturing, that either *Calabar*, *Princes*, the River *Gabone*, Cape *Lopez*, or *Annabona*, must be touched at for Water and Refreshment, tho' they should resolve to leave the Coast. As to the former at those Places, I have before observed, it was hazardous to think of, or rather impracticable; *Princes* had been a sower Grape to them, but being the first in the Way, she came before the Harbour the 20th, where learning no News, without loosing Time, steered for the River *Gabone*, and anchored at the Mouth of it *February* the 1st.

This River is navigable by two Channels, and has an Island about five Leagues up, called *Popaguays* or *Parrots*, where the *Dutch* Cruisers, for this Coast generally Clean, and where sometimes Pyrates come in to look for Prey, or to Refit, it being very convenient, by Reason of a soft Mud about it, that admits a Ship's lying on Shore, with all her Guns and Stores in, without Damage. Hither Captain *Ogle* sent his Boat and a Lieutenant, who spoke with a *Dutch* Ship, above the Island, from whom he had this Account, *viz.* That he had been four Days from Cape *Lopez*, and had left no Ship there. However, they beat up for the Cape, without regard to this Story, and on the 5th, at Dawning, was surprized with the Noise of a Gun, which as the Day brightened, they found was from Cape *Lopez* Bay, where they discovered three Ships at Anchor, the largest with the King's Colours and Pendant flying, which was soon after concluded to be Mr. *Roberts* and his Consorts; but the *Swallow* being to Windward, and unexpectedly deep in the Bay, was obliged to Steer off, for avoiding a Sand, called the *French Man's Bank*, which the Pyrates observed for some Time, and rashly interpreting it to be Fear in her, righted the *French Ranger*, which was then on the Heel, and ordered her to chase out in all hast, bending several of their Sails in the Pursuit. The Man of War finding they had foolishly mistaken her Design, humoured the Deceit, and kept off to Sea, as if she had been really afraid, and managed her Steerage so under the Direction of Lieutenant *Sun*, an experienced Officer, as to let the *Ranger* come up with her, when they thought they had got so far as not to have their Guns heard by her Consort at the Cape. The Pyrates had such an Opinion of their own Courage, that they could never dream any Body would use a Stratagem to speak with them, and so was the more easily drawn into the Snare.

The Pyrates now drew nigh enough to fire their Chase Guns; they hoisted the black Flag that was worn in *Whydah* Road, and got their Spritsail Yard along-ships, with Intent to board; no one having ever asked, all this while, what Country Ship they took the Chase to be; they would have her to be a *Portuguese*, (Sugar being then a Commodity among them,) and were swearing every Minute at the Wind or Sails to expedite so sweet a Chase; but, alass, all turned sour in an Instant: It was with the utmost Consternation they saw her suddenly bring to; and hawl up her lower Ports, now within Pistol-shot, and struck their black Flag upon it directly. After the first Surprize was over, they kept firing at a Distance, hoisted it again, and vapoured with their Cutlashes on the Poop; tho' wisely endeavouring at the same Time to get away. Being now at their Wits end, boarding was proposed by the Heads of them, and so to make one desperate Push; but the Motion not being well, seconded, and their Main-Top-Mast coming down by a Shot, after two Hours firing, it was declin'd; they grew Sick, struck their Colours, and called out for Quarters; having had 10 Men killed out right, and 20 wounded, without the loss or hurt of one of the King's Men. She had 32 Guns, mann'd with 16 *French* Men, 20 Negroes, and 77 *English*. The Colours were thrown over board, that they might not rise in Judgment, nor be display'd in Tryumph over them.

While the *Swallow* was sending their Boat to fetch the Prisoners, a Blast and Smoak was seen to pour out of the great Cabin, and they thought they were blowing up; but upon enquiry afterwards, found that half a dozen of the most Desperate, when they saw all Hopes fled; had drawn themselves round what Powder they had left in the Steerage, and fired a Pistol into it, but it was too small a Quantity to effect any Thing more, than burning them in a frightful Manner.

This Ship was commanded by one *Skyrme*, a *Welch* Man, who, tho' he had lost his Leg in the Action, would not suffer himself to be dressed, or carried off the Deck; but, like *Wid-rington*, fought upon his Stump. The rest appeared gay and brisk, most of them with white Shirts, Watches, and a deal of Silk Vests, but the Gold-Dust belonging to them, was most of it left in the *Little Ranger* in the Bay, (this Company's proper Ship,) with the *Royal Fortune*.

I cannot but take Notice of two among the Crowd, of those disfigured from the Blast of Powder just before mentioned, *viz. William Main* and *Roger Ball*. An Officer of the Ship seeing a silver Call hang at the Wast of the former, said to him, *I presume you are Boatswain of this Ship. Then you presume wrong*, answered he, *for I am Boatswain of the* Royal Fortune, *Captain* Roberts *Commander*. Then *Mr*. Boatswain *you will be hanged I believe*, replied the Officer. *That is as your Honour pleases*, answered he again, and was for turning away: But the Officer desired to know of him, how the Powder, which had made them in that Condition, came to take Fire. —*By G—* says he, *they are all mad and bewitched, for I have lost a good Hat by it*. (the Hat and he being both blown out of the Cabin Gallery, into the Sea.) *But what signifies a Hat Friend*, says the Officer. — *Not much* answer'd he, the Men being busy in stripping him of his Shoes and Stockings.—The Officer then enquired of him, whether *Roberts*'s Company were as likely Fellows as these.— *There are 120 of them*, (answered he) *as clever Fellows as ever trod Shoe Leather: Would I were with them! —No doubt on's*, says the Officer. —*By G —it is naked Truth*, answered he, looking down and seeing himself, by this Time, quite striped.

The Officer then approached *Roger Ball*, who was seated in a private Corner, with a Look as sullen as Winter, and asked him, how he came blown up in that frightful Manner. —*Why*, says he, John Morris *fired a Pistol into the Powder, and if he had not done it, I would*, (bearing his Pain without the least Complaint.) The Officer gave him to understand he was Surgeon, and if he desired it, he would dress him; but he swore it should not be done, and that if any Thing was applied to him, he would tear it off—Nevertheless the Surgeon had good Nature enough to dress him, tho' with much trouble: At Night he was in a kind of *Delirium*, and raved on the Bravery of *Roberts*, saying, he should shortly be released, as soon as they should meet him, which procured him a lashing down upon the Forecastle, which he resisting with all his Force, caused him to be used with the more Violence, so that he was tied down with so much Severity, that his Flesh being sore and tender with the blowing up, he died next Day of a Mortification.

They secured the Prisoners with Pinions, and Shackles, but the Ship was so much disabled in the Engagement, that they had once Thoughts to set her on Fire; but this would have given them the Trouble of taking the Pyrates wounded Men on Board themselves, and that they were certain the *Royal Fortune* would wait for their Consort's Return, they lay by her two Days, repaired her Rigging and other Damages, and sent her into *Princes*, with the *French* Men, and four of their own Hands.

On the 9th in the Evening, the *Swallow* gained the Cape again, and saw the *Royal Fortune* standing into the Bay with the *Neptune*, Captain *Hill*, of *London*: A good Presage of the next Day's Success; for they did not doubt but the Temptation of Liquor, and Plunder, they might find in this their new Prize, would make the Pyrates very confused; and so it happened.

On the 10th, in the Morning, the Man of War bore away to round the Cape. *Roberts*'s Crew discerning their Masts over the Land, went down into the Cabin, to acquaint him of it, he being then at Breakfast with his new Guest, Captain *Hill*, on a savory Dish of Solomongundy, and some of his own Beer. He took no Notice of it, and his Men almost as little, some saying she was a *Portuguese* Ship, others a *French* Slave Ship, but the major Part swore it was the *French Ranger* returning, and were merrily debating for some Time on the Manner of Reception, whether they should salute, or not; but as the *Swallow* approached nigher, Things appeared plainer, and though they were stigmatiz'd with the Name of Cowards, who shewed any Apprehension of Danger, yet some of them, now undeceived, declared it to *Roberts*, especially one *Armstrong*, who had deserted from that Ship, and knew her well: Those *Roberts* swore at as Cowards, who meant to dishearten the Men, asking them if it were so, whether they were afraid to fight, or no? And hardly refrained from Blows. What his own Apprehensions were, till she hawled up her Ports, and hoisted their proper Colours, is uncertain; but then being perfectly convinced, he slipped his Cable, got under Sail, and ordered his Men to Arms, without any shew of Timidity, dropping a first Rate Oath, *that it was a Bite*, but, at the same Time, resolved, like a gallant Rogue, to get clear, or die.

There was one *Armstrong*, as I just mention'd, a Deserter from the *Swallow*, whom they enquired of concerning the Trim and Sailing of that Ship; he told them she sail'd best upon a Wind, and therefore, if they designed to leave her, they should go before it.

The Danger was imminent, and Time very short, to consult of Means to extricate himself; his Resolution in this Streight, was as follows: To pass close to the *Swallow*, with all their Sails, and receive her Broadside, before they returned a Shot; if disabled by this, or that they could not depend on sailing, then to run on Shore at the Point, (which is steep to) and every one to shift for himself among the Negroes; or failing in these, to board, and blow up together, for he saw that the greatest Part of his Men were drunk, passively Couragious, unfit for Service.

Roberts himself made a gallant Figure, at the Time of the Engagement, being dressed in a rich crimson Damask Wastcoat and Breeches, a red Feather in his Hat, a Gold Chain round his Neck, with a Diamond Cross hanging to it, a Sword in his Hand, and two Pair of Pistols hanging at the End of a Silk Sling, slung over his Shoulders (according to the Fashion of the Pyrates;) and is said to have given his Orders with Boldness, and Spirit; coming, according to what he had purposed, close to the Man of War, received her Fire, and then hoisted his Black Flag, and returned it, shooting away from her, with all the Sail he could pack; and had he took *Armstrong's* Advice, to have gone before the Wind; he had probably es-

caped; but keeping his Tacks down, either by the Winds shifting, or ill Steerage, or both, he was taken a-back with his Sails;
and the *Swallow* came a second Time very nigh to him: He
had now perhaps finished the Fight very desperately, if Death,
who took a swift Passage in a Grape-Shot, had not interposed,
and struck him directly on the Throat. He settled himself on
the Tackles of a Gun, which one *Stephenson*, from the Helm,
observing, ran to his Assistance, and not perceiving him
wounded, swore at him, and bid him stand up and fight like
a Man; but when he found his Mistake, and that his Captain
was certainly dead, he gushed into Tears, and wished the next
Shot might be his Lot. They presently threw him over-board
with his Arms and Ornaments on, according to the repeated
Request he made in his Life-time.

Roberts was a tall black Man, near forty Years of Age, born
at *Newey-bagh*, nigh *Haverford-West* in *Pembrokshire*, of
good natural Parts, and personal Bravery, tho' he applied
them to such wicked Purposes, as made them of no Commendation, frequently drinking *D——n to him who ever
lived to wear a Halter.* He was forc'd himself at first among
this Company out of the *Prince*, Captain *Plumb* at *Anamaboe*,
about three Years before, where he served as second Mate,
and shed, as he us'd to tell the fresh *Men*, as many Crocodile
Tears then as they did now, but Time and good Company
had wore it off. He could not plead Want of Employment,
nor Incapacity of getting his Bread in an honest way, to
favour so vile a Change, nor was he so much a Coward as
to pretend it; but frankly own'd, it was to get rid of the
disagreeable Superiority of some Masters he was acquainted
with, and the Love of Novelty and Change, Maritime Per-
egrinations had accustom'd him to. *In an honest Service*, says
he, *there is thin Commons, low Wages, and hard Labour; in
this, Plenty and Society, Pleasure and Ease, Liberty and Power;
and who would not balance Creditor on this side when all the
Hazard that is run for it, at worst, is only a four Look or two
at choaking. No*, A merry Life and a short one, *shall be my
Motto.* Thus he preach'd himself into an Approbation of

what he at first abhorr'd; and being daily regal'd with Musick, Drinking, and the Gaiety and Diversions of his Companions, these deprav'd Propensities were quickly edg'd and
strengthen'd, to the extinguishing of Fear and Conscience.
Yet among all the vile and ignominious Acts he had per-
petrated, he is said to have had an Aversion towards forcing
Men into that Service, and had procured some their Discharge, notwithstanding so many made it their Plea.

When *Roberts* was gone, as tho' he had been the Life and
Soul of the Gang, their Spirits' sunk; many deserted their
Quarters, and all stupidly neglected any Means for Defence,
or Escape; and their Main-mast soon after being shot by the
Board, they had no Way left, but to surrender and call for
Quarters. The *Swallow* kept aloof, while her Boat passed,
and repassed for the Prisoners; because they understood they
were under an Oath to blow up; and some of the Desperadoes shewed a Willingness that Way, Matches being lighted,
and Scuffles happening between those who would, and those
who opposed it: But I cannot easily account for this Humour, which can be term'd no more than a false Courage,
since any of them had Power to destroy his own Life, either
by Pistol, or Drowning, without involving others in the same
Fate, who are in no Temper of Mind for it: And at best, it
had been only dying, for fear of Death.

She had 40 Guns, and 157 Men, 45 whereof were Negroes; three only were killed in the Action, without any Loss
to the *Swallow*. There was found upwards of 2000 *l.* in
Gold-Dust in her. The Flag could not be got easily from
under the fallen Mast, and was therefore recover'd by the
Swallow; it had the Figure of a Skeleton in it, and a Man
pourtray'd with a flaming Sword in his Hand, intimating a
Defyance of Death it self.

The *Swallow* returned back into Cape *Lopez* Bay, and
found the little *Ranger*, whom the Pyrates had deserted in
hast, for the better Defence of the Ship: She had been plunder'd, according to what I could learn, of 2000 l. in Gold-
Dust; (the Shares of those Pyrates who belonged to her;) and

Captain *Hill* in the *Neptune*, not unjustly suspected, for he would not wait the Man of War's returning into the Bay again, but sail'd away immediately, making no Scruple afterwards to own the Seizure of other Goods out of her, and surrender'd, as a Confirmation of all, 50 Ounces at *Barbadoes*, for which, see the Article at the End of this Book.

All Persons who after the 29th of Septem. 1690, &c.

To sum up the whole, if it be considered, first, that the sickly State of the Men of War, when they sail'd from *Princes*, was the Misfortune that hindered their being as far as *Sierraleon*, and consequently out of the Track the Pyrates then took. That those Pyrates, directly contrary to their Design, in the second Expedition, should get above Cape *Corso*, and that nigh *Axim*, a Chace should offer, that inevitably must discover them, and be soon communicated to the Men of War. That the satiating their evil and malicious Tempers at *Whydab*, in burning the *Porcupine*, and running off with the *French* Ship, had strengthened the *Swallow* with 30 Men. That the *Swallow* should miss them in that Road, where probably she had not, or at least so effectually obtained her End. That they should be so far infatuated at Cape *Lopez*, as to divide their Strength, which when collected, might have been so formidable. And lastly, that the Conquest should be without Bloodshed: I say, considering all these Circumstances, it shews that the Hand of Providence was concerned in their Destruction.

As to their Behaviour after they were taken, it was found that they had great Inclinations to rebel, if they could have laid hold of any Opportunity. For they were very uneasy under Restraint, having been lately all Commanders themselves; nor could they brook their Diet, or Quarters, without cursing and swearing, and upbraiding each other, with the Folly that had brought them to it.

So that to secure themselves against any mad desperate Undertaking of theirs, they strongly barricado'd the Gun-Room, and made another Prison before it; an Officer, with Pistols and Cutlashes, doing Duty, Night and Day, and the Prisoners within, manacled and shackled.

They would yet in these Circumstances be impudently merry, saying, when they viewed their Nakedness, *that they had not left them a halfpenny, to give old* Charon, *to ferry them over* Stix: And at their thin Commons, they would observe, that they fell away so fast, that they should not have Weight left to hang them. *Sutton* used to be very prophane; he happening to be in the same Irons with another Prisoner, who was more serious than ordinary, and read and pray'd often, as became his Condition; this Man *Sutton* used to swear at, and ask him, *what he proposed by so much Noise and Devotion? Heaven*, says the other, *I hope. Heaven, you Fool*, says *Sutton, did you ever hear of any Pyrates going whither? Give me H—ll, it's a merrier Place: I'll give* Roberts *a Salute of 13 Guns at Entrance*. And when he found such ludicrous Expressions had no Effect on him, he made a formal Complaint, and requested that the Officer would either remove this Man, or take his Prayer-Book away, as a common Disturber.

A Combination and Conspiracy was formed, betwixt *Moody, Ashplant, Magnes, Mare*, and others, to rise, and kill the Officers, and run away with the Ship. This they had carried on by Means of a Mulatto Boy, who was allow'd to attend them, and proved very trusty in his Messages, between the Principals; but the Evening of that Night they were to have made this Struggle, two of the Prisoners that sat next to *Ashplant*, heard the Boy whisper them upon the Project, and naming to him the Hour they should be ready, presently gave Notice of it to the Captain, which put the Ship in an Alarm, for a little Time; and, on Examination, several of them had made shift to break off, or lose, their Shackles, (no doubt for such Purpose;) but it tended only to procure to themselves worse Usage and Confinement.

In the same Passage to Cape *Corso*, the Prize, *Royal Fortune*, was in the same Danger. She was left at the island of St. *Thomas's*, in the Possession of an Officer, and a few Men, to take in some fresh Provisions, (which were scarce at Cape *Corso*) with Orders to follow the Ship. There were only some of the Pyrates Negroes, three or four wounded Prisoners, and *Scudamore*, their Surgeon; from whom they seemed to be under no Apprehension, especially from the last, who might have hoped for Favour, on Account of his Employ; and had stood so much indebted for his Liberty, eating and drinking constantly with the Officer; yet this Fellow, regardless of the Favour, and lost to all Sense of Reformation, endeavored to bring over the Negroes to his Design of murdering the People, and running away with the Ship. He easily prevailed with the Negroes to come into the Design; but when he came to communicate it to his Fellow Prisoners, and would have drawn them into the same Measures, by telling them, he understood, Navigation, that the Negroes were stout Fellows, and by a Smattering he had in the *Angolan* Language, he had found willing to undertake such an Enterprize and that it was better venturing to do this, run down the Coast, and raise a new Company, than to proceed to Cape *Corso*, and be hanged like a Dog, and Sun dry'd. One of them abhorring the Cruelty, or fearing the Success, discovered it to the Officer, who made him immediately a Prisoner, and brought the Ship safe.

When they came to be lodg'd in Cape *Corso-Castle*, their Hopes of this kind all cut off, and that they were assured they must there soon receive a final Sentence; the Note was changed among most of them, and from vain insolent jesting, they became serious and devout, begging for good Books, and joyning in publick Prayers, and singing of Psalms, twice at least every Day.

As to their Tryals, if we should give them at length, it may appear tedious to the Reader, for which Reason, I have, for the avoiding Tautology and Repetition, put as many of them together as were try'd for the same Fact, reserving the Circumstances which are most material, with Observations on the dying Behaviour of such of them, as came to my Knowledge.

And first, it may be observed from the List, that a great Part of these Pyrate Ships Crews, were Men entered on the Coast of *Africa*, not many Months before they were taken; from whence, it may be concluded, that the pretended Constraint of *Roberts*, on them, was very often a Complotment between Parties equally willing: And this *Roberts* several Times openly declared, particularly to the *Onslow's* People, whom he called aft, and ask'd of them, *who was willing to go, for he would force no Body?* As was deposed, by some of his best Hands, after Acquittal; nor is it reasonable to think, he should reject *Irish* Voluntiers, only from a Pique against *Kennedy*, and force others, that might hazard, and, in Time, destroy his Government: But their Behaviour soon put him out of this Fear, and convinc'd him, that the Plea of Force was only the best Artifice they had to shelter themselves under, in Case they should be taken; and that they were less Rogues than others, only in Point of Time.

It may likewise be taken Notice of, that the Country, wherein they happened to be tried, is among other Happinesses, exempted from Lawyers, and Law-Books, so that the Office of Register, of necessity fell on one, not versed in those Affairs, which might justify the Court in want of Form, more essentially supply'd with Integrity and Impartiality.

But, perhaps, if there was less Law, there might be more Justice, than in some other Courts; for, if the civil Law be a Law of universal Reason, judging of the Rectitude, or Obliquity of Mens Actions, every Man of common Sense is endued with a Portion of it, at least sufficient to make him distinguish Right from Wrong, or what the Civilians call, *Malum in se.*

Therefore, here, if two Persons were equally Guilty of the same Fact, there was no convicting one, and bringing the other off, by any Quirk, or turn of Law; for they form'd their Judgments upon the Constraint, or Willingness, the Aim, and Intention of the Parties, and all other Circumstances, which make a material Difference. Besides, in Crimes of this Nature, Men bred up to the Sea, must be more knowing, and much abler, than others more learned in the Law; for, before a Man can have a right Idea of a Thing, he must know the Terns standing for that Thing: The Sea-Terms being a Language by it self, which no Lawyer can be supposed to understand, he must of Consequence want that discriminating Faculty, which should direct him to judge right of the Facts meant by those Terms.

The Court well knew, it was not possible to get the Evidence of every Sufferer by this Crew, and therefore, first of all, considered how that Deficiency should be supplied; whether, or no, they could pardon one *Jo. Dennis*, who had early offered himself, as King's Evidence, and was the best read in their Lives and Conversations: Here indeed, they were at a Loss for Law, and concluded in the Negative, because it look'd like compounding with a Man to swear falsly, losing by it, those great Helps he could have afforded.

Another great Difficulty in their Proceedings, was, how to understand those Words in the Act of Parliament, of, *particularly specifying in the Charge, the Circumstances of Time, Place,* &c. i. e. so to understand them, as to be able to hold a Court; for if they had been indicted on particular Robberies, the Evidence had happened mostly from the Royal *African* Company's Ships, on which these Gentlemen of *Cape-Corso-Castle*, were not qualify'd to fit, their Oath running, *That they have no Interest directly, or indirectly, in the Ship, or Goods, for the Robbery of which, the Party stands accused:* And this they thought they had, Commissions being paid them, on such Goods: And on the other Side, if they were incapacitated, no Court could be formed, the Commission absolutely requiring three of them by Name.

To reconcile all Things, therefore, the Court resolved, to bottom the whole of their Proceedings on the *Swallow's* Depositions, which were clear and plain, and had the Circumstance of Time when, Place where, Manner how, and the like, particularly specified according to the Statute in that Case made, and provided. But this admitted only a general Intimation of Robbery in the Indictment, therefore *to approve their Clemency,* it looking Arbitrary on the Lives of Men, to lump them to the Gallows, in such a summary Way as must have been done, had they solely adhered to the *Swallow's* Charge, they resolved to come to particular Tryals.

Secondly, *That the Prisoners might not be ignorant whereon to answer*, and so have all fair Advantages, to excuse and defend themselves; the Court farther agreed with Justice and Equanimity, to hear any Evidence that could be brought, to weaken or corroborate the three Circumstances that compleat a Pyrate; first, being a Voluntier amongst them at the Beginning; secondly, being a Voluntier at the taking or robbing of any Ship; or lastly, voluntarily accepting a Share in the Booty of those that did; for by a Parity of Reason, where these Actions were of their own disposing, and yet committed by them, it must be believed their Hearts and Hands joyned together, in what they acted against his Majesty's Ship the *Swallow*.

❂ ❂ ❂ ❂ ❂ ❂ ❂ ❂ ❂ ❂ ❂ ❂ ❂ ❂ ❂ ❂ ❂ ❂ ❂ ❂

The TRYALS *of the* Pyrates,

Taken by his Majesty's Ship the Swallow, *begun at Cape* Corso-Castle, *on the Coast of* Africa, March *the 28th*, 1722.

THE COMMISSION impowered any three named therein, to call to their Assistance, such a Number of qualified Persons as might make the Court always consist of seven: And accordingly Summons were signed to Lieut. *Jo. Barnsley*, Lieut. *Ch. Fanshaw*, Capt. *Samuel Hartsease*, and Capt. *William Menzies, viz.*

By Virtue of a Power and Authority, to us given, by a Commission from the King, under the Seal of Admiralty, You are hereby required to attend, and make one of the Court, for the trying and adjudging of the Pyrates, lately taken on this Coast, by his Majesty's Ship the *Swallow*.

Given under our Hands this 28th of *March*, 1722, at Cape *Corso-Castle*.

Mungo Heardman,	Francis Boy,
James Phips,	Edward Hide.
Henry Dodson,	

The Commissioners being met in the Hall of the Castle, the Commission was first read, after which, the President, and then the other Members, took the Oath, prescribed in the Act of Parliament, and having directed the Form of that for Witnesses, as follows, the Court was opened.

I, A. B. solemnly promise and swear on the Holy Evangelists, to bear true and faithful Witness between the King and Prisoner, or Prisoners, in Relation to the Fact, or Facts, of Pyracy and Robbery, he or they do now stand accused of.

So help me God.

The Court consisted of
Captain *Mungo Heardman*, President

James Phips, *Esq; General of the Coast,*	Mr. Edward Hyde, *Secretary to the Company,*
Mr. H. Dodson, } *Mer.*	Lieut. John Barnsley,
Mr. F. Boye,	Lieut. Ch. Fanshaw

The following Prisoners, out of the Pyrate Ship *Ranger*, have been commanede dbefore them, the Charge, or Indictment, was exhibited.

Prisoners taken in the *Ranger*.

Mens Names.	Ships from	Time when.
* James Skyrm	*Greyhound* Sloop	*Oct.* 1720
* Rich. Hardy	Pyrate with *Davis*	1718
* Wm. Main	Brigantine Capt. *Peet*	*June* 1720
* Henry Dennis		1718
* Val. Ashplant }	Pyrates with Capt. *Davis*	1719
* Rob. Birdson		1719

Names	Ship	Date
* *Rich. Harris* * *D. Littlejohn* * *Thomas How*	*Phoenix* of *Bristol*, Capt. *Richards* at *Newfoundland*	*June* 1720
† *Her. Hunkins*	*Success* Sloop	
* *Hugh Harris* * *W. Mackintosh*	*Willing Mind*	
Thomas Wills † *John Wilden* * *Ja. Greenham* * *John Jaynson*	*Richard* of *Biddiford* *Mary* and *Martha* *Little York, Phillips* Mr. *Love* of *Lancaster*	*July* 1720
† *Chri. Lang*	*Thomas* Brigantine	*Sept.* 1720
* *John Mitchel* T. *Withstandenot*	*Norman* Galley	*Oct.* 1720
Peter la Fever * *Wm. Shurin*	*Jeremiah* and *Ann*	*Ap.* 1720
* *Wm. Wats* * *Wm. Davis*	*Sierraleon* } of Mr. *Glin* of Seig. *Josse*	*July* 1721
† *James Barrow* * *Joshua Lee*	*Martha* Snow Capt *Lady*	
Rob. Hartley (I) † *James Crane*	*Robinson* of *Leverpole* Capt. *Kanning*	*Aug.* 1721
George Smithson *Roger Pye* † *Rob. Fletcher* † *Ro. Hartley* (2)	*Stanwich* Galley Captain *Tarlton*	*Aug.* 1721
† *Andrew Rance*	A *Dutch* Ship	
* *Cuthbert Goss* * *Tho. Giles* * *Israel Hynde*	*Mercy* Galley of *Bristol* at *Callibar*	*Oct.* 1721
William Church *Philip Haak*	*Gertruycht* of *Holland* *Flushingham* of *ditto*	
William Smith *Adam Comry*	*Elizabeth* Capt. *Sharp*	
William Graves * *Peter de Vine* *John Johnson* *John Stodgill*	*King Solomon* Capt. *Tre-* *hern* of Cape *Appollonia*	
Henry Dawson *William Glass*	*Whydah* Sloop at *Jaquin*	
Josiah Robinson *John Arnaught* *John Davis* † *Henry Graves* *Tho. Howard* † *John Rimer* *Thomas Clephen*	*Tarlton* Capt. *Tho. Tarlton,*	*Jan.* 1727
Wm. Guineys † *James Cosins*	*Porcupine* Capt. *Fletcher*	

Too. Stretton		
* William Petty		
Mic. Lemmon		
* Wm. Wood	*Onslow* Capt. *Gee* at *Cesos*	Jan. 1721
* Ed. Watts		
* John Horn		

Pierre Ravon	Peter Grossey	
John Dugan	Rence Frogier	
James Ardeon	Lewis Arnaut	From the
Ettrien Gilliot	Rence Thoby	*French* ship
Ren. Marraud	Meth Roulac	in *Whydah*
John Gittin	John Gumar	Road *Feb.*
Jo. Richardeau	John Paquete	1721–2.
John Lavogue	Allan Pigan	
John Duplaissey	Pierce Shallot	

You, *James Skyrm, Michael Lemmon, Robert Hartley,* &c. Ye, *and every one of you, are in the Name, and by the Authority, of our dread Sovereign Lord,* George, *King of* Great Britain, *indicted as follows;*

Forasmuch as in open Contempt of the Laws of your Country, ye have all of you been wickedly united, and articled together, for the Annoyance and Disturbance of his Majesty's trading Subjects by Sea. And have in Conformity to the most evil and mischievous Intentions, been twice down the Coast of Africa, *with two Ships; once in the Beginning of* August, *and a second Time, in* January *last, sinking, burning, or robbing such Ships, and Vessels as then happened in your Way.*

Particularly, ye stand charged at the Instance, and Information of Captain Chaloner Ogle, *as Traytors and Pyrates, for the unlawful Opposition ye made to his Majesty's Ship, the* Shallow, *under his Command.*

For that on the 5th of February *last past, upon Sight of the aforesaid King's Ship, ye did immediately weigh Anchor from under Cape* Lopez, *on the Southern Coast of* Africa, *in a* French *built Ship of 32 Guns, called the* Ranger, *and did pursue and chase the aforesaid King's Ship, with such Dispatch and Precipitancy, as declared ye common Robbers and Pyrates.*

That about Ten of the Clock the same Morning, drawing within Gun-shot of his Majesty's aforesaid Ship the Swallow, *ye hoisted a pyratical black Flag, and fired several chace Guns, to deter, as much as ye were able, his Majesty's Servants from their Duty.*

That an Hour after this, being very nigh to the aforesaid King's Ship, ye did audaciously continue in a hostile Defence and Assault, for about two Hours more, in open Violation of the Laws, and in Defiance to the King's Colours and Commission.

And lastly, that in the acting, and compassing of all this, ye were all, and every one of you, in a wicked Combination, voluntarily to exert, and actually did, in your several Stations, use your utmost Endeavours to distress the said King's Ship, and murder his Majesty's good Subjects.

To which they severally pleaded, *Not Guilty.*

Then the Court called for the Officers of the *Swallow*, Mr. *Isaac Sun*, Lieutenant, *Ralph Baldrick*, Boatswain, *Daniel Maclauglin*, Mate, desiring them to view the Prisoners, whether they knew them? And to give an Account in what Manner they had attack'd and fought the King's Ship; and they agreed as follows.

That they had viewed all the Prisoners, as they stood now before the Court, and were assured they were the same taken out of one, or other, of the Pyrate Ships, *Royal Fortune*, or *Ranger*; but verily believe them to be taken out of the *Ranger*.

That they did in the King's Ship, at break of Day, on *Monday*, the 5th of *February*, 1721–2, discover three Ships at Anchor, under Cape *Lopez*, on the Southern Coast of *Africa*; the Cape bearing then W.S.W. about three Leagues, and perceiving one of them to have a Pendant flying, and having heard their Morning-Gun before, they immediately suspected them to be *Roberts* the Pyrate, his Consort, and a *French* Ship, they knew had been lately carried out of *Whydah* Road.

The King's Ship was obliged to hawl off N. W. and W. N. W. to avoid a Sand, called, the *French Man's Bank*, the Wind then at S. S. E. and found in half an Hour's time, one of the three had got under Sail from the Careen, and was bending her Sails, in a Chace towards them. To encourage this Rashness and Precipitancy, they kept away before the Wind, (as though afraid,) but with their Tacks on Board, their Main-Yard braced, and making, at the same Time, very bad Steerage.

About half an Hour after Ten, in the Morning, the Pyrate Ship came within Gun-shot, and fired four Chace Guns, hoisted a black Flag at the Mizen-Peek, and got their Sprit-sail Yard under their Bowsprit, for boarding. In half an Hour more, approaching still nigher, they Starboarded their Helm, and gave her a Broadside, the Pyrate bringing to, and returning the same.

After this, the Deponents say, their Fire grew slack for some Time, because the Pyrate was shot so far a Head on the Weather-Bow, that few of their Guns could Point to her; yet in this Interval their black Flag was either Shot away, or hawled down a little Space, and hoisted again.

At length, by their ill Steerage, and Favour of the Wind, they came near, a second Time; and about Two in the Afternoon shot away their Main-topmast.

The Colours they fought under, besides a black Flag, were a red *English* Ensign, a King's Jack, and a *Dutch* Pendant, which they struck at, or about, Three in the Afternoon, and called for Quarters; it proving to be a *French* built Ship of 32 Guns, called the *Ranger*.

> *Isaac Sun,*
> *Ralph Baldrick,*
> *Daniel Maclaughlin.*

When the Evidence had been heard, the Prisoners were called upon to answer, how they came on Board this Pyrate Ship; and their Reason for so audacious a Resistance, as had been made against the King's Ship.

To this, each, in his Reply, owned himself to be one of those taken out of the *Ranger*; that he had signed their pyratical Articles, and shared in their Plunder, some few only accepted, who had been there too short a Time. But that neither in this signing, or sharing, nor in the Resistance had been made against his Majesty's Ship, had they been Voluntiers, but had acted in these several Parts, from a Terror of Death; which a Law amongst them, was to be the Portion of those who refused. The Court then ask'd, who made those Laws? How those Guns came to be fired? Or why they had not deserted their Stations, and mutinied, when so fair a Prospect of Redemption offered? They replied still, with the same Answers, and could extenuate their Crimes, with no other Plea, than being forced Men. Wherefore the Court were of Opinion, that the Indictment, as it charged them with an unlawful Attack and Resistance of the King's Ship, was sufficiently proved; but then it being undeniably evident, that many of these Prisoners had been forced, and some of them of very short standing, they did, on mature Deliberation, come to this merciful Resolution;

That they would hear further Evidence for, or against, each Person singly, in Relation to those Parts of the Indictment, which declared them Voluntiers, or charged them with aiding and assisting, at the burning, sinking, or robbing of other Ships; for if they acted, or assisted, in any Robberies or Devastations, it would be a Conviction they were Voluntiers; here such Evidence, though it might want the Form, still carried the Reason of the Law with it.

The Charge was exhibited also against the following Pyrates taken out of the *Royal Fortune*.

* *Mich. Mare*	in the *Rover* 5 Years ago	
* *Chris. Moody*	under *Davis*	1718.
* *Mar. Johnson*	a *Dutch* Ship	18.
* *James Philips*	the *Revenge* Pyrate Sloop	17.
* *David Symson* } * *Tho. Sutton*	Pyrates with *Davis*	
* *Hag. Jacobson*	a *Dutch* Ship	1719
* *W. Williams* 1 } * *Wm. Fernon* * *W. Williams* 2 * *Roger Scot*	*Sadbury* Captain *Thomas* } *Newfoundland*	June 1720.

* *Tho. Owen*	*York* of *Bristol*	
* *Wm. Taylor* }		May 1720.
* *Joseph Nositer*	*Expedition* of *Topsham*	
* *John Parker*	*Willing Mind* of *Pool*	
* *Robert Crow*	*Happy Return* Sloop	
* *George Smith*	*Mary* and *Martha*	July 1720.
* *Ja. Clements*	*Success* Sloop	
* *John Walden*	*Blessing* of *Lymington*	
* *Jo. Mansfield*	from *Martinico*	
† *James Harris*	*Richard* Pink	
* *John Philips*	a fishing Boat	
Harry Glasby	*Samuel* Capt. *Cary.*	July 1720.
High Menzies }		
* *Wm. Magnus*		
* *Joseph Moor*	*May Flower* Sloop	Feb. 1720.
† *John du Frock*		
Wm. Champries	*Loyd* Gally Capt. *Hyng-*	May 1721.
George Danson	*ston*	
† *Isaac Russel*		
Robert Lilbourn		
* *Robert Johnson*	*Jeremiah* and *Ann*, Capt.	Ap. 1721.
Wm. Darling	*Turner*	
† *Wm. Mead*		
Thomas Diggles	*Christopher* Snow	
* *Ben. Jeffreys*	*Norman* Galley	
John Francia	a Sloop at St. *Nicholas*	
* *D. Harding*	a *Dutch* Ship	Ap. 1721.
* *John Coleman*	*Adventure* Sloop	
* *Charles Bunce*	a *Dutch* Galley	
* *R. Armstrong*	*ditto* run from the *Swallow*	
* *Abra. Harper*		
* *Peter Lesley*		
* *John Jessup* 1		
Thomas Watkins		
* *Philip Bill*	*Onslow* Capt. *Gee* at *Sestos,*	May 1721.
* *Jo. Stephenson*		
* *James Cromby*		
Thomas Garrat		
† *George Ogle*		
Roger Gorsuch	*Martha* Snow	Au. 1721.
John Watson }		
William Child	*Mercy* Gally at *Callabar*	Oct. 1721.
* *John Griffin*		
* *Pet. Scudamore* }		

Christ. Granger Nicho. Brattle James White Tho. Davis Tho. Sever * Rob. Bevins * T. Oughterlaney * David Rice	Cornwall Galley at Cal- labar	ditto.
* Rob. Haws Hugh Riddle Stephen Thomas	Joceline Capt. Loane Diligence Boat	Oct. 1721. Ja. 1721.
* John Lane * Sam. Fletcher * Wm. Philips Jacob Johnson * John King	King Solomon	ditto.
Benjamin Par William May Ed. Thornden	Robinson Capt. Kanning Elizabeth Capt. Sharp	ditto.
* George Wilson Edward Tarlton * Robert Hays	Tarlton of Leverpool at Cape la Hou	ditto.
Thomas Roberts John Richards John Cane	Charlton Capt. Allwright	Feb. 1721.
Richard Wood Richard Scot Wm. Davison Sam. Morwell Edward Evans	Porcupine Capt. Fletcher Whydah Road	Feb. 1721.
* John Jessup 2	surrender'd up at Princes	

You, *Harry Glasby, William Davison, William Champnies,*
Samuel Morwell, &c.
Ye, and every one of you, are, in the Name, and by the Authority
of our most dread Sovereign Lord. George, *King of* Great Britain, *indicted as follows.*

    Forasmuch as in open Contempt and Violation of the Laws
of your Country, to which ye ought to have been subject,) ye have
all of you been wickedly united and articled together, for the
Annoyance and Destruction of his Majesty's trading Subjects by
Sea; and in Conformity to so wicked an Agreement and Asso-
ciation, ye have been twice lately down this Coast of Africa, *once*

in August, *and a* Second Time *in* January *last, spoiling and destroying many Good and Vessels of his Majesty's Subjects, and other trading Nations.*

Particularly ye stand indicted at the Information and Instance of Captain Chaloner Ogle, *as Traytors, Robbers, Pyrates, and common Enemies to Mankind.*

For that on the 10th of February *last, in a Ship ye were possess'd of called the* Royal Fortune, *of 40 Guns, ye did maintain a hostile Defence and Resistance for some Hours, against his Majesty's Ship the* Swallow, *nigh Cape* Lopez Bay, *on the Southern Coast of* Africa.

That this Fight and insolent Resistance against the King's Ship, was made, not only without any Pretence of Authority, more than that of your own private depraved Wills, but was done also under a black Flag, flagrantly by that, denoting your selves common Robbers and Traitors, Opposers and Violators of the Laws.

And lastly, that in this Resistance, ye were all of you Voluntiers, and did, as such, contribute your utmost Efforts, for disabling and distressing the aforesaid King's Ship, and deterring his Majesty's Servants therein, from their Duty.

To which they severally pleaded, *Not Guilty.*

Whereupon the Officers of his Majesty's Ship, the *Swallow*, were called again, and testified as follows.

That they had seen all the Prisoners now before the Court, and knew them to be the same which were taken out of one or other of the Pyrate Ships, *Royal Fortune* or *Ranger*, and verily believe them to be those taken out of the *Royal Fortune*.

That the Prisoners were possess'd of a Ship of Guns, called the *Royal Fortune*, and were at an Anchor under Cape *Lopez*, on the Coast of *Africa*, with two others: When his Majesty's Ship the *Swallow*, (to which the Deponents belong'd, and were Officers,) stood in for the Place, on *Saturday* the 10th of *February* 1721–2: The largest had a Jack, Ensign and Pendant flying, (being this *Royal Fortune*,) who on Sight of them, had their Boats passing and repassing, from the other two, which they supposed to be with Men: The Wind not favouring the aforesaid King's Ship, she was obliged to make two Trips to gain nigh enough the Wind, to fetch in with the Pyrates; and being at length little more than random Shot from them, they found she slipped her Cable, and got under Sail.

At Eleven, the Pyrate was within Pistol-Shot, a Breast of them, with a black Flag, and Pendant hoisted at their Main-topmast Head. The Deponents say, they then struck the *French* Ensign that had continued hoisted at their Staff all the Morning till then; and display'd the King's Colours, giving her, at the same Time, their Broadside, which was immediately returned.

The Pyrate's Mizen-topmast fell, and some of her Rigging was torn, yet she still out sailed the Man of War, and slid half Gun-Shot from them, while they continued to fire without Intermission, and the other to return such Guns as could be brought to bear, till by favour of the Winds, they were advanced very nigh again; and after exchanging a few more Shot, about half an Hour past one, his Main-Mast came down, having received a Shot a little below the Parrel.

At Two she struck her Colours, and called for Quarters, proving to be a Ship, formerly call'd the *Onslow*, but by them, the *Royal Fortune*; and the Prisoners from her, assured them, that the smallest Ship of the two, then remaining in the Road, belong'd to them, by the Name of the *Little Ranger*, which they had deserted on this Occasion.

> *Isaac Sun,*
> *Ralph Baldrick,*
> *Daniel Maclaughlin.*

The Prisoners were asked by the Court, to the same Purpose the others had been in the Morning; what Exception they had to make against what had been sworn? And what they had to say in their Defence? And their Reply were much the same with the other Prisoners; that they were forc'd

Men, had not fired a Gun in this Resistance against the *Swallow*, and that what little Assistance they did give on this Occasion, was to the Sails and Rigging, to comply with the arbitrary Commands of *Roberts*, who had threaten'd, and they were perswaded would, have Shot them on Refusal.

The Court, to dispense equal Justice, mercifully resolved for these, as they had done for the other Pyrate Crew; that further Evidence should be heard against each Man singly, to the two Points, of being a Voluntier at first, and to their particular Acts of Pyracy and Robbery since: That so Men, who had been lately received amongst them, and as yet, had not been at the taking, or plundering, of any Ship, might have the Opportunity, and Benefit, of clearing their Innocence, and not fall promiscuously with the Guilty.

By Order of the Court,
John Atkins, *Register.*

Wm. Magnes, Tho. Oughterlauney, Wm. Main, Wm. Mackintosh, Val. Ashplant, John Walden, Israel Hind, Marcus Johnson, Wm. Petty, Wm. Fernon, Abraham Harper, Wm. Wood, Tho. How, John Stephenson, Ch. Bunce, and *John Griffin.*

Against these it was deposed by Captain *Joseph Trahern,* and *George Fenn,* his Mate, that they were all of them, either at the attacking and taking of the Ship King *Solomon,* or afterwards at the robbing and plundering of her, and in this Manner;

That on the 6th of *January* last their Ship riding at Anchor near Cape *Appollonia* in *Africa,* discovered a Boat rowing towards them, against Wind and Stream, from a Ship that lay about three Miles to Leeward. They judged from the Number of Men in her, as she nearer advanced, to be a Pyrate, and made some Preparation for receiving her, believing, on a nigher View, they would think fit to withdraw from an Attack that must be on their Side with great Disadvantage in an open Boat, and against double the Number of Men; yet by the Rashness, and the Pusillanimity of his own People (who laid down their Arms, and immediately called for Quarter) the Ship was taken, and afterwards robbed by them.

President. Can you charge your Memory with any Particulars in the Seizure and Robbery?

Evidence. We know that *Magnes*, Quarter-Master of the Pyrate Ship, commanded the Men in this Boat that took us, and assumed the Authority of ordering her Provisions and Stores out, which being of different Kinds, we soon found, were seized and sent away under more particular Directions; for *Main*, as Boatswain of the Pyrate Ship, carried away two Cables, and several Coils of Rope, as what belonged to his Province, beating some of our own Men for not being brisk enough at working in the Robbery. *Petty*, as Sail-maker, saw to the Sails and Canvas, *Harper*, as Cooper to the Cask and Tools; *Griffin*, to the Carpenter's Stores, and *Oughterlauney*, as Pilot, having shifted himself with a Suit of my Clothes, a new tye Wig, and called for a Bottle of Wine, ordered the Ship, very arrogantly, to be steered under Commodore *Robert's* Stern, (I suppose to know what Orders there were concerning her.) So far particularly. In the general, Sir, they were very outragious and emulous in Mischief.

President. Mr. *Castel*, acquaint the Court of what you know in Relation to this Robbery of the King *Solomon*; after what Manner the Pyrate-Boat was dispatch'd for this Attempt.

Tho. Castel. I was a Prisoner, Sir, with the Pyrates when their Boat was ordered upon that Service, and found, upon a Resolution of going, Word was passed through the Company, Who would go? And I saw all that did, did it voluntarily; no Compulsion, but rather pressing who should be foremost.

The Prisoners yielded to what had been sworn about the Attack and Robbery, but denied the latter Evidence, saying, *Roberts* hector'd, and upbraided them of Cowardice on this very Occasion; and told some, they were very ready to step on Board of a Prize when within Command of the Ship, but now there seem'd to be a Tryal of their Valour, backward and fearful.

President. So that *Roberts* forc'd ye upon this Attack.

Prisoners. Roberts commanded us into the Boat, and the Quarter-Master to rob the Ship; neither of whose Commands we dared to have refused.

President. And granting it so, those are still your own Acts, since done by Orders from Officers of your own Election. Why would Men, honestly disposed, give their Votes for such a Captain and such a Quarter-Master as were every Day commanding them on distastful Services?

Here succeeded a Silence among the Prisoners, but at length *Fernon* very honestly own'd, that he did not give his Vote to *Magnes*, but to *David Sympson* (the old Quarter-Master,) *for in Truth*, says he, *I took Magnes for too honest a Man, and unfit for the Business.*

The Evidence was plain and home, and the Court, without any Hesitation, brought them in *Guilty.*

William Church, Phil. Haak, James White, Nico. Brattle, Hugh Riddle, William Thomas, Tho. Roberts, Jo. Richards, Jo. Cane, R. Wood, R. Scot, Wm. Davidson, Sam. Morwell, Edward Evans, Wm. Guineys, and 18 *French* Men.

The four first of these Prisoners, it was evident to the Court, served as Musick on Board the Pyrate, were forced lately from the several Merchant Ships they belonged to; and that they had, during this Confinement, an uneasy Life of it, having sometimes their Fiddles, and often their Heads broke, only for excusing themselves, or saying they were tired, when any Fellow took it in his Head to demand a Tune.

The other *English* had been a very few Days on Board the Pyrate, only from *Whydah* to Cape *Lopez*, and no Capture or Robbery done by them in that Time. And the *French* Men were brought with a Design to reconduct their own Ship (or the *Little Ranger* in Exchange) to *Whydah* Road again, and were used like Prisoners; neither quarter'd nor suffered to carry Arms. So that the Court immediately acquiesced in, *Acquitting them.*

Tho. Sutton, David Sympson, Christopher Moody, Phil. Bill, R. Hardy, Hen. Dennis, David Rice, Wm. Williams, R. Harris, Geo. Smith, Ed. Watts, Jo. Mitchell and *James Barrow.*

The Evidence against these Prisoners, were *Geret de Haen*, Master of the *Flushingham*, taken nigh *Axim*, the Beginning of *January* last.

Benj. Kreft Master, and *James Groet* Mate of the *Gertruycht*, taken nigh *Gabone* in *December* last, and Mr. *Castel, Wingfield* and others, that had been Prisoners with the Pyrates.

The former deposed, that all these Prisoners (excepting *Hardy*) were on Board at the Robbery and Plunder of their Ships, behaving in a vile outragious Manner, putting them in bodily Fears, sometimes for the Ship, and sometimes for themselves; and in particular, *Kreft* charged it on *Sutton*, that he had ordered all their Gunner's Stores out; on which that Prisoner presently interrupted, and said, he was perjured, *That he had not taken half.* A Reply, I believe, not designed as any sawcy Way of jesting, but to give their Behaviour an Appearance of more Humanity than the *Dutch* would allow.

From Mr. *Castel, Wingfield* and others, they were proved to be distinguished Men, Men who were consulted as Chiefs in all Enterprizes; belonged most of them to the House of Lords, (as they call'd it,) and could carry an Authority over others. The former said, particularly of *Hardy*, (Quarter-Master of the *Ranger*,) that when the *Diligence* Sloop was taken, (whereto he belonged,) none was busier in the Plunder, and was the very Man who scuttled and sunk that Vessel.

From some of the Prisoners acquitted, it was farther demanded, whether the Acceptance or Refusal of any Office was not in their own Option? And it was declared, that every Officer was chose by a Majority of Votes, and might refuse, if he pleased, since others gladly embraced what brought with it an additional Share of Prize. *Guilty*

The Court on the 31st of *March*, remanded the following six before them, for Sentence, *viz. Dav. Sympson, Wm. Magnes, R. Hardy, Thomas Sutton, Christopher Moody*, and *Valen. Ashplant.*

To whom the President spoke to the following Purpose; *The Crime of Pyracy, of which all of ye have been justly convicted, is of all other Robberies the most aggravating and inhumane, in that being removed from the Fears of Surprize, in remote and distant Parts, ye do in Wantonness of Power often add Cruelty to Theft.*

Pyrates unmoved at Distress or Poverty, not only spoil and rob, but do it from Men needy, and who are purchasing their Livlihoods thro' Hazards and Difficulties, which ought rather to move Compassion, and what is still worse, do often, by Perswasion or Force, engage the inconsiderate Part of them, to their own and Families Ruin, removing from their Wives and Children, and by that, from the Means that should support them from Misery and Want.

To a trading Nation, nothing can be so Destructive as Pyracy, or call for more exemplary Punishment; besides, the national Reflection it infers: It cuts off the Returns of Industry, and those plentiful Importations that alone can make an Island flourishing; and it is your Aggravation, that ye have been the Chiefs and Rulers in these licentious and lawless Practices.

However, contrary to the Measures ye have dealt ye have been heard with Patience, and tho' little has, or possibly could, have been said in Excuse or Extenuation of your Crimes, yet Charity makes us hope that a true and sincere Repentance (which we heartily recommend) may entitle ye to Mercy and Forgiveness, after the Sentence of the Law has taken Place, which now remains upon me to pronounce.

You Dav. Simpson, William Magnes, R. Hardy, Tho. Sutton, Christopher Moody, *and* Val. Ashplant.

Ye, and each of you, are adjudged and sentenced, to be carried back to the Place from whence ye came, from thence to the Place of Execution, without the Gates of this Castle, and there within the Flood-Marks, to be hanged by the Neck till ye are dead.

After this, ye, and each of you shall be taken down, and your Bodies hanged in Chains.

Warrant for Execution.

PURSUANT to the Sentence given on Saturday, *by the Court of Admiralty, at* Cape-Corso-Castle, *against* Dav. Simpson, Wm. Magnes, R. Hardy, Tho. Sutton, Christopher Moody, *and* Valentine Ashplant.

You are hereby directed to carry the aforesaid Malefactors to the Place of Execution, without the Gates of this Castle, to Morrow Morning at Nine of the Clock, and there within the Flood-Marks, cause them to be hanged by the Neck till they are dead, for which, this shall be your Warrant. Given under my Hand, this 2d Day of April 1722.

To Joseph Gordyn,   Mungo Heardman.
    Provost-Marshal.

The Bodies remove in Chains, to the Gibbets already cited on the adjacent Hillocks.

                                                                M. H.

William Phillips.

It appeared by the Evidence of Captain *Jo. Trahern*, and *George Fenn*, Mate of the King *Solomon*, that this Prisoner was Boatswain of the same Ship, when she was attacked and taken off Cape *Appollonia*, the 6th of *January* last, by the Pyrate's Boat.

When the Boat drew nigh, (they say,) it was judged from the Number of Men in her, that they were Pyrates, and being hailed, answered, *Defiance*; at which the Commander snatched a Musquet from one of his Men, and fired, asking them at the same Time, whether they would stand by him, to defend the Ship? But the Pyrates returning a Volley, and crying out, they would give no Quarters if any Resistance was made; this Prisoner took upon him to call out for Quarters, without the Master's Consent, and mislead the rest to the laying down their Arms, and giving up the Ship, to half the Number of Men, and in an open Boat. It was further evident he became, after this, a Voluntier amongst them. First, because he was presently very forward and brisk, in robbing the Ship *King Solomon*, of her Provisions and Stores. Secondly because he endeavoured to have his Captain ill used; and lastly, because he had confessed to *Fenn*, that he had been obliged to sign their Articles that Night, (a Pistol being laid on the Table, to signify he must do it, or be shot,) when the whole appeared to be an Untruth from other Evidence, who also asserted his being armed in the Action against the *Swallow*.

In answer to this, he first observed upon the Unhappiness of being friendless in this Part of the World, which, elsewhere, by witnessing to the Honesty of his former Life, would, he believed, in a great Measure, have invalidated the wrong Evidence had been given of his being a Voluntier with the Pyrates. He owns indeed, he made no Application to his Captain, to intercede for a Discharge, but excuses it with saying, he had a dislike to him, and therefore was sure that such Application would have avail'd him nothing.

The Court observed the Pretences of this, and other of the Pyrates, of a Pistol and their Articles being served up in a Dish together, or of their being misused and forced from an honest Service, was often a Complotment of the Parties, to render them less suspected of those they came from, and was to answer the End of being put in a News-Paper or Affidavit: and the Pyrates were so generous as not to refuse a Compliment to a Brother that cost them nothing, and, at the same Time, secured them the best Hands; the best I call them, because such a Dependance made them act more boldly. *Guilty*.

Harry Glasby, Master.
There appearing several Persons in Court, who had been

taken by *Roberts*'s Ship, whereof the Prisoner was Master, their Evidence was accepted as follows.

Jo. Trahern, Commander of the *King Solomon*, deposed, the Prisoner, indeed, to act as Master of the Pyrate Ship (while he was under Restraint there) but was observed like no Master, every one obeying at Discretion, of which he had taken Notice, and complained to him, how hard a Condition it was, to be a Chief among Brutes; and that he was weary of his Life, and such other Expressions, (now out of his Memory,) as shew'd in him a great Disinclination to that Course of Living.

Jo. Wingfield, a Prisoner with them at *Calabar*, says the same, as to the Quality he acted in, but that he was Civil beyond any of them, and verily believes, that when the Brigantine he served on Board of, as a Factor for the *African* Company, was voted to be burnt, this Man was the Instrument of preventing it, expressing himself with a great deal of Sorrow, for this and the like malicious Rogueries of the Company he was in; that to him shewed, she had acted with Reluctancy, as one who could not avoid what he did. He adds further, that when one *Hamilton*, a Surgeon, was taken by them, and the Articles about to be imposed on him, he opposed, and prevented it. And that *Hunter*, another Surgeon, among them, was cleared at the Prisoner's Instance and Perswasion; from which last, this Deponent had it assured to him, that *Glasby* had once been under Sentence of Death, on Board of them, with two more, for endeavouring an Escape in the *West-Indies*, and that the other two were really shot for it.

Elizabeth Trengrove, who was taken a Passenger in the *African* Company's Ship *Onslow*, strengthen'd the Evidence of the last Witness; for having heard a good Character of this *Glasby*, she enquired of the Quarter-Master, who was then on Board a robbing, whether or no she could see him? And he told her, *No*; they never ventured him from the Ship, for he had once endeavoured his Escape, and they had ever since continued jealous of him.

Edward Crisp, Captain *Trengrove*, and Captain *Sharp*, who had all been taken in their Turns, acknowledge for themselves and others, who had unluckily fallen into those Pyrates Hands, that the good Usage they had met with, was chiefly thro' the Prisoner's Means, who often interposed, for leaving sufficient Stores and Instruments on Board the Ships they had robbed, alledging, they were superfluous and unnecessary there.

James White, whose Business was Musick, and was on the Poop of the Pyrate Ship in Time of Action with the *Swallow*, deposed, that during the Engagement, and Defence she made, he never saw the Prisoner busied about the Guns, or giving Orders, either to the loading or firing of them; but that he wholly attended to the setting, or trimming, of the Sails, as *Roberts* commanded; and that in the Conclusion, he verily believed him to be the Man who prevented the Ship's being blown up, by setting trusty Centinels below, and opposing himself against such hot-headed Fellows as had procured lighted Matches, and were going down for that Purpose.

Isaac Sun, Lieutenant of the Man of War, deposed, that when he came to take Possession of the Prize, in the King's Boat, he found the Pyrates in a very distracted and divided Condition; some being for blowing up, and others (who perhaps supposed themselves least culpable) opposing it: That in this Confusion he enquired for the Prisoner, of whom he had before heard a good Character; and thinks he rendered all the Service in his Power, for preventing it; in particular, he understood by all Hands, that he had seized, and taken, from one *James Philips*, a lighted Match, at the Instant he was going down to the Magazine, swearing, that he should send them all to H—l together. He had heard also, that after *Roberts* was killed, the Prisoner ordered the Colours to be struck; and had since shown, how opposite his Practice and Principles had been, by discovering who were the greatest Rogues among them.

The Prisoner, in his own Defence, says, when he had the

Misfortune of falling into the Pyrates Hands, he was chief Mate of the *Samuel*, of *London*, Captain *Cary*; and when he had hid himself, to prevent the Design of carrying him away, they found him, and beat and threw him over-board. Seven Days afterwards, upon his objecting against, and refusing to sign their Articles, he was cut and abus'd again: That tho' after this he ingratiated himself, by a more humble Carriage, it was only to make Life easy; the Shares they had given him, having been from Time to Time returned again to such Prisoners as fell in his Way; till of late, indeed, he had made a small Reservation, and had desired Captain *Loan* to take two or three Moidores from him, to carry to his Wife. He was once taken, he says, at making his Escape, in the *West-Indies*, and, with two more, sentenced to be shot for it, by a drunken Jury; the latter actually suffered, and he was preserved only by one of the chief Pyrates taking a sudden Liking to him, and bullying the others. A second time he ran away at *Hispaniola*, carrying a Pocket Compass, for conducting him through the Woods; but that being a most desolate and wild Part of the Island he fell upon, and he ignorant how to direct his Course, was obliged, after two or three Days wandering, to return towards the Ship again, denying with egregious Oaths, the Design he was charg'd with, for Fear they should shoot him. From this Time he hopes it will be some Extenuation of his Fault, that most of the acquitted Prisoners can witness, they entertained Jealousies of him, and *Roberts* would not admit him into his Secrets; and withal, that Captain *Cary*, (and four other Passengers with him) had made Affidavit of his having been forced from his Employ, which tho' he could not produce, yet he humbly hoped the Court would think highly probable from the Circumstances offered.

On the whole, the Court was of Opinion Artists had the best Pretension to the Plea of Force, from the Necessity Pyrates are sometimes under of engaging such, and that many Parts of his own Defence had been confirmed by the Evidence, who had afferted he acted with Reluctance, and had expressed a Concern and Trouble for the little Hopes remained to him, of extricating himself. That he had used all Prisoners (as they were called) well, at the hazard of ill Usage to himself. That he had not in any military Capacity assisted their Robberies. That he had twice endeavoured his Escape, with the utmost Danger.   *Acquitted him.*

Captain *James Skyrm.*

It appeared from the Evidence of several Prisoners acquitted, that this *Skyrm* commanded the *Ranger*, in that Defence she made against the King's Ship; that he ordered the Men to their Quarters, and the Guns to be loaded and fired, having a Sword in his Hand, to enforce those Commands; and beat such to their Duty whom he espied any way negligent or backward. That altho' he had lost a Leg in the Action, his Temper was so warm, as to refuse going off the Deck, till he found all was lost.

In his Defence, he says, he was forced from a Mate's Employ on Board a Sloop call'd the *Greyhound*, of St. *Christophers, Oct.* 1720. The Pyrate having drubbed him, and broke his Head, only for offering to go away when that Sloop was dismissed. Custom and Success had since indeed blunted, and, in some Measure, worn out the Sense of Shame; but that he had really for several Months past been sick, and disqualified for any Duty, and though *Roberts* had forced him on this Expedition much against his Will, yet the Evidence must be sensible, the Title of Captain gave him no Preeminence, for he could not be obeyed, though he had often called to them, to leave off their Fire, when he perceived it to be the King's Ship.

The Sickness he alledged, but more especially the Circumstance of losing his Leg, were Aggravations of his Fault, shewing him more alert on such Occasions, than he was now willing to be thought: As to the Name of Captain, if it were allowed to give him no Precedence out of Battle, yet here it was proved a Title of Authority; such an Authority as could direct an Engagement against the King's Colours, and therefore he was in the highest Degree, *Guilty*.

John Walden.

Captain *John Trahern*, and *George Fenn*, deposed, the Prisoner to be one of the Number, who, in an open Boat, pyratically assailed, and took their Ship, and was remarkably busy at Mischief, having a Pole-Ax in his Hand, which served him instead of a Key, to all the lock'd Doors and Boxes he come nigh: Also in particular, he cut the Cable of our Ship, when the other Pyrates were willing, and busied at heaving up the Anchor, saying, Captain, what signifies this Trouble of *Yo Hope*, and straining in hot Weather; there are more Anchors at *London*, and besides, your Ship is to be burnt.

William Smith, (a Prisoner acquitted,) says *Walden* was known among the Pyrates mostly, by the Nick-Name of *Miss Nanney* (ironically its presumed from the Hardness of his Temper) that he was one of the twenty who voluntarily came on Board the *Ranger*, in the Chace she made out after the *Swallow*, and by a Shot from that Ship, lost his Leg; his Behaviour in the Fight, till then, being bold and daring.

The *President*, called for *Harry Glasby*, and bid him relate a Character of the Prisoner, and what Custom was among them, in Relation to these voluntary Expeditions, out of their proper Ship and this of going on Board the *Ranger*, in particular.

And he gave in for Evidence, that the Prisoner was looked on as a brisk Hand, (*i. e.*, as he farther explained it, a stanch Pyrate, a great Rogue) that when the *Swallow* first appeared in Sight, every one was willing to believe her a *Portuguese*, because Sugar was very much in Demand, and had made some Jarring and Dissention between the two Companies, (the *Fortune's* People drinking Punch, when the *Ranger's* could not) that *Roberts*, on Sight of the *Swallow*, hailed the new *Ranger*, and bid them right Ship, and get under Sail;

there is, says he, Sugar in the Offing, bring it in, that we may have no more Mumbling; ordering at the same Time the Word to be pass'd among the Crew, who would go to their Assistance, and immediately the Boat was full of Men, to transport themselves.

President. Then every one that goes on Board of any Prize, does it voluntarily? Or were there here any other Reasons for it?

H. Glasby. Every Man is commonly called by List, and insists, in his Turn, to go on Board of a Prize, because they then are allowed a Shift of Cloaths, (the best they can find) over and above the Dividend from the Robbery, and this they are so far from being compelled to, that it often becomes the Occasion of Contest and Quarrel amongst them: But in the present, or such like Cases, where there appears a Prospect of Trouble, the Lazy and Timerous are often willing to decline this Turn, and yield to their Betters, who thereby establish a greater Credit.

The Prisoner, and the rest of those Men who went from the *Fortune* on Board the *Ranger*, to assist in this Expedition, were Voluntiers, and the trustiest Men among us.

President. Were there no Jealousies of the *Ranger's* leaving you in this Chace, or at any other Time, in order to surrender?

H. Glasby. Most of the *Ranger's* Crew were fresh Men, Men who had been enter'd only since their being on the Coast of *Guiney,* and therefore had not so liberal a Share in fresh Provisions, or Wine, as the *Fortune's* People, who thought they had born the Burthen and Heat of the Day, which had given Occasion indeed to some Grumblings and Whispers, as tho' they would take an Opportunity to leave us, but we never supposed (if they did) it would be with any other Design then setting up for themselves, they having (many of them) behaved with greater Severity than the old Standers.

The Prisoner appeared undaunted, and rather solicitous, about resting his Stump, than giving any Answer to the

Court, or making any Defence for himself, till called upon; then he related in a careless, or rather hopeless Manner, the Circumstances of his first Entrance, being forced, he said, out of the *Blessing* of *Lemmington*, at *Newfoundland*, about 12 Months past; this, he is sure, most of the old Pyrates knew, and that he was for some Time as sick of the Change as any Man; but Custom and ill Company had altered him, owning very frankly, that he was at the Attack, and taking of the *King Solomon*, that he did cut her Cable, and that none were forced on those Occasions.

As to the last Expedition in the *Ranger*, he confesses he went on Board of her, but that it was by *Roberts*'s Order; and in the Chace loaded one Gun, to bring her to, but when he saw it was a Bite, he declared to his Comrades, that it was not worth while to resist, forbore firing, and assisted to reeve the Braces, in order, if they could, to get away, in which sort of Service he was busied, when a Shot from the Man of War took off his Leg: And being asked, that supposing the Chace had proved a *Portuguese?* Why then, says he, I dont know what I might have done, intimating withal, that every Body then would have been ready enough at plundering. *Guilty.*

Peter Scudamore.

Harry Glasby, Jo. Wingfield, and *Nicholas Brattle,* depose thus much, as to his being a Voluntier with the Pyrates, from Capt. *Rolls,* at *Calabar.* First, That he quarrelled with *Moody,* (one of the Heads of the Gang) and fought with him, because he opposed his going, asking *Rolls,* in a leering manner, whether he would not be so kind, as to put him into the *Gazette,* when he came Home. And, at another Time, when he was going from the Pyrate Ship, in his Boat, a Turnado arose, *I wish,* says he, *the Rascal may be drowned, for he is a great Rogue, and has endeavoured to do me all the ill Offices he could among these Gentlemen,* (i. e., Pyrates).

And secondly, That he had signed the Pyrate's Articles with a great deal of Alacrity, and gloried in having been the first Surgeon that had done so, (for before this, it was their

Custom to change their Surgeons, when they desired it, after having served a Time, and never obliged them to sign, but he was resolved to break thro' this, for the good of those who were to follow,) swearing immediately upon it, he was now, he hoped, as great a Rogue as any of them.

Captain *Jo. Trahern*, and *George Fenn*, his Mate, deposed, the Prisoner to have taken out of the *King Solomon*, their Surgeon's capital Instruments, some Medicines, and a Back-Gammon Table; which latter became the Means of a Quarrel between one *Wincon*, and he, whose Property they should be, and were yielded to the Prisoner.

Jo. Sharp, Master of the *Elizabeth*, heard the Prisoner ask *Roberts* leave to force *Comry*, his Surgeon, from him, which was accordingly done, and with him, carried also some of the Ship's Medicines: But what gave a fuller Proof of the dishonesty of his Principles, was, the treacherous Design he had formed of running away with the Prize, in her Passage to Cape *Corso*, though he had been treated with all Humanity, and very unlike a Prisoner, on Account of his Employ and better Education, which had rendred him less to be suspected.

Mr. Child, (acquitted) depos'd, that in their Passage from the Island of St. *Thomas*, in the *Fortune* Prize, this Prisoner was several Times tempting him, into Measures of rising with the Negroes, and killing the *Swallow*'s People, shewing him, how easily the white Men might be demolished, and a new Company raised at *Angola*, and that Part of the Coast, *for*, says he, *I understand how to navigate a Ship, and can soon teach you to steer; and is it not better to do this, than to go back to* Cape-Corso, *and be hanged and Sun-dryed?* To which the Deponent replying, he was not afraid of being hanged, *Scudamore* bid him be still, and no Harm should come to him; but before the next Day-Evening, which was the designed Time of executing this Project, the Deponent discovered it to the Officer, and assured him, *Scudamore* had been talking all the preceeding Night to the Negroes, in *Angolan* Language.

Isaac Burnet heard the Prisoner ask *James Harry*, a Pyrate, (left with the wounded in the Prize,) whether he was willing to come into the Project of running away with the Ship, and endeavour the raising of a new Company, but turned the Discourse to Horse-Racing, as the Deponent crept nigher; he acquainted the Officer with what he had heard, who kept the People under Arms all Night, their Apprehensions of the Negroes not being groundless; for many of them having lived a long Time in this pyratical Way, were, by the thin Commons they were now reduced to, as ripe for Mischief as any.

The Prisoner in his Defence said, he was a forced Man from Captain *Rolls*, in *October* last, and if he had not shewn such a Concern as became him, at the Alteration, he must remark the Occasion to be, the Disagreement and Enmity between them; but that both *Roberts*, and *Val. Ashplant*, threat'ned him into signing their Articles, and that he did it in Terror.

The *King Solomon*, and *Elizabeth* Medicine-Chest, he owns he plundered, by Order of *Hunter*, the then chief Surgeon, who, by the Pyrates Laws, always directs in this Province, and Mr. *Child*, (tho' acquitted) had by the same Orders taken out a whole *French* Medicine-Chest, which he must be sensible for me, as well as for himself, we neither of us dared to have denied; it was their being the proper Judges, made so ungrateful an Office imposed. If after this he was elected chief Surgeon himself, both *Comry* and *Wilson* were set up also, and it might have been their Chance to have carried it, and as much out of their Power to have refused.

As to the Attempt of rising and running away with the Prize, he denies it altogether as untrue; foolish Words, but only by Way of Supposition, that if the Negroes should take it in their heads (considering the Weakness, and ill look-out that was kept;) it would have been an easy Matter, in his Opinion for them to have done it; but that he encouraged such a Thing, was false, his talking to them in the *Angolan* Language, was only a Way of spending his Time, and trying his skill to tell twenty, he being incapable of further Talk. As to his understanding Navigation, he had frequently acknowledg'd it to the Deponent *Child*, and wonders he should now so circumstantiate this Skill against him. *Guilty.*

Robert Johnson.

It appeared to the Court, that the Prisoner was one of the twenty Men, in that Boat of the Pyrates, which afterwards robb'd the *King Solomon*, at an Anchor near Cape *Appollonia*: That all Pyrates on this, and the like Service, were Voluntiers, and he, in particular, had contested his going on Board a second Time, tho' out of his Turn.

The Prisoner in his Defence, called for *Harry Glasby*, who witnessed to his being so very drunk, when he first came among their Crew, that they were forced to hoist him out of one Ship into the other, with a Tackle, and therefore without his Consent; but had since been a trusty Man, and was placed to the Helm, in that running Battle they made with the *Swallow*.

He insisted for himself likewise, on Captain *Turner's* Affidavit of his being forced, on which others (his Ship-mates) had been cleared.

The Court considering the Partiality that might be objested in acquitting one, and condemning another of the same standing, thought fit to remark it as a clear Testimony of their Integrity, that their Care and Indulgence to each Man, in allowing his particular Defence, was to exempt from the Rigour of the Law, such, who it must be allowed, would have stood too promiscuously condemned, if they had not been heard upon any other Fact than that of the *Swallow*; and herein what could better direct them, than a Character and Behaviour from their own Associates; for tho' a voluntary Entry with the Pyrates may be doubtful, yet his consequent Actions are not, and it is not so material how a Man comes among Pyrates, as how he acts when he is there. *Guilty.*

George Wilson.

John Sharp, Master of the *Elizabeth*, in which Ship the Prisoner was Passenger, and fell a second Time into the Pyrates Hands, deposes, that he took the said *Wilson* off from *Sestos*, on this Coast, paying to the Negroes for his Ransom, the Value of three Pound five Shillings in Goods, for which he had taken a Note, that he thought he had done a charitable Act in this, till meeting with one Captain *Canning*, he was ask'd, why he would release such a Rogue as *Wilson* was? For that he had been a Voluntier with the Pyrates, out of *John Tarlton*. And when the Deponent came to be a Prisoner himself, he found *Thomas*, the Brother of this *John Tarlton*, a Prisoner with the Pyrates also, who was immediately on *Wilson*'s Instigation, in a most sad manner misused and beat, and had been shot, through the Fury and Rage of some of those Fellows if the Town-side, (*i. e. Liverpool*) Men, had not hid him in a Stay-Sail, under the Bowsprit; for *Moody* and *Harper*, with their Pistols cock'd, searched every Corner of the Ship to find him, and came to this Deponent's Hammock, whom they had like fatally to have mistaken for *Tarlton*, but on his calling out, they found their Error, and left him with this comfortable Anodyne, That he was the honest Fellow who brought the Doctor. At coming away, the Prisoner asked about his Note, whether the Pyrates had it or no? Who not being able readily to tell, he reply'd, it's no Matter Mr. *Sharp*, I believe I shall hardly ever come to *England* to pay it.

Adam Comry, Surgeon of the *Elizabeth*, says, that altho' the Prisoner had, on Account of his Indisposition and Want, received many Civilities from him, before meeting with the Pyrates, he yet understood it was thro' his and *Scudamore*'s Means, that he had been compelled among them: The Prisoner was very alert and chearful, he says, at meeting with *Roberts*, hailed him, told him he was glad to see him, and would come on Board presently, borrowing of the Deponent a clean Shirt and Drawers, for his better Appearance and

Reception; he signed their Articles willingly, and used Arguments with him to do the same, saying, they should make their Voyage in eight Months, to *Brasil*, Share 6 or 700 *l.* a Man, and then break up. Again, when the Crew came to an Election of a chief Surgeon, and this Deponent was set up with the others, *Wilson* told him, he hoped he should carry it from *Scudamore*, for that a quarter Share (which they had more than others) would be worth looking after; but the Deponent missed the Preferment, by the good Will of the *Ranger's* People, who, in general, voted for *Scudamore*, to get rid of him, (the chief Surgeon being always to remain with the Commadore.)

It appeared likewise by the Evidence of Captain *Jo. Trahern, Tho. Castel*, and others, who had been taken by the Pyrates, and thence had Opportunities of observing the Prisoners Conduct, that he seem'd thoroughly satisfy'd with that Way of Life, and was particularly intimate with *Roberts*; they often scoffing at the Mention of a Man of War, and saying, if they should meet with any of the Turnip-Man's Ships, they would blow up, and go to H—ll together. Yet setting aside these silly Freaks, to recommend himself, his Laziness had got him many Enemies, even *Roberts* told him, (on the Complaint of a wounded Man, whom he had refused to dress) that he was a double Rogue, to be there a second Time, and threat'ned to cut his Ears off.

The Evidence further assured the Court, from Captain *Thomas Tarlton*, that the Prisoner was taken out of his Brother's Ship, some Months before, a first Time, and being forward to oblige his new Company, had presently ask'd for the Pyrates Boat, to fetch the Medicine Chest away; when the Wind and Current proving too hard to contend with, they were drove on Shore at Cape *Montzerado*.

The Prisoner called for *William Darling*, and *Samuel Morwel*, (acquitted) and *Nicholas Butler*.

William Darling deposed, the first Time the Prisoner fell into their Hands, *Roberts* mistook him for *Jo. Tarlton* the Master, and being informed it was the Surgeon who came to represent him, (then indisposed,) he presently swore he should be his Mess-Mate, to which *Wilson* reply'd, he hop'd not, he had a Wife and Child, which the other laughed at; and that he had been two Days on Board, before he went in that Boat, which was drove on Shore at Cape *Montzerado*. And at his second coming, in the *Elizabeth*, he heard *Roberts* order he should be brought on Board in the first Boat.

Samuel Morwel says, that he has heard him bewail his Condition, while on Board the Pyrate, and desired one *Thomas*, to use his Interest with *Roberts*, for a Discharge, saying, his Employ, and the little Fortune he had left at Home, would, he hop'd, exempt him the further Trouble of seeking his Bread at Sea.

Nicholas Butler, who had remained with the Pyrates about 48 Hours, when they took the *French* Ships at *Whydah*, deposes, that in this Space the Prisoner addressed him in the *French* Language, several Times, deploring the Wretchedness and ill Fortune of being confined in such Company.

The Prisoner desiring Liberty of two or three Questions, ask'd, whether or no he had not expostulated with *Roberts*, for a Reason of his obliging Surgeons to sign their Articles, when heretofore they did not; Whether he had not expressed himself glad of having formerly escaped from them? Whether he had not said, at taking the Ships in *Whydah* Road, that he could like the Sport, were it lawful? And whether if he had not told him, should the Company discharge any Surgeon, that he would insist on it as his Turn? The Deponent answered, Yes, to every Question separately; and farther, that he believes *Scudamore* had not seen *Wilson* when he first came and found him out of the *Elizabeth*.

He added, in his own Defence, that being Surgeon with one *John Tarlton*, of *Leverpool*, he was met a first Time on this Coast of *Guiney*, by *Roberts* the Pyrate; who, after a Day or two, told him, to his Sorrow, that he was to stay there, and ordered him to fetch his Chest, (not Medicines, as asserted,) which Opportunity he took to make his Escape; for the Boat's Crew happening to consist of five *French* and one

English Man, all as willing as himself, they agreed to push
the Boat on Shore, and trust themselves with the Negroes
of Cape *Montzerado*: Hazardous, not only in Respect of the
dangerous Seas that run there, but the Inhumanity of the
Natives, who sometimes take a liking to humane Carcasses.
Here he remained five Months, till *Thomas Tarlton*, Brother
to his Captain chanced to put in the Road for Trade, to
whom he represented his Hardships and starving Condition;
but was, in an unchristian Manner, both refused a Release
of this Captivity, or so much as a small Supply of Biscuit
and salt Meat, because, as he said, he had been among the
Pyrates. A little Time after this, the Master of a *French* Ship
paid a Ransom for him, and took him off; but, by Reason
of a nasty leperous Indisposition he had contracted by hard
and bad living, was, to his great Misfortune set ashore at
Sestos again, when Captain *Sharp* met him, and generously
procured his Release in the Manner himself has related, and
for which he stands infinitely obliged.—That ill Luck threw
him a second Time into the Pyrate's Hands, in this Ship
Elizabeth, where he met *Thomas Tarlton*, and thoughtlesly
used some Reproaches of him, for his severe Treatment at
Montzerado; but protests without Design his Words should
have had so bad a Consequence; for *Roberts* took upon him,
as a Dispenser of Justice, the Correction of Mr. *Tarlton*,
beating him unmercifully; and he hopes it will be belived,
contrary to any Intention of his it should so happen, because
as a Stranger he might be supposed to have no Influence,
and believes there were some other Motives for it.—He cannot remember he expressed himself glad to see *Roberts* this
second Time, or that he dropped those Expressions about
Comry, as are sworn; but if immaturity of Judgment had
occasioned him to slip rash and inadvertent Words, or that
he had paid any undue Compliments to *Roberts*, it was to
ingratiate himself, as every Prisoner did, for a more civil
Treatment, and in particular to procure his Discharge, which
he had been promised, and was afraid would have been re-
voked, if such a Person as *Comry* did not remain there to

supply his Room; and of this, he said, all the Gentlemen (meaning the Pyrates) could witness for him.

He urged also his Youth in Excuse for his Rashness.— The first time he had been with them (only a Month in all,) and that in no military Employ; but in particular, the Service he had done in discovering the Design the Pyrates had to rise in their Passage on Board the *Swallow*. *Guilty*.

But Execution respited till the King's Pleasure be known, because the Commander of the *Swallow* had declared, the first Notice he received of this Design of the Pyrates to rise, was from him.

Benjamin Jefferys

By the Depositions of *Glasby* and *Lillburn* (acquitted) against this Prisoner, it appeared, that his Drunkenness was what at first detained him from going away in his proper Ship, the *Norman* Galley; and next Morning, for having been abusive in his Drink, saying to the Pyrates, there was not a Man amongst them, he received for a Welcome, six Lashes from every Person in the Ship, which disordered him for some Weeks, but on Recovery was made Boatswain's Mate; the serving of which, or any Office on Board a Pyrate, is at their own Option, (tho' elected,) because others are glad to accept what brings an additional Share in Prize.

The Deponents further say, that at *Sierraleon* every Man had more especially the Means of escaping; and that this Prisoner, in particular, neglected it, and came off from that Place after their Ship was under Sail, and going out of the River.

The Prisoner, in his Defence, protests, he was at first forc'd; and that the Office of Boatswain's Mate was imposed on him, and what he would have been glad to have relinquish'd. That the barbarous Whipping he had received from the Pyrates at first, was for telling them, that none who could get their Bread in an honest Way, would be on such an Account. And he had certainly taken the Opportunity which

presented at *Sierraleon*, of ridding himself from so distastful
a Life, if there had not been three or four of the old Pyrates
on Shore at the same Time, who, he imagined, must know
of him, and would doubtless have served him the same, if
not worse, than they since had done *William Williams*; who,
for such a Design, being delivered up by the treacherous
Natives, had received two Lashes thro' the whole Ship's
Company.

The Court observed, the Excuses of these Pyrates, about
want of Means to escape, was oftentimes as poor and evasive
as their Pleas of being forced at first; for here, at *Sierraleon*,
every Man had his Liberty on Shore, and it was evident,
might have kept it, if he, or they, had so pleased. And such
are further culpable, who having been introduced into the
Society, by such uncivil Methods, as whipping, or beating,
neglect less likely Means of regaining Liberty; it shews
strong Inclinations to Dishonesty, and they stand inexcus-
ably, *Guilty.*

Jo. Mansfield.

It was proved against this Prisoner, by Captain *Trahern* and
George Fenn, that he was one of those Voluntiers who was
at the Attack and Robbery of the Company's Ship, called
the *King Solomon*: That he bully'd well among them who
dar'd not make any Reply, but was very easy with his Friends,
who knew him; for *Moody*, on this Occasion, took a large
Glass from him, and threatned to blow his Brains out, (a
favourite Phrase with these Pyrates) if he muttered at it.

From others acquitted, it likewise appeared, that he was
at first a Voluntier among them, from an Island call'd *Dominico*, in the *West-Indies*, and had to recommend himself, told
them, he was a Deserter from the *Rose* Man of War, and
before that, had been on the High-Way; he was always
drunk, they said, and so bad at the Time they met with the
Swallow, that he knew nothing of the Action, but came up
vapouring with his Cutlash, after the *Fortune* had struck her
Colours, to know who would go on Board the Prize; and it

was some Time before they could perswade him into the Truth of their Condition.

He could say little in Defence of himself, acknowledg'd this latter Part of Drunkenness; a Vice, he says, that had too great a Share in insnaring him into this Course of Life, and had been a greater Motive with him than Gold. *Guilty.*

William Davis.

William Allen deposed, he knew this Prisoner at *Sierraleon*, belonging to the *Ann* Galley; that he had a Quarrel with, and beat the Mate of that Ship, for which (as he said) being afraid to return to his Duty, he consorted to the idle Customs and Ways of living among the Negroes, from whom he received a Wife, and ungratefully sold her, one Evening, for some Punch to quench his Thirst. After this, having put himself under the Protection of Mr. *Plunket*, Governor there for the Royal *African* Company: The Relations and Friends of the Woman, apply'd to him for Redress, who immediately surrendered the Prisoner, and told them, he did not care if they took his Head off; but the Negroes wisely judging it would not fetch so good a Price, they sold him in his Turn again to Seignior *Jossee*, a Christian Black, and Native of that Place; who expected and agreed for two Years Service from him, on Consideration of what he had disbursed, for the Redemption of the Woman: But long before the Expiration of this Time, *Roberts* came into *Sierraleon* River, where the Prisoner, (as Seignior *Jossee* assured the Deponent,) entered a Voluntier with them.

The Deponent further corroborates this Part of the Evidence; in that he being obliged to call at Cape *Mount*, in his Passage down hither, met there with two Deserters from *Roberts*'s Ship, who assured him of the same; and that the Pyrates did design to turn *Davis* away the next Opportunity, as an idle good-for-nothing Fellow.

From *Glasby* and *Lilburn*, it was evident, that every Pyrate, while they stay'd at *Sierraleon*, went on Shore at Discretion. That *Roberts* had often assured Mr. *Glyn* and other Traders, at that Place, that he would force no Body; and in short, there was no Occasion for it; in particular, the Prisoner's Row-Mate went away, and thinks, he might have done the same, if he had pleased.

The Prisoner alleged his having been detained against his Will, and says, that returning with Elephants Teeth for *Sierraleon*, the Pyrate's Boat pursued and brought him on Board, where he was kept on Account of his understanding the Pilotage and Navigation of that River.

It was obvious to the Court, not only how frivolous Excuses of Constraint and Force were among these People, at their first commencing Pyrates, but also it was plain to them, from these two Deserters, met at Cape *Mount*, and the discretional Manner they lived in, at *Sierraleon*; thro' how little Difficulty several of them did, and others might, have escaped afterwards, if they could but have obtained their own Consents for it. *Guilty.*

This is the Substance of the Tryals of *Roberts*'s Crew, which may suffice for others, that occur in this Book. The foregoing Lists, shews, by a * before the Names, who were condemn'd; those Names with a † were referred for Tryal to the *Marshalsea*, and all the rest were acquitted.

The following Pyrates were executed, according to their Sentence, without the Gates of Cape *Corso-Castle*, within the Flood-Marks, *viz.*

Mens Names	Years of Age	Habitations
William Magnes	35	*Minehead.*
Richard Hardy	25	*Wales.*
David Sympson	36	*North-Berwick.*
Christopher Moody	28	
Thomas Sutton	23	*Berwick.*
Valentine Ashplant	32	*Minories.*
Peter de Vine	42	*Stepney.*
William Philips	29	*Lower-Shadwell.*

Philip Bill	27	St. *Thomas's*
William Main	28	
William Mackintosh	21	*Canterbury.*
William Williams	40	nigh *Plymouth.*
Robert Haws	31	*Yarmouth.*
William Petty	30	*Deptford.*
John Jaynson	22	nigh *Lancaster.*
Marcus Johnson	21	*Smyrna.*
Robert Crow	44	*Isle of Man.*
Michael Maer	41	*Ghent.*
Daniel Harding	26	*Croomsbury* in *Somersetshire*
William Fernon	22	*Somersetshire.*
Jo. More	19	*Meer* in *Wiltshire.*
Abraham Harper	23	*Bristol.*
Jo. Parker	22	*Winfred* in *Dorsetshire.*
Jo. Philips	28	*Alloway* in *Scotland.*
James Clement	20	*Jersey.*
Peter Scudamore	35	*Bristol.*
James Skyrm	44	*Wales.*
John Walden	24	*Somersetshire.*
Jo. Stephenson	40	*Whitby.*
Jo. Mansfield	30	*Orkneys.*
Israel Hynde	30	*Bristol.*
Peter Lesley	21	*Aberdeen.*
Charles Bunce	26	*Exeter.*
Robert Birtson	30	*Other* St. *Maries Devonshire.*
Richard Harris	45	*Cornwall.*
Joseph Nositer	26	*Sadbury* in *Devonshire.*
William Williams	30	Speechless at Execution.
Agge Jacobson	30	*Holland.*
Benjamin Jefferys	21	*Bristol.*
Cuthbert Goss	21	*Topsham.*
John Jessup	20	*Plymouth.*
Edward Watts	22	*Dunmore.*
Thomas Giles	26	*Mine-head.*

William Wood	27	*York.*
Thomas Armstrong	34	*London,* executed on board the *Weymouth.*
Robert Johnson	32	at *Whydah.*
George Smith	25	*Wales.*
William Watts	23	*Ireland.*
James Philips	35	*Antegoa.*
John Coleman	24	*Wales.*
Robert Hays	20	*Liverpool.*
William Davis	23	*Wales.*

The Remainder of the Pyrates, whose Names are under mentioned, upon their humble Petition to the Court, had their Sentence changed from Death, to seven Years Servitude, conformable to our Sentence of Transportation; the Petition is as follows.

To the Honourable the President and Judges of the Court of Admiralty, for trying of Pyrates, sitting at Cape Corso-Castle. *the 20th Day of* April, 1722.

The humble Petition of *Thomas How, Samuel Fletcher, &c.* Humbly sheweth,
That your Petitioners being unhappily, and unwarily drawn into that wretched and detestable Crime of Pyracy, for which they now stand justly condemned, they most humbly pray the Clemency of the Court, in the Mitigation of their Sentence, that they may be permitted to serve the Royal African *Company of* England, *in this Country for seven Years, in such a Manner as the Court shall think proper; that by their just Punishment, being made sensible of the Error of their former Ways, they will for the future become faithful Subjects, good Servants, and useful in their Stations, if it please the Almighty to prolong their Lives.*
And your Petitioners, as in Duty, *&c.*

The Resolution of the Court was,
That the Petitioners have Leave by this Court of Admiralty, to

interchange Indentures with the Captain General of the Gold
Coast, *for the Royal* African *Company, for seven Years Servi-*
tude, at any of the Royal African *Company's Settlements in*
Africa, *in such Manner as he the said Captain General shall*
think proper.

On Thursday *the 26th Day of* April, *the Indentures being*
all drawn out, according to the Grant made to the Petitioners,
by the Court held on Friday *the 20th of this Instant; each Pris-*
oner was sent for up, signed, sealed and exchanged them in the
Presence of

> *Captain* Mungo Herdman, *President,*
> James Phipps, *Esq;*
> *Mr.* Edward Hyde,
> *Mr.* Charles Fanshaw,
> *And Mr.* John Atkins, *Register.*

A Copy of the Indenture.

The Indenture of a Person condemned to serve abroad for
  Pyracy, which, upon the humble Petition of the Pyrates
  therein mentioned, was most mercifully granted by his
  Imperial Majesty's Commissioners and Judges appointed
  to hold a Court of Admiralty, for the Tryal of Pyrates at
  Cape *Corso-Castle*, in *Africa*, upon Condition of serving
  seven Years, and other Conditions, are as follows, *viz.*

This Indenture made the twenty sixth Day of April. Anno
Regni Regis Georgii magnæ Britanniæ &c. Septimo, Dom-
ini, Millessimo, Sepcentessimo viginti duo, *between* Roger
Scot, *late of the City of* Bristol *Mariner, of the one Part, and*
the Royal African *Company of* England, *their Captain General*
and Commander in Chief, for the Time being, on the other Part,
Witnesseth, *that the said* Roger Scot, *doth hereby covenant,*
and agree to, and with, the said Royal African *Company, their*
Captain General, and Commander in chief for the Time being,
to serve him, or his lawful Successors, in any of the Royal African
Company's Settlements on the Coast of Africa, *from the Day of*

the Date of these Presents, to the full Term of seven Years, from hence next ensuing, fully to be compleat and ended; there to serve in such Employment, as the said Captain General, or his Successors shall employ him; according to the Custom of the Country in like Kind.

In Consideration whereof, the said Captain General, and Commander in chief doth covenant and agree, to, and with, the said Roger Scot, to find and allow him Meat, Drink, Apparel and Lodging, according to the Custom of the Country.

In witness whereof, the Parties aforesaid, to these Presents, have interchangably put their Hands and Seals, the Day and Year first above written.

Signed, sealed and delivered, in the Presence of us, at Cape Corso-Castle, in Africa, where no stamp'd Paper was to be had.

Mungo Heardman, *President*,
John Atkins, *Register*, } Witnesses.

In like Manner was drawn out and exchanged the Indentures of

Thomas How of Barnstable, in the County of Devon.
Samuel Fletcher of East-Smithfield, London.
John Lane of Lambard-Street, London.
David Littlejohn of Bristol.
John King of Shadwell Parish, London.
Henry Dennis of Bidiford.
Hugh Harris of Cors-Castle, Devonshire.
William Taylor of Bristol.
Thomas Owen of Bristol.
John Mitchel of Shadwell Parish, London.
Joshua Lee of Leverpool.
William Shuren of Wapping Parish, London.
Robert Hartley of Leverpool.
John Griffin of Blackwall, Middlesex.
James Cromby of London, Wapping.
James Greenham of Marshfield, Gloucestershire.
John Horn of St. James's Parish, London.

John Jessop of *Wisbich, Cambridgeshire.*
David Rice of *Bristol.*

None of which, I hear, are now living, two others, *viz.*
George Wilson and *Thomas Oughterlaney*, were respited from
Execution, till his Majesty's Pleasure should be known; the
former dy'd abroad, and the latter came Home, and received
his Majesty's Pardon; the Account of the whole stands thus,

Acquitted,		74
Executed,		52
Respited,		2
To Servitude,		20
To the *Marshalsea*,		17
Kill'd {	In the *Ranger*,	10
	In the *Fortune*,	3
Dy'd {	In the passage to Cape *Corso*,	15
	afterwards in the Castle,	4
Negroes in both Ships,		70

Total, 267

I am not ignorant how acceptable the Behaviour and dying Words of Malefactors are to the generality of our Countrymen, and therefore shall deliver what occurr'd, worthy of
Notice, in the Behaviour of these Criminals.

The first six that were called to Execution were *Magnes,
Moody, Sympson, Sutton, Ashplant,* and *Hardy*; all of them
old Standers and notorious Offenders: When they were
brought out of the Hold, on the Parade, in order to break
off their Fetters, and fit the Halters; none of them, it was
observed, appeared the least dejected, unless *Sutton*, who
spoke faint, but it was rather imputed to a Flux that had
seiz'd him two or three Days before, than Fear. A Gentleman, who was Surgeon of the Ship, was so charitable at this
Time, to offer himself in the room of an Ordinary, and represented to them, as well as he was able, the Heinousness of
their Sin, and Necessity which lay on them of Repentance;

one particular Part of which ought to be, acknowledging the Justice they had met with. They seem'd heedless for the present, some calling for Water to drink, and others applying to the Soldiers for Caps, but when this Gentleman press'd them for an Answer, they all exclaim'd against the Severity of the Court, and were so harden'd, as to curse, and wish the same Justice might overtake all the Members of it, as had been dealt to them. *They were poor Rogues*, they said, *and so hang'd, while others, no less guilty in another Way, escaped.*

When he endeavoured to compose their Minds, exhorting them to dye in Charity with all the World, and would have diverted them from such vain Discourse, by asking them their Country, Age, and the like; some of them answered, 'What 'was that to him, they suffered the Law, and should 'give no Account but to God;' walking to the Gallows without a Tear, in Token of Sorrow for their past Offences, or shewing as much Concern as a Man would express at travelling a bad Road; nay, *Sympson*, at seeing a Woman that he knew, said, 'he had lain with that B—h three times, and now 'she was come to see him hang'd.' And *Hardy*, when his Hands were ty'd behind him, (which happened from their not being acquainted with the Way of bringing Malefactors to Execution,) observed, 'that he had seen many a Man hang'd, but 'this Way of the Hands being ty'd behind them, he 'was a Stranger to, and never saw before in his 'Life.' I mention these two little Instances, to shew how stupid and thoughtless they were of their End, and that the same abandoned and reprobate Temper that had carried them thro' their Rogueries, abided with them to the last.

Samuel Fletcher, another of the Pyrates ordered for Execution, but reprieved, seem'd to have a quicker Sense of his Condition; for when he saw those he was allotted with gone to Execution, he sent a Message by the Provost-Marshal to the Court, to be 'inform'd of the Meaning of it, and humbly desir'd 'to know whether they design'd him Mercy, or not? 'If they did, he stood infinitely oblig'd to them, and 'thought the whole Service of his Life an incompetent Return for so great a Favour; but that if he 'was to suffer, the sooner the better, *he said*, that 'he might be out of his Pain.'

There were others of these Pyrates the reverse of this, and tho' destitute of Ministers, or fit Persons to represent their Sins, and assist them with spiritual Advice, were yet always imploying their Time to good Purposes, and behaved with a great deal of seeming Devotion and Penitence; among these may be reckon'd *Scudamore, Williams, Philips, Stephenson, Jefferys, Lesly, Harper, Armstrong, Bunce*, and others.

Scudamore too lately discerned the Folly and Wickedness of the Enterprize, that had chiefly brought him under Sentence of Death, from which, seeing there was no Hopes of escaping, he petitioned for two or three Days Reprieve, which was granted; and for that Time apply'd himself incessantly to Prayer, and reading the Scriptures, seem'd to have a deep Sense of his Sins, of this in particular, and desired, at the Gallows, they would have Patience with him, to sing the first Part of the thirty first Psalm; which he did by himself throughout.

Armstrong, having been a Deserter from his Majesty's Service, was executed on Board the *Weymouth*, (and the only one that was;) there was no Body to press him to an Acknowledgement of the Crime he died for, nor of sorrowing in particular for it, which would have been exemplary, and made suitable Impressions on Seamen; so that his last Hour was spent in lamenting and bewailing his Sins in general, exhorting the Spectators to an honest and good Life, in which alone they could find Satisfaction. In the End, he desir'd they would join with him in singing two or three latter Verses of the 140th Psalm; and that being concluded, he was, at the firing of a Gun, tric'd up at the Fore-Yard-Arm.

Bunce was a young Man, not above 26 Years old, but made the most pathetical Speech of any at the Gallows. He first declaim'd against the guilded Bates of Power, Liberty, and Wealth, that had ensnar'd him among the Pyrates, his unexperienc'd Years not being able to withstand the Temptation;

but that the Briskness he had shewn, which so fatally had procured him Favour amongst them, was not so much a Fault in Principle, as the Liveliness and Vivacity of his Nature. He was now extreamly afflicted for the Injuries he had done to all Men, and begg'd their's and God's Forgiveness, very earnestly exhorting the Spectators to remember their Creator in their Youth, and guard betimes, that their Minds took not a wrong Byass, concluding with this apt Similitude, *That he stood there as a Beacon upon a Rock*, (the Gallows standing on one) *to warn erring Marriners of Danger.*

CHAPTER X.

of *Captain* ANSTIS, And his CREW.

*T*HOMAS *ANSTIS* ship'd himself at *Providence* in the Year 1718, aboard the *Buck* Sloop, and was one of six that conspired together to go off a pyrating with the Vessel; the rest were, *Howel Davis*, *Roberts*'s Predecessor, killed at the Island of *Princes; Dennis Topping*, killed at the taking of the rich *Portuguese* Ship on the Coast of *Brasil; Walter Kennedy*, hanged at *Execution-Dock*, and two others, which I forbear to name, because, I understand they are at this Day employ'd in an honest Vocation in the City.

What followed concerning *Anstis*'s Pyracies, has been in-cluded in the two preceeding Chapters; I shall only observe that the Combination of these six Men abovementioned, was the Beginning of that Company, that afterwards proved so formidable under Captain *Roberts*, from whom *Anstis* sepa-rated the 18th of *April* 1721, in the *Good Fortune* Brigantine, leaving his Commadore to pursue his Adventures upon the Coast of *Guiney*, whilst he returned to the *West-Indies*, upon the like Design.

About the Middle of *June*, these Pyrates met with one Captain *Marston*, between *Hispaniola* and *Jamaica*, bound on a Voyage to *New-York*; from whom they took all the wearing Apparel they could find, as also his Liquors and Provision, and five of his Men, but did not touch his Cargo; two or three other Vessels were also plundered by them, in this Cruise, out of whom they stocked themselves with Provision and Men; among the rest, I think, was the *Irwin*, Captain *Ross*, from *Cork* in *Ireland*; but this I won't be positive of, because they denied it themselves. This Ship had 600 Barrels of Beef aboard, besides other Provisions, and was taken off *Martinico*, wherein Colonel *Doyly* of *Montserrat*, and his Family were Passengers. The Colonel was very much abused and wounded, for endeavouring to save a poor Woman, that was also a Passenger, from the Insults of that brutish Crew; and the Pyrates prevailing, twenty one of them forced the poor Creature successively, afterwards broke her Back and flung her into the Sea. I say, I will not be positive it was *Anstis*'s Crew that acted this unheard of Violence and Cruelty, tho' the Circumstances of the Place, the Time, the Force of the Vessel, and the Number of Men, do all concur, and I can place the Villany no where else; but that such a Fact was done, there is too much Evidence for it to be doubted of.

When they thought fit to put an End to this Cruize, they went into one of the Islands to clean, which they effected without any Disturbance, and came out again, and stretching away towards *Burmudas*, met with a stout Ship, called the *Morning Star*, bound from *Guiney* to *Carolina*; they made Prize of her, and kept her for their own Use. In a Day or two, a Ship from *Barbadoes*, bound to *New-York*, fell into their Hands, and taking out her Guns and Tackle, mounted the *Morning Star* with 32 Pieces of Cannon, mann'd her with a 100 Men, and appointed one *John Fenn* Captain; for the Brigantine being of far less Force, the *Morning Star* would have fallen to *Anstis*, as elder Officer, yet he was so in Love with his own Vessel, (she being an excellent Sailor,) that he made it his Choice to stay in her, and let *Fenn*, who was, before, his Gunner, Command the great Ship.

Now, that they had two good Ships well mann'd, it may be supposed they were in a Condition to undertake something bold: But their Government was disturbed by Malecontents, and a Kingdom divided within it self cannot stand;

they had such a Number of new Men amongst them, that seem'd not so violently enclined for the Game; that whatever the Captain proposed, it was certainly carried against him, so that they came to no fix'd Resolution for the undertaking any Enterprize; therefore there was nothing to be done, but to break up the Company, which seemed to be the Inclination of the Majority, but the Manner of doing so, concerned their common Safety; to which Purpose various Means were proposed, at length it was concluded to send home a Petition to his Majesty (there being then no Act of Indemnity in Force) for a Pardon, and wait the Issue; at the same Time one *Jones*, Boatswain of the *Good Fortune*, proposed a Place of safe Retreat, it being an uninhabited Island near *Cuba*, which he had been used to in the late War, when he went a privateering against the *Spaniards*.

This being approved of, it was unanimously resolved on, and the underwritten Petition drawn up and signed by the whole Company in the Manner of what they call a *Round Robin*, that is, the Names were writ in a Circle, to avoid all Appearance of Pre-eminence, and least any Person should be mark'd out by the Government, as a principal Rogue among them.

To his most sacred Majesty George, *by the Grace of God, of* Great-Britain, France *and* Ireland, *King, Defender of the Faith,* &c.

The humble P E T I T I O N of the Company, now belonging to the Ship *Morning Star*, and Brigantine *Good Fortune*, lying under the ignominious Name and Denomination of P Y R A T E S.

Humbly sheweth,
That we your Majesty's most loyal Subjects, have, at sundry Times, been taken by Bartholomew Roberts, *the then Captain of the above said Vessels and Company, together with another Ship, in which we left him; and have been forced by him and*

his wicked Accomplices, to enter into, and serve, in the said Company, as Pyrates, much contrary to our Wills and Inclinations: And we your loyal Subjects utterly abhoring and detesting that impious way of Living, did, with an unanimous Consent, and contrary to the Knowledge of the said Roberts, *or his Accomplices, on, or about the 18th Day of* April 1721, *leave, and ran away with the aforesaid Ship* Morning Star, *and Brigantine* Good Fortune, *with no other Intent and Meaning than the Hopes of obtaining your Majesty's most gracious Pardon. And, that we your Majesty's most loyal Subjects, may with more Safety return to our native Country, and serve the Nation, unto which we belong, in our respective Capacities, without Fear of being prosecuted by the Injured, whose Estates have suffered by the said* Roberts *and his Accomplices, during our forcible Detainment, by the said Company: We most humbly implore your Majesty's most royal Assent, to this our humble Petition.*

And your Petitioners shall ever pray.

This Petition was sent home by a Merchant Ship bound to *England,* from *Jamaica,* who promised to speak with the Petitioners, in their Return, about 20 Leagues to Windward of that Island, and let them know what Success their Petition met with. When this was done, the Pyrates retires to the Island before proposed, with the Ship and Brigantine.

This Island (which I have no Name for) lies off the Southwest End of *Cuba,* uninhabited, and little frequented. On the East End is a Lagune, so narrow, that a Ship can but just go in, tho' there's from 15 to 22 Foot Water, for almost a League up: On both Sides of the Lagune grows red Mangrove Trees, very thick, that the Entrance of it, as well as the Vessels laying there, is hardly to be seen. In the Middle of the Island are here and there a small thick Wood of tall Pines, and other Trees scattered about in different Places.

Here they staid about nine Months, but not having Provision for above two, they were forced to take what the Island afforded, which was Fish of several Sorts, particularly Turtle, which latter was the chiefest Food they lived on, and was found in great Plenty on the Coasts of this Island; whether there might be any wild Hogs, Beer, or other Cattle, common to several Islands of the *West-Indies*, or that the Pyrates were too idle to hunt them, or whether they preferr'd other Provisions to that sort of Diet, I know not; but I was informed by them, that for the whole Time they eat not a Bit of any kind of Flesh-Meat, nor Bread; the latter was supply'd by Rice, of which they had a great Quantity aboard: This was boyl'd and squeez'd dry, and so eat with the Turtle.

There are three or four Sorts of these Creatures in the *West-Indies*, the largest of which will weigh 150 or 200 Pound Weight or more, but those that were found upon this Island were of the smallest Kind, weighing 10 or 12 Pounds each, with a fine natural wrought Shell, and beautifully clouded; the Meat sweet and tender, some Part of it eating like Chicken, some like Veal, *&c.* so that it was no extraordinary Hardship for them to live upon this Provision alone, since it affords variety of Meats to the Taste, of it self. The manner of catching this Fish is very particular; you must understand, that in the Months of *May*, *June* and *July*, they lay their Eggs in order to hatch their Young, and this three times in a Season, which is always in the Sand of the Seashore, each laying 80 or 90 Eggs at a time. The Male accompanies the Female, and come ashore in the Night only, when they must be watch'd, without making any Noise, or having a Light; as soon as they land, the Men that watch for them, turn them on their Backs, then haul them above high Water Mark, and leave them till next Morning, where they are sure to find them, for they can't turn again, nor move from the Place. It is to be observ'd, that besides their laying time, they come ashore to feed, but then what's very remarkable in these Creatures, they always resort to different Places to breed, leaving their usual Haunts for two or three Months, and 'tis thought they eat nothing in all that Season.

They pass'd their Time here in Dancing, and other Diversions, agreeable to these sort of Folks; and among the rest, they appointed a Mock Court of Judicature to try one an-

other for Pyracy, and he that was a Criminal one Day was
made Judge another. I had an Account given me of one of
these merry Tryals, and as it appeared diverting, I shall give
the Readers a short Account of it.

The Court and Criminals being both appointed, as also
Council to plead, the Judge got up in a Tree, and had a dirty
Taurpaulin hung over his Shoulders; this was done by Way
of Robe, with a Thrum Cap on his Head, and a large Pair
of Spectacles upon his Nose: Thus equipp'd, he settled himself in his Place, and abundance of Officers attending him
below, with Crows, Handpikes, &c. instead of Wands, Tip-
staves, and such like.—The Criminals were brought out,
making a thousand four Faces; and one who acted as
Attorney-General opened the Charge against them; their
Speeches were very laconick, and their whole Proceedings
concise. We shall give it by Way of Dialogue.

Attorn. Gen. An't please your Lordship, and you Gentlemen of the Jury, here is a Fellow before you that is a sad
Dog, a sad sad Dog; and I humbly hope your Lordship will
order him to be hang'd out of the Way immediately.—He
has committed Pyracy upon the High Seas, and we shall
prove, an't please your Lordship, that this Fellow, this sad
Dog before you, has escap'd a thousand Storms, nay, has got
safe ashore when the Ship has been cast away, which was a
certain Sign he was not born to be drown'd; yet not having
the Fear of hanging before his Eyes, he went on robbing and
ravishing Man, Woman and Child, plundering Ships Cargoes fore and aft, burning and sinking Ship, Bark and Boat,
as if the Devil had been in him. But this is not all, my Lord,
he has committed worse Villanies than all these, for we shall
prove, that he has been guilty of drinking Small-Beer; and
your Lordship knows, there never was a sober Fellow but
what was a Rogue.—My Lord, I should have spoke much
finer than I do now, but that, as your Lordship knows our
Rum is all out, and how should a Man speak good Law that
has not drank a Dram.—However, I hope, your Lordship
will order the Fellow to be hang'd.

Judge.—Hearkee me, Sirrah,—you lousy, pittiful, ill-look'd Dog; what have you to say why you should not be tuck'd up immediately, and set a Sun-drying like a Scare-crow?—Are you guilty, or not guilty?

Pris. Not guilty, an't please your Worship.

Judge. Not guilty! say so again, Sirrah, and I'll have you hang'd without any Tryal.

Pris. An't please your Worship's Honour, my Lord, I am as honest a poor Fellow as ever went between Stem and Stern of a Ship, and can hand, reef, steer, and clap two Ends of a Rope together, as well as e'er a He that ever cross'd salt Water; but I was taken by one *George Bradley* [the Name of him that sat as Judge,] a notorious Pyrate, a sad Rogue as ever was unhang'd, and he forc'd me, an't please your Honour.

Judge. Answer me, Sirrah,—How will you be try'd?

Pris. By G— and my Country.

Judge. The Devil you will.—Why then, Gentlemen of the Jury, I think we have nothing to do but to proceed to Judgment.

Attor. Gen. Right, my Lord; for if the Fellow should be suffer'd to speak, he may clear himself, and that's an Affront to the Court.

Pris. Pray, my Lord, I hope your Lordship will consider—

Judge. Consider!—How dare you talk of considering?—Sirrah, Sirrah, I never consider'd in all my Life.—I'll make it Treason to consider.

Pris. But, I hope, your Lordship will hear some Reason.

Judge. D'ye hear how the Scoundrel prates?—What have we to do with Reason?—I'd have you to know, Raskal, we don't sit here to hear Reason;—we go according to Law.—Is our Dinner ready?

Attor. Gen. Yes, my Lord.

Judge. Then heark'ee, you Raskal at the Bar; hear me, Sirrah, hear me.—You must suffer, for three Reasons; first, because it is not fit I should sit here as Judge, and no Body be hang'd.—Secondly, you must be hang'd, because you have a damn'd hanging Look:—And thirdly, you must be hang'd, because I am hungry; for know, Sirrah, that 'tis a Custom, that whenever the Judge's Dinner is ready before the Tryal is over, the Prisoner is to be hang'd of Course.—There's Law for you, ye Dog.—So take him away Goaler.

This is the Tryal just as it was related to me; the Design of my setting it down, is only to shew how these Fellows can jest upon Things, the Fear and Dread of which, should make them tremble.

The beginning of *August* 1722, the Pyrates made ready the Brigantine, and came out to Sea, and beating up to Windward, lay in the Track for their Correspondant in her Voyage to *Jamaica*, and spoke with her; but finding nothing was done in *England* in their Favour, as 'twas expected, they return'd to their consorts at the Island with the ill news, and found themselves under a necessity, as they fancied; to continue that abominable Course of Life they had lately practis'd; in order thereto, they sail'd with the Ship and Brigantine to the Southward, and the next Night, by intolerable Neglect, they run the *Morning Star* upon the *Grand Caimanes*, and wreck'd her; the Brigantine seeing the Fate of her Consort, hall'd off in Time, and so weather'd the Island. The next Day Captain *Anstis* put in, and found that all, or the greatest part of the Crew, were safe ashore, whereupon she came to an Anchor, in order to fetch them off; and having brought *Fenn* the Captain, *Philips* the Carpenter, and a few others aboard, two Men of War came down upon them, *viz.* the *Hector* and *Adventure*, so that the Brigantine had but just Time to cut their Cable, and get to Sea, with one of the Men of War after her, keeping within Gun-shot for several Hours, *Anstis* and his Crew were now under the greatest Consternation imaginable, finding the Gale freshen, and the Man of War gaining Ground upon them, so that, in all Probability, they must have been Prisoners in two Hours more; but it pleased God to give them a little longer Time, the Wind dying away, the Pyrates got out their Oars, and row'd for their Lives, and thereby got clear of their Enemy.

The *Hector* landed her Men upon the Island, and took 40 of the *Morning Star*'s Crew, without any Resistance made by them; but on the contrary, alledging, they were forc'd Men, and that they were glad of this Opportunity to escape from the Pyrates; the rest hid themselves in the Woods, and could not be found. *George Bradley* the Master, and three more, surrender'd afterwards to a *Burmudas* Sloop, and were carried to that Island.

The Brigantine, after her Escape, sail'd to a small Island near the Bay of *Honduras*, to clean and refit, and, in her Way thither, took a *Rhode Island* Sloop, Captain *Durfey*, Commander, and two or three other Vessels, which they destroy'd, but brought all the Hands aboard their own.

While she was cleaning, a Scheme was concerted between Captain *Durfey*, some other Prisoners, and two or three of the Pyrates, for to seize some of the Chiefs, and carry off the Brigantine; but the same being discovered before she was fit for sailing, their Design was prevented: However, Captain *Durfey*, and four or five more, got ashore with some Arms and Ammunition; and when the Pyrates Canoe came in for Water, he seiz'd the Boat with the Men; upon which *Anstis* ordered another Boat to be mann'd with 30 Hands and sent ashore, which was accordingly done; but Captain *Durfey*, and the Company he had by that Time got together, gave them such a warm Reception, that they were contented to betake themselves to their Vessel again.

About the beginning of *December*, 1722, *Anstis* left this Place and return'd to the Islands, designing to accumulate all the Power and Strength he could, since there was no looking back. He took in the Cruise a good Ship, commanded by Captain *Smith*, which he mounted with 24 Guns, and *Fenn*, a one handed Man, who commanded the *Morning-Star* when she was lost, went aboard to command her. They cruis'd together, and took a Vessel or two, and then went to the *Bahama Islands*, and there met with what they wanted, *viz.* a Sloop loaded with Provisions, from *Dublin*, called the *Antelope*.

It was time now to think of some Place to fit up and clean their Frigate lately taken, and put her in a Condition to do Business; accordingly they pitch'd upon the Island of *Tobago*, where they arrived the beginning of *April*, 1723, with the *Antelope* Sloop and her Cargo.

They fell to work immediately, got the Guns, Stores, and every Thing else out upon the Island, and put the Ship upon the Heel; and just then, as ill Luck would have it, came in the *Winchelsea* Man of War, by Way of Visit, which put the Marooners into such a Surprize, that they set Fire to the Ship and Sloop, and fled ashore to the Woods. *Anstis*, in the Brigantine, escap'd, by having a light Pair of Heels, but it put his Company into such a Disorder, that their Government could never be set to rights again; for some of the New-Comers, and those who had been tir'd with the Trade, put an End to the Reign, by shooting *Tho. Anstis* in his Hammock, and afterwards the Quarter-Master, and two or three others; the rest submitting, they put into Irons, and surrender'd them up, and the Vessel, at *Curacco*, a *Dutch* Settlement, where they were try'd and hang'd; and those concerned in delivering up the Vessel, acquitted.

But to return to Captain *Fenn*, he was taken stragling with his Gunner and three more, a Day or two after their Misfortune, by the Man of War's Men, and carry'd to *Antegoa*, where they were all executed, and *Fenn* hang'd in Chains. Those who remain'd, staid some Time in the Island, keeping up and down in the Woods, with a Hand to look out; at length Providence so order'd it, that a small Sloop came into the Harbour, which they all got aboard of, except two or three Negroes, and those they left behind. They did not think fit to pursue any further Adventures, and therefore unanimously resolved to steer for *England*, which they accordingly did, and in *October* last came into *Bristol* Channel, sunk the Sloop, and getting ashore in the Boat, dispersed themselves to their Abodes.

✗✗✗✗✗✗✗✗✗✗✗✗✗✗✗✗✗✗✗✗✗✗

CHAPTER XI.

of
Captain WORLEY,
And his CREW.

HIS REIGN was but short, but his Beginning somewhat particular, setting out in a small open Boat,
with eight others, from *New-York*. This was as resolute a Crew as ever went upon this Account: They took
with them a few Biscuits, and a dry'd Tongue or two, a little
Cag of Water, half a dozen old Muskets and Ammunition
accordingly. Thus provided, they left *New-York* the latter
End of *September* 1718, but it cannot be supposed that such
a Man of War as this, could undertake any considerable Voyage, or attempt any extraordinary Enterprize; so they stood
down the Coast, till they came to *Delaware* River, which is
about 150 Miles distant, and not meeting with any Thing
in their Way, they turn'd up the same River as high as *New-
castle*, near which Place they fell upon a Shallop belonging
to *George Grant*, who was bringing Houshold Goods, Plate,
&c. from *Oppoquenimi* to *Philadelphia*; they made Prize of
the most valuable Part of them, and let the Shallop go. This
Fact could not come under the Article of Pyracy, it not being
committed *Super altum Mare*, upon the High-Sea, therefore
was a simple Robbery only; but they did not stand for a Point
of Law in the Case, but easing the Shallop Man of his Lading, the bold Adventurers went down the River again.

The Shallop came straight to *Philadelphia*, and brought
the ill News thither, which so alarm'd the Government, as

if War had been declared against them; Expresses were sent to *New-York*, and other Places, and several Vessels fitted out against this powerful Rover, but to no manner of Purpose; for after several Days Cruize, they all return'd, without so much as hearing what became of the Robbers.

Worley and his Crew, in going down the River, met with a Sloop of *Philadelphia*, belonging to a Mulatto, whom they call'd *Black Robbin*; they quitted their Boat for this Sloop, taking one of *Black Robin*'s Men along with them, as they had also done from *George Grant*, besides two Negroes, which encreased the Company one Third. A Day or two after, they took another Sloop belonging to *Hull*, homeward bound, which was somewhat fitter for their Purpose; they found aboard her, Provisions and Necessaries, which they stood in need of, and enabled them to prosecute their Design, in a manner more suitable to their Wishes.

Upon the Success of these Rovers, the Governor issued out a Proclamation, for the apprehending and taking all Pyrates, who had refused or neglected to surrender themselves, by the Time limited in his Majesty's Proclamation of Pardon; and thereupon, ordered his Majesty's Ship *Phoenix*, of 20 Guns, which lay at *Sandy Hook*, to Sea, to cruize upon this Pyrate, and secure the Trade to that, and the adjoining Colonies.

In all probability, the taking this Sloop sav'd their Bacons, for this Time, tho' they fell into the Trap presently afterwards; for they finding themselves in tolerable good Condition; having a Vessel newly cleaned, with Provisions, &c. they stood off to Sea, and so missed the *Phænix*, who expected them to be still on the Coast.

About six Weeks afterwards they returned, having taken both a Sloop and a Brigantine, among the *Bahama* Islands; the former they sunk, and the other they let go: The Sloop belonged to *New-York*, and they thought the sinking of her good Policy, to prevent her returning to tell Tales at Home.

Worley had by this Time encreased his Company to about

five and twenty Men, had six Guns mounted, and small
Arms as many as were necessary for them, and seem'd to be
in a good thriving sort of a Way. He made a black Ensign,
with a white Death's Head in the Middle of it, and other
Colours suitable to it. They all signed Articles, and bound
themselves under a solemn Oath, to take no Quarters, but
to stand by one another to the last Man, which was rashly
fulfill'd a little afterwards.

For going into an Inlet in *North-Carolina*, to clean, the
Governor received Information of it, and fitted out two
Sloops, one of eight Guns, and the other with six, and about
seventy Men between them. *Worley* had clean'd his Sloop,
and sail'd before the *Carolina* Sloops reached the Place, and
steered to the Northward; but the Sloops just mentioned,
pursuing the same Course, came in sight of *Worley*, as he
was cruising off the Capes of *Virginia*, and being in the Of-
fin, he stood in as soon as he saw the Sloops, intending
thereby to have cut them off from *James* River; for he verily
believed they had been bound thither, not imagining, in the
least, they were in Pursuit of him.

The two Sloops standing towards the Capes at the same
Time, and *Worley* hoisting of his black Flag, the Inhabitants
of *James* Town were in the utmost Consternation, thinking
that all three had been Pyrates, and that their Design had
been upon them; so that all the Ships and Vessels that were
in the Road, or in the Rivers up the Bay, had Orders immediately to hale in to the Shore, for their Security, or else
to prepare for their Defence, if they thought themselves in
a Condition to fight. Soon after two Boats, which were sent
out to get Intelligence, came crowding in, and brought an
Account, that one of the Pyrates was in the Bay, being a
small Sloop of six Guns. The Governor expecting the rest
would have followed, and altogether make some Attempt to
land, for the sake of Plunder, beat to Arms, and collected all
the Force that could be got together, to oppose them; he
ordered all the Guns out of the Ships, to make a Platform,

and, in short, put the whole Colony in a warlike Posture; but was very much surprised at last, to see all the supposed Pyrates fighting with one another.

The Truth of the Matter is, *Worley* gained the Bay, thinking to make sure of his two Prizes, by keeping them from coming in; but by the hoisting of the King's Colours, and firing a Gun, he quickly was sensible of his Mistake, and too soon perceived that the Tables were turned upon him; that instead of keeping them out, he found himself, by a superiour Force kept in. When the Pyrates saw how Things went, they resolutely prepar'd themselves for a desperate Defence; and tho' three to one odds, *Worley* and his Crew determined to fight to the last Gasp, and receive no Quarters, agreeably to what they had before sworn; so that they must either Dye or Conquer upon the Spot.

The *Carolina* Men gave the Pyrate a Broadside, and then Boarded him, one Sloop getting upon his Quarter, and the other on his Bow; *Worley* and the Crew, drew up upon the Deck, and fought very obstinately, Hand to Hand, so that in a few Minutes, abundance of Men lay weltering in their Gore; the Pyrates proved as good as their Words, not a Man of them cry'd out for Quarter, nor would accept of such, when offered, but were all killed except the Captain and another Man, and those very much wounded, whom they reserved for the Gallows. They were brought ashore in Irons, and the next Day, which was the 17th of *February* 1718–19, they were both hanged up, for fear they should dye, and evade the Punishment as was thought due to their Crimes.

CHAPTER XII.

of
Capt. GEORGE LOWTHER,
And his CREW.

GEORGE LOWTHER sailed out of the River of *Thames*, in one of the Royal *African* Company's Ships, call'd the *Gambia Castle*, of 16 Guns and 30 Men, *Charles Russel* Commander; of which Ship, the said *Lowther* was second Mate. Aboard of the same Ship, was a certain Number of Soldiers, commanded by one *John Massey*, who were to be carried to one of the Company's Settlements, on the River of *Gambia*, to Garrison a Fort, which was sometime ago taken and destroy'd by Captain *Davis* the Pyrate.

In *May* 1721, the *Gambia Castle* came safe to her Port in *Africa*, and landed Captain *Massey* and his Men on *James*'s Island, where he was to Command under the Governor, Colonel *Whitney*, who arrived there at the same Time, in another Ship: And here, by a fatal Misunderstanding, between the military Folks and the Trading People, the Fort and Garrison not only came to be lost again to the Company, but a fine Galley well provided, and worth 10000 *l.* turned against her Masters.

The Names of Governor and Captain sounded great, but when the Gentlemen found that the Power that generally goes along with those Title, was oversway'd and born down by the Merchants and Factors, (mechanick Fellows as they thought them) they grew very impatient and disatisfy'd, especially *Massey*, who was very loud in his Complaints against them, particularly at the small Allowance of Provisions to him and his Men; for the Garrison and Governor too, were victualled by the Merchants, which was no small Grievance and Mortification to them. And as the want of eating was the only Thing that made the great *Sancho* quit his Government, so did it here rend and tare their's to Pieces: For *Massey* told them, *that he did not come there to be a* Guiney *Slave, and that he had promised his Men good Treatment, and Provisions fitting for Soldiers: That as he had the Care, of so many of his Majesty's Subjects, if they would not provide for them in a handsome Manner, he should take suitable Measures for the Preservation of so many of his Countrymen and Companions.*

The Governor at this Time was very ill of a Fever, and, for the better Accomodation in his Sickness, was carried aboard the Ship *Gambia Castle*, where he continued for about three Weeks, and therefore could have little to say in this Dispute, tho' he resolved not to stay in a Place, where there was so little Occasion for him, and where his Power was so confin'd. The Merchants had certainly Orders from the Company, to issue the Provisions out to the Garrison, and the same is done along the whole Coast; but whether they had cut them short of the Allowance that was appointed them, I can't say, but if they did, then is the Loss of the Ship and Garrison owing principally to their ill Conduct.

However, an Accident that happened on Board the Ship, did not a little contribute to this Misfortune, which was a Pique that the Captain of her took against his second Mate, *George Lowther*, the Man who is the Subject of this short History; and who losing his Favor, found Means to ingratiate himself into the good liking of the common Sailors, insomuch that when Captain *Russel* ordered him to be punish'd, the Men took up Handspikes, and threat'ned to knock that Man down, that offered to lay hold of the Mate. This served but to widen the Differences between him and the Captain, and more firmly attach'd *Lowther* to the Ship's Company, the greatest Part of which, he found ripe for any Mischief in the World.

Captain *Massey* was no wit the better reconciled to the Place, by a longer Continuance, nor to the Usage he met with there, and having often Opportunities of conversing with *Lowther*, with whom he had contracted an Intimacy in the Voyage; they aggravated one another's Grievances to such a height, that they resolved upon Measures to curb the Power that controul'd them, and to provide for themselves after another Manner.

When the Governor recover'd of his Fever, he went ashore to the Island, but took no Notice of *Massey*'s Behaviour, tho' it was such as might give Suspicion of what he designed; and *Lowther*, and the common Sailors, who were in the Secret of Affairs, grew insolent and bold, even refusing to obey when commanded to their Duty by Captain *Russel* and the chief Mate. The Captain seeing how Things were carried, goes ashore early one Morning to the Governor and Factory, in order to hold a Council, which *Lowther* apprehending, was in order to prevent his Design, sent a Letter in the same Boat to *Massey*, intimating it to him, and *that he should repair on Board, for it was high Time to put their Project in Execution.*

As soon as *Massey* received this Letter, he went to the Soldiers at the *Barracks*, and said to them, and others, *You that have a Mind to go to* England, *now is your Time*; and they generally consenting, *Massey* went to the Store-Room, burst open the Door, set two Centinels upon it, and ordered that no Body should come near it; then he went to the Governor's Apartment, and took his Bed, Baggage, Plate and Furniture, (in Expectation that the Governor himself, as he had promised *Massey*, would have gone on Board, which he afterwards refused, by Reason, as he said, he believed they were going a-pyrating; which at first, whatever *Lowther* designed, *Massey* certainly proposed only the going to *England*;) when this was done, he sent the Boat off to the chief Mate, with this Message, *That he should get the Guns ready, for that the King of* Barro [a Negro Kingdom near the Royal *African* Settlement] *would come aboard to Dinner.* But *Lowther* understanding best, the meaning of those Orders, he confined the chief Mate, shotted the Guns, and put the Ship in a Condition for sailing. In the Afternoon *Massey* came on Board with the Governor's Son, having sent off all the Provisions of the Island, and eleven Pipes of Wine, leaving only two half Pipes behind in the Store-House, and dismounted all the Guns of the Fort.

In the Afternoon they weigh'd one Anchor, but fearing to be too late to get out of the River, they slipp'd the other, and so fell down; in doing of which, they run the Ship aground. *Massey* shew'd himself a Soldier upon this Accident, for as soon as the Misfortune happen'd, he left the Ship with about sixteen Hands, and rows directly to the Fort, remounts the Guns, and keeps Garrison there all the Night, while the Ship was ashore; and obliged some of the Factory to assist in getting her clear. In the mean while, *Russel* came off, but not being suffered to come on Board, he call'd to *Lowther*, and offered him and the Company, whatever Terms they would be pleased to accept of, upon Condition of surrendering up the Ship, which had no effect upon any of them. In the Morning they got her afloat, and *Massey* and his Men came aboard, after having nailed up and dismounted all the Cannon of the Fort: They put the Governor's Son, and two or three others ashore, who were not willing to go without the Governor, and sail'd out of the River, having exchanged several Shot with the *Martha, Otter &c.* that lay there, without doing Execution on either Side.

When the Ship came out to Sea, *Lowther* called up all the Company, and told them, *it was the greatest Folly imaginable, to think of returning to* England, *for what they had already done, could not be justifyed upon any Pretence whatsoever, but would be look'd upon, in the Eye of the Law, a capital Offence, and that none of them were in a Condition to withstand the Attacks of such powerful Adversaries, as they would meet with at Home; for his Part he was determined not to run such a Hazard, and therefore if his Proposal was not agreed to, he desired to be set a Shore in some Place of Safety: That they had a good ship under them, a parcel of brave Follows in her, that* it was not their Business to starve, or be made Slaves; and therefore, if they were all of his Mind, they should seek their Fortunes upon the Seas, as other Adventurers had done before them. They one and all came into the Measures, knocked down the Cabins, made the Ship flush fore and aft, prepared black Colours, new named her, *the Delivery*, having about 50 Hands and 16 Guns, and the following short Articles were drawn up, signed and sworn to upon the Bible.

The Articles of Captain *George Lowther*, and his Company.

1. *The Captain is to have two full Shares; the Master is to have one Share and a half; the Doctor, Mate, Gunner, and Boatswain, one Share and a quarter.*

2. *He that shall be found Guilty of taking up any unlawful Weapon on Board the Privateer, or any Prize, by us taken, so as to Strike or abuse one another, in any regard, shall suffer what Punishment the Captain and Majority of the Company shall think fit.*

3. *He that shall be found Guilty of Cowardize, in the Time of Engagement, shall suffer what Punishment the Captain and Majority shall think fit.*

4. *If any Gold, Jewels, Silver, &c. be found on Board of any Prize or Prizes, to the Value of a Piece of Eight, and the Finder do not deliver it to the Quarter-Master, in the Space of 24 Hours, shall suffer what Punishment the Captain and Majority shall think fit.*

5. *He that is found Guilty of Gaming, or Defrauding another to the Value of a Shilling, shall suffer what Punishment the Captain and Majority of the Company shall think fit.*

6. *He that shall have the Misfortune to lose a Limb, in Time of Engagement, shall have the Sum of one hundred and fifty Pounds Sterling, and remain with the Company as long as he shall think fit.*

7. *Good Quarters to be given when call'd for.*

8. *He that sees a Sail first, shall have the best Pistol, or Small-Arm, on Board her.*

It was the 13th of *June*, that *Lowther* left the Settlement, and on the 20th, being then within twenty Leagues of *Barbadoes*, he came up with a Brigantine, belonging to *Boston*, called the *Charles, James Douglass* Master, which they plundered in a pyratical Manner, and let the Vessel go; but least she should meet with any of the Station Ships, and so give Information of the Robbery, *in Terrorem*, to prevent a Pursuit, *Lowther* contrived a sort of a Certificate, which he directed the Master to shew to their Consort, if they should meet with her; and upon Sight of it the Brigantine would pass unmolested: This Consort, he pretended, was a 40 Gun Ship, and cruising thereabouts.

After this the *Delivery* proceeded to *Hispaniola*; near the West End of the Island she met with a *French* Sloop Loaden with Wine and Brandy; aboard of this Vessel went Captain *Massey*, as a Merchant, and ask'd the Price of one Thing, and then another, bidding Money for the greatest Part of the Cargo; but after he had trifled a while, he whisper'd a Secret in the *French* Man's Ear, *viz. That they must have it all without Money. Monsieur* presently understood his Meaning, and unwillingly agreed to the Bargain. They took out of her thirty Casks of Brandy, five Hogsheads of Wine, several Pieces of Chintzes, and other valuable Goods, and about 70 *l. English*, in Money; of which *Lowther* generously return'd five Pounds back to the *French* Master for his Civilities.

But as all Constitutions grow old, and thereby shake and totter, so did our Commonwealth in about a Month of its Age, feel Commotions and intestine Disturbances, by the Divisions of its Members, which had near hand terminated in its Destruction; these civil Discords were owing to the following Occasion. Captain *Massey* had been a Soldier almost from his Infancy, but was but very indifferently acquainted with Maritime Affairs, and having an enterprizing Soul, nothing would satisfy him, but he must be doing Business in his own Way, therefore he required *Lowther* to let him have thirty Hands to land with, and he would attack the *French* Settlements, and bring aboard the Devil and all of Plunder.

Lowther did all that he could do, and said all that he could say, to disswade *Massey* from so rash and dangerous an Attempt; pointing out to him the Hazard the Company would run, and the Consequences to them all, if he should not succeed, and the little Likelihood there was to expect Success from the Undertaking: But 'twas all one for that, *Massey* would go and attack the *French* Settlements, for any thing *Lowther* could say against it; so that he was obliged to propose the Matter to the Company, among whom *Massey* found a few Fellows as resolute as himself; however, a great Majority being against it, the Affair was over-ruled in Opposition to Captain *Massey*, notwithstanding which, *Massey* grew fractious, quarrelled with *Lowther*, and the Men divided into Parties, some siding with the Land Pyrate, and some with the Sea Rover, and were all ready to fall together by the Ears, when the Man at the Mast-Head cry'd out, A Sail! A Sail! then they gave over the Dispute, set all their Sails, and steered after the Chace. In a few Hours they came up with her, she being a small Ship from *Jamaica*, bound to *England*; they took what they thought fit out of her, and a Hand or two, and then *Lowther* was for sinking the Ship with several Passengers that were in her, for what Reason I know not, but *Massey* so that he interposed, prevented their cruel Fate, and the Ship safely arrived afterwards in *England*.

The next Day they took a small Sloop, an interloping Trader, which they detain'd with her Cargo. All this while *Massey* was uneasy, and declar'd his Resolution to leave them, and *Lowther* finding him a very troublesome Man to deal with, consented that he should take the Sloop, last made Prize of, with what Hands had a Mind to go with him, and shift for himself. Whereupon *Massey*, with about ten more Malecontents, goes aboard and Sloop, and comes away in her directly for *Jamaica*.

Notwithstanding what had passed, Captain *Massey* puts a bold Face upon the Matter, and goes to Sir *Nicholas Laws*, the Governor, informs him of his leaving *Lowther* the Pyrate, owns, *That he assisted in going off with the Ship, at the River* Gambia; but said, 'twas to *save so many of his Majesty's Subjects from perishing, and that his Design was to return to* England; *but* Lowther *conspiring with the greater Part of the Company went a pyrating with the Ship; and that he had taken this Opportunity to leave him, and surrender himself and Vessel to his Excellency.*

Massey was very well received by the Governor, and had his Liberty given him, with a Promise of his Favour, and so forth; and, at his own Request, he was sent on Board the *Happy* Sloop, Captain *Laws*, to cruise off *Hispaniola*, for *Lowther*; but not being so fortunate as to meet with him, Captain *Massey* returned back to *Jamaica* in the Sloop, and getting a Certificate, and a Supply of Money, from the Governor, he came home Passenger to *England*.

When *Massey* came to Town, he writes a long Letter to the Deputy Governor and Directors of the *African* Company, wherein he imprudently relates the whole Transactions of his Voyage, the going off with the Ship, and the Acts of Pyracy he had committed with *Lowther*; but excuses it as Rashness and Inadvertency in himself, occasioned by his being ill used, contrary to the Promises that had been made him, and the Expectations he had entertained; but own'd, that he deserved to dye for what he had done; yet, if they had Generosity enough to forgive him, as he was still capable to do them Service, as a Soldier, so he should be very ready to do it; but if they resolved to prosecute him, he begg'd only this Favour, that he might not be hang'd like a Dog, but to die like a Soldier, as he had been bred from his Childhood, that is, that he might be shot.

This was the Substance of the Letter, which, however, did not produce so favourable an Answer as he hoped for, Word being brought back to him, *That he should be fairly hang'd*. Whereupon, *Massey* resolved not to be out of the Way, when he found what important Occasion there was likely to be for him, but takes a Lodging in *Aldersgate-Street*, the next Day went to the Lord Chief Justice's Chambers, and enquired, if my Lord had granted a Warrant against Captain *John Massey*, for Pyracy: But being told by the Clerks, that they knew of no such Thing; he informed them, he was the Man, that my Lord would soon be apply'd to for that Purpose, and the Officer might come to him at such a Place, where he lodg'd: They took the Directions in Writing, and, in a few Days, a Warrant being issued, the Tipstaff went directly, by his own Information, and apprehended him, without any other Trouble, than walking to his Lodging.

There was then no Person in Town to charge him with any Fact, upon which he could be committed; nor could the Letter be proved to be of his Hand-Writing, so that they had been obliged to let him go again, if he had not helped his Accusers out at Pinch: The Magistrate was reduced to the putting of this Question to him, *Did you write this Letter?* He answered, *He did:* And not only that, but confessed all the Contents of it; upon which, he was committed to *Newgate*, but was afterwards admitted to a hundred Pounds Bail, or thereabouts.

On the 5th of *July* 1723, he was brought to his Tryal, at a Court of Admiralty held at the *Old-Baily*, when Captain *Russel*, Governor *Whitney*'s Son, and others, appeared as Evidences, by whom the Indictment was plainly proved against him; which, if it had not been done, the Captain was of such an heroick Spirit, that he would have deny'd nothing; for instead of making a Defence, he only entertained the Court with a long Narrative of his Expedition, from the first setting out, to his Return to *England*, mentioning two Acts of Pyracy committed by him, which he was not charged with, often challenging the Evidences to contradict him, if in any Thing he related the least Syllable of an Untruth; and instead of denying the Crimes set forth in the Indictment, he charged himself with various Circumstances, which fixed the Facts more home upon him. Upon the whole, the Captain was found Guilty, received Sentence of Death, and was executed three Weeks after, at *Execution-Dock*.

We return now to *Lowther*, whom we left cruising off *Hispaniola*, from whence he plyed to Windward, and, near *Porto Rico*, chased two Sail, and spoke with them; they proving to be a small *Bristol* Ship, commanded by Captain *Smith*, and a *Spanish* Pyrate, who had made Prize of the said Ship. *Lowther* examined into the *Spaniard*'s Authority for taking an *English* Vessel, and threat'ned to put every Man of them to death, for so doing; so that the *Spaniards* fancied themselves to be in a very pittiful Condition, till Matters cleared up, and they found their Masters as great Rogues as themselves, from whom some Mercy might be expected, in regard to the near Relation they stood with them, as to their Profession; in short, *Lowther* first rifled, and then burnt both the Ships, sending the *Spaniards* away in their Launch, and turning all the *English* Sailors into Pyrates.

After a few Days Cruise, *Lowther* took a small Sloop belonging to St. *Christophers*, which they mann'd and carried along with them to a small Island, where they cleaned, and stay'd some Time to take their Diversions, which consisted in unheard of Debaucheries, with drinking, swearing and rioting, in which there seemed to be a kind of Emulation among them, resembling rather Devils than Men, striving who should out do one another in new invented Oaths and Execrations.

They all got aboard about *Christmas*, observing neither Times nor Seasons, for perpetrating their villainous Actions, and sailed towards the Bay of *Honduras*; but stopping at the *Grand Caimanes* for Water, they met with a small Vessel with 13 Hands, in the same honourable Employment with themselves; the Captain of this Gang was one *Edward Lowe*, whom we shall particularly discourse of in a Chapter by it self: *Lowther* received them as Friends, and treated them with all imaginable Respect, inviting them, as they were few in Number, and in no Condition to pursue the Account, (as they called it) to join their Strength together, which on the Consideration aforesaid, was accepted of, *Lowther* still continuing Commander, and *Lowe* was made Lieutenant: The

Vessel the new pyrates came out of, they sunk, and the Confederates proceed on the Voyage as *Lowther* before intended.

The 10th of *January*, the Pyrates came into the Bay, and fell upon a Ship of 200 Tun, called the *Greyhound, Benjamin Edwards* Commander, belonging to *Boston*. *Lowther* hoisted his pyratical Colours, and fired a Gun for the *Greyhound* to bring to, which she refusing, the *Happy Delivery* (the Name of the Pyrate) edg'd down, and gave her a Broad-side, which was returned by Captain *Edwards* very bravely, and the Engagement held for an Hour; but Captain *Edwards*, finding the Pyrate too strong for him, and fearing the Consequence of too obstinate a Resistance against those lawless Fellows, ordered his Ensign to be struck. The Pyrates Boat came aboard, and not only rifled the Ship, but whipp'd beat, and cut the Men in a cruel Manner, turned them aboard their own Ship, and then set Fire to their's.

In cruising about the Bay, they met and took several other Vessels without any Resistance, *viz.* two Brigantines of *Boston* in *New-England*, one of which they burnt, and sunk the other; a Sloop belonging to *Connecticut*, Captain *Airs*, which they also burnt; a Sloop of *Jamaica*, Captain *Hamilton*, they took for their own Use; a Sloop of *Virginia* they unladed, and was so generous as to give her back to the Master that own'd her. They took a Sloop of 100 Ton, belonging to *Rhode Island*, which they were pleased to keep, and mount with eight Carriage, and ten Swivel Guns.

With this little Fleet, *viz.* Admiral *Lowther*, in the *Happy Delivery*; Captain *Low*, in the *Rhode Island* Sloop; Captain *Harris*, (who was second Mate in the *Greyhound* when taken,) in *Hamilton's* Sloop, and the little Sloop formerly mentioned, serving as a Tender; I say, with this Fleet the Pyrates left the Bay, and came to *Port Mayo* in the Gulph of *Matique*, and there made Preparations to careen; they carried ashore all their Sails, and made Tents by the Water-Side, wherein they laid their Plunder, Stores, *&c.* and fell to work; and at the Time that Ships were upon the Heel, and the good Folks employ'd in heaving down, scrubing, tallow-

ing, and so forth; of a sudden came down a considerable
Body of the Natives, and attack'd the Pyrates unprepared.
As they were in no Condition to defend themselves, they
fled to their Sloops, leaving them Masters of the Field and
the Spoil thereof, which was of great Value, and set Fire to
the *Happy Delivery*, their capital Ship.

Lowther made the best Provision he could in the largest
Sloop, which he called the *Ranger*, having ten Guns and
eight Swivels, and she sailing best, the Company went all
aboard of her, and left the other at Sea. Provisions was now
very short, which, with the late Loss, put them in a confounded ill Humour, insomuch that they were every now and
then going together by the Ears, laying the Blame of their
ill Conduct sometimes upon one, then upon another.

The Beginning of *May* 1722, they got to the *West-Indies*,
and near the Island of *Diseada*, took a Brigantine, one *Payne*
Master, that afforded them what they stood in need of,
which put them in better Temper, and Business seemed to
go on well again. After they had pretty well plundered the
Brigantine, they sent her to the Bottom. They went into the
Island and watered, and then stood to the Northward, intending to visit the Main-Coast of *America*.

In the Latitude of 38, they took a Brigantine called the
Rebecca of *Boston*, Captain *Smith*, bound thither from St.
Christophers. At the taking of this Vessel, the Crews divided;
for *Low*, whom *Lowther* joined at the *Grand Caimanes*, proving always a very unruly Member of the Commonwealth,
always aspiring, and never satisfy'd with the Proceedings of
the Commander; he thought it the safest Way to get rid of
him, upon any Terms; and according to the Vote of the
Company, they parted the Bear Skin between them: *Low*
with 44 Hands went aboard the Brigantine, and *Lowther*
with the same Number stay'd in the Sloop, and separated
that very Night, being the 28th of *May* 1722.

Lowther proceeding on his Way to the Main-Coast, took
three or four fishing Vessels off *New-York*, which was no

great Booty to the Captors. The 3d of *June*, they met with a small *New-England* Ship, bound home from *Barbadoes*, which stood an Attack a small Time, but finding it to no Purpose, yielded herself a Prey to the Booters: The Pyrates took out of her fourteen Hogsheads of Rum, six Barrels of Sugar, a large Box of *English* Goods, several Casks of Loaf Sugar, a considerable Quantity of Pepper, six Negroes, besides a Sum of Money and Plate, and then let her go on her Voyage.

The next Adventure was not so fortunate for them, for coming pretty near the Coast of *South-Carolina*, they met with a Ship just come out, on her Voyage to *England;* *Lowther* gave her a Gun, and hoisted his pyratical Colours; but this Ship, which was called the *Amy*, happening to have a brave gallant Man to command her, who was not any ways daunted with that terrible Ensign, the black Flag, he instead of striking immediately, as 'twas expected, let fly a Broadside at the Pyrate. *Lowther* (not at all pleased with the Compliment, tho' he put up with it for the present) was for taking Leave; but the *Amy* getting the Pyrate between her and the Shore, stood after him to clap him aboard; to prevent which, *Lowther* run the Sloop a-ground, and landed all the Men with their Arms. Captain *Gwatkins*, the Captain of the *Amy*, was obliged to stand off, for fear of running his own Ship ashore; but at the same Time thought fit for the publick Good, to destroy the Enemy; and thereupon went into the Boat, and rowed towards the Sloop, in order to set her on Fire; but before he reached the Vessel, a fatal Shot from *Lowther's* Company ashore, put an End to their Design and Captain *Gwatkin's* Life. After this unfortunate Blow, the Mate returned aboard with the Boat, and not being enclined to pursue them any farther, took Charge of the Ship.

Lowther got off the Sloop after the Departure of the *Amy*, and brought all his Men aboard again, but was in a poor shattered Condition, having suffered much in the Engagement, and had a great many Men kill'd and wounded: He made Shift to get into an Inlet somewhere in *North-Carolina*, where he staid a long while before he was able to put to Sea again.

He and his Crew laid up all the Winter, and shifted as well as they could among the Woods, divided themselves into small Parties, and hunted generally in the Day Times, killing of black Cattle, Hogs, *&c.* for their Subsistance, and in the Night retired to their Tents and Huts, which they made for Lodging; and sometimes when the Weather grew very cold, they would stay aboard of their Sloop.

In the Spring of the Year 1723, they made Shift to get to Sea, and steered their Course for *Newfoundland*, and upon the Banks took a Scooner, call'd the *Swift, John Hood* Master; they found a good Quantity of Provisions aboard her, which they very much wanted at that Time, and after taking three of their Hands, and plundering her of what they thought fit, they let her depart. They took several other Vessels upon the Banks, and in the Harbour, but none of any great Account; and then steering for a warmer Climate, in *August* arrived at the *West-Indies*. In their Passage thither, they met with a Brigantine, called the *John* and *Elizabeth, Richard Stanny* Master, bound for *Boston*, which they plundered, took two of her Men, and discharged her.

Lowther cruised a pretty while among the Islands without any extraordinary Success, and was reduced to a very small Allowance of Provisions, till they had the luck to fall in with a *Martinica* Man which proved a seasonable Relief to them; and after that, a *Guiney* Man had the ill Fortune to become a Prey to the *Rovers*; she was called the *Princess*, Captain *Wicksted* Commander.

It was now thought necessary to look out for a Place to clean their Sloop in, and prepare for new Adventures: Accordingly the Island of *Blanco* was pitched upon for that Purpose, which lies in the Latitude of 11° 50 m. N. about 30 Leagues from the Main of the *Spanish America*, between the Islands of *Margarita* and *Rocas*, not far from *Tortuga*. It is a low even Island, but healthy and dry, uninhabited, and about two Leagues in Circumference, with Plenty of Lignum Vitæ Trees thereon, growing in Spots, with shrubby Bushes of other Wood about them. There are, besides Turtle, great Numbers of Guanoes, which is an amphibious Creature like a Lizard, but much larger, the Body of it being as big as a Man's Leg; they are very good to eat, and are much used by the Pyrates that come here: They are of divers Colours, but such as live upon dry Ground, as here at *Blanco,* are commonly yellow. On the N. W. End of this Island, there is a small Cove or Sandy Bay, all round the rest of the Island is deep Water, and steep close to the Island. Here *Lowther* resorted to, the Beginning of *October* last, unrigged his Sloop, sent his Guns, Sails, Rigging, &c. ashore, and put his Vessel upon the Careen. The *Eagle* Sloop of *Barbadoes,* belonging to the *South-Sea* Company, with 35 Hands commanded by *Walter Moore,* coming near this Island, in her Voyage to *Comena,* on the *Spanish* Continent, saw the said Sloop just careen'd, with her Guns out, and Sails unbent, which she supposed to be a Pyrate, because it was a Place where Traders did not commonly use, so took the Advantage of attacking her, as she was then unprepared; the *Eagle* having fired a Gun to oblige her to shew her Colours, the Pyrate hoisted the St. *George's* Flag at their Topmast-Head, as it were to bid Defiance to her; but when they found *Moore* and his Crew resolved to board them in good earnest, the Pyrates cut their Cable and hawled their Stern on Shore, which obliged the *Eagle* to come to an Anchor a-thwart their Hawse, where she engaged them till they called for Quarter and struck; at which Time *Lowther* and twelve of the Crew made their Escape out of the Cabin Window. The Master of the *Eagle* got the Pyrate Sloop off, secured her, and went ashore with 25 Hands, in Pursuit of *Lowther* and his Gang; but after five Day's search, they could find but five of them, which they brought aboard, and then proceeded with the Sloop and Pyrates to *Comena* aforesaid, where they soon arrived.

The *Spanish* Governor being informed of this brave Action, condemned the Sloop to the Captors, and sent a small Sloop with 23 Hands to scower the Bushes and other Places of the Island of *Blanco,* for the Pyrates that remained there, and took four more, with seven small Arms, leaving behind them Captain *Lowther,* three Men, and a little Boy, which they could not take; the above four the *Spaniards* try'd and condemned to Slavery for Life; three to the Gallies, and the other to the Castle of *Arraria.*

The *Eagle* Sloop brought all their Prisoners afterwards to St. *Christopher*'s, where the following were try'd by a Court of Vice Admiralty, there held *March* the 11th, 1722, *viz. John Churchill, Edward Mackdonald, Nicholas Lewis, Richard West, Sam. Levercott, Robert White, John Shaw, Andrew Hunter, Jonathan Delve, Matthew Freebarn, Henry Watson, Roger Grange, Ralph Candor,* and *Robert Willis*; the three last were acquitted, the other thirteen were found Guilty, two of which were recommended to Mercy by the Court, and accordingly pardoned; and the rest executed at that Island, on the 20th of the same Month.

As for Captain *Lowther,* it is said that he afterwards shot himself upon that fatal Island, where his Pyracies ended, being found, by some Sloop's Men, dead, and a Pistol burst by his Side.

CHAPTER XIII.

of
Captain EDWARD LOW,
And his CREW.

EDWARD LOW was born in *Westminster*, and had his Education there, such as it was, for he could neither write or read. Nature seem'd to have designed him for a Pyrate from his Childhood, for very early he began the Trade of plundering, and was wont to raise Contributions among all the Boys of *Westminster*; and if any were bold enough to refuse it, a Battle was the Consequence; but *Low* was so hardy, as well as bold, there was no getting the better of him, so that he robbed the Youths of their Farthings, with Impunity; when he grew bigger he took to Gaming in a low Way, for it was commonly among the Footmen in the *Lobby* of the House of Commons, where he used to play the whole Game, (as they term it,) that is, cheat all he could, and those who pretended to dispute it with him, must fight him.

The Virtues of some of his Family were equal to his; one of his Brothers was a Youth of Genius, when he was but seven Years old, he used to be carried-in a Basket, upon a Porter's Back, into a Crowd, and snatch Hats and Wigs: According to the exact Chronology of *Newgate*, he was the first who practised this ingenious Trick. After this, he applied himself to picking of Pockets; when he increased in Strength, he attempted greater Things, such as Housebreaking, *&c.* But after he had run a short Race, he had the

Misfortune of ending his Days at *Tyburn*, in Company with *Stephen Bunce*, and the celebrated *Jack Hall* the Chimney-Sweeper.

But to return to *Ned*, when he came to Man's Estate, at his eldest Brother's Desire, he went to Sea with him, and so continued for three or four Years, and then parted; and *Ned* work'd in a Rigging-House in *Boston* in *New-England*, for a while About six Years ago, he took a Trip home to *England*, to see his Mother, who is yet Living. His Stay was not long here; but taking Leave of his Friends and Acquaintance, for the last Time he should see them; for so he was pleased to say; he returned to *Boston*, and work'd a Year or two longer at the Rigging Business. But being too apt to disagree with his Master, he left them, and shipp'd himself in a Sloop that was bound to the Bay of *Honduras*.

When the Sloop arrived in the Bay, *Ned Low* was appointed Patron of the Boat, which was employ'd in cutting of Logwood, and bringing it aboard to lade the Ship; for that is the Commodity they make the Voyage for: In the Boat were twelve Men besides *Low*, who all go arm'd, because of the *Spaniards*, from whom this Logwood is but little better than stole. It happened that the Boat one Day came aboard just before Dinner, was ready, and *Low* desired that they might stay and Dine; but the Captain, being in a Hurry for his Lading, ordered them a Bottle of Rum, and to take t'other Trip, because no Time should be lost: This provoked the Boat's Crew, but particularly *Low*, who takes up a loaded Musquet and fires at the Captain, but missing him, shot another poor Fellow thro' the Head, then put off the Boat, and with his twelve Companions goes to Sea: The next Day they took a small Vessel, and go in her, make a black Flag, and declare War against all the World.

They then proceeded to the Island of the *Grand Caimanes*, intending to have fitted up their small Vessel, and prepare themselves as well as their Circumstances would permit, for their honourable Employment; but falling in Company with *George Lowther*, another Pyrate there, who paying his Compliments to *Low*, as great Folks do to one another when they meet, and offering himself as an Ally; *Low* accepted of the Terms, and so the Treaty was presently sign'd without Plenipo's or any other Formalities.

We have already given an Account of their joynt Pyracies, under *Lowther* as chief Commander, till the 28th of *May*, 1722, when they took a Brigantine of *Boston*, bound thither from St. *Christophers*, at which Time they parted, and *Edward Low* went into the Brigantine, with forty four others, who chose him their Captain: They took with them two Guns, four Swivels, six Quarter-Casks of Powder, Provisions and some Stores, and so left *Lowther* to prosecute his Adventures, with the Men he had left.

Their first Adventure in the Brigantine, was on *Sunday* the 3rd Day of *June*, when they took a Vessel belonging to *Amboy*, *John Hance* Master, whom he rifled of his Provisions, and let go; the same Day he met with a Sloop, *James Calqudron* Master, off of *Rhode Island*, bound into that Port, whom he first plundered, and then cut away his Boltsprit, and all his Rigging; also his Sails from the Yards, and wounded the Master, to prevent his getting in to give Intelligence, and then stood away to the South-Eastward, with all the Sail he could make, there being then but little Wind.

Low judged right in making sail from the Coast, for a longer stay had proved fatal to him, for notwithstanding the disabled Condition he had rendered the Sloop in, she made shift to get into *Block Island*, at 12 o'Clock that Night, and immediately dispatched a Whale-Boat to *Rhode Island*, which got thither by seven the next Morning, with an Account of the Pyrate, his Force, and what had happened to him: As soon as the Governor had received this Information, he ordered a Drum to beat up for Volunteers, and two of the best Sloops then in the Harbour, to be fitted out: He gave Commissions to one Captain *John Headland*, and Captain *John Brown*, jun. for ten Days; the former had eight Guns and two Swivels, and the latter six Guns, well fitted with small Arms, and in both Sloops 140 stout Fellows; all this was performed with so much Expedition, that before Sun-set, they were under Sail, turning out of the Harbour, at the same Time the Pyrate was seen from *Block Island*, which gave great Hopes that the Sloops would be Masters of her the next Day, which however did not happen, for the Sloops returned into Harbour some Days afterwards, without so much as seeing their Enemy.

After this Escape, Captain *Low*, went into Port, upon the Coast, for he had not fresh Water enough to run to the Islands, where he staid a few Days, getting Provisions and what Necessaries the Crew wanted, and then sailed for Purchase, (as they call it) steering their Course towards *Marblehead*.

About the 12th of *July*, the Brigantine sailed into the Harbour of Port *Rosemary*, and there found thirteen Ships and Vessels, but none of Force, at Anchor, they spread their black Flag, and ran in among them; *Low* telling them from the Brigantine, they should have no Quarters if they resisted; in the mean Time they mann'd and arm'd their Boat, and took Possession of every one of them, plundered them of what they thought fit, and converted one to their own Use, *viz.* a Scooner of 80 Tuns, aboard of which they put 10 Carriage Guns, and 50 Men, and *Low* himself went Captain, and nam'd her the *Fancy*, making one *Charles Harris*, (who was at first forced into their Service out of the *Greyhound* of *Boston*, by *Lowther*, of which Ship *Harris* was second Mate) Captain of the Brigantine: Out of these Vessels they took several Hands, and encreased the Company to 80 Men, who all signed the Articles, some willingly, and a few perhaps by Force, and so sailed away from *Marblehead*.

Some Time after this, they met with two Sloops bound for *Boston*, with Provisions for the Garrison, and the Scooner coming up first, attacked them, but there happening to be an Officer and some Soldiers on Board, who gave them a warm Reception, *Low* chose to stay till he should be joyned by the Brigantine; in the mean while the Sloops made the best of their Way, and the Pyrates gave them Chace two Days, and at last lost sight of them in a Fog.

They now steered for the Leeward Islands, but in their Voyage met with such a Hurricane of Wind, that the like had not been known; the Sea ran Mountains high, and seemed to threaten them every Moment with Destruction; it was no Time now to look out for Plunder, but to save themselves, if possible, from perishing. All Hands were continually employed Night, and Day, on Board the Brigantine, and all little enough, for the Waves went over her, so that they were forced to keep the pump constantly going, besides baling with Buckets; but finding themselves not able to keep her free, and seeing the utmost Danger before their Eyes, they turn'd to the Takle, and hoisted out their Provisions, and other heavy Goods, and threw them over-board, with six of their Guns, so that by lightening the Vessel, she might rise to the Top of the Sea with the Waves: They were also going to cut away their Mast; but considering how dangerous it would be, to be left in such a Condition, they resolved to delay it to the last, which was Prudence in them to do; for a Ship without Masts or Sails, lies like a Log upon the Water, and if attack'd, must fight with Disadvantage, the working of her being the most artful Part of the Engagement, because she may sometimes bring all her great Guns on one Side, to bear upon her Enemy, when the disabled Ship can do little or nothing.

But to proceed; by their throwing over-board the heavy Goods, the Vessel made considerable less Water, and they could keep it under with the Pump only, which gave them Hopes and new Life; so that instead of cutting all away, they took necessary Measures to secure the Mast, by making Preventor-Shrowds, &c. and then wore and lay too upon the other Tack, till the Storm was over. The Scooner made somewhat better Weather of it, of the two, but was pretty roughly handled notwithstanding, having split her Mainsail, sprung her Boltsprit, and cut her Anchors from her

Bows. The Brigantine by running away to Leeward, when she were wore upon the Larboard Tack, had lost Sight of the Scooner; but not knowing whether she might be safe or not, as soon as the Wind abated, she set her Main-Sail and Top-Sail, and made short Trips to Windward; and the next Day had the good Fortune to come in Sight of their Consort, who, upon a Signal, which the other knew, bore down to her, and the Crew were overjoy'd to meet again, after such ill Treatment from the Winds and Seas.

After the Storm, *Low* got safe to a small Island, one of the Weathermost of the *Caribbees*, and there fitted their Vessels, as well as the Place could afford; they got Provisions of the Natives, in exchange for Goods of their own; and as soon as the Brigantine was ready, 'twas judg'd necessary to take a short Cruize, and leave the Scooner in the Harbour till her Return. The Brigantine sail'd out accordingly, and had not been out many Days before they met a Ship at Sea, that had lost all her Masts; on Board of whom they went, and took from her in Money and Goods, to the Value of 1000 *l.* and so left her in the Condition they found her: This Ship was bound home from *Barbadoes*, but losing her Masts in the late Storm, was making for *Antegoa* to refit, where she afterwards arriv'd.

The Storm just spoken of, was found to have done incredible Damage in those Parts of the World; but however, it appear'd to have been more violent at *Jamaica*, both to the Island and Shipping, there was such a prodigious Swell of the Sea, that several hundred Tuns of Stones and Rocks, were thrown over the Wall of the Town of *Port Royal*, and the Town it self was overflowed, and above half destroy'd, there being the next Morning five Foot Water from one End to the other; the Cannon of Fort *Charles* were dismounted, and some washed into the Sea, and four hundred people lost their Lives; a more melancholly Sight was scarce ever seen when the Water ebb'd away, all the Streets being covered with Ruins of Houses, Wrecks of Vessels, and a great Number of dead Bodies, for forty Sail of Ships, in the Harbour, were cast away.

The Brigantine return'd to the Island, where she had left the Scooner, who being ready to sail, it was put to the Vote of the Company, what Voyage to take next; and herein they follow'd the Advice of the Captain, who thought it not adviseable to go any farther to Leeward, because of the Men of War who were cruising in their several Stations, which they were not at all fond of meeting, and therefore it was agreed to go to the *Azores*, or Western Islands.

The latter End of *July*, *Low* took a *French* Ship of 34 Guns, and carried her along with him to the *Azores*. He came into St. *Michael*'s Road the 3d of *August*, and took seven Sail that were lying there, *viz.* the *Nostre Dame*, *Mere de Dieu*, Captain *Roach* Commander; the *Dove*, Capt. *Cox*; the *Rose* Pink, formerly a Man of War, Capt. *Thompson*; another *English* Ship, Capt. *Chandler*; and three other Vessels. He threatened all with present Death who resisted, which struck such a Terror to them, that they yielded themselves up a Prey to the Villains, without firing a Gun.

The Pyrates being in great Want of Water and fresh Provisions, *Low* sent to the Governor of St. *Michael*'s for a Supply, and promised upon that Condition to release the Ships he had taken, but otherwise to burn them all; which Demand the Governor thought it not prudent to refuse, but sent the Provision he required, upon which he released six of the Ships, (after he had plundered them of what he thought fit,) and the other, *viz.* the *Rose* Pink, was made a Pyrate Ship, which *Low* himself took the Command of.

The Pyrates took several of the Guns out of the *French* Ship, and mounted them aboard the *Rose*, which proved very fit for their Turn, and condemned the former to the Flames. They took all the Crew out of her, but the Cook, who, they said, being a greazy Fellow would fry well in the Fire; so the poor Man was bound to the Main-Mast, and burnt in the Ship, to the no small Diversion of *Low* and his *Mirmidons*.

Low ordered the Scooner to lye in the Fare between St. *Michael*'s and St. *Mary*'s, where, about the 20th of *August*, Captain *Carter* in the *Wright* Galley, had the ill Fortune to come in her Way; and because at first they shewed Inclinations to defend themselves, and what they had, the Pyrates cut and mangled them in a barbarous Manner; particularly some *Portuguese* Passengers, two of which being Friers, they triced up at each Arm of the Fore-Yard, but let them down again before they were quite dead, and this they repeated several Times out of Sport.

Another *Portuguese*, who was also Captain *Carter*'s Passenger, putting on a sorrowful Countenance at what he saw acted, one of this vile Crew attacked him upon the Deck, saying, *he did not like his Looks*, and thereupon gave him one Blow a-cross his Belly with his Cutlash, that cut out his Bowels, and he fell down dead without speaking a Word. At the same Time another of these Rogues cutting at a Prisoner, missed his Mark, and Captain *Low* standing in his Way, very opportunely received the Stroke upon his under Jaw, which laid the Teeth bare; upon this the Surgeon was called, who immediately stitched up the Wound, but *Low* finding fault with the Operation, the Surgeon being tollerably drunk, as it was customary for every Body to be, struck *Low* such a Blow with his Fist, that broke out all the Stitches, and then bid him sew up his Chops himself and be damned, so that *Low* made a very pitiful Figure for some Time after.

When they had plundered Captain *Carter*'s Ship, several of them were for burning her, as they had done the *French* Man, but it was otherwise resolved at last; for after they had cut her Cables, Rigging and Sails to Pieces, they left her to the Mercy of the Sea.

After these Depredations, they steered for the Island of *Madera*, where missing other Booty, they took up with a Fishing-Boat, with two old Men and a Boy in her, one of which they detained on Board, but sent the other ashore with a Flag of Truce, demanding a Boat of Water of the Governor, on Pain of taking away the old Man's Life, whom they threatened to hang at the Yard-Arm, upon their refusal; but the Thing being complied with, the old Man was honourably (as the Pyrates say) discharged, and all the three much handsomer cloathed than when they took them. From this Island they sailed to the *Canaries*, but meeting with no Prey there, they continued their Course for the *Cape de Verd* Islands, and at *Bonavista*, took a Ship called the *Liverpool Merchant*, Captain *Goulding*, from whom they stole a great Quantity of Provisions and dry Goods, 300 Gallons of Brandy, two Guns and Carriages, a Mast, Yard and Hawsers, besides six of his Men, and then would not let them Trade there, nor at St. *Nicholas*, but obliged Captain *Goulding* to go with his Ship, to the Isle of *May*.

The Pyrate also took among these Islands, a Ship belonging to *Liverpool, Scot* Commander; two *Portuguese* Sloops bound for *Brasil*; a small *English* Sloop trading there, *James Peace* Master, bound to *Santa Cruz*, and three Sloops from St. *Thomas* bound to *Curaso*, the Masters Names were *Lilly*, *Staples* and *Simpkins*, all which they plundered, and then let go about their Business, except one Sloop which they fitted up for the following Purpose.

Low had heard by one of the above mentioned Ships, that two small Gallies were expected every Day at the *Western Islands*, viz. the *Greyhound*, Captain *Glass*, and the *Foliff*, Captain *Aram*; the former of which was designed to be fitted for the pyratical Trade to *Brasil*, if Things had happened to their Minds. They mann'd the Sloop, and sent her in Quest of one or both of these Ships to the *Western Islands*, aforesaid, whilst they carreen'd their Ship *Rose*, at one of the *Cape de Verds*: But now Fortune that had hitherto been so propitious to them, left her Minions, and baffled for the present all their Hopes, for the Sloop missing of their Prey, was reduced to great Necessities for want of Provisions and Water, so that they ventured to go ashore at St. *Michael*'s for a Supply, and pass for a Trader; but they play'd their Parts so awkwardly, that they were suspected by the Governor to be what they really were, and he was soon put out of doubt by a Visit some *Portuguese* made them, who happened unluckily to be Passengers in Captain *Carter*'s Ship, when *Low* took her, and knew the Gentlemen's Faces very well; upon which the whole Crew was conducted into the Castle, where they were provided for as long as they liv'd.

Low, in the mean Time, did not fare quite so ill, but had his intended Voyage to *Brasil* spoil'd, by the oversetting of his Ship, when she was upon the Careen, whereby she was lost, so that he was reduc'd to his old Scooner, which he called the *Fancy*, aboard of which they all went, to the Number of 100, as vile Rogues as ever ended their Lives at *Tyburn*. They proceeded now to the *West-Indies*, but before they had gotten far on their Voyage, they attack'd a rich *Portuguese* Ship, call'd the *Nostre Signiora de Victoria*, bound home from *Bahia*, and after some Resistance, took her. *Low* tortur'd several of the Men, to make them declare where the Money, (which he suppos'd they had on Board) lay, and extorted by that Means, a Confession that the Captain had, during the Chace, hung out of the Cabin Window, a Bag with 11,000 Moidores, which, assoon as he was taken, he cut the Rope off, and let it drop into the Sea.

Low, upon hearing what a Prize had escap'd him, rav'd like a Fury, swore a thousand Oaths, and ordered the Captain's Lips to be cut off, which he broil'd before his Face, and afterwards murdered him and all the Crew, being thirty two Persons.

After this bloody Action, they continued their Course, till they came to the Northward of all the Islands, and there cruiz'd for about a Month, in which Time they made Prizes of the following Vessels, *viz.* a Snow from *New-York* to *Curacoa*, *Robert Leonard* Master; a Sloop from the Bay, bound to *New-York*, *Craig* Master; a Snow from *London* and *Jamaica*, bound to *New-York*; and the *Stanhope*, Pink, *Andrew Delbridge* Master, from *Jamaica* to *Boston* which last they burnt, because of *Low*'s irreconcileable Aversion to *New-England* Men.

After this Cruize, they went into one of the Islands and clean'd, and then steered for the Bay of *Honduras*, where they arrived about the Middle of *March* 1722–3, and met a Sloop turning out of the said Bay. The Pyrates had hoisted up

Spanish Colours, and continued them till they drew near the Sloop, then they hall'd them down, hoisted their black Flag, fired a Broadside, and boarded her. This Sloop was a *Spaniard* of six Guns, and 70 Men, that came into the Bay that Morning, and meeting there with five *English* Sloops, and a Pink, made Prizes of them all, plundered them, and brought the Masters of the Vessels away Prisoners, for the ransom of the Logwood; their Names were *Tutbill, Norton, Newbury, Sprafort, Clark and Parrot.* The *Spaniards* made no Resistance, so that the *English* Pyrates soon became their Masters and fell to rifling; but finding the above-mentioned People in the Hold, and several *English* Goods, they consulted *Low* the Captain thereupon, and without examining any further, the Resolution pass'd to kill all the Company; and the Pyrates, without any Ceremony, fell Pell-Mell to Execution with their Swords, Cutlashes, Poll-Axes and Pistols, cutting, flashing and shooting the poor *Spaniards* at a sad Rate. Some of the miserable Creatures jump'd down into the Hold, but could not avoid the Massacre; they met Death every where, for it they escaped it from one Hand, they were sure to perish by another; the only Prospect they had of Life, was to fly from the Rage of those merciless Men, and to trust to the more merciful Sea; and accordingly a great many leap'd overboard, and swam for the Shore; but *Low* perceiving it, ordered the Canoa to be mann'd, and sent in pursuit of them, by which Means several of the poor unhappy Men were knock'd in the Head in the Water, as they were endeavouring to get to Land; however, about 12 of them did reach the Shore, but in a miserable Condition, being very much wounded, and what became of them afterwards was not known, except one, who while the Pyrates were at their Sports and Pastimes ashore, finding himself very weak and fainting with his Wounds, and not knowing where to go for Help and Relief, in this Extremity, he came back to them, and begg'd for God sake, in the most earnest Manner possible, that they would give him Quarters; upon which, one of the Villains took hold of him, and said, *G—d—n him, he*

would give him good Quarters presently, and made the poor
Spaniard kneel down on his Knees, then taking his Fusil, put
the Muzzle of it into his Mouth, and fired down his Throat.
'Twas thought the rest did not long survive their miserable
Condition, and could only prolong their Lives, to add to the
Misery of them.

When the murdering Work was over, they rumaged the
Spanish Pyrate, and brought all the Booty aboard their own
Vessels: The six Masters aforementioned, found in the Hold,
they restored to their respective Vessels: They forced away
the Carpenter from the Pink, and then set Fire to the *Spanish*
Sloop, and burnt her; which last Scene concluded the Destruction of their Enemy, Ship and Crew.

Low set the Masters of the Vessels free, but would not
suffer them to steer for *Jamaica*, where they were then bound,
for fear the Men of War should get Intelligence of them,
but forced them all to go to *New-York*, threat'ning them with
Death, when they met them again, if they refused to comply
with their Demands.

In the next Cruize, which was between the Leeward Islands and the Main, they took two Snows, bound from *Jamaica* to *Liverpool*, and a Snow from *Jamaica* to *London*,
Bridds Master; as also a Ship from *Biddford* to *Jamaica*, *John
Pinkham* Commander; and two Sloops from *Jamaica* to *Virginia*.

On the 27th of *May*, *Low* and his Consort *Harris*, came
off *South-Carolina*, and met with three good Ships, *viz.* the
Crown, Captain *Lovereigne*, the *King William*, the *Carteret*,
and a Brigantine, who all came out of *Carolina* together two
Days before. The Pyrates were at the Trouble of chacing
them, and Captain *Lovereigne* being the sternmost, she fell
first a Prey into their Hands; and they spent all the Day in
coming up with the rest.

Within a few Days they took a Ship called the *Amsterdam
Merchant*, Captain *Willard*, from *Jamaica*, but belonging to
New-England; as *Low* let none of that Country depart with-
out some Marks of his Rage, he cut off this Gentleman's

Ears, slit up his Nose, and cut him in several Places of his Body, and, after plundering his Ship, let him pursue his Voyage.

After this he took a Sloop bound to *Amboy, William Frazier*, Master, with whom Mr. *Low* happening to be displeased, he ordered lighted Matches to be ty'd between the Mens Fingers, which burnt all the Flesh off the Bones; then cut them in several Parts of their Bodies with Knives and Cutlashes; afterwards took all their Provisions away, and set some of them ashore in an uninhabited Part of the Country.

The *Kingston*, Captain *Estwick*, another Ship, one *Burrington* Master, two Brigantines from *Carolina* to *London*; a Sloop from *Virginia* to *Bermudas*; a Ship from *Glasgow* to *Virginia*; a Scooner from *New-York* to *South-Carolina*; a Pink from *Virginia* to *Dartmouth*, and a Sloop from *Philadelphia* to *Surinam*, fell a Prey to these Villains, upon this Cruize, besides those above-mentioned.

It happened that at this Time one of his Majesty's Ships was upon a Cruize, on this Station, and got Intelligence of some of the mischievous Actions of this Miscreant, by one of the Vessels that had been plundered by him, who steering as directed, came in Sight of the Pyrates by break of Day, on the 10th of *June*, of all Days in the Year. The Rovers looking out for Prey, soon saw, and gave Chace to the Man of War, which was called the *Greyhound*, a Ship of 20 Guns, and 120 Men, rather inferiour in Force to the two Pyrate Vessels: The *Greyhound* finding them so eager, was in no doubt what they should be, and therefore tack'd and stood from them, giving the Pyrates an Opportunity to chace her for two Hours, till all Things were in Readiness for an Engagement, and the Pyrates about Gun-shot off; then the *Greyhound* tack'd again, and stood towards the two Sloops, one of them called the *Fancy*, commanded by *Low* himself, and the other the *Ranger*, commanded by *Harris*, both which hoisted their pyratical Colours, and fired each a Gun. When the *Greyhound* came within Musquet-shot, she halled up her Main-sail, and clapp'd close upon a Wind, to keep the Pyrates from running to Leeward, and then engaged: But when the Rogues found who they had to deal with, they edg'd away under the Man of War's Stern, and the *Greyhound* standing after them, they made a running Fight for about two Hours; but little Wind happening, the Sloops gained from her, by the help of their Oars; upon which the *Greyhound* left off firing, and turned all Hands to her own Oars, and at three in the Afternoon came up with them. The Pyrates haul'd upon a Wind to receive the Man of War, and the Fight was immediately renewed, with a brisk Fire on both Sides, till the *Ranger's* Main-Yard was shot down, and the *Greyhound* pressing close upon the disabled Sloop, *Low*, in the other, thought fit to bear away and leave his Consort a Sacrifice to his Enemy, who (seing the Cowardice and Treachery of his Commadore and Leader, having ten or twelve Men killed and wounded, and that there was no possibility of escaping,) called out for *Quarters*, and surrendered themselves to Justice, which proved severe enough to them a-while afterwards.

The Conduct of *Low* was surprizing in this Adventure, because his reputed Courage and Boldness, had, hitherto, so possess'd the Minds of all People, that he became a Terror, even to his own Men; but his Behaviour throughout this whole Action, shewed him to be a base cowardly Villain, for had *Low's* Sloop fought half so briskly as *Harris's* had done, (as they were under a solemn Oath to do,) the Man of War, in my Opinion, could never have hurted them.

The *Greyhound* carried in their Prize to *Rhode Island*, to the great Joy of the whole Province, tho' it had been more compleat, if the great *LOW* himself had grac'd the Triumph. The Prisoners were strongly secured in a Goal, till a Court of Vice-Admiralty could be held for their Tryals, which begun on the 10th of *July*, at *Newport*, and continued three Days. The Court was made up of the following Gentlemen.

William Dummer, Esq; Lieutenant Governor of the
Massachusets, President.

Nathaniel Paine, Esq;	*John Valentine*, Esq;
Addington Davonport, Esq;	Advocate-General.
Thomas Fitch, Esq;	*Samuel Cranston*, Governor
Spencer Phipps, Esq;	of *Rhode-Island*
John Lechmere, Esq;	*John Menzies*, Esq; Judge of
Surveyor-General.	the Admiralty,

Richard Ward, Esq; Register.

Mr. *Fahleel Brinton*, Provost-Marshal.

Robert Auchmuta, Esq; was assigned, by the Court, Council
for the Prisoners here under mention'd.

Prisoners Names.	Ages.	Places of Birth.
Charles Harris, Captain	25	*London.*
William Blads	28	*Rhode-Island.*
Daniel Hide	23	*Virginia.*
Thomas Powel, jun.	21	*Connecticut, N.E.*
Stephen Mundon	20	*London.*
Thomas Huggit	30	*London.*
William Read	35	*Londonderry, Ireland.*
Peter Kneeves	32	*Exeter* in *Devon.*
James Brinkly	28	*Suffolk* in *England.*
Joseph Sound	28	City of *Westminster.*
William Shutfield	40	*Lancaster* in *England.*
Edward Eaton	38	*Wrexham* in *Wales.*
John Brown	29	County of *Durham.*
Edward Lawson	20	*Isle of Man.*
Owen Pice	27	*South-Wales.*
John Tomkins	23	*Gloucestershire.*
John Fitzgerrald	21	*Limerick* in *Ireland.*
Abraham Lacy	21	*Devonshire.*
Thomas Linister	21	*Lancashire.*
Francis Leyton	39	*New-York.*
John Waters, Quart.-Mr.	35	County of *Devon.*
William Jones	28	*London.*

Charles Church	21	*St. Margaret*'s, *Westm.*
Thomas Hazel	50	— — —
John Bright	25	— — — —

These 25 were found guilty, and executed the 19th of
July, 1723, near *Newport* in *Rhode-Island.*

John Brown	17	*Liverpoole.*
Patrick Cunningham	25	— — —

These two were found guilty, but respited for one Year,
and recommended to the King's Favour.

John Wilson	23	*New-London* County
Henry Barnes	22	*Barbadoes.*
Thomas Jones	17	*Flur* in *Wales.*
Joseph Switzer	24	*Boston* in *New-England.*
Thomas Mumper, Indian.		*Mather's Vineyard N.E.*
John Hincher, Doctor	22	Near *Edinburgh, Scot.*
John Fletcher	17	— — —
Thomas Child	15	— — —

These eight were found Not Guilty.

The destroying this Pyrate was look'd upon by the Province, to be of such a signal Service to the Publick, and particular Advantage to the Colony of *New-York*, that it was thought necessary to make some handsome Acknowledgement to Captain *Peter Solgard* for it; and therefore it was resolved, in an Assembly of the Common-Council, to compliment him with the Freedom of their Corporation. The Resolution, together with the Preamble of the Captain's Freedom, being curious in their Kind, I subjoin them for the Satisfaction of the Reader.

Resolution of the Mayor and Common-Council of the City
of *New-York*, at a Common-Council held at the City Hall
of the said City, on *Thursday* the 25th of *July, Anno. Dom.*
1723.

Present *Robert Walter*, Esq; Mayor.

City of New-York, ss.
*This Court having taken into their Consideration the great
Service lately done to this Province in particular, as well as to
all other his Majesty's good Subjects in general, by Captain*
Peter Solgard, *Commander of his Majesty's Ship the* Greyhound, *the Station Ship of the Province, who lately in a Cruize upon this Coast, in due Execution and Discharge of his
Duty, upon Intelligence given him, sought for, pursued and
engaged two Pyrate Sloops, commanded by one* Low, (*a notorious and inhumane Pyrate,*) *one of which Sloops he took,
after a resolute Resistance, and very much shattered the other,
who by the Favour of the Night escaped. Twenty six of which
Pyrates so taken, being lately executed at* Rhode Island, *not
only eased this City and Province of a very great Trouble, but
of a very considerable Expence,* &c. *It is therefore resolved*
(Nemine Contradicente) *that this Corporation do present the
said Captain* Solgard *with the Freedom of this Corporation,
as a Mark of the great Esteem they have for his Person, as
well as for the aforesaid great and good Services; and that the
Seal of the said Freedom be enclosed in a Gold Box; that Mr.*
Recorder *and Mr.* Bickley *do draw the Draught of the said
Freedom, signifying therein, the grateful Sense of this Corporation, for so signal a Service to the Publick, and Benefit and
Advantage of Mankind. That Alderman* Kip, *and Alderman*
Cruger, *do prepare the said Box; that the Arms of the Corporation be engraved on one Side thereof, and a Representa-
tion of the Engagement on the other, with this Motto,* (viz.)
[Quesitos Humani Generos Hostes Debellare superbum,
10 Junii, 1723.] *That the Town-Clerk cause the same Free-*

*dom to be handsomly engrossed on Parchment, and that the whole Corporation do wait upon him, to present the same.
By Order of the Common-Council.*

William Sharpas, *Clerk.*

The Preamble of Captain *Peter Solgard's* Copy of his Freedom.
Robert Walter, Esq; Mayor, and the Aldermen of the City of *New-York.*

City of *New-York, SS.*

To all whom these Persents shall come, send Greetings. WHEREAS, Captain Peter Solgard, *Commander of his Majesty's Ship the* Greyhound, *(the present Station Ship of this Province,) in his Cruize, having Intelligence of two Pyrate Sloops of considerable Force in Consortship, under the Command of one* Low, *a notorious Pyrate, that had for upward of two Years, committed many Depredations, Murders and Barbarities, upon many of his Majesty's Subjects and Allies, lately come upon this Coast, hath, with great Diligence, and utmost Application, pursued, overtaken, and after a stubborn Resistance, vanquished and overcome both of them, taking one, and driving the other from our Coast; which Action, as it is glorious in it self, so it is glorious in the publick Benefits and Advantages that flow from it, (to wit) The Safety and Freedom of our own Trade and Commerce, and of all the neighbouring Provinces on this Continent, such signal Service done against the Enemies of Mankind, merits the Applause of all good Men, but more immediately from those of this Province, who are appointed his particular Care and Charge. WE therefore, the Mayor, Aldermen and Commonalty of the City of* New-York, *assembled in Common Council, to express our grateful Sense and Acknowledgment, to the said Captain* Peter Solgard, *for so noble and faithful a Discharge of his Duty, and as a particular Mark of the great Esteem and just Regard we bear to his kind Acceptance of the Freedom of the Corporation of this City of* New-York, *and that he will please to become a Fellow Citizen with us.* These are* therefore *to certify and declare, that the said Captain* Peter Solgard *is hereby admitted, received and allowed a Freeman and Citizen of the said City of* New-York, *to have, hold, enjoy and partake of all and singular Advantages, Benefits, Liberties, Privileges, Franchises, Freedoms and Immunities whatsoever, granted or belonging to the same City:* In Testimony *thereof, the said Mayor hath hereunto subscribed his Name, and caused the Seal of the said City to be affix'd the 25th Day of* July, *in the ninth Year of the Reign of our Sovereign Lord* George, *by the Grace of God, King of* Great Britain, France *and* Ireland, *Defender of the Faith,* &c. Anno. Dom. 1723.

William Sharpas,   R. Walter *Mayor*
Clerk.

This narrow Escape of *Low* and his Companions, one would have thought might have brought them to a little Consideration of their black and horrid Crimes, and to look upon this Interval as an Opportunity put into their Hands by Providence, to reconcile themselves to God, by a hearty and sincere Repentance. But alass they were dead to all Goodness, and had not so much as one Spark of Virtue to stir them up to be thankful for such an eminent Deliverance: But instead thereof, vented a Million of Oaths and Curses upon the Captain of the *Greyhound,* vowing to execute Vengeance upon all they should meet with afterwards, for the Indignity he put upon them.

The first Prey that they met with, after their Flight was a small Sloop belonging to *Nantucket,* a Whale-Fishing, about 80 Miles from Land; the Master of which, one *Nathan Skiff,* a brisk young Fellow, the Pyrates cruelly whipp'd naked about the Deck, making his Torture their Sport; after which they cut of his Ears, and last of all shot him through the Head, and then sunk his Vessel; putting the rest of the Hands into their Whale-Boat, with a Compass, a little Water, and a few Biskets; and it being good Weather, they providentially got safe to *Nantucket,* beyond all Expectation.

There was another Whale-Boat belonging to this Sloop

last mentioned, which happened to be at some Distance from her, and perceiving what was doing, rowed with all speed to another Sloop not far off, to acquaint her with the Misfortune, that the Men might take Care of themselves; and she happily got away in Time. Some Days after, *Low* took a Fishing-Boat off of *Block Island*, but did not perpetrate so much Cruelty to her, contenting himself with only cutting off the Master's Head: But after taking two Whale-Boats near *Rhode Island*, he caused one of the Master's Bodies to be ripp'd up, and his Intrails to be taken out; and cut off the Ears of the other, and made him eat them himself with Pepper and Salt; which hard Injunction he comply'd with, without making a Word. Several other Persons he would have murthered, but Humanity prevailing in the tender Hearts of his Companions, they refused to put his savage Orders in Execution.

From the Coast of *New-England*, *Low* sailed directly for *Newfoundland*, and, near Cape *Briton*, took two or three and twenty *French* Vessels; and one of them of 22 Guns he mann'd with Pyrates, making a sort of a Man of War of her; with which he scower'd the Harbours and Banks of *Newfoundland*, and took sixteen or eighteen other Ships and Vessels, all which they plundered, and some destroyed.

Thus these inhumane Wretches went on, who could not be contented to satisfy their Avarice only, and travel in the common Road of Wickedness; but, like their Patron, the Devil, must make Mischief their Sport, Cruelty their Delight, and damning of Souls their constant Employment. Of all the pyratical Crews that were ever heard of, none of the *English* Name came up to this, in Barbarity; their Mirth and their Anger had much the same Effect, for both were usually gratified with the Cries and Groans of their Prisoners; so that they almost as often murthered a Man from the Excess of good Humour, as out of Passion and Resentment; and the Unfortunate could never be assured of Safety from them, for Danger lurked in their very Smiles. An Instance of this had liked to have happened to one Captain *Graves*, Master of a *Virginia* Ship last taken; for as soon as he came aboard of the Pyrate, *Low* takes a Bowl of Punch in his Hand, and drinks to him, saying, *Captain* Graves, *here's half this to you.* But the poor Gentleman being too sensibly touched at the Misfortune of falling into his Hands, modestly desired to be excused, for that he could not drink; whereupon *Low* draws out a Pistol, cocks it, and with the Bowl in tother Hand, told him, he should either take one or the other: So *Graves*, without Hesitation, made Choice of the Vehicle that contained the Punch, and guttled down about a Quart, when he had the least Inclination that ever he had in his Life to be merry.

The latter End of *July*, (1723,) *Low* took a large Ship, called the *Merry Christmas*, and fitted her for a Pyrate, cut several Ports in her, and mounted her with 34 Guns. *Low* goes aboard of this Ship, assumes the Title of Admiral, and hoists a black Flag, with the Figure of Death in red, at the Main-topmast Head, and takes another Voyage to the *Western Islands*, where he arrived the Beginning of *September*. The first Vessel he met with there, was a Brigantine, formerly an *English* Sloop, commanded by *Elias Wild*, but lately bought by a *Portuguese* Nobleman, and altered: She was manned partly with *English*, and partly *Portuguese*; the latter *Low* caused to be hang'd, by Way of Reprisal, for some of his own Men sent thither in a Sloop from the *Cape de Verd* Islands, as has been mentioned: The *English* Men he thrust into their own Boat, to shift for themselves, and set Fire to the Vessel.

At St. *Michaels*, they sent in their Boats and cut out of the Road, a new *London* built Ship of 14 Guns, commanded by Captain *Thompson*, who was taken there the Year before, by *Low*, in the *Rose* Pink. The Boats had fewer Men than the Ships and Captain *Thompson* would have defended himself, but his Men through Cowardize, or too great an Inclination of becoming Pyrates themselves, refused to stand by him, and he was obliged to surrender; and when he came aboard the Pyrate, had his Ears cut off close to his Head, for only proposing to resist Admiral *Low*'s black Flag; they gave him one of his own Boats, and burnt his Ship.

The next was a *Portuguese* Bark that fell into their Hands, whose Men came off somewhat better than usual, for they only cut them with their Cutlashes, out of Wantonness, turned them all into their Boat, and set their Vessel on Fire. When the Boat was going from the Side of the Ship, one of *Low*'s Men, who, we may suppose, was forced into his Gang, was drinking with a Silver Tankard at one of the Ports, and took his Opportunity to drop into the Boat among the *Portuguese*, and lye down in the Bottom, in order to escape along with them: After he had stowed himself in the Boat, so as not to be seen, it came into his Head, that the Tankard might prove of some Use to him, where he was going; so he got up again, laid hold of the Utensil, and went off, without being discover'd: In which Attempt had he failed, no doubt his Life, if not the Lives of all the People in the Boat, would have paid for it: The Name of this Man is *Richard Hains*.

Low took his old Tour to the *Canaries, Cape de Verd* Islands, and so to the Coast of *Guiney*; but nothing extraordinary happened till they arrived near *Sierraleon* in *Africa*, where they met with a Ship call'd the *Delight*, Captain *Hunt* Commander; this Ship they thought fit for their own Purpose, for she had been a small Man of War, and carried 12 Guns; however, they mounted 16 on Board her, mann'd her with 60 Men, and appointed one *Spriggs*, who was then their Quarter-Master, to be Captain of her, who, two Days after, separated from the Admiral, and went to the *West-Indies* a-pyrating, upon his own, and particular Company's, Account, where for the present we shall leave him.

In *January* Last, *Lew* took a Ship, called the *Squirrel*, Captain *Stephenson*; but what became of him afterwards, I can't tell; we have had no News concerning him come to *England*, since this I have now mentioned; but I have heard that he talk'd of going to *Brazil*; and if so, it is likely we may too soon hear of some Exploit or other; tho' the best Information we could receive, would be, that he and all his Crew were at the Bottom of the Sea.

❇ ❇

CHAPTER XIV.

of
Capt. JOHN EVANS,
And his CREW.

JOHN EVANS was a *Welch* Man, had been formerly Master of a Sloop belonging to *Nevis*, but losing his Employ there, he sailed for some Time out of *Jamaica* as Mate, till happening in Company of three or four of his Comrades, and Wages not being so good as formerly, and Births scarce, because of the great Number of Seamen; they agreed to go abroad in search of Adventures. They sailed, or rather rowed out of *Port Royal* in *Jamaica*, the latter End of *September* 1722, in a Canoa; and coming on the North-Side of the Island, went ashore in the Night, broke open a House or two, and robb'd them of some Money, and every Thing else they could find that was portable, and brought the Booty on Board the Canoa.

This was very well for the first Time, but this kind of Robbery did not please so well, they wanted to get out to Sea, but having no Vessel but their Canoa, they were prevented in their laudable Design; however, they kept a good look out, and traversed the Island, in Expectation that Providence would send some unfortunate Vessel as a Sacrifice, and in a few Days their Wishes were accomplished; for at *Duns Hole*, they round a small Sloop at an Anchor, belonging to *Bermudas*: They made bold and went aboard, and *Evans* informed the Folks that belonged to her, that he was Captain of the Vessel, which was a Piece of News they knew not

before. After they had put their Affairs in a proper Disposition aboard, they went ashore to a little Village for Refreshments, and lived jovially the remaining Part of the Day,
at a Tavern, spending three Pistols, and then departed. The
People of the House admired at the merry Guests they had
got, were mightily pleased, and wished for their Company
at another Time, which happened too soon for their Profit;
for, in the middle of the Night, they came ashore all Hands,
rifled the House, and carried what they could aboard their
Sloop.

The next Day they weighed in the Sloop, aboard of which
they mounted four Guns, called her the *Scowerer*, and sailed
to *Hispaniola*; on the North Part of which Island they took
a *Spanish* Sloop, which proved an extraordinary rich Prize,
as it fell among so few Persons as this Company consisted
of, for they shared upwards of 150 *l.* a Man.

In Pursuance of the Game, and beating up for the Wind-
ward Islands, the *Scowerer* met with a Ship from *New-
England*, bound to *Jamaica*, 120 Tons called the *Dove*,
Captain *Diamond* Master, off *Porto Rico*: They plundered
her, and strengthened their own Company, by taking out
the Mate, and two or three other Men; they discharged the
Prize, and run into one of the Islands for fresh Water and
Necessaries, and staid there some Time.

The next Prize they made, was the *Lucretia and Catherine*,
Captain *Mills*, of 200 Ton Burthen; they came up with her
near the Island *Disseada, January* 11th. Upon seizing of this
Ship, the Pyrates began to take upon themselves the Distri-
bution of Justice, examining the Men concerning their Master's Usage of them, according to the Custom of other
Pyrates; but the Captain over-hearing the Matter, put an
End to the judicial Proceedings, and fell to rumaging the
Ship, saying to them; *What have we to do to turn Reformers,
'tis Money we want*; And speaking to the Prisoners, he asked
them, *Does your Captain give you Victuals enough?* And they
answering in the Affirmative: *Why then*, said he, *he ought to
give you Work enough.*

After the taking of this Prize, they went to the little Island of *Avis*, with a Design to clean, and carried the *Lucretia* along with them, in order to heave down the *Scowerer* by her; but meeting there with a Sloop, the Pyrate gave Chace till the Evening, when she was within Gun-Shot of her; but fearing to lose Company with the *Lucretia*, who was a heavy Sailor, they left off, and saw her no more. This Chace brought them to Leeward of their Port, so that they were obliged to look out for another Place of Retreat, and the Island of *Ruby* not being far distant, they steered for that, and anchored there accordingly; but the next Day a *Dutch* Sloop coming as it were, into their Mouths, they could not forbear dealing, and so making her their Prize, they plundered her of what came, when shared, to fifty Pounds a Man.

They found this Sloop more for their Purpose than the *Lucretia*, to clean their own Sloop by, as being much lower in the Wast, and therefore capable of heaving her Bottom farther out of the Water, so she was discharged, and the *Dutch* Man kept in her Room; but not thinking it convenient to lay up here, for fear a discovery should be made, they turned their Thoughts another Way, and steered to the Coast of *Jamaica*, where they took a Sugar Drover, and then run to the *Grand Caimanes*, about 30 Leagues to Leeward of *Jamaica*, with Intention to clean there; but an unhappy Accident put an End to their Pyracies, which hitherto had proved very successful to them.

The Boatswain of the Pyrate being a noisy surly Fellow, the Captain had at several Times Words with him, relating to his Behaviour, who thinking himself ill treated, not only returned ill Language, but also challenged the Captain to fight him on the next Shore they came to, with Pistols and Sword, as is the Custom among these Outlaws. When the Sloop arrived, as abovementioned, the Captain proposed the Duel; but the cowardly Boatswain refused to fight, or go ashore, tho' it was his own Challenge. When Captain *Evans* saw there was nothing to be done with him, he took his Cane, and gave him a hearty drubbing; but the Boatswain not being able to bear such an Indignity, drew out a Pistol and shot *Evans* thro' the Head, so that he fell down dead; and the Boatswain immediately jumped over-board, and swam towards the Shore; but the Boat was quickly mann'd and sent after him, which took him up and brought him aboard.

The Death of the Captain in that Manner, provoked all the Crew, and they resolved the Criminal should die by the most exquisite Tortures; but while they were considering of the Punishment, the Gunner, transported with Passion, discharged a Pistol, and shot him thro' the Body; but not killing him outright, the Delinquent in very moving Words, desired a Week for Repentance only; but another stepping up to him, told him, *that he should repent and be damned to him*, and without more ado shot him dead.

I should have observed, that when the *Lucretia* and *Katharine* was suffered to go away, the Pyrates detained their Mate, who was now the only Man aboard, who understood Navigation, and him they desired to take upon him the Command of the Sloop, in the Room of Captain *Evans* deceased; but he desired to be excused that Honour, and at length positively refused it; so they agreed to break up the Company, and leave the Mate in Possession of the Vessel: Accordingly they went ashore at the *Caimanes*, carrying with them about nine thousand Pounds among thirty Persons; and it being fair Weather, the Mate and a Boy brought the Vessel into *Port Royal*, in *Jamaica*.

※ ※ ※ ※ ※ ※ ※ ※ ※ ※ ※ ※ ※ ※ ※ ※ ※ ※ ※ ※

CHAPTER XV.

of
Captain JOHN PHILLIPS,
And his CREW.

JOHN PHILLIPS was bred a Carpenter, and sailing to *Newfoundland* in a West-Country Ship, was taken by *Anstis* in the *Good Fortune* Brigantine, the next Day after he had left his Consort and Commadore, Captain *Roberts*. *Phillips* was soon reconciled to the Life of a Pyrate, and being a brisk Fellow, was appointed Carpenter of the Vessel, for at first his Ambition reach'd no higher; there he remain'd till they broke up at *Tabago*, and was one of those who came home in a Sloop that we have mentioned to be sunk in *Bristol* Channel.

His Stay was not long in *England*, for whilst he was paying his first Visits to his Friends in *Devonshire*, he heard of the Misfortune of some of his Companions, that is, of their being taken and committed to *Bristol* Goal; and there being good Reason for his apprehending Danger from a Wind that blew from the same Quarter, he mov'd off immediately to *Topsham*, the nearest Port, and there shipp'd himself with one Captain *Wadham*, for a Voyage to *Newfoundland*, and home again; which, by the way, Mr. *Phillips* never design'd to perform, or to see *England* any more. When the Ship came to *Peter* Harbour in *Newfoundland* aforesaid, he ran away from her, and hired himself a Splitter in the Fishery, for the Season: But this was only till he could have an Opportunity of prosecuting his intended Rogueries; in order to which, he combined with several others, in the same Employ, to go off with one of the Vessels that lay in the Harbour, upon the pyratical Account; accordingly the Time was fix'd, *viz.* the 29th of *August* 1723, at Night; but whether Remorse or Fear prevented their coming together, I know not, but of sixteen Men that were in the Combination, five only kept the Appointment: Notwithstanding which, *Phillips* was for pushing forward with that small Number, assuring his Companions, that they should soon encrease their Company; and they agreeing, a Vessel was seiz'd on, and out of the Harbour they sailed.

The first Thing they had now to do, was to chuse Officers, draw up Articles, and settle their little Commonwealth, to prevent Disputes and Ranglings afterwards; so *John Phillips* was made Captain, *John Nutt*, Master, (or Navigator) of the Vessel; *James Sparks*, Gunner; *Thomas Fern*, Carpenter; and *William White* was the only private Man in the whole Crew: When this was done, one of them writ out the following Articles (which we have taken *verbatim*) and all swore to 'em upon a Hatchet for want of a Bible.

The Articles on Board the *Revenge*.

I.

Every Man shall obey civil Command; the Captain shall have one full Share and a half in all Prizes; the Master, Carpenter, Boatswain and Gunner shall have one Share and quarter.

2.

If any Man shall offer to run away, or keep any Secret from the Company, he shall be marroon'd, with one Bottle of Powder, one Bottle of Water, one small Arm, and Shot.

3.

If any Man shall steal any Thing in the Company, or game, to the Value of a Piece of Eight, he shall be marroon'd or shot.

4.

If at any Time we should meet another Marrooner [that is
Pyrate,] *that Man that shall sign his Articles without the Con-*
sent of our Company, shall suffer such Punishment as the Cap-
tain and Company shall think fit.

5.

That Man that shall strike another whilst these Articles are
in force, shall receive Mofes's *Law (that is,* 40 *Stripes lacking*
one) on the bare Back.

6.

That Man that shall snap his Arms, or smoak Tobacco in the
Hold, without a Cap to his Pipe, or carry a Candle lighted
without a Lanthorn, shall suffer the same Punishment as in the
former Article.

7.

That Man that shall not keep his Arms clean, fit for an En-
gagement, or neglect his Business, shall be cut off from his Share,
and suffer such other Punishment as the Captain and the Com-
pany shall think fit.

8.

If any Man shall lose a Joint in time of an Engagement, shall
have 400 *Pieces of Eight; if a Limb,* 800.

9.

If at any time you meet with a prudent Woman, that Man
that offers to meddle with her, without her Consent, shall suffer
present Death.

Thus prepar'd, this bold Crew set out, and before they left
the Banks they made Prize of several small Fishing-Vessels, out
of which they got a few Hands, some *French* and some *English*,
and then sail'd for the *West-Indies*; in one of these Vessels they

took out one *John Rose Archer*, who having been a Pyrate under the famous *Black-beard*, was immediately preferr'd over other People's Heads, to be Quarter-Master to the Company; which sudden Promotion so disgusted some of the older Standers, especially *Fern*, the Carpenter, that it occasioned some Mischief to follow, as we shall shew by and by.

The Pyrates came off *Barbadoes* the beginning of *October*, and cruised there, and among other Islands, above three Months, without speaking with a Vessel, so that they were almost starv'd for want of Provisions, being reduc'd to a Pound of Meat a Day between ten; at length they fell in with a *Martinico* Man of 12 Guns and 35 Hands, far superior in Force, and what they would not have ventur'd on at another Time, but *Hunger will break down Stone Walls*; they were resolved to shew the *French* Men their black Flag; and if that would not do, they must seek out elsewhere; accordingly, they boldly ran up a-long-side of the Sloop, with their pyratical Colours flying, and told them, if they did not strike immediately, they would give them no Quarters; which so intimidated the *Frenchmen*, that they never fired a Gun. This proved a seasonable Supply; they took her Provisions, and four of her Men, and let her go. They took presently after, a Sloop belonging to *New-York*, and a *Virginia* Man, *Huffam* Master.

Having now occasion to clean their Vessel, *Phillips* propos'd *Tobago*, where the Company he formerly belong'd to, under *Anstis* and *Fenn*, broke up; to induce them to it, he told them when he left the Island, there was left behind six or eight of their Company that were not willing to go to *England*, with three Negroes: Whereupon they sail'd to the Island, and after a careful Search, found only one of the Negroes, whose Name was *Pedro*, who inform'd Captain *Phillips*, that those that were left behind were taken by a Man of War's Crew, and hang'd at *Antegoa*, among whom was *Fenn*, their Captain.

They took *Pedro* on Board, and then fell to Business, careening their Vessel; and just as they had finished their

Work, a Man of War's Boat came into the Harbour, the
Ship being cruising to Leeward of the Island. It was easily
guessed upon what Errant she was sent, and therefore they
lost no Time, but, as soon as the Boat went away, warp'd
out, and ply'd to Windward for Security, but left the four
French Men, they took out of the *Martinico* Sloop, behind.

In a few Days they took a Snow with a few Hands, and
Fern, the Carpenter, one *William Phillips, Wood* and *Taylor*,
went aboard to take Possession of her. *Fern*, not forgetting
the Affront of having *Archer* preferr'd before him, resolv'd to
go off with the Prize, and brought the rest into the same
Measures; however *Phillips*, the Captain, keeping a good
Look-out, perceiv'd their Design, and gave them Chace,
who coming up with the Vessel, a Skirmifh ensu'd, wherein
Wood was kill'd and *Taylor* wounded in his Leg; upon which
the other two surrender'd. There was no Surgeon aboard,
and therefore it was advis'd, upon a learned Consultation,
that *Phillips*'s Leg should be cut off; but who should perform
the Operation was the Dispute; at length the Carpenter was
appointed, as the most proper Man: Upon which, he fetch'd
up the biggest Saw, and taking the Limb under his Arm, fell
to Work, and separated it from the Body of the Patient, in
as little Time as he could have cut a Deal Board in two; after
that he heated his Ax red hot in the Fire, and cauteriz'd the
Wound, but not with so much Art as he perform'd the other
Part, for he so burnt his Flesh distant from the Place of
Amputation, that it had like to have mortify'd; however nature perform'd a Cure at last without any other Assistance.

From *Tobago* they stood away to the Northward and took
a *Portugueze* bound for *Brazil*, and two or three Sloops from
Jamaica, in one of which, *Fern* the Carpenter, endeavouring
to go off, was kill'd by *Phillips* the Captain, pursuant to their
Articles; another had the same Fate some Days after for the
like Attempt. These Severities made it dangerous for any to
consult or project an Escape; the Terror of which made several sign their Articles and set down quietly, waiting impa-
tiently for Redemption, which as yet they saw no great

likelyhood of, and should they have been taken before such Circumstances appear'd in their Actions or Characters, as afterwards happen'd, to denote their Innocence, they might have lost their Lives upon a Tryal at a Court of Admiralty; for pretty strong Evidence is expected in their Favour, to ballance that of being taken aboard a Vessel which is prov'd to be in actual Pyracy, and they assisting therein.

Thus was many an honest Man's Case made most desperate by the consummate Villany of a few hardned Wretches, who fear neither God or Devil, as this *Phillips* us'd often blasphemously to express himself.

On the 25th of *March* they took two Ships from *Virginia* for *London, John Phillips*, the Pyrate Captain's Namesake, was Master of one, and Captain *Robert Mortimer*, the other, a brisk young Fellow, that deserv'd a better Fate than he met with. *Phillips* the Pyrate staid on Board of Captain *Mortimer*'s Ship, while they transported the Crew to the Sloop, and the Boat returning along side, one of the Pyrates therein calls to *Phillips*, and tells him, there was a Mutiny aboard their Vessel, *Mortimer* had two Men in his Ship, and the Pyrate Captain had two, therefore thought it a good Opportunity to recover his Ship, and directly took up a Handspike and struck *Phillips* over the Head, giving him a dangerous wound, but not knocking him down, he recovered and wounded *Mortimer* with his Sword; and the two Pyrates that were aboard coming in to Captain *Phillips*'s Assistance, Captain *Mortimer* was presently cut to Pieces, while his own two Men stood by and did nothing.

This was the first Voyage that *Mortimer* had the Command of a Vessel, by whose Death is a poor disconsolate Widow made miserable, more in regard of the mutual Love and Fidelity they lived in, than the Loss of what would have been a handsome and comfortable Provision for themselves and Children, which, I think, now ought to be made up by the Publick, since 'twas in the publick Service he fell; for had his Attempt succeeded, in all Probability he would not only have regained his own Ship, but entirely subdued and destroy'd the Enemy, there being several, as it afterwards proved, that would have seconded such an Enterprize when ever they found a Beginning made.

This Affair ended without any other consequence than a strict Search after a Brother of Captain *Mortimer*, who was on Board, in order to have put him likewise to death; but he had the good Fortune to meet with a Townsman among the Crew, who hid him for four and twenty Hours in a Stay-Sail, till the Heat of their Fury was over, and by that Means happily missed of the Fate designed him.

Out of the other *Virginia* Man before spoken of they took one *Edward Cheeseman*, a Carpenter, to supply the Place of their late Carpenter, *Fern*. He was a modest sober young Man, very averse to their unlawful Practice, and a brave gallant Fellow. There was one *John Philmore* of *Ipswich*, formerly taken by them, ordered to row *Cheeseman* aboard of *Mortimer's* Ship, which the Pyrates possess'd themselves of, who, seeing with what Reluctance and Uneasiness *Cheeseman* was brought away, told him, he would join with him, in some Measures, to over-throw the pyratical Government, telling him withal, their present Condition, what Difficulties *Phillips* had met with to make up his Company, and how few voluntary Pyrates there were on Board, and the like. But, however specious this seemed, *Cheeseman* out of Prudence rejected his Offers of Assistance, till he saw some Proofs of his Sincerity, which after a few Days he was convinced of, and then they often consulted; but as the old Pyrates were always jealous of the new Comers, and consequently observant of their Behaviour; this was done with the utmost Caution, chiefly when they were lying down together, as tho' asleep, and, at other Times, when they were playing at Cards; both which they seigned often to do for that Purpose.

The Pyrates went on all the while, plundering and robbing several Ships and Vessels, bending their Course towards *Newfoundland*, where they designed to raise more Men, and do all the Mischief they could on the Banks, and in the Harbours.

Newfoundland is an Island on the North Continent of *America*, contained between the 46 and 53° of N. Latitude, discovered first by St. *Sebastion Cabot* A. D. 1497, but never settled till the Year 1610; when Mr. *Guy* of *Bristol* revived the Affair, and obtained a Patent, and himself to be Governor. The Island is deserted by the Natives and neglected by us, being desolate and Woody, and the Coast and Harbour only held for the Conveniency of the Cod Fishery, for which alone they were settled.

The Bays and Harbours about it, are very numerous and convenient, and being deeply indented, makes it easy for any Intelligence quickly to pass from one Harbour to another over Land; especially the principal, St. *John*'s and *Placentia*, when the Appearance of an Enemy makes them apprehend Danger.

They are able to cure and export about 100000 Quintals (100 Weight each) of Fish, annually, which returns to *England* in Money, or the necessary Commodities of *Portugal, Spain* and *Italy*. As it therefore expends abundance of Rum, Molossus and Sugar, the Product of our *West-India* Colonies, and employs a Number of Fishermen from home every Season, by whose Industry and Labour only this Fish is purchased, it may very well be reckon'd an advantagious Branch of Trade.

But the present Design of this Digression being not to give an exact Description of the Country or Fishery; but rather how it accidentally contributes to raise, or support the Pyrates already rais'd, I shall observe.

First, That our West Country Fishing-Ships, *viz.* from *Topsham, Barnstable* and *Bristol*, who chiefly attend the Fishing Seasons, transport over a considerable Number of poor Fellows every Summer, whom they engage at low Wages, and are by their Terms to pay for Passage back to *England*. When the *Newfoundland* Ships left that Country, towards Winter, in the Year 1720, these Passengers muster'd 1100, who, during the Season of Business, (the Hardness of their

Labour, and Chilness of the Nights, pinching them very much) are mostly fond of drinking Black Strap, (a strong Liquor used there, and made from Rum, Molossus, and Chowder Beer;) by this the Majority of them out-run the Constable, and then are necessitated to come under hard Articles of Servitude for their Maintenance in the Winter; no ordinary Charge, indeed, when the Barrenness of the Country is consider'd, and the Stock of Provision laid in, happen to fall short, in Proportion to the Computation made of the People remaining there the Winter, which are generally about 17 or 1800. The Masters residing there think Advantages taken on their Necessities, no more than a just and lawful Gain; and either bind such for the next Summer's Service, or sell their Provisions out to them at extravagant Rates; Bread from 15s. to 50, immediately at the departing of the Ships, and so of other sorts of Food in Proportion; wherefore not being able to subsist themselves, or in any likely Way of clearing the Reckoning to the Masters, they sometimes run away with Shallops and Boats, and begin on pyratical Exploits, as *Phillips* and his Companions, whom we are now treating of, had done.

And secondly (which is more opportunely for them,) they are visited every Summer, almost, by some Set of Pyrates or other, already rais'd, who call here for the same Purpose, (if young Beginners) and to lay in a Store of Water and Provisions, which they find imported, much or little, by all the Ships that use the Trade.

Towards this Country *Phillips* was making his Way, and took on the Voyage, besides those above-mentioned, one *Salter*, in a Sloop off the Isle of *Sables*, which Vessel they made use of themselves, and gave back *Mortimer's* Ship to the Mate and Crew. The same Day, *viz.* the 4th of *April*, took a Scooner, one *Chadwell*, Master, which they scuttled, in order to sink; but Capt. *Phillips* understanding that she belong'd to Mr. *Minors* at *Newfoundland*, with whose Vessel they first went off a pyrating, a Qualm of Conscience came athwart his Stomach, and he said to his Companions, *We have done him Injury enough already*; so order'd the Vessel immediately to be repair'd, and return'd her to the Master.

That Afternoon they chac'd another Vessel, and at Night came up with her, the Master of which was a Saint of *New-England*, nam'd *Dependence Ellery*, who taking *Phillips* for a Pyrate, he told him was the Reason that he gave him the Trouble of chacing so long; which being resented by these Men of Honour, they made poor *Dependance* dance about the Deck till he was weary.

Within few Days several other Vessels had the same Misfortune, the Masters Names were as follow, *Joshua Elwell, Samuel Elwell*, Mr. *Combs*, Mr. *Lansly, James Babston, Edward Freeman*, Mr. *Start, Obediah Beal, Erick Erickson* and *Benjamin Wheeler*.

The 14th of *April* they took a Sloop belonging to Cape *Ann, Andrew Harradine* Master; they look'd upon this Vessel more fit for their Purpose, and so came aboard, keeping only the Master of her Prisoner, and sending *Harradine*'s Crew away in *Salter*'s Vessel, which they, till this Time, detain'd. To this *Harradine, Cheeseman* the Carpenter, broke his Mind, and brought him into the Confederacy to destroy the Crew, which was put in Execution four Days afterwards.

Harradine and the rest were for doing the Business in the Night, as believing they might be more opportunely surpriz'd; for *Nut*, the Master, being a Fellow of great Strength, and no less Courage, it was thought dangerous to attack him without Fire-Arms, however, *Cheeseman* was resolute to have it perform'd by Day-light, as the least liable to Confusion; and as to the Master, he offer'd to lay Hands on him first: Upon this 'twas concluded on; 12 at Noon was the appointed Time; in order for the Business *Cheeseman* leaves his working Tools on the Deck, as though he had been going to use them, and walked aft; but perceiving some Signs of Timidity in *Harradine*, he comes back, fetches his Brandy Bottle and gives him and the rest a Dram, then drank to *Burril*, the Boatswain, and the Master, *To their next merry Meeting*, and up he puts the Bottle; then he takes a Turn with *Nut*, asking what he thought of the Weather, and such like: In the mean while *Filemore* takes up the Axe, and turns it round upon the Point, as if at Play, then both he and *Harradine* wink at him, thereby letting him know they were ready; upon which Signal he seizes *Nut* by the Collar, with one Hand between his Legs, and toss'd him over the Side of the Vessel, but, he holding by *Cheeseman*'s Sleeve, said, *Lord have Mercy upon me! what are you going to do, Carpenter?* He told him it was an unnecessary Question, *For*, says he, *Master, you are a dead Man*, so strikes him over the Arm, *Nut* looses his Hold, tumbles into the Sea, and never spoke more.

By this time the Boatswain was dead; for as soon as *Filemore* saw the Master laid hold of, he raised up the Axe, and divided his Enemy's Head in two: The Noise brought the Captain upon Deck, whom *Cheeseman* saluted with the Blow of a Mallet, which broke his Jaw-Bone, but did not knock him down; *Harradine* came in then with the Carpenter's Adds, but *Sparks*, the Gunner, interposing between him and Captain *Phillips*, *Cheeseman* trips up his Heels, and flung him into the Arms of *Charles Joymay*, one of his Consorts, who that Instant discharg'd him into the Sea; and at the same Time *Harradine* compassed his Business with the Captain aforesaid: *Cheeseman* lost no Time, but from the Deck jumps into the Hold, and was about to beat out the Brains of *Archer*, the Quarter-Master, having struck him two or three Blows with his blunt Weapon the Mallet, when *Harry Giles*, a young Lad, came down after him, and desir'd his Life might be spar'd, as an Evidence of their own Innocence; that he having all the Spoil and Plunder in his Custody, it may appear, that these tragick Proceedings were not undertaken with any dishonest View of seizing or appropriating the Effects to themselves; which prudent Advice prevail'd, and he and three more were made Prisoners, and secured.

The Work being done, they went about Ship, altered the Course from *Newfoundland* to *Boston*, and arrived safe the 3d of *May* following, to the great Joy of that Province.

On the 12th of *May*, 1724, a special Court of Admiralty was held for the Tryal of these Pyrates, when *John Filmore, Edward Cheeseman, John Combs, Henry Giles, Charles Ivymay, John Bootman*, and *Henry Payne*, the seven that confederated together for the Pyrates Destruction, were honourably acquitted; as also three *French* Men, *John Baptis, Peter Taffery*, and *Isaac Lassen*, and three Negroes, *Pedro, Francisco*, and *Pierro*. And *John Rose Archer*, the Quarter-Master, *William White, William Taylor*, and *William Phillips*, were condemned; the two latter were reprieved for a Year and a Day, in order to be recommended (though I don't know for what) as Objects of his Majesty's Mercy. The two former were executed on the 2d of *June*, and dy'd very penitently, making the following Declarations at the Place of Execution, with the Assistance of two grave Divines that attended them.

The dying Declarations of John Rose Archer *and* William White, *on the Day of their Execution at* Boston, June 2, 1724, *for the Crimes of Pyracy.*

First, separately, of *Archer*.

I Greatly bewail my Profanations of the Lord's Day, and my Disobedience to my Parents.

And my Cursing and Swearing, and my blaspheming the Name of the glorious God.

Unto which I have added, the Sins of Unchastity. And I have provoked the Holy One, at length, to leave me unto the Crimes of Pyracy and Robbery; wherein, at last, I have brought my self under the Guilt of Murder also.

But one Wickedness that has led me as much as any, to all the rest, has been my brutish Drunkenness. By strong Drink I have been heated and hardened into the Crimes that are now more bitter than Death unto me.

I could wish that Masters of Vessels would not use their Men with so much Severity, as many of them do, which exposes to great Temptations.

And then of *White*.

I am now, with Sorrow, reaping the Fruits of my Disobedience to my Parents, who used their Endeavours to have me instructed in my Bible, and my Catechism.

And the Fruits of my neglecting the publick Worship of God, and prophaning the holy Sabbath.

And of my blaspheming the Name of God, my Maker.

But my Drunkenness has had a great Hand in bringing my Ruin upon me. I was drunk when I was enticed aboard the Pyrate.

And now, for all the vile Things I did aboard, I own the Justice of God and Man, in what is done unto me.

Of both together.

We hope, we truly hate the Sins, whereof we have the Burthen lying so heavy upon our Consciences.

We warn all People, and particularly young People, against such Sins as these. We wish, all may take Warning by us.

We beg for Pardon, for the sake of Christ, our Saviour; and our Hope is in him alone. Oh! *that in his Blood our Scarlet and Crimson Guilt may be all washed away!*

We are sensible of an hard Heart in us, full of Wickedness. And we look upon God for his renewing Grace upon us.

We bless God for the Space of Repentance which he has given us; and that he has not cut us off in the Midst and Heighth of our Wickedness.

We are not without Hope, that God has been savingly at work upon our Souls.

We are made sensible of our absolute Need of the Righteousness of Christ; that we may stand justified before God in that. We renounce all Dependance on our own.

We are humbly thankful to the Ministers of Christ, for the great Pains they have taken for our Good. The Lord Reward their Kindness.

We don't Despair of Mercy; but hope, through Christ,

that when we dye, we shall find Mercy with God, and be received into his Kingdom.

We wish others, and especially the Sea-faring, may get Good by what they see this Day befalling of us.

Declared in the Presence of   J. W. D. M.

CHAPTER XVI.

of
Captain SPRIGGS,
And his CREW.

SPRIGGS sailed with *Low* for a pretty while, and I believe came away from *Lowther*, along with him; he was Quarter-Master to the Company, and consequently had a great Share in all the Barbarities committed by that execrable Gang, till the Time they parted; which was about *Christmas* last, when *Low* took a Ship of 12 Guns on the Coast of *Guiney*, called the *Delight*, (formerly the *Squirrel* Man of War commanded by Captain *Hunt*. *Spriggs* took Possession of the Ship with eighteen Men, left *Low* in the Night, and came to the *West-Indies*. This Separation was occasioned by a Quarrel with *Low*, concerning a Piece of Justice *Spriggs* would have executed upon one of the Crew, for killing a Man in cold Blood, as they call it, one insisting that he should be hang'd, and the other that he should not.

A Day or two after they parted, *Spriggs* was chose Captain by the rest, and a black Ensign was made, which they called *Jolly Roger*, with the same Device that Captain *Low* carried, *viz.* a white Skeliton in the Middle of it, with a Dart in one Hand striking a bleeding Heart, and in the other, an Hour-Glass; when this was finished and hoisted, they fired all their Guns to salute their Captain and themselves, and then looked out for Prey.

In their Voyage to the *West-Indies*, these Pyrates took a *Portuguese* Bark, wherein they got valuable Plunder, but not contented with that alone, they said they would have a little Game with the Men, and so ordered them a Sweat, more for the Brutes Diversion, than the poor Men's Healths; which Operation is performed after this Manner; they stick up lighted Candles circularly round the Mizon-Mast, between Decks, within which the Patients one at a Time enter; without the Candles, the Pyrates post themselves, as many as can stand, forming another Circle, and armed with Pen-Knives, Tucks, Forks, Compasses &c. and as he runs round and round, the Musick playing at the same Time, they prick him with those Instruments; this usually lasts for 10 or 12 Minutes, which is as long as the miserable Man can support himself. When the Sweating was over, they gave the *Portuguese* their Boat with a small Quantity of Provisions, and set their Vessel on Fire.

Near the Island of St. *Lucia*, they took a Sloop belonging to *Barbadoes*, which they plundered, and then burnt, forcing some of the Men to sign their Articles, the others they beat and cut in a barbarous Manner, because they refused to take on with the Crew, and then sent them away in the Boat, who all got safe afterwards to *Barbadoes*.

The next was a *Martinico* Man, which they served as bad as they had done the others, but did not burn their Ship. Some Days afterwards in running down to Leeward, they took one Captain *Hawkins*, coming from *Jamaica*, loaden chiefly with Logwood; they took out of her, Stores, Arms, Ammunition, and several other Things, as they thought fit, and what they did not want they threw over-board or destroy'd; they cut the Cables to pieces, knocked down the Cabins, broke all the Windows, and in short took all the Pains in the World to be Mischievous. They took by Force, out of her, Mr. *Burridge* and Mr. *Stephens*, the two Mates, and some other Hands; and after detaining the Ship from the 22d of *March*, to the 29th, they let her go. On the 27th they took a *Rhode Island* Sloop, Captain *Pike*, and all his Men were obliged to go aboard the Pyrate; but the Mate being a grave sober Man, and not inclinable to stay, they told him, he should have his Discharge, and that it should be immediately writ on his Back; whereupon he was sentenced to receive ten Lashes from every Man in the Ship, which was rigorously put in Execution.

The next Day Mr. *Burridge*, Captain *Hawkins*'s Mate, sign'd their Articles, which was so agreeable to them (he being a good Artist and Sailor) that they gave three Huzza's, fir'd all the Guns in the Ship, and appointed him Master: The Day was spent in boysterous Mirth, roaring and drinking of Healths, among which was, by Mistake, that of King *George* the II. for you must know, now and then the Gentry are provok'd to sudden Fits of Loyalty, by the Expectation of an Act of Grace: It seems Captain *Pike* had heard at *Jamaica* that the King was dead, so the Pyrates immediately hoisted their Ensign Half-Mast (the Death Signal) and proclaim'd his Royal Highness, saying, *They doubted not but there would be a general Pardon in a twelve Month, which they would embrace and come in upon, but damn 'em if they should be excepted out of it, they would murder every* Englishman *that should fall into their Hands.*

The second of *April*, they spy'd a Sail, and gave her Chace till 12 o'Clock at Night, the Pyrates believed her to be a *Spaniard*, when they came close up to her, they discharged a Broadside, with small and great Shot, which was follow'd by another, but the Ship making a lamentable Cry for Quarters, they ceas'd firing, and ordered the Captain to come aboard, which he did, but how disappointed the Rogues were when they found 'twas their old Friend Captain *Hawkins*, whom they had sent away three Days before, worth not one Penny? This was such a Baulk to them, that they resolved he should suffer for falling in their Way, tho' it was so contrary to his own Inclinations: About 15 of them surrounded the poor Man with sharp Cutlashes, and fell upon him, whereby he was soon laid flat on the Deck; at the Instant *Burridge* flew amongst the thickest of the Villains, and begg'd earnestly for his Life, upon whose Request 'twas granted. They were now most of 'em drunk, as is usual at this Time of Night, so they unanimously agreed to make a Bonfire of *Hawkins*'s Ship, which was immediately done, and in half an Hour she was all of a Blaze.

After this, they wanted a little more Diversion, and so Captain *Hawkins* was sent for down to the Cabin to Supper; what should the Provision be, but a Dish of Candles, which he was forced to eat, having a naked Sword and a Pistol held to his Breast all the while; when this was over, they buffeted him about for some Time, and sent him forward amongst the other Prisoners, who had been treated with the same Delicacies.

Two Days afterwards, they anchor'd at a little uninhabited Island, call'd *Rattan*, near the Bay of *Honduras*, and put ashore Captain *Hawkins*, and several other Men, (one of them his Passenger) who dy'd there of the Hardships he under went. They gave them Powder and Ball, and a Musquet, with which they were to shift as they could, sailing away the next Day for other Adventures.

Captain *Hawkins*, and his unfortunate Companions, staid 19 Days upon this Island, supplying themselves with both Fish and Fowl, such as they were, at which Time came two Men in a Canoe, that had been left upon another maroon Island near *Benacca*, who carry'd the Company at several Times thither, it being more convenient in having a good Well of fresh Water, and plenty of Fish, &c. Twelve Days afterwards they spy'd a Sloop off at Sea, which upon their making a great Smoke, stood in, and took them off; she was the *Merriam*, Captain *Jones*, lately escaped out of the Bay of *Honduras*, from being taken by the *Spaniards*.

At an Island to the Westward, the Pyrates clean'd their Ship, and sail'd towards the Island of St. *Christophers*, to wait for one Captain *Moor*, who commanded the *Eagle* Sloop, when she took *Lowther*'s upon the Careen at *Blanco*; *Spriggs* resolved to put him to Death, whenever he took him, for falling upon his Friend and Brother, but instead of *Moor*, he found a *French* Man of War, from *Martinico*, upon the Coast, which *Spriggs* not thinking fit to contend with, run

away with all the Sail he could make; the *French* Man
crowded after him, and was very likely to speak with Mr.
Spriggs, when unfortunately his Main-Top-Mast came by
the Board, which obliged him to give over the Chace.

Spriggs then stood to the Northward, towards *Burmudas*,
or the *Summer Isles*, and took a Scooner belonging to *Boston*;
he took out all the Men and sunk the Vessel, and had the
Impudence to tell the Masters, that he designed to encrease
his Company on the Banks of *Newfoundland*, and then
would sail for the Coast of *New-England* in quest of Captain
Solgard, who attack'd and took their Consort *Charles Harris;*
Spriggs being then in *Low*'s Sloop, very fairly run for it. The
Pyrate ask'd the Master if he knew Captain *Solgard*, who
answering No; he ask'd another the same Question, and then
a third, who said he knew him very well, upon which *Spriggs*
ordered him to be sweated, which was done in the Manner
before describ'd.

Instead of going to *Newfoundland* as the Pyrates
threat'ned, they came back to the Islands, and to Windward
of St. *Christophers*, on the 4th of *June* 1724 took a Sloop,
Nicholas Trot Master, belonging to St. *Eustatia*, and wanting
a little Diversion, they hoisted the Men as high as the Main
and Fore Tops and let them run down amain, enough to
break all the Bones in their Skins, and after they had pretty
well Cripled them by this cruel Usage, and whipp'd them
along the Deck, they gave *Trot* his Sloop, and let him go,
keeping back only 2 of his Men, besides the Plunder of the
Vessel.

Within two or three Days they took a Ship coming from
Rhode-Island to St. *Christophers*, loaders with Provisions and
some Horses; the Pyrates mounted the Horses and rid them
about the Deck backwards and forwards a full Gallop, like
Madmen at *New-Market*, cursing swearing and hollowing at
such a Rate, that made the Creatures wild. At length two or
three of them throwing their Riders, they fell upon the Ship's
Crew, and whip'd, cut, and beat them in a barbarous Manner, telling them, it was for bringing Horses without Boots

and Spurs, for want of which they were not able to ride like Gentlemen.

After this he was so bold as to cruise off of *Port Royal* in the Island of *Jamaica*, and in sight thereof, take a Sloop and plunder her, upon which the *Diamond* and *Spence*, two Men of War that lay there, gave Chace to the Pyrate, but missing of her on the Coast of the Island, one of them returned into the Harbour, and the other continued in pursuit to the Bay of *Honduras*, whither the Man of War thought she might probably be gone, which happened accordingly; for *Sprigg* taking a Sloop a little before, put in one *Shipton* with about 40 Hands, and sailed to the aforesaid Bay, and there took ten or twelve *English* Ships and Vessels that came thither for Logwood, *&c.* and while he was plundering his Prizes, the Man of War came down and gave the Pyrates a Broadside. The Pyrates were in great Consternation, but however, return'd several Shot at the Man of War, tho' they did not think fit to contest the Honour of the Day, for they got out their Oars with the utmost Expedition, and, there being but little Wind, made shift to row into Shoal Water and escape.

By this seasonable Assistance, the Owners recovered most of their Ships, but not without Loss, the Pyrates having taken several Goods, Stores, and Money from them, besides several of their Men. From the Bay they sail'd through the Gulph, and the Channel of the *Bahama*'s for the Continent of North *America*, in which Run they were almost starv'd for want of Provisions; in the Way they met with a Sloop in the Service of the *South-Sea* Company bound from *Jamaica* to the Havanna with Negroes, whom they took out, and brought on board their Ship and Sloop, which help'd to consume the little Provision they had left. In a Day or two, which was about the beginning of the New Year, they took a Ship bound from *Jamaica* to *New England*, which, after they had plunder'd, they were about to put all the Negroes aboard that were taken in the abovemention'd Sloop, but the Captain representing his great want of Provisions, and the Danger of their perishing by Famine if he took them in, he was set at Liberty upon his taking only ten of them, which he carried to South *Carolina*, whither he was forc'd to put in for a fresh Supply of Provisions.

After this *Sprigg* met with Captain *Durfy*, off *Rhode Island*, whom he plunder'd in the usual manner, but resolv'd the Negroes should go along with him, so they put 25 aboard his Vessel, and took his Mate and all the rest of his Hands, leaving Captain *Durfy* alone to manage his black Troop as well as he could.

Sprigg having got Provisions and Necessaries out of the Vessels lately taken, he altered his Voyage because of the Cold Weather and hard Gales of Wind, and came into a warmer Latitude, and having clean'd and refresh'd at a small Island, he with his Company agreed to pay another Visit to the Bay of *Honduras*, where he went and took sixteen Vessels, one of which, Commanded by Captain *Kelsey*, he burnt, to whom he gave the Longboat belonging to his Ship for his whole Company, and it being fair Weather, they all came safe to the uninhabited Island of *Bonaco*; afterwards a Sloop came by and took them off the said Island.

Sprigg and *Shipton* left the Bay that Night, in order to have gone to the *Bahama* Islands, but off the West End of Cuba was met with again by the aforesaid Man of War, who chac'd them over to the *Elerida* Shore, where *Shipton*'s Sloop run aground and was lost, the Men got safe to Land, but falling into the Hands of the *Indians*, they kill'd and eat 16 of them, and carried about 40 to the *Havana*. *Shipton* the Captain, and 12 more got off in a Canoe, but being pursued by the Man of War's Boats, he was forc'd to quit her again, and the Canoe, with four Negroes, and one Pyrate, and about 3000 1, in Gold, fell a Prize to the *Diamond*.

As to *Sprigg*, he got clear off, sail'd away towards the Main, took several more Prizes, and is still cruising, as I am inform'd by Letters from *New-England*, dated *April* 26. 1725.

CHAPTER XVII.

of
Captain JOHN SMITH.

JOHN SMITH, was about 27 Years of Age, born at *Cathness,* in the North of *Scotland,* but liv'd with Relations at *Carisston* in the *Orkneys,* most of his Time; when he grew up to Maturity, he sail'd in several Vessels, and came in one to *Ratterdam* in a Mate's Employ, from whence he Ship'd himself in the *George* Galley, named so by a Gentleman who purchas'd her there, she being an *English* built Ship, and formerly call'd the *Princess Carolina.*

This Ship was commanded by *Oliver Ferneau,* an elderly Man, who appointed this *Smith* 2d Mate, and Gunner; and having got in the Ships Lading, they fell down to the *Texel,* in order to prosecute their Voyage to *Sancta Cruze,* in South *Barbary,* whither they were bound. On the first of *August,* the Ship weigh'd from the *Texel,* and arriv'd at the intended Port about a Month afterwards, in good Condition. While the Ship lay here, *Smith,* and one *James Williams* a Foremast Man, had diverse Consults in what Manner to seize the Ship and go a Pyrating in her, which, 'tis thought, they design'd when they first came aboard at *Ratterdam.* The Master, Captain *Ferneau,* was a cross pevish old Man, had pinch'd the Sailors in their Provisions, and otherways disobliged them, so that as these Conspirators apprehended they would be all glad enough of a Change, and indeed the ill Usage such poor Wretches receive under a severe Master is too often the Oc-

casion of Revolts of this Nature; it being Natural to all Men
to prefer a full Meal and an easy Life to Hunger and hard
Labour; especially in such a Case where their Revenge is
gratified on the Authors of their Distress at the same time
as they, in their Opinions, have provided for their better
Accommodation.

To accomplish this Design, all were to be taken off that
stood in their Way; these were the Captain, Chief Mate,
Surgeon, and the Merchant's Clark, who was a sort of a
Super-Cargo; these were doom'd to Death, and no doubt
many others had been involved in the Massacre, had they
expected any Opposition from them, but indeed they were,
too much inclin'd in favour of the Villainy; and tho' no more
than eight Persons agreed to be concern'd in the Execution,
yet there were others privy to the Design, but were not yet
so hard'ned as to imbrue their Hands in Innocent Blood,
tho' such Men by the Law of *England*, as well as by the
Divine Law, are certainly as guilty of the Murther, in per-
mitting, or, which is the same Thing, in not preventing it,
as any of those who were Actors in the bloody Tragedy.

On the third Day of *November*, the *George* Galley weigh'd
from *Sancta Cruz*; having taken in a Loading of Wax with
other Commodities, which was intended to be carry'd to
Marseilles up the *Mediteranean*; but *Smith* and his Confederates had other things in View, and resolv'd to alter the
Course that very Night; accordingly about ten, when one
Watch was turn'd into their Hammocks, the Assassines assembled upon Deck, and from thence dispers'd to the several
Stations assign'd, in order to perform the bloody Operation,
which was compleated after this manner.

The first Alarm was given, by crying out, That a Man was
tumbled overboard. This brought the Captain to the Ships
Side, to look after the Man who was supposed to have fallen
in the Sea, when he was immediately seiz'd by two of the
Conspirators, *William Melvin* and *Peter Rolson*, who endeavour'd to throw him over and drown him; but in struggling he got away from them, tho' at that Instant met with

one *Winter* with a Knife in his Hand, coming up from cutting the Surgeons Throat, with which he also cut his Throat, but missing his Windpipe, the former two took hold of him again, trying to fling him overboard, but he still struggling with them, *Smith*, the then second Mate, came up, to him, and with a Pistol Shot him thro' the Body, and then they threw him into the Sea.

While this was doing *Daniel Machally* went to the Clerk (or *Schrivan* as the *Dutch* call it) who was asleep in his Hammock, and cut his Throat, but not doing it effectually, he waked and got out of Bed, after *Maccally* went away; *John Peterson* at the same time went to the Chief Mate's Cabbin, *Bonadventure Jelphs*, and cut his Throat likewise, but not killing him, *Melvin* assisted in dragging him out of the Hold where he lay, which *Williams* seeing, puts a Pistol into a Boys Hand, one *Michael Moore*, and told him, if he did not Shoot him he would hang him the next Morning at the Yard Arm, which he instantly did, and kill'd him upon the Spot, in the mean while the said *Williams* goes forward and meets the poor Schrivan crawling along to whom he claps a Pistol to his Head, but he beg'd earnestly for a little Time to say his Prayers, but the Villain not mov'd thereat, said *D—n you, This is no Time to say Prayers*. And so shot him dead. The Surgeon, *Thomas Guy*, came up after his Throat was cut and fell cross the Tiller, from whence they took him and flung him overboard after the Captain.

The Company was now alarm'd by the noise of the Pistols, and Groans of the dying Persons, so that they all came up from between Decks, some of them readily joyn'd with the Pyrates, and the others thought fit to comply in Appearance, for indeed there was no resisting; *Smith*, being Gunner of the Ship, took Care to secure all the Arms but what his own Gang had Possession of, and those he most doubted, he kept Prisoners in the Cabbin, and clapt a Sentry over them; of these were the Boatswain and Carpenter, till such time that the new Government should be settled, and every one had sign'd to it.

Assoon as the Confusion was over, *Williams* came upon the Quarter Deck and Salutes *Smith* with the Title of Captain, with no other Ceremony than striking his Cutlass upon one of the great Guns, and saying, *Captain* Smith *You're Welcome! Welcome to your new Command*; then *Williams* had the Compliment made him of the Honour and Post of Lieutenant, *Peter Rolson* was appointed Gunner, and *James Belvin* who was then lock'd up in the Great Cabbin, accepted of his own Post, *viz.* that of Boatswain, very readily, and told them he was sorry they did not let him into the Cabal, for that he would have lent them a Hand in the Murthers with all his Heart. The new Captain made a short Speech to the Crew, wherein he told them, he would have no two Persons whisper together on Pain of Death; *and* says he, *if any of you refuse my Orders, let every such Man to depend upon it, that he shall certainly go the same Way as those that are now gone before.*

Thus they Set out upon their Pyratical Adventures. The Captain order'd the Carpenter to Work to fit up the Ship for that Purpose, he new nam'd her the *Revenge*, and than steer'd away to the North Eastward in quest of Business.

It was not long before they had an Opportunity of exercising their Villainy upon other honest Traders, for meeting with two Ships, the *Delight* Captain *Cross*, and the *Batchellor* Captain *Wise*, one *November* 18, and the other *December* the 18th, from *Newfoundland* bound to *Cadiz*; plunder'd them of what they thought fit, especially Stores, Money, Apparel, and Guns; and sunk them to the bottom of the Sea, to prevent their giving any Intelligence of them.

From the Southward Cape, they ranged along the Coast to Cape *Finisterre*; having out of the above mention'd Ships, strengthen'd their own, to the amount of 22 Guns, and 16 Pattereroes, and their Company was encreas'd to 38 Men. In this Range they took a Scotch Snow, bound from *Glasgow* to *Leghorn*, and a *French* Ship with 12 Men, bound from *Cadiz* to *Brest*, they plunder'd them both, and were about to sink these as they had done the others, but the Majority prevailing, on Consideration that they design'd no long Stay in that Station, they were pleased to detain them in their Hands till the Cruise was over.

Presently after (*viz.* the 6th. of *January*) they took the *Triumvirate* Captain, *Joel Davis*, within Thirty Leagues of *Vigo*, which they detain'd in like manner taking the Captain aboard their own Ship, and putting some Hands they could depend on aboard their Prize. Some Days afterwards they came up with a *French* Ship, whom they fired upon, but she being a Ship of some Force, seem'd resolved to defend herself, which the Pyrate Captain finding, hoisted his Topsails and stood away from her. This so provok'd *Williams* the Lieutenant, that he fired a Pistol at the Captain's Head, upbraided him with Cowardise, gave him a great deal of opprobrious Language, and swore he would be no further concern'd with him, for his letting such a Ship go that would, he said, have made them all.

However the Captain's Conduct was rather approv'd of than condemn'd by the Company; but had it been otherwise they said he ought to have had a fair Hearing, and not to be knock'd in the Head, thro the obstinacy and Caprice of a Particular Fellow, and if such Actions receiv'd Counteance, there would be an End, at once, of not only their own Projects but their Lives too; therefore some mov'd loud enough that *Williams* should be try'd and punish'd for his Offence, but such an Uproar follow'd, and being unskill'd in Matters of Judicature, they could agree in nothing but the turning him off aboard the *Triumvirate*, which they, intending to leave the Coast, thought fit to discharge, with others that had been detain'd for fear of allarming their Enemies: So *Williams* was put into Irons and sent aboard accordingly, which Ship arriv'd at *Lisbon* in a few Days, and Captain *Davis* surrender'd him to the Captain of the *Argyle* Man of War, who brought him home to *England*, and at *Sheerness* deliver'd him to the Marshal of the Admiralty, from whence he was carry'd to Town and committed to the *Marshalsea* Prison in *Southwark*.

When Captain *Davis* came into *Lisbon*, there lay in that River, besides the *Argyle* abovementioned, the *Ludlow Castle* one of his Majesty's fifth Rate Men of War, who, assoon as she had been inform'd of the Matter, weigh'd and sail'd in quest of the *Revenge*, but after 15 Days Cruise, not finding her on the Coast, return'd to *Lisbon*, she supposing the Pyrate to have gone off to the *West Indies*, the common Rendezvous of those Vermine.

It was indeed the Opinion of several of the Rogues, that it was best to bend their Course to those warm Climates, since now they had, in all probability, made those Quarters too hot for their longer Continuance in them; but the Captain was for returning to his own Country, assuring his Company, *That they might clean and refit there with all the safety imaginable, and pass for an East Country Trader, but that at worst, if by any Accident they should be discover'd, it would not be in the Power of all the Country to molest them, so that there could be no Possibility of failing in the Enterprize; and that after they had cleaned, fitted up their Ship, and taken in Provisions and Necessaries, they might,* he said *sail for the* West Indies, *or what Part of the World they pleased upon New Adventures,* This Advice was adhered to, and they put away with a Westerly Wind, round *Ireland*, to the *Orkneys*, and came into one of the Isles thereof, call'd *Cariston*, with as much Assurance as if they had belong'd to the Place. Here Captain *Smith* was accquainted and had long courted a young Woman of the Place, to whom he was fond of appearing a Commander, and there with told her a formal Story of his acquiring that Preferment, with other Gallantries, not worth taking Notice of here.

While the Ship was upon the Careen, eight of the Crew, who perhaps might not have voluntarily come into the Measures of the rest, got into the Longboat, and put cross the *Frith* no doubt with Design to leave their Comrades, and in passing over they were met by the Custom House Boat belonging to *Queen's Ferry*. They readily acquainted the Officers what they were, whence they came, and the Adventures they were upon; and so they were brought ashore and put into Prison.

When *Smith* saw the Desertion of his Men, he could not be insensible of the Circumstance he stood in, he knew a Discovery must follow, and tho' there was no Force there to take him, he could not tell what Accidents might happen, therefore he goes ashore, takes what Necessaries he could get off the Island, Rights the Ship and brings her under Sail, standing away to the Northward, but there being but little Wind and a pretty strong Current running, the Ship was move ashore near a Place called *Calf Sound*, about 2 Mile from *Cariston*, which proved their Destruction; for losing their Longboat, they had no other fit to carry out an Anchor to get the Ship off. Under this Extremity, the Boatswain, with three or four more well arm'd, goes ashore in a Yawl to a small Fishing Town, and applies for Assistance, which at first was promised him; but they hearing from *Cariston* what Lay they were upon, directed the Boatswain to a Publick House, to wait till a Boat and other Materials were got ready to help them; but assoon as the Boatswain entered, he was seiz'd by three or four Fellows plac'd there for that Purpose, who took three Pair of Pistols from him, bound him, and then went after the others who came ashore with him, whom they likewise made Prisoners.

The Captain finding no Assistance come off, neither the Men he sent ashore, fear'd the worst, and seeing no Prospect of getting his Ship afloat, came ashore himself, hoping to treat for his Liberty and those that remain'd in the Ship, but he was secur'd and made Prisoner with the rest. The Gunner then kept the Ship with the residue of the Crew for three or four Days, not in Expectation of escaping, for now they were past Hopes, But as there was a good Quantity of Wine and Brandy aboard, they resolved not to leave the Liquor behind them, remembering the Proverb, and so sate to it Night and Day, emptied the Casks, and then came away in as drunken a Pickle as can be imagined.

Thus ended the short Reign of this Pyratical Crew, who might have done considerable more Mischief, had not they been so infatuated, as to Court, as it were, their own Ruin. None had been before so hardy, as to run into the Ports of this Kingdom for shelter (after so many Violences committed in our own Seas) where if any Mis-Conduct, or cross. Accident happen'd would prove their Overthrow as it befell them here; for Providence wisely determin'd that strict Justice should suddenly be executed upon Villains that had been no common Offenders, in that they deliberately resolved to lay the first Scene of their Roguery in Blood and upon that Design, several of them had conspir'd before they went aboard in Holland, as has been before taken Notice of.

From *Scotland* they were brought to *England* by the *Greyhound* Man of War, and deposited in the *Marshalsea* Prison, whence they were taken, preparatory to their Tryal, and examin'd at *Doctor's Commons*. Five of which, the Carpenter and four more, appearing to have had no Hand either in the Murthers or Revolt, were made use of as Evidences against the rest, at the *Old Baily*, where on Wednesday the 26 of *May* 1725, the following Criminals were found Guilty and receiv'd Sentence of Death *viz. John Smith* (who in this Expedition took the Surname of *Gow*) Captain, *James Williams* the Lieutenant, *Daniel Machanly, Peter Roltson, John Peterson, William Melvin, Robert Winter, James Belvin*, and *Alexander Rob,*—*William Harvey, Robert Teague and Robert Read* were acquitted; and those who ran away with the Longboat were not brought to any Tryal.

John Smith refus'd to Plead, for which the Court order'd that his Thumbs should be ty'd together with Whipcord, which was done several Times, by the Executioner and another Officer, they drawing the Cord till it broke, but he still continuing in an obstinate Refusal, the Court pronounced that Sentence upon him which the Law appoints in such Cases, that is, That he should be press'd to Derek The Jaylor was ordered to carry him back to *Newgate*, and to see the

Sentence executed next Morning. Then the Court proceeded in the Tryals of the other Prisoners.

This Punishment is rarely executed in *England*, and suffered only for the sake of saving their Estates to their Families, which, upon Conviction of a Capital Crime, is forfeited to the King; for without Pleading, that is, without the Prisoners answering *Guilty*, or *Not Guilty*, to the Indictment, the Court cannot proceed to Tryal, and consequently cannot be convicted of the Offence he stands indicted for; (unless in Cases of High Treason.) The pretence of this harden'd Pyrate's standing contumacious, was that he had an Estate in Reversion, and therefore would not deprive his Heirs; but without entering into this Point we shall give a short Account of the Punishment it self.

The Prisoner is laid in a low dark Room in the Press Yard at *Newgate*, all naked but his Privy Parts, his Back upon the bare Ground, his Arms and Legs stretch'd with Cords, and fasten'd to the several Quarters of the Room. This done, he has a great weight of Iron and Stone laid upon him. His Diet, till he dies, is only three Morsels of Barley Bread without Drink the next Day; and if he lives longer, he has nothing daily, but as much foul Water as he can drink three several Times, and that without any Bread, till he expires.

To return to *Smith*, the Prisoner, when he understood the Nature of the Press, and the manner how the Pain was inflicted, his Resolution fail'd him, and he sent to pray the Court that he should be admitted, which the Court granted; he was thereupon arraign'd a-new upon an Indictment for the Murther of *Oliver Ferneau*, the former Captain of the *GeorgeGalyl*, and upon several other Indictments for Felony and Pyracy on the High Seas, to all which he pleaded *Not Guilty*, but the Facts being plainly prov'd, and he having little or nothing to say in his Defence, but that the Pistol with which he Shot Captain *Ferneau* went off accidentally, he was found Guilty.

John Winter, James Williams, Daniel Maccawly, Peter Rolson, John Peterson, William Melvin, Michael Moore, and *Rob-*

ert Read, were indicted upon nine several Indictments, *viz.*
For the Murther of *Bonadventure Felphs*. For the Murther
of *John Guy*. For the Murther of *Stephen Algier*. For the Murther of *Oliver Ferneau*. For Felony and Pyracy, in betraying
their Trust, and running away with the *George Galley*. For
Felony and Pyracy in taking and robbing the *Delight of Pool*.
For Felony and Pyracy in taking and robbing the Ship *Batchellor*. For Felony and Pyracy in taking and robbing a *French*
Ship call'd the *Lewis* and *Joseph*. For Felony and Pyracy in
taking and robbing the Ship *Triumvirate*; of all which they
were found Guilty, except *Robert Read*, who was acquitted
of every one

    James Belvin was Tryed upon the four last Indictments,
and *Alexander Rob* upon the three last, and *William Harvey*
and *Robert Teague* on the two last: *Belvin* was acquitted of
the first of them, but found Guilty of the other three Indictments, and *Harvey* and *Teague* acquitted of all.

    On the 11th Day of *June*, *Smith* the Captain, *Williams* the
Lieutenant, *Rolson* the Gunner, *Belvin* the Boatswain, *Daniel Maccawly*, *John Peterson*, *John Winter*, and *William Melvin*
are to be executed at *Execution Dock* in *Wapping*, and the
two first will be afterwards hang'd in Chains.

    The Merchants Letters from the *West Indies* in from us
of a new Pyrate in those Seas, which has taken two or three
Vessels, but I have no particulars of her except what these
Letters mention, *viz.* That she was called the *Mary-Woodly*,
Sloop-built, 14 Hands, 4 great Guns and two Swivels, and
several small Arms, Captain *Thomas Scrogbarn* Commander.
This Sloop was lying at the Island *Corocoa* in *January* last,
and in the Absence of the said Captain and two or three
Hands, who had row'd the said Captain ashore, the rest of
the Men rose up against the Mate, cut their Cables and went
away with the Vessel before the Master could get aboard
again, and so turn'd Pyrates.

CHAPTER XVIII.

of

Captain ROBERT KIDD.

W E ARE now going to give an Account of one whose Name is well known in England. The Person we mean is Capt. *Kidd*, whose public Trial and Execution here, rendered him the Subject of all Conversation, so that his actions have been chaunted about in Ballads. However, it is now a considerable Time since these Things passed, and though the People knew in general that Capt. *Kidd* was hanged, and that his Crime was Pyracy, yet there were scarce any, even at that time, who were acquainted with his Life or Actions, or could Account for his turning Pyrate.

In the beginning of King *William*'s War, Captain *Kidd* commanded a Privateer in the *West-Indies*, and by several adventurous Actions acquired the Reputation of a brave Man, as well as an experienced Seaman. About this time the Pyrates were very troublesome in those Parts: wherefore Capt. *Kidd* was recommended by the Lord *Bellamont*, then Governor of *Barbadoes*, as well as by several other Persons, to the government here, as a Person very fit to be entrusted with the Command of a government Ship, and to be employed in cruising upon the pyrates as knowing those Seas perfectly well, and being acquainted with all their lurking Places; but what Reasons governed the Politics of those Times, I cannot tell, but this Proposal met with no encouragement here, though it is Certain it would have been of great Consequences to the Subject, our Merchants suffering incredible Damages by those Robbers.

Upon this Neglect, the Lord *Bellamont* and some others, who knew what great Captures had been made by the Pyrates, and what a prodigious Wealth must be in their Possession, were tempted to fit out a Ship at their own private Charge, and to give the Command of her to Capt. *Kidd*; and to give the Thing a greater Reputation, as well as to keep their Seamen under the better Command, they procured the King's Commission for the said Capt. *Kidd*, of which the following is an exact Copy.

William Rex,
"WILLIAM THE THIRD, by the Grace of God, King of *England, Scotland, France* and *Ireland*, defender of the Faith, &c. To our trusty and well beloved Capt. *ROBERT KIDD*, Commander of the Ship the *Adventure* Gallery, or to any other the Commander of the same for the time being, GREETING: Whereas we are informed, that Capt. *Thomas Too, John Ireland*, Capt. *Thomas Wake*, and Capt. *William Maze*, or *Mace*, and other Subjects, Natives or Inhabitants of *New-York*, and elsewhere, in our Plantations in *America*, have associated themselves, with Divers others, wicked and ill-disposed Persons, and do, against the Law of Nations, commit many and great Piracies, Robberies and Depredations on the Seas, upon the Parts of America, and in other Parts, to the great hindrance and discouragement of Trade and Navigation, and to the great Danger and Hurt of our loving Subjects, our Allies, and all others; navigating the Seas upon their lawful Occasions. NOW KNOW YE, that we being desirous to prevent the aforesaid Mischiefs, and as much as in us lies, to bring the said Pyrates, Free-booters and Sea-rovers to Justice, have thought Fit, and do hereby give and grant to the said *ROBERT KIDD* (to

whom our Commissioners for exercising the Office of Lord High Admiral of *England,* have granted a Commission as a private Man of War, bearing Date the 11th day of *December,* 1695,) and unto the Commander of the said Ship for the Time being, and unto the Officers, Mariners, and others, which shall be under your command, full power and authority to apprehend, seize, and take into custody as well the said Capt. *Thomas Too. John Ireland,* Capt. *Thomas Wake,* and Capt. *William Maze,* or *Mace,* as all such Pyrates. Free-booters, and Sea-rovers, being either our Subjects, or of other Nations associated with them, which you shall meet with upon the Seas or Coasts of *America,* or upon any other Seas or Coasts, with all their Ships and Vessels, and all such Merchandizes, Money, Goods and Wares as shall be found on board or with them, in case they shall willingly yield themselves; but if they will not yield without fighting, then you are by force to compel them to yield. And we also require you to bring, or cause to be brought, such Pyrates, Free-booters, or Sea-rovers, as you shall seize, to a legal Trial, to the end they may be proceeded against according to the Law in such Cases. And we do hereby command all our Officers, Ministers, and other our loving Subjects whatsoever, to be aiding and assisting to you in the Premises. And we do hereby enjoin you to keep an exact Journal of your proceedings in the Execution of the Premises, and set down the Names of such Pyrates, and of their Officers and Company, and the Names of such Ships and Vessels as you shall by Virtue of these Presents take and seize, and the quantities of Arms, Ammunitions, Provision and Lading of such Ships, and the true value of the same, as near as you Judge. And we do hereby strictly charge and command you, as you will answer the contrary at your Peril, that you do not, in any manner, offend or molest our Friends or Allies, their Ships, or Subjects, by Colour or Pretence of these Presents, or the Authority thereby granted. *In Witness whereof,* we have caused our great Seal of *England* to be affixed to these Presents. Given at our Court of *Kensington,* the 26th day of *January,* 1693, in the seventh Year of our Reign."

Capt. *Kidd* had also another Commission, which was called a Commission of Reprisals; for it being then War Time, this Commission was to justify him in the taking of *French* merchant Ships, in case he should meet with any; but as this Commission is nothing to our present Purpose, we shall not burthen the Reader with it.

With these two Commissions he sailed out of *Plymouth* in *May,* 1696, in the *Adventure* Galley, of 30 Guns, and 80 Men; the Place he first designed for was *New-York;* in his Voyage thither he took a *French* Banker, but this was no act of Pyracy, he having a Commission for that Purpose, as we have just observed.

When he arrived at *New-York,* he put up Articles for engaging more Hands, it being necessary to his Ship's Crew, since he proposed to deal with a desperate Enemy. The Terms he offered were, that every Man should have a share of what was taken, reserving for himself and owners forty Shares. Upon which Encouragement he soon increased his Company to 155 Men.

With this Company he sailed first for *Madeira,* where he took in Wine and some other necessaries from thence he proceeded to *Bonavista,* one of the *Cape-de-Verd* Islands, to furnish the ship with Salt and from thence went immediately to St. *Jago,* another of the *Cape-de-Verd* Islands, in order to stock himself with Provisions. When all this was done, he bent his Course to *Madagascar,* the known Rendezvous of Pyrates. In his way he fell in with Capt. *Warren,* Commodore of three Men of War: he acquainted them with his Design, kept them Company two or three Days, and then leaving them, made the best of his way for *Madagascar*, where he arrived in *February*, 1697, just nine Months from his departure from *Plymouth*.

It happened that at this Time the Pyrate Ships were most of them out in search of Prey; so that according to the best Intelligence Capt. *Kidd* could get, there was not one of them at that Time about the Island: wherefore, having spent some Time in watering his Ship, and taking in more Provisions, he thought of trying his Fortune on the Coast of *Malabar*, where he arrived in the Month of *June* following, four Months from his reaching *Madagascar*. Hereabouts he made an unsuccessful Cruise, touching sometimes at the Island of *Mohila*, and sometimes at that of *Johanna*, between *Malabar* and *Madagascar*. His Provisions were every Day wasting, and his Ship began to want repair: wherefore, when he was at *Johanna*, he found means of borrowing a Sum of Money from some *Frenchmen* who had lost their Ship, but saved their Effects, and with this he purchased Materials for putting his Ship in good repair.

It does not appear all this while that he had the least Design of turning Pyrate; for near *Mohila* and *Johanna* both, he met with several *Indian* Ships richly Laden, to which he did not offer the least Violence, though he was strong enough to have done what he pleased with them; and the first Outrage or Depredation I find he committed upon Mankind, was after his repairing his Ship, and leaving *Johanna*: he touched at a place called *Mabbee*, upon the *Red Sea*, where he took some *Guinea* Corn from the Natives, by Force. After this, he sailed to *Bab's Key*, a place upon a little Island at the Entrance of the *Red Sea*. Here it was that he first began to open himself to his Ship's Company, and let them Understand that he intended to change his Measures; for, happening to talk to the *Mocha* Fleet, which was to sail that way, he said, *We have been unsuccessful hitherto; but Courage, my Boys, we'll make our Fortunes out of this Fleet*: and finding that none of them appeared Averse to it, he ordered a Boat out, well manned, to go upon the Coast to make discoveries, commanding them to take a Prisoner and bring to him, or get Intelligence any way they could. The Boat returned in a few Days, bringing him Word, that they saw fourteen or fifteen Ships ready to sail, some with *English*, some with *Dutch*, and some with *Moorish* Colours.

We cannot account for this sudden change in his Conduct, otherwise than by supposing that he first meant well, while he had hopes of making his Fortune by taking of Pyrates; but now, weary of ill Success, and fearing lest his Owners, out of humour at their great Expences, should dismiss him, and he should want Employment, and be marked out for an unlucky Man; rather, I say, than run the hazard of Poverty, he resolved to do his Business one way, since he could not do it another.

He therefore ordered a man continually to watch at the Mast Head, lest this Fleet should go by them; and about four Days after, towards Evening, it appeared in Sight, being convoyed by one *English* and one *Dutch* Man of War. *Kidd* soon fell in with them, and getting into the midst of them, fired at a *Moorish* ship which was next him; but the Men of War taking the Alarm, bore down upon *Kidd*, and firing upon him, obliged him to sheer off, he not being strong enough to contend with them. Now he had begun Hostilities, he resolved to go on, and therefore he went and cruised along the Coast of *Malabar*. The first Prize he met was a small Vessel belonging to *Aden*; the Vessel was *Moorish*, and the Owners were *Moorish* Merchants, but the Master was an *Englishman*; his Name was *Parker*. *Kidd* forced him and a *Portuguese* that was called *Don Antonio*, which were all the *Europeans* on board, to take on with him; the first he designed as a Pilot, and the last as an Interpreter. He also used the Men very cruelly, causing them to be hoisted up by the Arms, and drubbed with a naked Cutlash, to force them to discover whether they had Money on Board, and where it lay; but as they had neither Gold nor Silver on Board, he got nothing by his cruelty; however, he took from them a bale of Pepper, and a bale of coffee, and so let them go.

A little Time after he touched at *Carawar*, a Place upon the same Coast, where, before he arrived, the News of what he had done to the *Moorish* Ship had reached them; for some of the *English* Merchants there had received an Account of it from the Owners, who corresponded with them, wherefore, as soon as Kidd came in, he was suspected to be the person who committed this Pyracy; and one Mr. *Harvey* and Mr. *Mason*, two of the *English* factory, came on Board and asked for *Parker*, and *Antonio* the *Portuguese*; but *Kidd* denied that he knew any such Persons, having secured them both in a private Place in the hold, where they were kept for seven or eight Days, that is, till *Kidd* sailed from thence.

However, the Coast was alarmed, and a *Portuguese* Man of War was sent out to cruise. *Kidd* met with her, and fought her about six Hours, gallantly enough; but finding her too Strong to be taken, he quitted her; for he was able to run away from her when he would. Then he went to a Place called *Porca*, where he watered the Ship, and bought a number of Hogs of the Natives to victual his company.

Soon after this, he came up with a *Moorish* Ship, the Master whereof was a *Dutchman*, called *Schipper Mitchel*, and chased her under *French* Colours, which they observing, hoisted *French* colours too when he came up with her, he hailed her in *French*, and they having a *Frenchman* on Board, answered him in the same Language; upon which he ordered them to send their Boat on Board; they were obliged to do so, and having examined who they were, and from whence they came, he asked the *Frenchman*, who was a passenger, if he had a *French* Pass for himself; the *Frenchman* gave him to understand that he had. Then he told the *Frenchman* he must pass for Captain, and by—, says he, you are the Captain: the *Frenchman* durst not refuse doing as he would have him. The Meaning of this was, that he would seize the Ship as fair Prize, and as if she had belonged to *French* Subjects, according to a Commission he had for that Purpose; though, one would think, after what he had already done, that he need not have recourse to a quibble to give his actions a Colour.

In short, he took the Cargo and sold it some time after; yet still he seemed to have some Fears upon him, lest these Proceedings should have a bad End; for, coming up with a *Dutch* Ship some time after, when his men thought of nothing but attacking her, *Kidd* opposed it; upon which a Mutiny arose, and the majority being for taking the said Ship, and arming themselves to man the Boat to go and seize her, he told them, such as did, never should come on Board him again; which put an End to the Design, so that he kept Company with the said Ship some time, without offering her any Violence. However, this Dispute was the Occasion of an Accident, upon which an Indictment was afterwards grounded against *Kidd*; for *Moor*, the Gunner, being one Day upon Deck, and talking with *Kidd* about the said *Dutch* Ship, some Words arose between them, and *Moor* told *Kidd*, that he had ruined them all; upon which, *Kidd*, calling him dog, took up a Bucket and struck him with it, which breaking his Skull, he died the next Day.

But *Kidd*'s penitential Fit did not last long, for coasting along *Malabar*, he met with a great Number of Boats, all which he plundered. Upon the same Coast he also fell in with a *Portuguese* Ship, which he kept Possession of a Week, and then having taken out of her some Chests of *India* Goods, thirty Jars of Butter, with some Wax, Iron, and a hundred Bags of Rice, he let her go.

Much about the same Time he went to one of the *Malabar* Islands for Wood and Water, and his Cooper being ashore, was murdered by the Natives; upon which *Kidd* himself landed, and burnt and pillaged several of their Houses, the People running away; but having taken one, he caused him to be tied to a tree, and commanded one of his Men to shoot him; then putting to sea again he took the greatest Prize which fell into his Hands while he followed this Trade; this was a Moorish Ship of 400 Tons, richly laden, Named the

Queda Merchant, the Master whereof was an *Englishman*, by the Name of *Wright*; for the *Indians* often make use of *English* or *Dutchmen* to command their Ships, their own Mariners not being so good Artists in Navigation. *Kidd* chased her under *French* Colours, and having come up with her, he ordered her to hoist out her Boat, and to send on Board of him, which being done, he told Wright he was his prisoner; and informing himself concerning the said Ship, he understood there were no *Europeans* on board, except two *Dutch*, and one *Frenchman*, all the rest being *Indians* or *Armenians*, and that the *Armenians* were part Owners of the Cargo. *Kidd* gave the *Armenians* to understand, that if they would offer any Thing that was worth his taking for their Ransom, he would hearken to it. Upon which, they proposed to pay him 20,000 Rupees, not quite 3000 *l.* Sterling; but *Kidd* judged this would be making a bad Bargain, wherefore he rejected it, and setting the Crew on shore, at different Places on the Coast, he soon sold as much of the Cargo as came to near 10,000 Pounds. With part of it he also trafficked, receiving in exchange Provisions, or such other Goods as he wanted; by degrees he disposed of the whole Cargo, and when the Division was made, it came to about 200 Pounds a Man; and having reserved forty Shares to Himself, his dividend amounted to about 8000 *l.* Sterling.

The *Indians* along the Coast came on Board and trafficked with all Freedom, and he punctually performed his Bargains, till about the Time he was ready to sail; and then thinking he should have no further Occasion for them, he made no Scruple of taking their Goods, and setting them on Shore without any payment in Money or Goods, which they little expected; for as they had been used to deal with Pyrates, they always found them Men of Honor in the way of Trade; a People, Enemies to deceit, and that scorned to rob but in their own way.

Kidd put some of his Men on Board the *Queda Merchant*, and with this Ship and his own, sailed for *Madagascar*. As soon as he had arrived and cast Anchor, there came on Board of him a Canoe, in which were several *Englishmen*, who had formerly been well acquainted with *Kidd*. As soon as they saw him they saluted him, and told him, they were informed he was come to take them, and hang them, which would be a little unkind in such an old Acquaintance. *Kidd* soon dissipated their Doubts, by swearing he had no such Design, and that he was now in every Respect their Brother, and just as bad as they; and calling for a Cup of Bomboo, drank their Captain's Health.

These Men belonged to a Pyrate Ship, called the *Resolution*, formerly the *Mocha* Merchant, whereof one Capt. *Culliford* was Commander, and which lay at an Anchor not far from them. *Kidd* went on Board with them, promising them his Friendship and Assistance, and *Culliford* in his turn came on Board of *Kidd*; and *Kidd*, to testify his Sincerity in iniquity, finding *Culliford* in want of some Necessaries, made him a Present of an Anchor and some Guns, to fit him out for Sea again.

The *Adventure* Galley was now so old and leaky, that they were forced to keep two Pumps continually going, wherefore *Kidd* shifted all the Guns and Tackle out of her into the *Queda Merchant*, intending her for his Man of War; and as he had divided the Money before, he now made a Division of the Remainder of the Cargo: soon after which, the greatest part of the Company left him, some going on Board Capt. *Culliford*, and others absconding into the Country, so that he had not above 40 Men left.

He put to Sea, and happened to touch at *Amboyna*, one of the *Dutch Spice* Islands, where he was told, that the News of his actions had reached *England*, and that he was there declared a Pyrate.

The Truth of it is, his pyracies so alarmed our Merchants, that some motions were made in Parliament, to enquire into the Commission that was given him, and the Persons who fitted him out. These proceedings seemed to lean a little hard upon Lord *Bellamont*, who thought himself so much touched thereby, that he published a Justification of himself in a Pamphlet, after *Kidd*'s execution. In the mean Time it was thought advisable, in order to stop the course of these pyracies, to publish a Proclamation, offering the King's free pardon to all such pyrates as should voluntarily surrender themselves, whatever pyracies they had been guilty of, at any time before the last Day of *April*, 1699—that is to say, for all pyracies committed Eastward of the *Cape of Good Hope*, to the Longitude and Meridian of *Socatora*, and *Cape Cormorin*; in which Proclamation, *Avery* and *Kidd* were excepted by Name.

When *Kidd* left *Amboyna* he knew nothing of this Proclamation, for certainly had he had Notice of his being excepted in it, he would not have been so infatuated, as to run himself into the very Jaws of Danger; but relying upon his interest with the Lord *Bellamont*, and fancying that a *French* pass or two he found on Board some of the Ships he took, would serve to countenance the Matter, and that part of the Booty he got would gain him new Friends—I say, all these Things made him flatter himself that all would be hushed, and that Justice would but wink at him.—Wherefore he sailed directly for *New-York*, where he was no sooner arrived, but by the Lord *Bellamont*'s orders, he was secured with all his Papers and Effects. Many of his Fellow-Adventurers, who had forsook him at *Madagascar*, came over from thence Passengers, some to *New-England*, and some to *Jersey*; where hearing of the king's Proclamation for pardoning of Pyrates, they surrendered themselves to the Governor of those Places. At first they were admitted to bail, but soon after were laid in strict Confinement, where they were kept for some Time, till an opportunity happened of sending them with their Captain over to *England* to be tried.

Accordingly a Sessions of admiralty being held at the *Old Baily*, in *May*, 1701, Capt. *Kidd, Nicholas Churchill, James How, Robert Lumley, William Jenkins, Gabriel Loff, Hugh Parrot, Richard Barlicorn, Abel Owens*, and *Darby Mullins*, were arraigned for pyracy and robbery on the high Seas, and all found guilty, except three: these were *Robert Lumley*,

William Jenkins, and *Richard Barlicorn*, who proving themselves to be Apprentices to some of the Officers of the Ship, and producing their indentures in Court, were acquitted.

The three above mentioned, though they were proved to be concerned in taking and sharing the Ship and Goods mentioned in the Indictment, yet, as the Gentlemen of the long Robe rightly distinguished, there was a great difference between their Circumstances and the rest; for there must go an intention of the Mind and a freedom of the Will to the committing an act of felony or piracy. A Pyrate is not to be understood to be under constraint, but a free Agent; for in this case, the bare Act will not make a man Guilty, unless the will make it so.

Now a Servant, it is true, if he go voluntarily, and have his Proportion, he must be accounted a Pyrate, for then he acts upon his own Account, and not by Compulsion; and these Persons, according to the Evidence, received their part, but whether they accounted to their Masters for their shares afterwards, is the matter in question, and what distinguishes them as free Agents or Men, that did go under the Compulsion of their Masters, which being left to the Consideration of the Jury, they found them *not Guilty*.

Kidd was tried upon an Indictment of Murder also, *viz.* for killing *Moor*, the Gunner, and found Guilty of the same. *Nicholas Churchill* and *James How* pleaded the king's Pardon, as having surrendered themselves within the Time limited in the Proclamation, and Col. *Bass*, Governor of *West Jersey*, to whom they surrendered, being in court, and called upon, proved the same. However, this Plea was over-ruled by the Court, because there being four Commissioners named in the Proclamation, *viz.* Capt. *Thomas Warren, Israel Hayes, Peter Delannoye*, and *Christopher Pollard*, Esquires, who were appointed Commissioners, and sent over on purpose to receive the Submissions of such Pyrates as should surrender, it was adjudged no other Person was qualified to receive their Surrender, and that they could not be entitled to the Benefit of the said Proclamation, because they had not in all Circumstances complied with the Conditions of it.

Darby Mullins urged in his Defence, that he served under the king's Commission, and therefore could not disobey his Commander without incurring great punishments; that whenever a ship or ships went out upon any expedition under the king's Commission, the Men were never allowed to call their Officers to an Account, why they did this or why they did that, because such a Liberty would destroy all discipline; that if any thing was done which was unlawful, the Officers were to answer it, for the men did no more than their Duty in obeying Orders. He was told by the Court, that acting under the Commission justified in what was lawful, but not in what was unlawful. He answered, he stood in need of nothing to justify him in what was lawful, but that the Case of Seamen must be very hard, if they must be brought into such Danger for obeying the Commands of their Officers, and punished for not obeying them; and if they were allowed to dispute the Orders, there could be no such thing as Command kept up at Sea.

This seemed to be the best Defence the Thing could bear; but his taking a Share of the Plunder, the seamen's mutinying on Board several times, and taking upon them to controul the captain, shewed there was no obedience paid to the commission; and that they acted in all Things according to the Custom of Pyrates and Free-Booters, which weighing with the Jury, they brought him in guilty with the rest.

As to Capt. *Kidd*'s Defence, he insisted much upon his own Innocence, and the Villany of his men. He said, he went out in a landable Employment, and had no occasion, being then in good circumstances, to go a pyrating; that the men often mutinied against him, and did as they pleased; that he was threatened to be shot in his Cabin, and that ninety-five left him at one Time, and set fire to his boat, so that he was disabled from bringing his Ship Home, or the Prizes he took, to have them regularly condemned, which he said were taken by virtue of a Commission under the broad Seal, they having

French passes. The Captain called one Col. *Hewson* to his reputation, who gave him an extraordinary Character, and declared to the Court, that he had served under his Command, and been in two Engagements with him against the French, in which he fought as well as any Man he ever saw; that there were only *Kidd*'s Ship and his own against Monsieur *du Cass*, who commanded a squadron of six Sail, and they got the better of him. But this being several Years before the facts mentioned in the Indictment were committed, proved of no Manner of Service to the Prisoner on his Trial.

As to the Friendship shewn to *Culliford*, a notorious Pyrate, *Kidd* denied, and said, he intended to have taken him, but his Men being a Parcel of rogues and villains refused to stand by him, and several of them ran away from his Ship to the said Pirate.—But the evidence being full and particular against him, he was found Guilty as before mentioned.

When *Kidd* was asked what he had to say why Sentence should not pass against him, he answered, that *he had nothing to say, but that he had been sworn against by perjured, wicked People.* And when sentence was pronounced, he said, *my Lord, it is a very hard sentence. For my part, I am the most innocent Person of them all, only I have been sworn against by perjured Persons.*

Wherefore about a Week after, Capt. *Kidd*, *Nicholas Churchill*, *James How*, *Gabriel Loff*, *Hugh Parrot*, *Abel Owen*, and *Darby Mullins*, were executed at *Execution Dock*, and afterwards hung up in Chains, at some distance from each other, down the River, where their Bodies hung exposed for many Years.

❀ ❀ ❀ ❀ ❀ ❀ ❀ ❀ ❀ ❀ ❀ ❀ ❀ ❀ ❀ ❀ ❀ ❀ ❀

A Relation of Five Men setting up for a Company of Pyrates

THIS WAS a strange adventurous Crew, who without Arms, Men, Navigators, or any other Necessaries more than a Vessel poorly provided, could venture themselves in the wide World to make War upon all Nations, but the Success was answerable to the Rashness of the Attempt, for before they had an Opportunity of trying their Fortune, in that Life of Gallantry, a Stop was happily put to their Designs, as we shall find by the following Account.

A Brigantine belonging to *Bristol*, of which one Mr. *Rowry* was Master, had been trading to *Gambia*, in *Africa*, and falling as low as Cape *Mount*, to finish the slaving of the Vessel, he had, by a Misfortune usual at that Part of the Coast, his Mate, Surgeon, and two more of his Men, *Panyarr'd by the Negroes. The Remainder of his Company, which was not above 5 or 6 in Number, took this Opportunity, and seiz'd the Vessel in the Road, making the Master Prisoner.

You will think it prodigious impudent that so small a Number should undertake to proceed a pyrating, especially when neither of them had sufficient Skill in Navigation: Yet this they did, leaving those People, their Ship-Mates abovemention'd, to the Mercy of the barbarous Natives, and sail'd away down the Coast, making them a black Flag, which they merrily said, would be as good as 50 Men more, *i. e.* would carry as much Terror; and that they did not doubt of soon increasing their Crew, to put them in an enterprizing Ca-

---

*Term for stealing of Men used all over the Coast.

pacity; but their vain Projection was soon happily frustrated, and after this Manner.

The Master whose Life they had preserved, (perhaps only for supplying their own Unskillfulness in Navigation,) advised them, that since contrary to their Expectations, they had met with no Ship between *Cape Mount*, and the *Bite* of *Calabar*, to proceed to the Island of St. *Thomas*'s, where they might recruit with Provisions and Water, and sell off the Slaves (about 70 of them) which they perceived would be a useless Lumber, and incommodious to their Design. They arrived there in *August* 1721 and one Evening, while Part of them were on Shore, applying for this Purpose to the Governor, and the other Part carelesly from the Deck, Mr. *Rowry* stepp'd into the Boat belonging to the Vessel, and pushed off, very suddenly: They heard the Noise it made, and soon were upon Deck again, but having no other Boat to pursue, nor a Musket, ready to fire, he got safe on Shore, and ran to the Governor with his Complaint, who immediately imprisoned those already there, and sent a Launch off to take the rest out of the Ship.

The *Swallow* arrived at St. *Thomas*'s the Beginning of *October* following, where, on Mr. *Rowry*'s Remonstrance, Application was made to the *Portuguese* Governor of that Island, for a Surrendery of these five *English* Prisoners then in the Castle; but he not only peremptorily excused himself from it, as a Matter out of his Power, without particular Direction from the Court of *Portugal*; but withal insinuated, that they had only taken Refuge there from the Hardships and Severity they had met with from their Master. The manner of Denial, and the avaritious Temper of the Gentleman, which I had Occasion to be acquainted with, makes it very suspicious, that he proposed considerable Gains to himself; for if Mr. *Rowry* had not made such an Escape to him, the Slaves had been his for little or nothing, as a Bribe to silence his Suspicions, which any Man, less acute than he, must have had from the awkward and unskilful Carriage of such Merchants. But enough of this; perhaps he is not the only Governor abroad that finds an Interest in countenancing these Fellows.

An Account of the Pyracies and Murders committed by Philip Roche, &c.

*P*HILIP ROCHE was born in *Ireland*, and from his Youth had been bred up to the Sea; he was a brisk genteel Fellow, of 30 Years of Age at the Time of his Death; one whose black and savage Nature did no ways answer the Comliness of his Person, his Life being almost one continued Scene of Villany, before he was discovered to have committed the horrid Murders we are now speaking of.

This inhumane Monster had been concerned with others, in insuring Ships to a great Value, and then destroying them; by which Means, and other Rogueries, he had got a little Money; and being Mate of a Ship, was dilligent enough in trading for himself between *Ireland* and *France*, so that he was in a Way of getting himself a comfortable Livelihood: But, as he resolved to be rich, and finding fair Dealing brought in Wealth but slowly, he contriv'd to put other Things in Execution, and certainly had murthered several innocent Persons in the Prosecution of his abominable Schemes; but as I have now forgot the particular Circumstances of those Relations, I shall confine my self at present to the Fact for which he suffer'd.

Roch getting acquainted with one *Neal*, a Fisherman at *Cork*, whom he found ready for any villainous Attempt, he imparted his Design to him, who being pleas'd with the Project, brings one *Pierce Cullen* and his Brother into the Confederacy, together with one *Wise*, who at first was very unwilling to come into their Measures, and, indeed, had the least Hand in the Perpetration of what follows.

They pitch'd upon a Vessel in the Harbour, belonging to *Peter Tartoue*, a *French* Man, to execute their cruel Intentions upon, because it was a small one, and had not a great Number of Hands on Board, and 'twas easy afterwards to exchange it for one more fit for Pyracy; and therefore they apply'd themselves to the Master of her, for a Passage to *Nantz*, whereto the Ship was bound; and accordingly, the Beginning of *November* 1721, they went aboard; and when at Sea, *Philip Roche* being an experienced Sailor, the Master of the Vessel readily trusted him with the Care of her, at times, while he and the Mate went to rest.

The 15th of *November*, at Night, was the Time designed for the Tragedy; but *Francis Wise* relented, and appear'd desirous to divert them from their bloody Purposes. *Roche* (sometimes called Captain) told him, *That as* Cullen *and he had sustained great Losses at Sea, unless every* Irishman *present would assist in repairing their Losses, by murthering all the* French *Rogues, and running away with the Ship, he should suffer the same Fate with the* French *Men*; but if all would assist, all should have a Share in the *Booty*. Upon this, they all resolved alike, and Captain *Roche* ordered three *Frenchmen* and a Boy up to hand the Topsails, the Master and Mate being then asleep in their Cabins, The two first that came down, they beat out their Brains and threw them over-board: The other two seeing what was done, ran up to the Topmast Head, but *Cullen* followed them, and taking the Boy by the Arm, tost him into the Sea; then driving down the Man, those below knocked him on the Head, and threw him overboard.

Those who were asleep, being awakened by the dismal Skrieks and Groans of dying Men, ran upon Deck in Confusion, to enquire into the Cause of such unusual Noises; but the same Cruelty was immediately acted towards them, e'er they could be sensible of the Danger that threat'ned them.

They were now (as *Roche* himself afterwards confess'd) *all over as wet with the Blood that had been spilt, as if they had been dipp'd in Water, or stood in a Shower of Rain, nor did they regard it any more.* *Roche* said, Captain *Tartoue* used many Words for Mercy, and asked them, if he had not used them with Civility and Kindness? If they were not of the same Christian Religion, and owned the same blessed *Jesus*, and the like? But they, not regarding what he said, took Cords and bound the poor Master and his Mate Back to Back, and while that was doing, both of them begged with the utmost Earnestness, and used the most solemn Intreaties, that they would at least allow them a few Minutes to say their Prayers, and beg Mercy of God for the various Sins and Offences of their Lives: But it did not move them, (though all the rest were dead, and no Danger could be apprehended from them two alone) for the bound Persons were hurry'd up and thrown into the Sea.

The Massacre being finished, they washed themselves a little from the Blood, and searched the Chests and Lockers, and all Places about the Ship, and then set down in the Captain's Cabin, and refreshed themselves with some Rum they found there, and (as *Roche* confessed) were never merrier in their Lives. They invested *Roche* with the Command of the Ship, and calling him Captain, talked over their Liquor, what rare Actions they would perform about Cape *Briton, Sable Isle,* and the Banks of *Newfoundland,* whither they designed to go as soon as they had recruited their Company, and got a better Ship, which they proposed speedily to do.

Roche taking upon himself the Command of the Vessel, *Andrew Cullen* was to pass for a Merchant or Super-cargo; but when they bethought themselves, that they were in Danger of being discovered by the Papers of the Ship, relating to the Cargo, as Bills of Lading, *&c.* therefore they erase and take out the Name of the *French* Master, and instead thereof, inserted the Name of *Roche,* so that it stood in the Ship's Papers, *Peter Roche* Master; that then having so few Hands on Board, they contrived if they met any Ships, to give out, that they had lost some Hands by their being washed overboard in a Storm, and by that Means screen themselves from being suspected of having committed some such wicked Act, by Reason of the Fewness of their Hands on Board; and also might prevail with some Ship to spare them some, on Consideration of their pretended Disaster.

In going to *Cales* they were in Distress by the Weather, and being near *Lisbon*, they made Complaint to a Ship, but obtained no Assistance. They were then obliged to sail back for *England*, and put into the Port of *Dartmouth*; but then they were in fear least they might be discovered, therefore to prevent that, they resolve to alter the Ship, and getting Workmen, they take down the Mizzen-Mast, and build a Spar Deck, and made Rails, (on pretence that the Sailors had been wash'd overboard) to secure the Men. Then they took down the Image of St. *Peter* at the Head of the Ship, and put up a Lion in its Place, and painted over the Stern of the Ship with Red, and new nam'd her the *Mary* Snow. The Ship being thus alter'd that they thought it could not be known, they fancy'd themselves pretty secure; but wanting Money to defray the Charge of these Alterations, *Roche*, as Master of the Vessel, and *Andrew Cullen*, as Merchant, apply themselves to the Officers of the Customs for Liberty to dispose of some of the Cargo, in order to pay the Workmen; which they having obtained, they sold fifty eight Barrels of Beef, and having hired three more Hands, they set Sail for *Ostend*, and there having sold more Barrels of Beef, they steer their Course to *Rotterdam*, dispose of the rest of the Cargo, and took in one Mr. *Annesly*, who freighted the Ship for *England*; but in their Passage, in a stormy Night, it being very dark, they took up Mr. *Annesly* their Passenger, and threw him into the Sea, who swam about the Ship a pretty while, calling out for Life, and telling them they should have all his Goods, if they would receive him again into the Vessel: But in vain were his Cries!

After this, they were obliged to put into several Ports, and by contrary Winds, came to the Coast of *France*, and hearing there was an Enquiry made after the Ship, *Roche* quits her at *Havre de Grace*, and leaves the Management to *Cullen* and the rest; who having shipp'd other Men, sail'd away to *Scotland*, and there quitted the Vessel, which was afterwards seized and brought into the River of *Thames*.

Some Time after this, *Philip Roche* came to *London*, and making some Claim for Money, he had made Insurance of, in the Name of *John Eustace*, the Officer was apprized of the Fraud, and he arrested and flung into the Compter; from whence directing a Letter to his Wife, she shewed it to a Friend, who discovered by it, that he was the principal Villain concerned in the Destruction of *Peter Tartoue*, and the Crew. Upon this, an Information was given to my Lord *Carteret*, that the Person who went by the Name of *John Eustace*, was *Philip Roche*, as aforesaid; and being brought down by his Lordships Warrant, he stifly deny'd it for some Time, notwithstanding a Letter was found in his Pocket, directed to him by the Name of *Roche*; but being confronted by a Captain of a Ship, who knew him well, he confessed it, but prevaricated in several Particulars; whereupon he was committed to *Newgate* upon violent Suspicions, and the next Day was brought down again at his own Request, confessed the whole, desired to be made an Evidence, and promised to convict three Men worse than himself. Two were discovered by him, who died miserably in the *Marshalsea*, and *Roche* himself was afterwards try'd, (no more being taken,) found Guilty of the Pyracy, and executed.

@ @ @ @ @ @ @ @ @ @ @ @ @ @ @ @ @ @ @

An Abstract of the Civil Law and Statute Law now in Force, in Relation to PYRACY.

*A*PYRATE is Hostis humanis generis, *a common Enemy, with whom neither Faith nor Oath is to be kept, according to* Tully. *And by the Laws of Nature, Princes and States are responsible for their Neglect, if they do not provide Remedies for restraining these sort of Robberies. Though Pyrates are called common Enemies, yet they are properly not to be term'd so. He is only to be honour'd with that Name, says* Cicero, *who hath a* Commonwealth, *a Court, a Treasury, Consent and Consord of Citizens, and some Way, if Occasion be, of Peace and League: But when they have reduced themselves into a Government or State, as those of* Algier, Sally, Tripoly, Tunis, *and the like, they then are allowed the Solemnities of War, and the Rights of Legation.*

If Letters of Marque *be granted to a Merchant, and he furnishes out a Ship, with a Captain and Mariners, and they, instead of taking the Goods, or Ships of that Nation against whom their Commission is awarded, take the Ship and Goods of a Friend, this is Pyracy; and if the Ship arrive in any Part of his Majesty's Dominions, it will be seized, and for ever lost to the Owners; but they are no way liable to make Satisfaction.*

If a Ship is assaulted and taken by the Pyrates, for Redemption of which, the Master becomes a Slave to the Captors, by the Law Marine, *the Ship and Lading tacitly obliged for his Redemption, by a general Contribution; but if it happen through his own Folly, then no Contribution is to be made.*

If Subjects in Enmity with the Crown of England, *are abord an* English *Pyrate, in Company with* English, *and a Robbery is committed, and they are taken; it is Felony in the* English, *but not in the Stranger; for it was no Pyracy in them, but the Depredation of an Enemy, and they will be tried by a Martial Law.*

If Pyracy is committed by Subjects in Enmity with England, *upon the* British *Seas, it is properly only punishable by the Crown of* England, *who have* istud regimen & Dominnm *exclusive of all other Power.*

If Pyracy be committed on the Ocean, and the Pyrates in the Attempt be overcome, the Captors may, without any Solemnity of Condemnation, hang them up at the Main-Yard; if they are brought to the next Port, and the Judge rejects the Tryal, or the Captors cannot wait for the Judge, without Peril or Loss, Justice may be done upon them by the Captors.

If Merchandize be delivered to a Master, to carry to one Port, and he carries it to another, and sells and disposes of it, this is not Felony; but if, after unlading it at the first Port, he retakes it, it is Pyracy.

If a Pyrate attack a Ship, and the Master for Redemption, gives his Oath to pay a Sum of Money, tho' there be nothing taken, yet it is Pyracy by the Law Marine.

If a Ship is riding at Anchor, and the Mariners all ashore, and a Pyrate attack her, and rob her, this is Pyracy.

If a Man commit Pyracy upon the Subjects of any Prince, or Republick, (though in Amity with us,) and brings the Goods into England, *and sells them in a Market* Overt *the same shall bind, and the Owners are for ever excluded.*

If a Pyrate enters a Port of this Kingdom, and robs a Ship at Anchor there, it is not Pyracy, because not done, super altum Mare; *but is Robbery at common Law, because* infra Corpus Comitatus. *A Pardon of all Felonies does not extend to Pyracy, but the same ought to be especially named.*

By 28 H. 8. *Murthers and Robberies committed upon the Sea, or in other Places, where the Admiral pretends Jurisdiction, shall be enquired into, try'd, heard, and determined, in such*

Places and counties within the Realm, as shall be limited by the King's Commission, in like Manner as if such Offences were done at Land. And such Commissions (being under the Great Seal) shall be directed to the Lord Admiral, his Lieutenant or Deputy, and to three or four such others as the Lord Chancellor shall name.

The said Commissioners, or three of them, have Power to enquire of such Offences by twelve lawful Men of the County, so limited in their Commission, as if such Offences were done at Land, within the same County; and every Indictment so found and presented, shall be good in Law; and such Order, Progress, Judgment, and Execution shall be used, had, done, and made thereupon, as against Offenders for Murder and Felony done at Land. Also the Tryal of such Offences (if they be denied) shall be had by twelve Men of the County, limited in the said Commission, (as aforesaid,) and no Challenge shall be had for the Hundred: And such as shall be convict of such Offences, shall suffer Death without Benefit of Clergy, and forfeit Land and Goods, as in Case of Felonies and Murders done at Land.

This Act shall not prejudice any Person, or Persons, (urged by Necessity) for taking Victuals, Cables, Ropes, Anchors or Sails, out of another Ship that may spare them, so as they either pay ready Money, or Money worth for them, or give a Bill for the Payment thereof; if on this Side the Straits of Gibraltar, within four Months; if beyond, within twelve Months.

When any such Commission shall be sent to any Place within the Jurisdiction of the Cinque-Ports, it shall be directed to the Warden of the said Ports, or his Deputy with three or four other Persons, as the Lord Chancellor shall Name; and the Inquisition or Tryal of such Offences, there, shall be made and had, by the Inhabitants of the said Ports, and Members of the same.

By 11 and 12 W. 3. c. 7. If any natural born Subjects or Denizons of England, commit Pyracy, or any Act of Hostility, against his Majesty's Subjects at Sea, under Colour of a Commission or Authority, from any foreign Prince or State, or Person whatsoever, such Offenders shall be adjudged Pyrates.

If any Commander or Master of a Ship, or Seaman or Mariner, give up his Ship, &c. to Pyrates, or combine to yield up, or run away with any Ship, or lay violent Hand on his Commander, or endeavour to make a Revolt in the Ship, he shall be adjudged a Pyrate.

All Persons who after the 29th of September 1720, *shall set forth any Pyrate (or be aiding and assisting to any such Pyrate,) committing Pyracy on Land or Sea, or shall conceal such Pyrates, or receive any Vessel or Goods pyratically taken, shall be adjudged accessary to such Pyracy, and suffer as Principals.*

By 4. G. c. 11. Sect. 7. *All Persons who have committed, or shall commit any Offences, for which they ought to be adjudged Pyrates, by the Act* 11 *and* 12 W. 3. c. 7. *may be tried for every such Offence, in such Manner as the Act* 28 H. 8. c. 15. *is directed for the Tryal of Pyrates; and shall not have the Benefit of Clergy.*

Sect. 8. *This Act shall not extend to Persons convicted or attainted in* Scotland.

Sect. 9. *This Act shall extend to his Majesty's Dominions in* America, *and be taken as a publick Act.*